The Riches of Paris

ALSO BY MARIBETH CLEMENTE

The Riches of France:
A Shopping and Touring Guide to the French Provinces

AS MARIBETH RICOUR DE BOURGIES

The Chic Shopper's Guide to Paris

The Riches of Paris

A SHOPPING AND TOURING GUIDE

Second Edition

Maribeth Clemente

ST. MARTIN'S GRIFFIN
NEW YORK

Book design by Mary A. Wirth
Maps by David Lindroth

ISBN-13: 978-0-312-36163-1
ISBN-10: 0-312-36163-7

Second Edition: May 2007

10 9 8 7 6 5 4 3 2 1

To all those who love Paris and things French,
with the wish that this book will help you to become
better travelers and further appreciate the French

Contents

PART THREE: MORE SHOPPING

Acknowledgments

Thank you to George Witte, editor in chief at St. Martin's Press, for giving the go-ahead to this new edition of *The Riches of Paris: A Shopping and Touring Guide*. Thank you to Tom Mercer at St. Martin's for moving this work forward and for having found many ways to improve upon it. Tom, I really appreciate your insight, expertise, and enthusiasm in helping me to reshape and reorganize the material in my book. Your ideas contributed greatly to this new edition of *The Riches of Paris*. I also want to thank my current editor, David Moldawer at St. Martin's, for having jumped right into this project with such skill and know-how that it seemed as though he had been with me on it from the beginning. David, you are a fine editor, and I am grateful for all the work you have done on this book. This is my fourth book with St. Martin's, and with each one, I'm continually impressed by the smarts and professionalism of those I work with at this publishing house. Thank you to Valerie Saint-Rossy, who did an extraordinary job with the copyediting of the manuscript. Your attention to detail—particularly with the accents on certain French words—truly wowed me. Thanks also to Michael Storrings for such a lovely cover design.

Many other people touched me in numerous ways throughout the research and writing of this work. So many people—from travel book aficionados to booksellers to casual tourists—took the time to provide me with invaluable feedback on the first edition of *The Riches of Paris*. Your comments, notes, and e-mails have helped me to reaffirm my own way of presenting Paris and its marvelous goods to discriminating shoppers and travelers. Please continue to provide input when you are so inspired. Thank you to the shop owners, hoteliers, restaurateurs, and countless other passionate people in Paris who shared their stories with me. Your enthusiasm for the riches of Paris helped me many times to forget my tired feet and weary countenance when pounding the Paris pavement. And on both sides of the Atlantic I have been buoyed up by many, many good friends. You know who you are, and I think you know you played a special part. Thank you especially to Victoria Wolff, Marie Châtelier, and Michèle Brothers, who tirelessly debriefed me on all that was new and noteworthy in Paris. These acknowledgments would not be complete without mentioning Peter Hazard, who has been a dear friend to me through thick and thin these past seven years. I also want to recognize the undying love and support that my parents, Frank and Mary Ellen Clemente, have shown me throughout my life. And, of course, big hugs to my furry little friends, Leo and Clara, who have provided me with heaps of love and companionship in recent years.

A New Discovery Around Every Corner

My love for shopping in Paris grew out of a desire to discover boutiques full of charm, authenticity, and a uniqueness that is intrinsically French. I'll never forget the time I stumbled upon a centuries-old Left Bank antique shop at the tender age of sixteen, the day I first crossed the threshold of a great Paris couture house, or the cold, grey Sunday afternoon I made my first trip to the flea markets. Each time I found something new, I realized that I was experiencing something far beyond any of the places I knew back home in America.

The idea of a boutique—or rather a shopping showplace—is inherently French and, even more so, Parisian. The first trading places in Paris were set up along bridges, where people could bargain for their essential goods as they plodded along on the route from northern Europe to the Mediterranean. The actual shops during the mid-seventeenth-century were merely storerooms for the goods lined up outdoors; store windows didn't begin to appear until the end of the seventeenth century. But somehow I imagine that the Parisians found their own alluring way of displaying their wares, an expertise that has grown with every passing century, an art whose effect is more inviting than ever before.

Behind each shopwindow is a story. In this new edition of *The Riches of Paris: A Shopping and Touring Guide*, I've tried to highlight these stories even more. The tales are about the boutiques and other types of establishments I've included here, the people behind them, and the areas where they reside. I'd like to think that this book provides you with another way to discover Paris and French culture and history in addition to visiting the Louvre and the Eiffel Tower. In Paris I relish the idea of entering a boutique that is quaint, enticingly decorated, and, most of all, has a soul all its own. I hope you, too, will feel a connection with these establishments, whether the setting is in a seventeenth-century town house in the Marais or a new, glittery showplace on the rue du Faubourg-Saint-Honoré. The French have a flair for personally embellishing their goods, and there's much to appreciate even if you buy only a few treasured *souvenirs*. I feel that in knowing these stories, the products and places I describe will have greater meaning for you.

Some of you might wonder how I became such an expert on Paris shopping. For seven years, I operated the Chic Promenade shopping service in Paris. (I lived in the French capital for eleven years, not counting the numerous visits I've made there over nearly three decades.) During my Chic Promenade days, I became firmly committed to sharing the joys of Paris—shopping-wise *and* otherwise—with visitors to the capital, whether they were ardent boutique explorers or wide-eyed tourists. Little did I know at the time that I would learn as much from them as they learned from me; shoppers have such different tastes and desires that I soon developed a comprehensive repertory of addresses serving all interests.

When my little black book reached a certain point, I knew it was time to write a real book. My first book on Paris shopping was *The Chic Shopper's Guide to Paris*. As time went on, I exchanged my tour guide cap for a reporter's plume and went on to write *The Riches of France: A Shopping and Touring Guide to the French Provinces*. That book revealed the rich culture, history, and tradition that are so much a part of France, including French goods. I then wrote *The Riches of Paris: A Shopping and Touring Guide*, a sort of update of *The Chic Shopper's Guide* written more in the style of *The Riches of France*.

This new edition of *The Riches of Paris* has allowed me to reaffirm my love for Paris shops and the neighborhoods that proudly feature them. And yes, my love for the French has been reaffirmed as well. It is the French, in fact, who are responsible for all this beauty and goodness that we come to enjoy. Sure, there have been some changes and, sadly, a handful of my favorite stores have disappeared. But the French haven't disappointed me in the slightest. I find them to be as warm and welcoming toward Americans as they have always been. I was actually amazed by how many more English words have been integrated into the French language in recent years. (Instead of saying something is *très mode*, or very fashionable, for example, people now often say it's *très fa-shun*.)

The French are as quirky as ever, but they still know how to pull it all together. And they seem to be doing just that more than ever before—I have never seen Paris glimmer as it does now. Every other boutique, café, restaurant, hotel, and museum has been buffed and polished, redone and done up to a magnificent splendor. Never before has Paris been so divine.

This book will help you fall in love with Paris, perhaps even more than you already are. As you read, I hope that you, too, will be touched by some of the impressions that enchanted me when I first ventured to that magical place at sweet sixteen.

How to Use This Guidebook

This book is divided into three main parts: "The Essentials," "The Districts," and "More Shopping." "The Essentials" provides an introduction to the Paris shopping scene and useful information that you will need to know when shopping and touring around the City of Light.

"The Districts" reveals the unique characteristics of each area of Paris and the establishments found therein. "The Districts" is broken into categories. Within each category, the establishments are listed alphabetically. Symbols indicate 🛍 boutiques, ✗ restaurants, ★ beauty services, or some combination of the three. These are meant to inform you that, although I've placed an establishment in a certain category, it may include other features of interest to you as well.

BOXES

Boxes throughout the text feature everything from the history of the English-language bookstores and department stores to the origins of the grandest hotels. Many tips—from how to achieve the French look to what books to read—have also been boxed. You'll find auction houses and antiques centers separated into boxes as well. Few individual establishments have been boxed, with the exception of the Paris cabarets, which are in a league of their own.

I recommend you read over the description of each district and mark off the establishments that tempt you the most. You can use the street name and the Métro station I've included for each entry to gain a greater sense of where these places are located within the districts, and consequently which particular areas interest you most.

At the end of each district, you'll find "Favorite Tours," a section of suggested itineraries. Some are longer than others, particularly the ones suggested on the Left Bank, which could take weeks to investigate thoroughly. The Passages, on the other hand, can easily be explored in an afternoon. Of course, you may also prefer to explore the various boutiques and neighborhoods on your own.

The book is arranged so that you can approach Paris shopping and touring in a logical manner, leaving plenty of room to accommodate your particular needs and interests. Whether you are on foot, traveling by Métro, cabbing it, or riding in your own chauffeured limo, you should have no problem locating your favorite boutiques, restaurants, and shop-filled streets of the French capital.

The third part of the book, "More Shopping," lists flea markets, boutiques, neighborhoods, and other establishments outside "The Districts." I think you'll find that it's worth going out of your way for many of these stores and places of interest.

Certain information is provided (when possible) for each listing mentioned in this book: the name of the establishment; the address (written the French way); the telephone, and, when possible, fax number (if there's no Web site or e-mail address); the closest Métro stop; the opening and closing hours for the establishment described; and the Web site or e-mail address. (If by any chance you want to send a letter to any of these establishments, the zip code for Paris is always 75 plus three digits, the last one or two being the number of the arrondissement, or area of Paris. When you see 8e, for example, it refers to the eighth arrondissement, and the address is 75008 Paris.) If store hours are listed after two or three different addresses for the same boutique, the hours are the same at each branch. If an address is listed after the store hours, assume there is some variation in hours for that branch.

For stores that have many different addresses in Paris, I have listed only a special selection of them. (The district in which I describe the boutique is where I think you should go—generally the motherhouse.) I've cross-referenced at times when I think it would be helpful to you to visit a branch store, particularly when there's not much of a difference between the various addresses. Many stores have multiple branches throughout Paris but I might have listed only one or two. If this is the case, and you find a store that catches your eye, look it up in the index to see if I've described it in a different section of the book.

Be sure to consult the Quick Reference at the end of the book. This should be a very handy tool for you—so much so that you may want to begin there! Call it Maribeth's picks, if you will, but I recommend you use it as a frame of reference, not as an absolute.

With all this information in hand, you should have no problem finding your way around the world's greatest shopping and touring capital: Paris!

PART ONE

The Essentials

1

Setting Out

Best Buys

Yes, it's true the bargains have not been earth-shattering in Paris these past few years with the less than favorable exchange of dollars to euros, but there's still some smart purchasing to be had. The following categories provide some guidelines, but know that there's much more out there than what you read below.

Beauty Treatments and Hairstyles and Cuts

You'll notice that I've accorded a good amount of space to the world of beauty in this book. To go to a spa or hair salon in Paris is truly extraordinary for all the obvious reasons, but these services are also quite reasonably priced, particularly in comparison to those in the United States. A sixty-five-minute facial at the renowned **Institut Clarins,** for example, rings in at €75—I pay considerably more than that here in Telluride, Colorado.

Wines and Spirits

You have to know where to go and what to buy to experience significant savings in wines and spirits in Paris. It's important to be able to trust your wine seller's recommendations in order to find a delicious wine that sells for considerably less in France. Go first to **Les Caves Augé,** where you will be steered in the right direction. **Caves Taillevent** also does a good job of pointing out smart purchases, and both of these establishments conduct Saturday tastings that are fun and informative. For spirits, however, my all-time favorite address is **Ryst-Dupeyron**. They sell a delicious armagnac in an astonishingly wide range of years, and you can also have the bottle personalized—terrific for gift giving.

Fancy and Not-So-Fancy Foods

It is, of course, more interesting price-wise and otherwise to buy truffles (not the chocolate kind!) at the **Maison de la Truffe** in Paris. But you can also purchase many ordinary French food products, such as Carte Noire coffee, hot and spicy *moutardes de Dijon* (just the regular mustards that the French pick up for themselves as frequently as we buy ketchup), cans of *flageolets* (a delicious bean almost like our northern beans, but green, which the French often serve with roasted lamb), and much more, from regular supermarkets. It's most fun to go to **Hédiard** and **Fauchon** (for high-end goods), **La Grande Epicerie** and **Lafayette Gourmet**, and, of course, the wonderful outdoor markets.

Table Arts

You'll still encounter tremendous savings (25 to 40 percent off) on luxury table arts from big names such as **Bernardaud, Haviland, Christofle, Baccarat, Lalique, Gien,** and many more. Go to "More Shopping" description p. 289 for the complete breakdown. The smaller tabletop shops offer originality and charm and many products that are also priced noticeably less than in the United States. **Dîners en Ville** is one such shop, and here I encourage you to purchase one of their stunning, vibrantly colored tablecloths from **Beauvillé**—I guarantee it will transform the whole look of your kitchen, dining room, or deck at home. Antique house linens also represent good value and fine craftsmanship.

Women's Fashion Accessories

Sure there's a great demand for stylish fashion accessories in Paris, but there's also a tremendous supply of high-quality, superalluring jewelry, bags, shoes, and hats that scintillate with a spirit that is fabulously

French. Not all of the accessory shops that I feature in this book sell to the United States, but in the case of many of those that do, the prices are remarkably higher stateside. Not-to-be-missed shops include: **Dominique Denaive, A la Bonne Renommée, Louise Gelinas, Mi Amor/Sic Amor, Hervé Chapelier, Marie Mercier,** and oh so many more!

Scarves and Shawls

The overall quality of fabrics in France leaves a long-lasting impression. Nowhere is this more evident than in the jewel-colored silk scarves and shawls, most of which are confectioned in Lyons. **Hermès** comes to mind first, but there are other boutiques big and small that will seduce you with their silky creations. A trip to **Wolff & Descourtis** is a must—not only to purchase a scarf or a shawl sure to become a lifelong treasure—but also to visit the glorious galerie Vivienne.

Perfumes and Beauty Products

Perfumes and beauty products rank among France's biggest exports. The savings vary from great (as much as 50 percent with the tax refund) to small, depending on the product. You'll really get a handle on all this at **Catherine,** one of the most reputable *parfumeurs* in Paris. I also love the lesser-known fragrance emporiums such as **Creed, Comptoir Sud Pacifique, Editions de Parfums Frédéric Malle, Les Salons du Palais Royal** (Serge Lutens), **Detaille,** and **P. de Nicolaï,** where the prices and the unique products and places truly warrant a visit. Know also that French scented candles are of superior quality. They may cost more than their American counterparts, but they're worth it.

Antiques and Bric-a-Brac

Just remember that hordes of antiques dealers, decorators, and shop owners from the United States come to France every year to buy. Their hefty markups have to cover their trip, their efforts, and the cost of shipping and showcasing those goods back home. So while you're enjoying your travels in Paris, why not pick up that special memento of the Old World? Know also that the prices on certain old items such as silver are typically less than on newly made goods.

Pharmacy Finds

I always seem to spend a ridiculous amount of money at *la pharmacie* when I go to France. This is partly because I tend to become sick more often when I travel, but it's also due to the wide assortment of tempting products. I'm hooked on the candylike vitamin C *comprimés* that are also handy for travel and some of the special herbal teas *(tisanes)* available for all kinds of ailments. The skin-care products most pharmacies typically carry are among the best in France. They're not cheap, but they still cost less than in the United States. And there's always something new and different to pick up such as a lip balm with an inventive way of opening or a toothbrush that is hopelessly *dee-zine* (design). Most of the people working in the pharmacies speak English—especially in the more tourist-trodden areas—so if they're not busy, go ahead and ask away.

Treasures from the Five-and-Ten

I've never been big on buying cheap stuff in cheap places, but the French five-and-tens do have a certain attraction. Poke around at **Prisunic, Monoprix,** and—if you're really adventuresome—**Tati** to see what is new and different from what you find at home. My favorite five-and-ten gift purchases include Donge almond-scented soaps with a *gant de toilette* (a washcloth in the shape of a fingerless mitt—very French) and pairs of fashion knee-highs.

When to Go

Deciding when to go to Paris depends largely on what you want out of the city in terms of shopping, tourism, and, of course, weather. I consider spring and fall to be good times to visit the French capital: The weather is grey to great, the selections in the boutiques are full and fresh, and the city is not overrun with tourists. If you come in May, choose your dates carefully because most stores are closed on the three different holidays (the dates vary except for May 1) that take place during that month. Note that the other two are Ascension Day and Pentacost. During July and August you have to battle crowds of visitors at the museums and monuments, but it can be a good time for shopping because the boutiques aren't as crowded. Some shops close in August, however, so keep that in mind. Many close for one week midmonth, few actually close for the whole month. In July and August you can get in on the sales, while September offers the first glimpse of the new season's fashions. If you don't mind bleak, drizzly weather and little sunshine, January is an excellent time to go to Paris because the sales are fabulous. Christmas in Paris is a disappointment for many Americans, but those looking to get away from the commercialization of the holidays in the United States will enjoy themselves.

What and Where to Buy *and* Tour

The types of goods worth buying in Paris are not only those that cost less than in the United States but also those for which a better selection is offered in France. I also place a lot of emphasis on the places where you buy them. Ambiance is really important to me, and I'm sure it is to many of you, or else you wouldn't be in (or going to) France. Where and how your little treasure is purchased can make all the difference in the world. (Don't you think champagne tastes better out of a crystal flute than a plastic cup?) The majority of stores in this book will provide you with more local flavor—grand or rustic—than any Hollywood set designer could muster. I encourage you to leave your planning to serendipity; but if you prefer a few guidelines, consider the following themes, which also happen to coincide with the categories within each district.

Boutiques de Luxe

Today's luxury boutiques carry an increasingly broad line of products for men, women, sometimes children, and often for the home, as well. Savings vary somewhat depending on the products. As a general rule, you can count on saving 5 to 15 percent (20 to 30 percent with the tax refund) on most of your purchases. What is most exceptional about buying from these big names in Paris is that the selection of goods and overall shopping experience at the motherhouse far exceed anything you'll encounter in their other stores.

Keep in mind also that a lot of designer fashions sold in the United States have been manufactured with licensing agreements. (These styles are often different and usually less expensive than those of a better quality sold in France.) So the big names in Paris sell only their "boutique" collection—just make sure you always compare apples with apples.

RICHES OF PARIS TIP

If you want to become familiar with who's hot and who's not, read Suzy Menkes's fashion reports during the collections in the *International Herald Tribune*—they're great!

Food and Wine Purveyors

The selection of gourmet foods, fine wines, and spirits in Paris is astounding, providing endless gift ideas in a wide range of prices. If you want to pick up a few gifts in the €5 to €10 bracket, it's best to consider smallish comestibles such as jars of fine-quality jams, mustards, or herbs from Provence—all welcome additions to anyone's pantry. More expensive items include foie gras, truffles, or a cocoa-brown box of chocolates from **La Maison du Chocolat.**

As far as wines and spirits are concerned, it seems a crime not to take advantage of your customs allowance and bring back a fine bottle of Château Margaux that will last you an evening, or a superb vintage of armagnac that will last you a year!

Table and Kitchen Arts, Home Décor, and Linens

The French home is generally filled with originality, much like the French wardrobe. You don't see many cookie-cutter interiors, and if a family has not been fortunate enough to inherit all kinds of interesting bibelots, you won't know it from the home décor. The stores in Paris are filled with legions of charming *objets,* most of which are sure to enhance your home, no matter where you live or what style you embrace. Think creative pell-mell. Also consider Paris's tabletop shops as a wonderful source of inspiration—you don't have to buy a thing to walk away with an abundance of ideas on how to put together what you have at home.

TEN WAYS TO ACHIEVE THE FRENCH LOOK FOR YOUR HOME

I think French interiors are usually far more interesting than those in America. If you would like your home to look a little more French, let these suggestions help you.

Mix Old with New Even if you have a penchant for *le contemporain,* make sure you have a few old knickknacks that will add character and charm. Old postcards and prints, for example, work well in all kinds of interiors.

Mix Good with Not-So-Good You'll sometimes find scrap metal pieces (wrought ironwork intended for the garden, for example) mixed in with fine antiques in French interiors. You'll find some of the best inspiration for this sort of mixing and matching at the famed Paris flea markets. No wonder you seldom see nondescript interiors in France!

Beautiful Fabrics This must be an influence from the Sun King, who draped Versailles in an astonishing array of rich fabrics. (Curtains and slipcovers were even replaced for the summer and winter seasons.) I've always been amazed by my French friends' sumptuous choice of fabrics in their draperies and home furnishings. The quality is so good and the materials so handsome that they last for ages.

Lots of Color The French love color and it is rarely used sparingly. Be dramatic, and while you're at it, don't be afraid to use lots of different patterns as well.

Eclectic Okay. I think I've already established that the French have flair—it seems as though there's a little bit of *l'artiste* in all of them. You can do it, too. Pick up something that was intended for one purpose and use it for another. You could, for example, ask to take home a restaurant menu from Paris and then have it framed to hang on your wall back home.

Use Trays There's always a good measure of decorum in France, and serving trays are a good end result. They're highly practical as well. You can find them for cheap or very pricey in many stores throughout Paris. Plus they're easy to pack in a suitcase.

Set a Nice Table After they've served their *apéritif* (with an ever so tiny amount of chips) on a tray, the French sit down to a beautifully set table—even for everyday meals. You'll find everything needed and more to achieve this in the various tabletop shops I've outlined. Remember: The right backdrop is always a good start, so think tablecloths.

Pillows and Throws The French are big on comfort and enjoy accessorizing their homes as much as themselves. You'll find lots of incredibly attractive pillows and throws for sale throughout the Paris boutiques.

Silver Out The French use their finery. They don't keep a whole lot stuffed away for "special occasions." They'll have silver candlesticks (heirloom or otherwise) out on a table amid some casual clutter—and it all works.

Lovely Lamps You rarely see a boring, purely functional lamp in a French home. It seems as though each one has a story—old or new—waiting to be told. Since the French possess a highly developed sense of aesthetics, they realize that the right lighting—preferably soft and low—makes everything and *everyone* look a whole lot better.

Art, Antiques, and Collectibles

Whether you buy at the flea markets, the auctions, from an art or antiques dealer, or in a curio shop, the selection and good value of art, antiques, and collectibles in France is for the most part unbeatable. In "The Districts," I indicate antiques stores, art galleries, and boutiques that, aside from being my favorites, tend to appeal to visitors who enjoy the thrill of unearthing something that is old, charming, or difficult to find at home. Those addresses only scratch the surface of the Gallic capital: There's much you'll discover on your own.

Note for art-gallery hoppers: The entertainment guide Pariscope—sold in kiosks—lists the current exhibitions throughout the capital.

HEIRLOOM PURCHASING

Nearly all the important Paris antiques and art dealers handle shipping arrangements and customs formalities. Be sure to verify that the proper documents regarding authenticity and age have been provided. If you have a certificate proving that your purchase is at least one hundred years old, you will not have to pay duty on it, or French sales tax. Find out the cost of shipping and insurance before you decide to send home an eighteenth-century armoire and, above all, remember that bargaining down 10 to 25 percent, even in the finer shops, is the name of the game. If you do purchase something of truly exceptional quality, whether at an antiques shop, an auction, or at the flea markets, find out ahead of time whether you might have difficulty bringing it out of the country. For truly valuable pieces, the store (or even the stand at the flea markets) should provide a letter from an expert along with the bill of sale. This letter or *certificat* should furnish a descriptive account of the nature of the piece, the approximate date at which it was made, any particular markings (such as the signature of the craftsperson), and so forth. For more modest purchases, a less formal note is sufficient. The shop owner should write up a brief description of the purchase and its approximate age. Make sure this includes the name of the store, its address, and the date. This simple act binds the seller to his or her word; if a dealer tells you that the porcelain tea service you are buying dates back to the mid-nineteenth century, for example, make sure you have that in writing.

Jewelry, Shoes, and Accessories

This category includes fine and costume jewelry as well as women's and men's shoes, hats, bags, belts, and small leather goods. The variety and quality of these goods are excellent, and not all the brands I write about in this book have broken through stateside. Certainly the world's leaders in high-style costume jewelry, Paris's costume jewelry designers sell creations that range from chic to mod, and the value for your money on these pieces is excellent. Finely crafted leather (real and faux) shoes, bags, and small leather goods don't cost any more than their U.S. equivalents, and are priced about 15 percent less than their French counterparts in the United States. As far as French hats are concerned, there's absolutely no comparison!

Womenswear

Know that most of the shops I include within this category also sell women's accessories. Some might even sell women's bathing suits and lingerie, which is why I've grouped the pure lingerie stores under Womenswear as well. Most of the designers and labels I feature here are well liked by the French, but perhaps less known by Americans. Boutiques such as **Lolita Lempicka, Chacok,** and **Popy Moreni** offer selection, value, and a style that is *typiquement français.*

TEN WAYS TO FIND THE FRENCH LOOK FOR YOU

If you do strive to exude more of a French flair, let these suggestions help you on your shopping and touring forays.

Get a French Haircut The French really know how to cut hair! Their training is far more extensive than what is required in the United States and all stylists must apprentice for three years.

Accessorize Many French women live with a limited wardrobe of basic black dresses, jeans, cream silk blouses, a few smart skirts, and a handful of cashmere sweaters, but they change their look fifty times over with the addition of up-to-the-minute accessories. It's all about adornment. Just look at their pastries (which they call *gâteaux,* or cakes)—they certainly put our most fancy layer cakes to shame.

Wear a Scarf or a Shawl Yes, these are accessories, but they are *the* quintessential French fashion accessories. I swear most French women are born knowing how to tie a scarf. But truly the secret is not to fuss too much. And make sure there's a gap between your neck and the scarf or shawl—that's way more seductive.

Know Where, When, and How to Wear a Hat For part of the research for this book, I was in Paris during a brutally cold time in January. I couldn't believe how few people wore warm hats. You can bet, though, that I donned my warmest (which one of my French friends called *un pot à fleur,* or a flower pot). I live in the Rockies, so I'm accustomed to having flat hair all winter long, but apparently the French don't buy it. No, in France hats are definitely for fashion—not practicality—and, of course, it's considered *gauche* to wear a hat inside (a home, restaurant, or bar) in the evening.

Sport Capris or Bermudas—Not Short Shorts Few people—men or women—can pull off shorts really well, and that becomes even more challenging in a cosmopolitan city such as Paris. I hardly ever see my slim French friends (or their teenaged daughters) in shorts. Best to go for a bit more length for men *and* women.

Keep Your Makeup Very Natural The French devote a lot of energy toward their personal skin-care regime from an early age, and I think it shows. They also know how to keep their makeup light—much more so than their American sisters. Strive for that healthy glow even if you achieve it through just the right touch of *maquillage*.

The Shoes and the Bag Tell It All I think the French believe that you can tell a woman by her shoes and bag. (And—I guess—a man by his watch.) So these key accessories should be of fine quality. No wonder the French classics such as **Hermès, Chanel, Dior,** and **Louis Vuitton** have been so immensely successful with their handbags. And if you need to wear shoes that are both comfortable and practical (which I highly recommend), make sure they're stylish. Oh, and no flip-flops!

Start with a Skirt Once you have your accessories rounded up, think about buying one or more articles of clothing that say "I've been to Paris." A skirt is a good place to start. Just think of the ruckus Christian Dior made with his "new look" when he created a skirt fashioned out of yards and yards of fabric in postwar Paris! This second oldest garment in the world (loincloth being the first) can be many different things—feminine and flirtatious but also luxurious and daring, which is why *une jupe* so poetically sings the praises of France.

Signature Style Whether it's a fountain pen or a ballpoint, make sure your writing instrument is elegant. The French were among the world's more prolific letter writers during the eighteenth century, and that mantle (like many others of Louis XIV) continues to reverberate in French society today.

Personal Style The French are masters at that certain *je ne sais quoi* that reflects their personality. Always infuse your style with personal touches. Mix and match—and even if you're classic, add *une petite touche* that is distinctly yours.

And you thought it was all about wearing a beret. *Au contráire!*

RICHES OF PARIS TIP
Do what the French do, buy less but buy better quality. (That's also how they stay so thin—they eat rich, wonderful food, but not much of it.)

Menswear

As *chez les femmes,* the bulk of the stores here feature both men's fashions and accessories. I think that French men are some of the best dressed on the planet, so I hope men will make good use of my shopping suggestions as well.

Women's and Men's Fashions

As the title indicates, you will find boutiques full of both women's and men's fashions and accessories under this heading. Some, such as **Marithé & François Girbaud,** are very well known internationally, while others are French favorites I thought you might enjoy.

Children's Clothing, Shoes, and Furnishings

Children's fashions tend to cost more in France than in the United States, but their quality and craftsmanship is superior. If you're looking for something special, Paris offers many beautiful children's clothing boutiques specializing in timeless styles. Clothing from **Bonpoint, Petit Faune, La Châtelaine,** and **Tartine et Chocolat** may be expensive, but it is cheaper to buy these brands in France than in the United States. As far as shoes and furnishings go, the places I highlight for these products will surely astound you.

Department Stores and Other Biggies

I often discourage people from department store shopping in Paris for several reasons: The smaller, more charming boutiques provide a more attractive setting for shopping *à la parisienne,* the salespeople in these same boutiques are friendlier and considerably more helpful than department store clerks, and, most of all, the merchandise in French department stores is not generally as attractively presented as in their U.S. counterparts. The Paris department stores do, however, provide you with the opportunity to see a tremendous amount of French merchandise together under one roof—a factor that is far from negligible, especially if you are in town for only a few days. I also want to emphasize that most of the major department stores of Paris have made strides in recent years to spiff up their images, and have invested bundles of money in creating departments (and in some cases whole stores) that have become major attractions. **La Grande Epicerie** at **Le Bon Marché, Lafayette Gourmet,** and the new table arts store **Lafayette Maison** at **Galeries Lafayette** make up the strong points of the Paris department store experience in my book.

If you do plan to go shopping in one of Paris's sprawling *grands magasins* and want to beat the crowds, I suggest you go early in the morning and never on Saturdays. The shopping system in Paris's larger stores differs from that of the smaller boutiques. Here, the salesperson only writes up and packages your purchases—it is up to you to go to the cashier *(caisse)* in a separate area to actually pay. Once this is taken care of, you go back to the salesperson to pick up your merchandise. Often the clerk is no longer at his or her post or is busy chatting with a coworker; this, of course, creates confusion, frustration, and a great loss of time. In order to minimize this sort of hassle and to avoid long lines at several different cashiers, you may want to accumulate all your purchase slips (or have all the purchases put on one slip) and pay everything together at the end. Totaling your purchases will also help you to attain the minimum balance required for your tax reduction.

RICHES OF PARIS TIP

Consult with the welcome desk in each store regarding its own policies and benefits for foreign shoppers, and most of all, pick up your 10 percent discount card (good for most purchases except for food items) that is their extra little gift for you. (Sometimes hotels and travel companies also provide this card.) And keep in mind that nearly all the major stores ship.

Although the Christmas decorations within the major department stores are somewhat disappointing, their mechanical, toy-filled windows—especially at Galeries Lafayette—depict whimsical storybook scenes that delight young and old alike. Most of the stores are open on the three Sundays before Christmas and, like the smaller boutiques, they hold sales in January and July (some for three-day periods on other occasions as well).

Keep in mind also that many of Paris's department stores are actually divided up into several different buildings, so you may want to consult the store directory before you go charging through!

You'll notice, too, that "Other Biggies" I've included in this category are not department stores, and I wouldn't consider them to be very boutiquelike, either.

YES, IT ALL BEGAN IN FRANCE: HISTORY OF DEPARTMENT STORES

It was in fact a Frenchman, Aristide Bouçicaut, who opened the world's first department store, Au Bon Marché (now called **Le Bon Marché**), in 1852. The rising capitalist tide, brought on by the Industrial Revolution and the new phenomenon of fixed prices (prior to which customers had to haggle for fair prices), whetted shoppers' appetites for a more abundant selection of goods. Monsieur Bouçicaut emphasized the shopper's right to browse freely, to return unwanted purchases, and to pay the same price as the next person for merchandise that was presented in an orderly fashion for all to see. Other retailers caught on fast, and by the end of the nineteenth century,

Paris had witnessed the birth of several major department stores, including **Au Printemps, Galeries Lafayette, La Samaritaine,** and **Le Bazaar de l'Hôtel de Ville** (BHV).

If you look beyond the jumble of displays that are sure to captivate your attention in Paris's department stores, you'll discover handsome architectural elements from the end of the nineteenth century and the beginning of the twentieth. Massive glass cupolas, flowery *art nouveau* paintings, and intricate hand-forged framework give evidence of a time when these commercial spaces were Paris's most comely shopping emporia. Encircled in spindly gold-leaf metal bannisters and crowned with a cathedral-high, stained-glass dome, the main floor of Galeries Lafayette merits a special trip just to see one of the French capital's most perfect examples of *fin de siècle* splendor.

Discount Shops

For each district I've tried to highlight *the best* shops or areas for buying reduced-price merchandise. Keep in mind that the discount-shopping scene in Paris is not nearly as alluring as what exists in the United States, but there are some great bargains to be found. Of course, if you're a seasoned shopper, you'll fare better than a casual browser. Most of the stores—with the exception of **Anna Lowe** and **Miss Griffes**—sell last year's collection at about 50 percent off.

Books and Music

I heartily encourage you to peek into the various book and music stores I've indicated throughout Paris. Most of these places are true bastions of culture, old and new, French and Anglo-Saxon. And for the latter, they are indeed veritable institutions, marvelous gathering places where events frequently take place. You might just have a better chance of meeting your favorite author in Paris than at home! And the largest stores, such as **FNAC** and **Virgin,** sell such an outstanding selection of music (and books) that there's no reason not to go home with a bit of today's French pop tucked carefully into your bag. Know that music and books (particularly those published overseas) cost a fair amount more in France, but I hope that won't deter you too much since much of what you'll find in these places will be hard to come by back home.

HISTORY OF THE ENGLISH-LANGUAGE BOOKSTORES

Merchants first began selling English books in Paris toward the end of the seventeenth century. But their grand epoch began about a hundred years ago when booksellers decided to open up shop in the Opéra-Concorde neighborhood. This area was a real hub of American culture at that time, due partly to the proximity of the American and British embassies and other important Anglo-American businesses and associations. Venerable booksellers such as **Brentano's** and **W. H. Smith** opened at that time (**Galignani** already existed) and they soon became places of notability, tradition, and chic. These bookstores may not seem that way today, loaded with camera-toting tourists clad in shorts (remember most French people rarely wear shorts in Paris) and terribly inelegant sneakers. But even if the look of the patrons has changed a bit from when women wore bustles and men donned top hats, the rich spirit of these bookstores lives on.

Other bookshops popped up later—most on the other side of the Seine—furnishing a decidedly Left Bank twist to their image and bookselling approach. Now, lovers of the language of Shakespeare may also shop in the Marais at **The Red Wheelbarrow Bookstore.** We'll take over the Bastille next!

Markets

Every visitor to Paris should experience at least one of the city's lively open-air food markets. Whether you are just strolling through or shopping for provisions for a picnic on the banks of the Seine, *les marchés de Paris* promise a colorful glimpse of how ordinary Parisians lead their lives.

Most Parisians still shop on a daily basis even if it's just to pick up a crisp baguette, a ripe red tomato, or a perfectly creamy piece of Camembert. Here you encounter local housewives and discriminating gourmets carefully selecting (you seldom touch anything yourself—you are served) ingredients for their midday and evening repasts. Row after row of meticulously arranged sweet red peppers; green baby courgettes; and plump, juicy grapes provide a feast for the eyes, and the animated and often exaggerated gestures of the market vendors entertain the heart and soul. As you walk down the bountiful alleys and see the merchants selling everything from freshly killed pheasant to the Mediterranean's choicest stingray, you will certainly feel a long way away from your local supermarket back home.

There are three different types of markets in Paris: roving markets, market streets, and covered markets. Each of these markets has its own personality, fostered by the neighborhood clientele. In addition to food items, most of the Paris markets also sell typically French gift ideas, including honey-scented soaps from Provence, country French ceramic dishes, and porcelain demitasses and teapots.

Be sure to dress casually and bring cash—sorry, no plastic. I have indicated some of the most interesting markets in each district, but the inclusions are by no means exhaustive. If you want to find out about the markets closest to your hotel, your concierge will be able to indicate where and when you should go. Have fun!

More Specialty Boutiques

This is a catchall category that includes a variety of shops that don't fit neatly into the other categories. Here you'll find smoke, bike, stationery, fabric, toy, and art-supply shops, dancewear specialists, fan and embroidery workshops, and eye- and sunglass boutiques. There's even an umbrella shop and a plumbing fixtures store (you should see their sinks!) A few of the specialties have a theme, as is the case with Provençal fabrics: I put both Souleiado and Les Olivades here because they sell so many different products—from clothing to table arts to miscellaneous gifts—in their wonderful print patterns that it was hard to classify them under one specific category. Within "More Specialty Boutiques" you'll find other themes, including gardening, French country, and more!

Note: I've placed each entry under its strongest category. You will find, for example, that some of the Table and Kitchen Arts, Home Décor, and Linens boutiques might also sell clothing and vice versa. These categories should serve as guidelines—not the rule.

Beauté and *Parfums* (Beauty Services, Products, and Perfumes)

The savings potential on French perfumes, beauty products, and cosmetics is somewhat similar to that of designer fashion. Here's my best advice for both: Know what you're dealing with and what the equivalent price is back home. Not all French products bear the "made in France" label; many of them, such as Lancôme products, are made by U.S. subsidiaries. As a rule, if you (or your friend, or the friend of your cousin) have a favorite French beauty product that you want to pick up in France, write down its U.S. price before you go shopping abroad so that you can compare it with prices in Paris. Don't automatically assume that you will save on French perfumes or cosmetics just because you buy them in Paris. Know that you *will* save most of the time—it's just a matter of how much. In this category I have included fragrance boutiques, beauty institutes, and hair salons. There's always an abundance of wonderful products sold at the spas and *coiffeurs,* so even if you don't go there for a treatment, you can pop in to shop.

TIPS FROM PARIS'S TOP BEAUTY INSTITUTES AND HAIR SALONS

A visit to one of Paris's top beauty insitutes and hair salons will leave you feeling relaxed and beautiful, and—if you so desire—informed. Most of the estheticians and stylists in these stronghouses of French *beauté* speak English and are more than happy to dispense a bit of advice to their clients. I always pick up at least one new tidbit every time.

Shed a Layer Make sure to do exfoliations on your face and body regularly so that your moisturizing creams will work better.

Easy Way to Look Younger Don't style your hair as much. A more casual, breezy coif will make you appear more youthful.

Prioritize Your Creams Invest in a good sun protection cream *before* an antiwrinkle cream.

Scrub for Stronger, Healthier Hair Use your body scrub once a month as a scalp scrub, then shampoo. Your hair and scalp will thank you.

Seductive Mouth Apply a touch of white iridescent eye shadow to the center of your lips to make them look fuller.

Silky Scrub Add a touch of oil to your exfoliation product so that it will penetrate better and leave your skin feeling like velvet.

Bigger Pouf Add more volume to your hair by rinsing it with mineral water (mixed with fresh mint and juice from a lemon).

For That Dewy Look Mix two drops of your foundation into your daily moisturizer for that fresh, natural look.

Oil Equals Shine Add olive, palm, or other types of oil to your hair once a week just a few minutes before shampooing to keep your locks healthy and silky smooth.

Use Your Tonic Always use a skin toner, or *tonique*, on your face after cleansing in order to remove any mineral residue left from water.

Thank you to **Spa George V, Institut Lancôme, Carita, Institut Clarins,** and **Caudelie Spa** for sharing some of their beauty secrets with me.

Note: There's no rule concerning tipping for beauty and hair services in France. However, ten percent is considered the norm.

Perfect Respites

If you haven't guessed it already, I'll tell you right away that my approach is not at all shop till you drop. I encourage you to take many breaks along the way, and I offer respites where I think you might enjoy spending some time, whether for a meal or some quick refreshment. These are some of my very favorite places, many of which I've been going to for years.

Recommended Hotels

I have tried to select hotels that best reflect the tone and spirit of each district. Many of these establishments house not-to-be-missed restaurants or bars. Pop in and look around—these are integral stops on your tour. And some even offer fine shopping.

Favorite Tours

At the end of each chapter, I've suggested itineraries. Of course, you might set up a whole different itinerary for yourself, depending on your own interests. Just make sure you allow yourself to get lost within the old streets of Paris on more than one occasion.

MUSEUM SHOPS

Virtually all the museums in Paris have shops, and many are quite wonderful. I've mentioned some museums—usually the less obvious—in "Favorite Tours," but there are many, many more to discover. For museum store shopping, my favorites include those at the **Louvre,** the **Musée des Arts Décoratifs,** the **Musée d'Orsay,** the **Opéra de Paris** (at Palais Garnier and the Bastille), the **Musée National d'Histoire Naturelle,** the **Musée de la Mode et du Textile,** and the **Pompidou Center.** Those are the biggies, but I also find smaller ones such as the boutique at the **Musée Carnavalet,** the **Musée de la Monnaie,** the **Musée Jacquemart-André,** the **Musée de la Poste,** and the **Musée du Moyen Age** to be delightful. You can buy everything from classic posters and postcards to reproductions of Venus de Milo or the pendant worn by one of the elegantly dressed ladies in Renoir's *Le Moulin de la Galette.* Some shops, such as **La Librairie des Jardins du Musée du Louvre** (in the Tuileries inside the Concorde gate), are tucked away; others, such as that of the Louvre (or of the **Musée d'Erotisme!**), boldly announce the treasures of the museum even before you've entered the exhibition halls. They all are quite different, and you'll encounter many during your museum-visiting expeditions throughout the city.

The museum restaurants warrant a whole other chapter. I long to go back to the elegant tearoom at the **Musée Jacquemart-André,** a real haven of loveliness, perfectly suited to the supreme collection of works housed in this spectacular private mansion in the northwest quadrant of Paris. Brunch on the terrace at the **Café de la Musique** only enhances your jazzy experience at the **Musée de la Musique at La Villette.** This rhapsodic gathering spot was orchestrated by the Costes brothers, the men responsible for injecting a lot of pizzazz into the café, dining, and hotel scene throughout Paris. Pick up a *Pariscope* or the *Paris Free Voice* for a complete list of museums.

RICHES OF PARIS TIP

The best museums that reveal the world of perfume are in the provinces, but in Paris, you can visit the **Musée de la Parfumerie Fragonard** (9 rue Scribe, 9e; tel.: 01.47.42.93.40; Métro: Opéra), a private museum/boutique housed in a lovely nineteenth-century town house.

Money

A Few Words About Prices

I've tried to provide indications within each of my descriptions concerning the price of goods or services for each establishment. I don't always spell it out, but the way I describe a certain place should say it all. The goods, for example, in the Boutiques de Luxe section tend to be high priced, but this should not deter price-conscious shoppers from taking a peek inside, because most of the houses also sell little trinkets that won't leave you gasping. Shopping on the Right Bank, in general, *is* considerably more upmarket than in areas such as the Left Bank, the place des Victoires and Les Halles, and the Marais. Boutiques within the Passages, the Bastille and République, and the Sixteenth tend to sell goods that are even more moderately priced.

Exchange Rates and Cashing In

Know that the rate you receive in most banks is slightly lower than the one announced in the newspapers, on CNN, or on Web sites such as www.xe.com. It was generally thought that you'd get the best rate by paying with a credit card. However, many credit card companies are now charging 3 percent for the fund conversion, which can really add up. Best to check with your credit card company about their added fees before you go charging up a storm.

Note: At this writing, $1 equals approximately € 0.80—a so-so exchange.

Shop around during your trip for the best exchange rates. Major banks typically give the best exchange, although some of the *bureaux de change* provide competitive exchanges as well. Always look at the exchange rate *and* any other fees that may be tacked on per transaction. You'll receive a slightly higher rate for traveler's checks. If you're looking to exchange U.S. $100 bills, you might find that they are refused at certain banks and exchange offices due to counterfeit concerns, so I suggest you travel with smaller denominations. It's best to avoid exchanging currencies in hotels—not to mention in boutiques or restaurants.

Banks usually open at 9 A.M. Some still close for lunch, and most close for the day at 5 P.M.; few are open on Saturdays. The following bank stays open later than most:

HSBC; 123 av des Champs-Elysées, 8e; tel.: 01.40.70.16.50; Métro: George V; Open Monday–Friday 9 A.M.–6:15 P.M.

Another key address for money-changing and more:

American Express; 11 rue Scribe, 9e; tel.: 01.47.77.79.28; Métro: Opéra; Open Monday–Friday 9 A.M.–6:30 P.M.; Saturday 9 A.M.–5:30 P.M.

If you are a cardholder, you may cash personal checks here or draw on your card for cash advances; you may also receive mail and messages addressed to you care of AMEX.

If you're down to your last fifty euros and you've reached your maximum credit limit on all your major credit cards, you can have cash (up to €7,600) quickly wired to you through Western Union. Most of the transfers may be picked up at the post office or certain banks. You may call 08.25.00.98.98 in Paris; the U.S. number is 800-325-6000; www .westernunion.com.

Automatic Banking Machines

Travelers have come to rely more and more upon automatic banking machines (ATMs) throughout France—so much so, in fact, that there's no real need to carry traveler's checks. Most of the machines are connected to the Cirrus and PLUS networks, and the logos are clearly visible. Using ATMs is a cinch, since the instructions are always listed in several languages and there are so many of them located throughout the capital.

Note: Most banks charge you a transaction fee when you use machines abroad, so it's best to withdraw large sums of money rather than making lots of withdrawals in small increments. Depending on your bank or credit card, the interest might pile up significantly with each withdrawal. It's best to check with your credit card company about these matters and daily cash withdrawal limits before you leave for your trip.

RICHES OF PARIS TIP

Withdraw some cash at the ATM machine upon arrival at the airport. The exchange will be better than at the airport *bureau de change* and the line shouldn't be nearly as long.

Payment

Most major credit cards are widely accepted throughout Paris, although generally speaking, the shops mostly take Visa or MasterCard. (American Express may be more readily used for hotels and restaurants.) The French people's credit cards necessitate PIN numbers when making purchases, whereas yours probably won't; if by any chance an absent-minded person in a boutique or any other establishment tries to run your card through a handheld gizmo, you may want to indicate that your card does not require you to punch in a PIN number.

Note: I have indicated which shops absolutely do not take credit cards; the rest accept at least one of the major cards.

If you have a debit card, it will most likely function at an ATM in Paris. Once again, check with your bank at home before you leave to learn how to best use it on your trip and whether any fees are involved.

Thinking about doing some antiquing in Paris or at the flea markets? Make doubly sure to bring a fair amount of cash with you. Not only will many of the dealers (especially at the flea markets) refuse credit cards, cash will also give you more leverage in bargaining.

Even if you're not antiquing, it's always good to have some cash with you. (You never know when you might encounter an open-air market!) But don't ever pay in American dollars or traveler's checks, unless you don't care about losing out on the exchange.

For lost or stolen credit cards or to obtain emergency cash, call:

American Express; tel.: 01.47.77.72.00 or to the United States at 336-393-1111 (may call collect).

Diners Club; tel.: 01.49.06.17.76 or to the United States at 800-234-6377.

MasterCard; tel.: 08.00.90.23.90 or to the United States at 800-307-7309.

Visa; tel.: 08.36.69.08.80 or to the United States at 800-428-1858.

RICHES OF PARIS TIP

Some credit card companies offer protection from purchases that have gone sour, but this may not apply abroad. Check with your credit card provider before you leave home to be sure.

Tax Refunds

The key word to savings in France is *détaxe*, which loosely translates to making a purchase without being charged the tax. The tax amount, which is included in nearly all prices listed in France, is often called TVA or VAT and ranges from 5.5 to 25 percent on various goods and services. (Important: Most stores give a tax refund of about 10 to 15 percent.) Nonresidents of France and the European Community are entitled to a tax refund if their total purchases in one boutique add up to at least €175. Certain luxury goods stores require a higher minimum purchase. There is no *détaxe* on antiques that are one hundred years old or more.

Your greatest savings occur when you take advantage of the *détaxe*, and it's worthwhile to shop in several well-chosen boutiques in order to achieve the minimum balance required in each establishment, instead of picking up a lot of odds and ends in fifteen different Paris shops. Keep in mind that if your total purchases fall just a small amount shy of the €175 marker, throwing in another little something is like getting it for free. Also, if you are shopping with friends, you may group your purchases together on one tax form in order to benefit from the *détaxe*. This does not mean that one person has to pay for everyone else's purchases; it does mean, however, that only one person will directly benefit from the tax refund. (He or she can then treat the rest of you to tea once you're back home in the States.)

The *détaxe* is very simple. Once you have reached your minimum balance of €175, you will most likely be reimbursed for the tax amount on your credit card whether you pay with a credit card or cash. (There are Tax Free Shopping and *Détaxe* bureaus that will reimburse you in cash before leaving Paris—as long as you show your plane ticket and passport—but it's best to ask the store where you make the purchase for information regarding these companies.)

At the moment of your purchase, the salesperson will help you fill out the tax forms. (You need to have your passport or passport number with you at this time.) Show these papers, along with your plane ticket and passport, to the customs officer at the airport, train station, port, or border (if you're in a car) on the day of your departure from France. Do this before you check your luggage, or have your purchases with you in a carry-on; chances are slim that you will be required to show your goods, but if you are asked where they are, you should at least have your bags with you. The customs official will stamp your tax forms and show you which one to mail back to the establishment as proof that you have indeed left the country. (The mailbox is right at the customs counter.)

Once your tax form has been received, your account should be credited for the tax amount (less certain small fees). If you don't go through with the paperwork, you will, of course, be charged for the tax amount.

Note: If you have not received compensation for filing within ninety days, you may want to contact the store where you made the purchase or the French consulate in your country, or both. Claims are valid a year after the date of purchase. If your purchases totaling €175 or more are shipped directly to you from the store, the tax is automatically withdrawn, and you do not have to go through this paperwork process.

DUTY-FREE AIRPORT SHOPPING

Duty-free shopping at the French airports is actually very good; I have found myself picking up more and more items at these mini airport boutiques over the years. An American friend of mine recently turned me on to their cheeses, which were particularly fine, just like the rest of their selection of gourmet foods, wines, and a cargo load full of other gift ideas. Count on saving at least 15 percent off regular French retail prices, sometimes considerably more. These little emporiums don't have the charm of the Paris boutiques, but they are convenient.

Facing the Music: Your Country's Customs and Duties

Going through customs can be a breeze or a living nightmare—it all depends on who you are up against and how you play the game. It's risky business, and if you try to smuggle in a suitcase full of Hermès scarves, you may get stuck paying the duty and a stiff penalty. Whatever route you decide to take, dress appropriately: If you wheel through with a set of matching Gucci bags, you will probably be stopped. Here's what you should know before you go.

Leaving France with your goods is easy unless you've just purchased a major hunk of France's *patrimoine national* or a near-priceless work of art. The dealer from whom you bought such a treasure will alert you to the fact that the French government may have reservations about letting it out of the country. If you have any doubts about French customs information, you may contact:

Douanes (Centre de Renseignements); 84 rue d'Hauteville, 75010 Paris; tel.: 08.25.36.82.63.

Reentering the United States is considerably more complicated. Here is a brief synopsis of what you really need to know:

- Articles totaling $800 or less may be entered free of duty as long as you have not already benefited from this exemption within the past thirty days; this total includes items purchased in the duty-free shops, gifts, and, believe it or not, any repairs or alterations made to your belongings while you were away.
- Each individual family member, including infants and children, is entitled to the $800 exemption; joint declarations may be made for all members. A family of four, for example, could make a single declaration and be exempt for $3,200 worth of goods.
- You pay a flat rate of 3 percent duty on the next $1,000 worth of goods above the $800 allowance. If your total purchases amount to $1,800, you pay $30 duty. ($1,000 \times .03 = 30$)
- If you have acquired more than $1,800 worth of merchandise abroad, duty is calculated separately for each additional item. Duty fees vary considerably, so you may want to research this a bit if you plan to do a ton of shopping. For more information, go to the Harmonized Tariff Schedule at www.usitc.gov.
- Duty-free items include fine art and antiques at least one hundred years old (with certificate of authenticity).
- All agricultural and food items must be declared. Canned pâté and other comestibles are for the most part okay. (These regulations vary according to particular meat or chicken alerts.) Bakery products and cheese (excepting those in liquid form) are also acceptable. For more detailed information on food items, consult www.aphis.usda.gov.
- You are entitled to one liter of wine or spirits if you are at least 21 years of age (although duty on wine and spirits per liter is nominal once over the $1,800 limit).
- If the customs officer really wants to come down on you, he or she may ask you to pay duty on possessions that you might have acquired

on a previous trip to Europe. In order to avoid such a fiasco, you may want to register susceptible goods (or carry proof of previous purchase) before you leave home.

- Any item you received as a gift must be declared.
- Duty is not collected on gifts sent home declared at a value less than $100. Know that if you declare a gift to be valued at more than $100, the recipient will have to pay duty.

Be cooperative and courteous to the customs officer, and your life will be made a lot easier. For more information about U.S. customs and duty, call the U.S. embassy in Paris at 01.43.12.74.00 or contact the U.S. Customs Service for a free and detailed guide titled *Know Before You Go:*

U.S. Customs Service; tel.: 202-354-1000; www.cbp.gov.

RICHES OF PARIS TIP
Customs officers often look through wallets and purses for sales receipts.

Shop Talk

Hours of Operation

Although store hours are indicated for each boutique, the French are rather inconsistent about set hours in general. Confirm the store hours by telephone if you are making a special trip. You're apt to encounter at least one sign on a store window saying "Be back in five minutes." Of course, five minutes is never five minutes, so be prepared to sit it out in a nearby café. The same rule applies to holidays, birthdays, and impromptu days off; it's not unusual for a French shopkeeper to spontaneously decide to close for the rest of the day. Only a handful of establishments close for the whole month of August, and I have indicated them to the best of my ability, but be prepared for variations. If there is a boutique you really want to see during a holiday week (Easter time, the winter holidays, or Assumption Day, on August 15), call ahead to see if it's open.

Note: Many stores are closed on Mondays, either all day or just until 2 P.M. Most stores are closed on Sundays, although more and more remain open, particularly in the Marais, along the Champs-Elysées, and in other tourist areas such as rue de Rivoli. Museum shops, the various antiques villages, and, of course, the flea markets are also open on Sundays. Many stores are open the three Sundays before Christmas.

Sales

There is strict governmental regulation regarding the practice of sales (or *soldes*) in France, which explains why—with only a few exceptions—they take place only twice a year: in January and July. (Some begin around the third week of December and June.) It's definitely worth the wait, though, since prices are marked down 20 to 50 percent (mostly 50!). If you're willing to push and shove with the rest of the Parisians, you can find some real bargains, especially on designer fashions. Most stores give tax refunds at this time, too, but not all take credit card payments.

The major department stores also have short, three-day sales during a week in March and October. Most sales are announced in *Le Figaro* newspaper the week of the sale.

Returns

French merchants aren't as flexible as American ones, and it is extremely difficult to make exchanges in most boutiques. If you hesitate about what you are buying, tell the salesperson that you have some reservations and want to show it to your husband or friend back at the hotel. If what you were considering buying doesn't work out—and if you are charming and clever enough—you may be able to bring the merchandise back the next day for a store credit.

If you have a horror story boutique experience, (such as paying a small fortune for a handbag advertised as handmade leather, and then discovering it's machine-stitched vinyl) you should file a consumer complaint. Of course, you should try to come to an agreement with the boutique, but if this gets you nowhere, send a letter (in French or English) to the address that follows. Be sure to include all necessary information, such as a copy of your receipt, the name and address of the shop, and an explanation of your complaint.

Direction Départementale de la Concurrence, de la Consommation, et de la
Répression des Fraudes de Paris/Ile-de-France

8 rue Froissart

75003 Paris

Tel.: 01.40.27.16.00; fax: 01.42.71.09.77 or 01.42.71.09.14.

Note: The above bureau prefers to receive complaints by letter or fax. Don't rely on it for settling complaints about antiques or artwork unless you have received a certificate of authenticity stating an exact description of the item.

Size Conversions and Other Size-Related Information

There is a chart of U.S., French, and British size conversions on page 33. Don't, however, refer to it as if it's the Word of God. Not only are there a lot of size discrepancies among different labels and cuts, I've usually found that it's difficult to provide exact equivalents for French sizes. In some stores you may be a 42, in others you may be a 40. Overall, salespeople are very helpful and quite effective with sizing you up. If you're buying gifts, it's best to buy large—it can always be taken in later. If you're buying for yourself, take the time to try on clothing and shoes.

Shopping for shoes can be a tiresome task in France (depending on your shoe size), because French shoes do not come in varying widths. Half sizes are not often easy to come by either, and the selection of women's shoes drops off considerably for larger sizes 40 and 41. Large women will have some trouble shopping for clothing in Paris because most shops only carry up to size 44 (many go only to 42). The big-name boutiques are usually well supplied with 46s, but you can also find plus sizes at **Vicky Tiel, Popy Moreni, Animale, Maud Defossez, Fred Lansac,** and other boutiques that also do custom work in addition to their regular ready-to-wear collection. Much to my chagrin, **Marina Rinaldi**—which is actually Italian—is the only boutique in my book that specializes in fashions for large-sized women.

You'll also find a lot of clothing (especially men's and women's shirts and sweaters) marked S, M, L, and XL or 1, 2, 3, and 4—for small, medium, and large.

SIZE-CONVERSION CHART

WOMEN

Coats, dresses, blouses, pants, and skirts *(manteaux, robes, chemisiers, pantaloons, et jupes)*

USA	6	8	10	12	14	16
F	36	38	40	42	44	46
GB	8	10	12	14	16	18

Shoes *(chaussures)*

USA	5	6	7	8	9	10
F	36	37	38	39	40	41
GB	3½	4½	5½	6½	7½	8½

MEN

Suits *(costumes)*

USA/GB	36	38	40	42	44	46
F	46	48	50	52	54	56

Shirts *(chemises)*

USA/GB	14	14½	15	15½	16	16½	17
F	36	37	38	39	40	41	42

Shoes *(chaussures)*

USA	6	7	7½	8½	9	10	11
F	39	40	41	42	43	44	45
GB	5½	6½	7	8	8½	9½	10½

CHILDREN

See text, p. 34, for clothing sizes.

Shoes *(chaussures)*

USA	8	9	10	11	12	13	1	2	3
F	24	25	27	28	29	30	32	33	34
GB	7	8	9	10	11	12	13	1	2

I've provided the conversions for children's shoe sizes, and clothing sizes are much easier to figure. Children's clothing sizes run according to the age of the child; sizes run in months for babies ages 3, 6, 12, and 18 months, and in years for kids ages 2, 3, 4, 6, 8, 10, 12, 14, and 16 years.

Alterations

If you find something in a shop that you really like but it needs to be altered, don't hesitate to buy it. Alterations *(retouches)* may be accomplished easily enough in most Paris boutiques and often in no time at all. Many shops require a week to ten days to carry out alterations; however, if they know that you're leaving tomorrow, most establishments will carry out the job by the end of the day. This is particularly true for the couture houses, and once the alteration has been made, they will have the item dropped off to you at your hotel. Unfortunately, most of these big-name boutiques charge for alterations, whereas the smaller, lesser-known shops usually won't. Service has its price.

Shopping from Your Home and via the Internet

With more of us shopping from our homes these days, it's nice to know that we can stretch our shopping landscape as far as France. Of course, nothing can replace the delight of entering a quaint little Left Bank boutique filled from its creaky floorboards to its rafters with centuries-old goods, but it's nice to know that we can begin to learn more about (or even buy) these treasures from afar.

I have included store Web sites in this book whenever possible. I think they will help you a lot. Consider them as visual descriptions of each of the entries I have included. Before you even begin to think about packing your bags, you may want to check them out to better plan your shopping and touring itinerary. Some of them are mere showcases; others allow you to buy the goods online. A certain number of the sites—particularly the ones trying to be extremely creative—are rather annoying since the download times are so long. But maybe even that will improve within the next year or two. The Internet is still relatively new in France. In any event, I'm quite sure that having these sites will be valuable to you. You have everything you need to be a perfect armchair traveler and shopper from the comfort of your own home.

RICHES OF PARIS TIP

I've found the Web site www.wayp.com helpful to look up phone numbers, addresses, and even sometimes Web sites of establishments in France.

Where to Rent

If you find that you have just been invited to a ball at Versailles or to some other fancy occasion, and you have nothing to wear—nor the time or money to shop for it—why not rent?

A.B.C.D. SOIRÉES Cocktail and evening dresses, prim suits (perfect for French weddings!), hats, bags, and shawls in a festival of colors may be rented from this sixteenth-arrondissement establishment. Prices begin at €80 for a simple dress and escalate up to €400 for *une création* from one of Paris's top designers. Reserve in advance for more of a selection.

8 rue Mignard, 16e; tel.: 01.45.03.50.03; Métro: Pompe; Open Monday 2–7 P.M.; Tuesday–Saturday 10:30 A.M.–7 P.M.; www.abcdsoirees.com.

AU COR DE CHASSE This is Paris's most distinguished address for men's formalwear rentals. Tuxedos run about €95 with a €350 guaranty; accessories such as gloves, shirts, and cuff links must be purchased separately. The store also has a selection of formalwear for sale.

25 rue de Condé, 6e; tel./fax: 01.43.26.51.89; Métro: Odéon; Open Monday 10 A.M.–6 P.M.; Tuesday–Saturday 9:30 A.M.–6:30 P.M. (come at least an hour before closing for fittings); www.aucordechasse.fr.

Note: Although most rental shops prefer that you call several days in advance, they will try to outfit you the day of your soirée.

Special Care

Soigné types will want to drop off their finery at **Delaporte** (62 rue François 1er, 8e; tel.: 01.43.59.82.11; Métro: Franklin-Roosevelt), Paris's most prestigious dry cleaner. Little gold chairs, bronze sconces, and a white and grey Dioresque interior announce the sort of approach that is employed here when caring for couture gowns and the like.

You may want to have your shoes shined at **Salon Baba** at 34 rue Jean-Mermoz (tel.: 01.42.56.35.53; Métro: Saint-Philippe-du-Roule), a side street off rue du Faubourg-Saint-Honoré, not far from place Saint-Philippe-du-Roule. People go to Salon Baba to relax and to receive an expert shine made special by a considerable amount of elbow grease. Incidentally, the folks from this little shop pointed out to me that you don't see many clean shoes in Paris—quite unlike London—since French people don't like to shine shoes. It's surprising you don't encounter more shoeshine shops in Paris! Salon Baba does repairs as well.

Bringing and Sending Home the Goods

BY HAND   Even with the airlines' crackdowns in recent years regarding luggage entitlements—particularly for carry-ons—it is still possible to bring home many of your purchases yourself (assuming, of course, that you didn't go overboard with the wardrobe you brought to Paris).

Ask the shops to properly wrap your purchases for you. Most will do this gladly and are very conscientious about protecting the more fragile items in Bubble Wrap. Note also that the French do a magnificent job of gift wrapping, often simply by using their own beautiful store bags, to which they affix a fancy bow and ribbon.

RICHES OF PARIS TIP

I ask for the wrappings to be given to me separately; then I can lay them flat in my luggage and do the prettying up myself once I'm back at home.

BY AIRMAIL   Many stores will mail your purchases for you. If you are staying in a luxury hotel, the concierge should be able to handle this as well. Otherwise, you will have to organize the mailing yourself. FedEx, DHL, and UPS are easy to find in Paris (check with your hotel), or you can also mail packages from *La Poste* (France's postal system). You may choose from several different classes of mail service, all of which work extremely well. (I've yet to lose a package.) The postal service provides a variety of different-shaped boxes, but you may not have a pleasant experience at *La Poste*. Both the postal workers and the people waiting in line tend to be gruff and impatient. Going there used to traumatize me when I first lived in France (much like dealing with the cashiers at supermarkets), but then it just became part of the downside of living in this beautiful country. Maybe you'll encounter more friendly faces.

RICHES OF PARIS TIP

As soon as you find a place in Paris that sells poster tubes, you may want to buy one for the *affiches* and prints you might pick up along the way; oddly enough, such tubes are not always easy to locate. You will most likely find them at the museum gift stores and the larger souvenir shops.

SHIPPING   Whatever you buy—no matter how big or fragile—there's a way to ship it home. Most stores and art and antiques dealers are more than happy to make the arrangements for you directly.

Know that shipping costs can be steep, particularly since there is usually a lot of careful packing and crating involved. But depending on the value of the piece, this expense is more than worth it. Be particularly vigilant about the paperwork. For antiques, the paperwork includes the certificate of authenticity of your purchase and usually two different receipts: one that indicates the value for customs purposes and one you might want to use for insurance appraisal once the piece has arrived at your home. (Know that these amounts are typically different.) Take pictures that clearly show the condition of the piece at the time of purchase in case it is damaged in transit. You must insure your purchase for this very reason, and if by any chance you are shipping more than one piece, ask for an itemized inventory list instead of a grouped one. (This will facilitate your cashing in on a claim in case only part of the shipment arrives damaged.) The trip home can be a long one (two to three months, depending on where the shipment is going). This voyage will probably have your newly acquired piece passed from truck to ship to truck and so on, so you need to take every precaution possible and always read the fine print. If you do all of that, everything should work out splendidly.

A Few Packing Tips

Developing a system for packing is crucial. When I travel, I truly live out of my suitcase. (I have done this for as many as seven weeks!) Unpacking is a real luxury, and that is only done when my belongings are in such disarray that I have to unpack and repack in order to fit everything in. I put what I am least likely to wear on the bottom, and generally leave room for three short stacks of clothing that consist of T-shirts, sweaters, pajamas, and a reserve of scarves and lightweight shawls. I leave the other quarter of my suitcase available for toiletry, makeup, and jewelry cases as well as other miscellaneous little bags. Shoes I tuck in front of a stack at the top of the suitcase or, if need be, on the sides. This is all pretty standard, but my best trick involves all of my plastic-covered garments. I leave my favorite clothes—blouses, tops, jackets, pants—that I have selected for my trip on their hangers. I then cover them—two or three at a time—with dry cleaner bags and fold them down into the suitcase on top of my little stacks. The bags trap the air, creating a perfect cushion that prevents the clothing from wrinkling. I learned this from the head of haute couture at Chanel, and my clothing has been far more presentable ever since. With this technique, you only have to remove your toiletry and other small cases and hang up your clothing in the plastic bags once you have arrived. Now, what to pack?

It's very Parisian to have lots of accessories (they allow you to change your look many times over). Think knits and silk, too. They're both extremely low maintenance and virtually the only way you can avoid those silly travel irons (which always seem to short out the electricity where you're staying anyway). Even if you can afford to stay in the fanciest hotels, I'm sure you will be appalled by the prices charged to do a little *pressing*. The old "hanging it out in the shower" trick works best for me.

Don't lose track of the fact that part of your mission here is to buy. So, as much as it's nice to have your favorite outfits with you, it's not a bad tactic to be just a little short on something—you'll inevitably find it (or something very close) in your travels. Do try to bring at least one bag—collapsible or otherwise (although always have one hard suitcase for the more breakable items)—that you can fill with all your loot for your trip home. This should not be difficult, given the size of luggage today (my father has a piece that looks like a small walk-in closet) and also since so many bags come equipped with wheels that actually work. When I saw that Louis Vuitton came out with a piece of luggage complete with wheels and a functional pop-up handle I knew that we had entered a new era, a time of practicality and high style. Let that be your mantra next time you begin to pack for Paris.

Keep in mind, too, that a lot has changed in recent years, so you have to be even more careful with your packing. Since bags are opened more than ever before by airport security specialists, make doubly sure that valuables and fragile goods are with you at all times in your carry-on. (That includes film, since much of the equipment used to screen bags can damage film.) Consider investing in a special Transportation Security Administration (TSA)–accepted lock that allows screeners to open and relock your bags. It's also best not to overpack since that makes it more difficult for these people to carefully close your bags. Be conscious of airline weight limits as well since we're no longer allowed to check such heavy bags. (Most airlines have reduced their limit to fifty pounds per bag from seventy.) Last but not least, make sure you haven't packed any prohibited items—particularly in your carry-on. For the complete list of these off-limit items, go to www.tsa.gov.

RICHES OF PARIS TIP

I always travel with a couple of candles or some incense to freshen up stale rooms and surround myself with familiar and comforting smells. If you *really* like to be cozy, tuck a hot-water bottle into your luggage. It helps with assorted aches and pains and warms up a cold and unfamiliar bed.

Dealing with Lost or Stolen Items

I once had all my luggage stolen out of the trunk of my car in the south of France, a devastating experience that taught me to be vigilant at all times. I also learned that it's possible to live happily with one of those famous core wardrobes, even one that might consist of just a few interchangeable outfits, two pairs of shoes (you were probably wearing a pair when the drama occurred), and yes, just one tube of lipstick! A good homeowner's or renter's insurance policy should cover all replacement costs (eventually), but be prepared to pursue your insurance company doggedly. (Since then, I keep piles of receipts, just in case something like it happens again.)

My apple (or should I say, shopping?) cart was also upended in Paris when I lost my extremely dog-eared copy of *The Chic Shopper's Guide to Paris*—the master copy with all my personal notations and updates for the first edition of *The Riches of Paris*. Prayers and a very attentive doorman at the Hôtel Plaza Athénée helped me recover my loss. I had taken a taxi from the Plaza and absentmindedly left my "bible" in the cab. Within twenty-four hours, the taxi driver returned to the Plaza for another fare, and the doorman alerted him to the stack of papers and torn-up book littering his cab. People can really go out of their way to make things right for you in France.

Let's hope that nothing even remotely similar happens to you, but if it does, you can seek out your loss at Paris's lost and found:

Objets Trouvés/Préfecture de Police; 36 rue des Morillons, 75015 Paris; tel.: 01.55.76.20.74; Métro: Convention.

Note: Anything lost at the airports, in the Métro, in taxis, and elsewhere in Paris would most likely be turned in to the above address. Most major train stations in Paris have their own lost and found.

You and the French (Breaking Down the Myth)

Stop! Don't turn on your heels and walk out of a Parisian boutique just because you have received a less than friendly welcome from a somewhat reserved French salesperson. Breaking down the icy barriers that sometimes exist between Americans and French salespeople is not as difficult as you may think (or may have heard). Like much of life in France, it begins with a greater understanding of the French and their approach to serving their clients. In the United States, it is easy to enter a boutique anonymously and to browse freely and at your leisure. This is rarely the case in France, which explains why many Americans sometimes feel bothered or uncomfortable when dealing with French salespeople.

My Chic Promenade boutique tours were created in part to facilitate shopping experiences for visitors to the French capital. The presence of someone who not only speaks the language but, even more important, understands the quirks that make French shop owners and salespeople tick reassures the shopper that their little foray will go as smoothly as possible. Some of my (and my clients') most rewarding exchanges with French salespeople occurred when I made the effort to engage in conversation with them. Some of you may balk at this idea, especially if you have ever been greeted with a rather snooty *"Bonjour, madame."* (Remember that the lack of a bubbly hello does not mean that the French are unfriendly, it's just a different approach.) If you feel slightly uncomfortable in a store because a salesperson is giving you the once-over, turn the tables and warm up to them. In most instances your interactions with the salespeople will turn out to be a sort of game. For example, start off with comments like "I've come to look at your new collection" (this only works at the beginnings of the seasons), "I've heard you specialize in so-and-so," or even something as banal as "It's good to get in out of the rain." Compliments go even further in France than in the United States, so if you start chattering about some element of the décor you're halfway there. The more you share yourself with them, the more they'll open up to you.

If you don't feel comfortable uttering a few words in French (such as *cette lampe est superbe!*), say it in English, but if you engage in conversation with the shopkeepers, ask first whether or not they speak your language. Many Americans make the mistake of interpreting standoffishness as anti-American sentiment. *Au contraire!* The French not only have a great fondness for Americans, but many also rely upon American tourists for a large part of their livelihoods.

Now that I've helped to break down the myth of the nasty Parisian salesperson, it's up to you to break down the myth of the Ugly American. It is important to treat Parisian shop owners and salespeople with the respect they merit. First of all, greetings and salutations are extremely important in

France, so remember to always add *monsieur* or *madame* onto a hello, a thank-you, or a good-bye, otherwise you may be considered impolite. Looking the part is key: If you go shopping on avenue Montaigne (the home of French couture), for example, try to look as elegant as the avenue itself. It's okay to dress down for sightseeing, but spiff up your look when you go shopping.

Appearances count for a lot in France, and you should look as chic as the boutiques you intend to visit. Accessorize, put on a dab of makeup, wear a few baubles, and remember to save your ultracasual footwear for the museums. (These shoes, though practical, still aren't part of being well dressed for shopping in Paris. I, for example, virtually live in sports sandals in my Rocky Mountain town of Telluride, Colorado, in the summer, but I can't imagine the day when I would wear them in Paris!)

Touring in Paris

Key Information

This is by no means an exhaustive repertory of all the Paris boutiques. (Yes, there're more!) I've selected the ones that best represent the riches of Paris and most clearly reflect the personality of the neighborhoods. This is a big tip of the iceberg, but here are some other important sources for help in planning a successful voyage:

Paris Convention & Visitors Bureau; 25 rue des Pyramides, 75001 Paris; tel.: 08.92.68.30.00; Métro: Pyramides; www.parisinfo.com.

Maison de la France; 444 Madison Avenue, 16th Floor, New York, NY 10022; Call the hotline to receive information: 514-288-1904.

Note: Every year, Maison de la France publishes FranceGuide, an info-packed glossy magazine. Receive a free copy by contacting info.us@franceguide.com or read the magazine online at www.franceguide.com.

If you are a real France-info junkie, I suggest you think about subscribing to one or more of the following publications:

La Belle France; tel.: 800-225-7825; www.lbfrance.com.

ENTREE (not exclusively on Paris or France); tel.: 805-969-5848; www.entreenews.com.

France Magazine; tel.: 202-944-6069; www.francemagazine.org.

France Today; tel.: 800-232-1549 or 415-981-9088; www.francetoday.com.

Journal Français (from the same publishers as *France Today,* but in French); tel.: 800-232-1549 or 415-981-9088; www.journalfrancais.com.

Paris Notes; tel.: 800-677-9660; www.parisnotes.com.

And for up-to-the-minute entertainment and arts coverage, pick up these publications when in Paris: *The Paris Voice*—available in English-language bookstores and American restaurants and bars throughout Paris, www.parisvoice.com, and *Pariscope*—sold for a few euros in kiosks around town, www.pariscope.fr.

The following Web sites provide even more information on Paris, some in the form of free newsletters:

www.anamericaninparis.com

www.bonjourparis.com

www.francemonthly.com

www.franceonyourown.com

www.insiderparisguides.com

www.parlerparis.com

www.paris-expat.com

www.parisinsites.com

Note: Be sure to check out my Web site, www.therichesof.com, for even more information on Paris, the French provinces, and beyond!

SOME OF MY FAVORITE READS

Pick up one of the following titles to read before, during, or after your trip to Paris. (There's a mix of fiction and nonfiction here, but I'll let you have fun looking them up on your own.) I assure you, however, that each one will provide you with copious amounts of insight about France and the French.

Almost French by Sarah Turnbull

Fatale by Edith F. Kunz

French or Foe? by Polly Platt

French Toast by Harriet Welty Rochefort

Into a Paris Quartier, *Le Divorce*, *Le Mariage*, and *L'Affaire*, all four books by
Diane Johnson

Paris, Paris by David Downie

Pariswalks (try touring with the audio version in Paris) by Alison and Sonia
Landes

Telephoning in France and Other Important Tidbits

In 1996, the telephone system changed in France, dividing the country into five different zones or area codes: 01 for Paris and its environs; 02 for the northwest; 03 for the northeast; 04 for the southeast, including Corsica; and 05 for the southwest. For all calls inside France, dial 0 before the nine-digit number.

Making telephone calls from hotels can be easy but quite expensive. To call abroad from France, dial 00. If you want to use a calling card to call outside of France, be sure you know the access code ahead of time. To call all numbers in France from outside the country, dial the nine digits (without the 0) after the access code 33 for France. (A call to Paris from the United States might read like this: 011-33-1-12-34-56-78.)

Note: Most of the better hotels provide Internet access either directly in your room or in the lobby. Some charge a fee for this, some don't. If this is important to you, it's best to inquire ahead of time.

RICHES OF PARIS TIP

It's a good idea to purchase phone cards (similar to the ones you buy at the post office in the United States) from a *tabac* or *La Poste* to make calls from phone booths in France. (Few public telephones take coins, although you can place a call with these phone cards or your regular calling card.)

Making Your Travel Plans to and from Paris and Beyond

The Internet has changed the way we research, plan, and book travel. Shop around and do price comparisons for products of equal (or at least similar) value. We're so lucky to have this resource at our fingertips—we just have to be careful how we use it.

The Internet—along with the airlines' elimination of travel agents' commissions on ticket sales—provoked many changes for the travel agency industry as well. Many were forced to close, but those that remained became better than ever. Today travel agencies charge fees and are even more highly regarded by their clients for the valuable services they provide. Just try making an unexpected change on your own from a ticket purchased on the Internet. Or see what happens if that hotel/cruise/tour you booked ends up looking nothing like what you thought you had purchased online? If you're looking for someone to help you to plan the best possible trip, find yourself a good travel agent. Word of mouth is a good start.

There are many options for finding your way to Paris by plane. In addition to the major carriers such as Air France, American Airlines, Delta, and United, you may want to look into buying a package from one of the many tour operators. They can usually provide you with a nicely reduced airfare and/or accommodations even if you forgo a set tour.

Air France Holidays; tel.: 800-2-France (800-237-2623); www.airfrance-holidays.com.

American Airlines Vacations; tel.: 800-321-2121; www.aavacations.com.

United Vacations; tel.: 800-328-6877; www.unitedvacations.com

Once you arrive in Paris by plane, you have many different options. I sometimes take a taxi for door-to-door service or, if I'm not too weary or loaded down, I take one of the Air France buses that ferries travelers in from Orly and Charles-de-Gaulle to different drop-off points in Paris (one-way trip from CDG to Etoile: €12).

You can also take the RER (commuter train) from CDG/Roissy into Paris. This works great if you are a light traveler, but if you're traveling with a full wardrobe (which you should be to some extent!), a taxi or the Air France buses are the best bet.

Chances are pretty good that at some point you will travel either into or out of Paris by train. The Eurostar, a sleek and luxurious train, is the mode of choice transportation to and from London. (Yes, this train takes you under the Channel.) It's totally divine and works like clockwork. For traveling to other cities in style, including Brussels, Amsterdam, Antwerp, Cologne, and Düsseldorf—all with links to Paris—I recommend the lovely Thalys, another magnificent example of today's technology that puts our Amtrak trains to shame. It's amazing how all these slick trains have made so many places within easy reach throughout Europe! For more information about these trains and the rest of Europe's train system (including the granddaddy of them all, France's TGV, or high-speed train), contact Rail Europe:

Rail Europe; tel.: 888-382-7245; www.raileurope.com.

Rail Europe also has a number of rail-and-drive packages that will help you with your travels outside Paris.

You may also consult the French rail system's Web site: www.sncf.com.

MY TOP THREE ALL-TIME FAVORITE TOURISTY THINGS TO DO IN PARIS

- Take a boat ride on the Seine, particularly at night when all the monuments and riverbanks are illuminated.
- Stroll through the Tuileries and/or the Luxembourg Gardens.
- Check out the view from the Pont (or *passerelle*) des Arts; then walk along the Seine to the Pont Neuf; tuck into place Dauphine; then wander through the rest of Ile-de-la-Cité down around Notre Dame and cross over to Ile-Saint-Louis.

Selecting the Right Culinary Experience and Lodging

I've indicated many places to stay the night or to enjoy a meal— simple or grand. All these places have been selected either because I have a great fondness for them or because I think they truly embody the flavor of the neighborhood—and oftentimes for both reasons. My description of each establishment should help to steer you when planning your trip or just deciding where to have a bite for lunch during your day of shopping and touring. There wasn't enough room to list all my favorite hotels and (especially) restaurants, but the ones I have included throughout the book are certainly at the top of my list.

Note: For gratuities in restaurants and cafés, be aware that although a 15 percent service charge is included, it is customary to leave a little extra—ten or twenty centimes for a café, considerably more for a nice dinner—3 to 5 percent of the total bill.

RICHES OF PARIS TIP

Speak up! If you don't like your room, just say so, and chances are you'll quickly be installed in another room far more to your liking.

The following list of lodging providers should help you to further solidify your plans:

Bestwestern; tel.: 800-528-1234; www.bestwestern.fr.

Châteaux et Hôtels de France; tel.: 888-924-2832; 0892.23.00.75 from France; www.chateauxhotels.com.

Concorde Hotels; tel.: 800-888-4747; 0800.05.00.11 from France; www.concorde-hotels.com.

Esprit de France; www.espritdefrance.com.

Four Seasons; tel.: 800-332-3442; www.fourseasons.com.

Inter-Continental Hotels; tel.: 800-327-0200; 0800.908.555 from France; www.interconti.com.

The Leading Hotels of the World; tel.: 800-223-6800; 0800.136.136 from France; www.lhw.com.

Libertel Hotels; tel.: 800-44-UTELL; www.libertel-hotels.com.

Relais & Châteaux; tel.: 800-735-2478; 01.45.72.96.50 from France; www.relaischateaux.com.

Sofitel and Demeure Hotels; tel.: 800-SOFITEL; 0825.885.555 from France; www.sofitel.com.

Warwick International Hotels; tel.: 800-203-3232; www.warwickhotels.com.

Note: Some of the companies above offer hotel rooms of varying categories and price ranges. There are often real deals to be had, depending on the time of year and your perseverance. Don't hesitate to look and ask for bargains, and keep in mind that there is generally a big difference between Right Bank and Left Bank hotels. The rooms and amenities in Left Bank hotels are directly proportionate to the more accessible pricing practiced on this rive gauche side of the Seine. The little boutique hotels may not be such a good idea for business travelers or for those in need of pampering, but for visitors seeking charm and a more relaxed atmosphere, the Left Bank is the way to go.

RICHES OF PARIS TIP

If you are able to include a road trip outside of Paris for a minimum of seventeen days (a perfect amount of time in which to enjoy *The Riches of France*), contact the following car-leasing agencies to rent a brand-new car:

Auto France; tel.: 800-572-9655; www.autofrance.net.
Renault USA; tel.: 800-221-1052; www.Renault-usa.com.

RICHES OF PARIS TIP

During the busiest periods (September through October, and March), you may have better luck booking hotels directly or through your travel agent than with tour companies—but try the companies anyway.

And if you're looking to become more of a Parisian—for a week or more—you can rent an apartment. The following agencies and numbers should prove most helpful to you:

Chez Vous; tel.: 415-331-2535; fax: 415-331-5296; www.chezvous.com.

Just France; tel.: 610-407-9633; fax: 610-407-0213; www.justfrance.com.

Rentals in Paris; tel./fax: 516-977-3318; www.rentals-paris.com.

Vacances Provençales Vacations; tel.: 800-263-7152; www.vacancesprovencales.com.

Ville et Village; tel.: 510-559-8080; www.villeetvillage.com.

And there're many more at www.therichesof.com!

If you're looking to buy your own special hideaway in France, contact **Just France Sales;** tel.: 610-407-9633; fax: 610-407-0213; www.justfrance sales.com.

RICHES OF PARIS TIP

Go to www.fusac.fr for a plethora of classified ads and advertisements on everything from apartment rentals to French lessons for the English-speaking community. You can also pick up the free *FUSAC* magazine at Anglo-frequented locations throughout Paris.

Sending You on Your Way

Now that you know all the essential information about shopping in Paris, you're probably eager to set out on your own. Although Paris is a maze of centuries-old streets that don't bear even the slightest resemblance to the grid pattern of most major American cities, you'll find it amazingly easy to find your way around.

The city is divided into twenty districts or *arrondissements,* a most organized system developed by Haussmann, Napoleon III's great city planner. The first one is in the center of Paris near Les Halles; the others spin out in a spiral-like formation. As long as you know in which arrondissement an address is located, it is easy for you to visualize in what part of the city that establishment may be found.

One of the most efficient forms of transportation is the Paris subway (or Métro). Not only is it easy to figure out, it also prevents you from being caught up in the city's frenzied traffic jams. Unless you plan on taking the subway or bus at least twice a day for a month (in which case you would buy a pass), it's most economical to buy ten Métro tickets at a time (total cost €70); ask for a *carnet* (pronounced "car-NAY").

These same tickets may be used for the Paris city buses (sometimes you need two if you're going a distance), which may be picked up throughout the city. At each bus stop there is a map with the names of the stops on that bus's route; once you have determined if that bus is going where you want to go, make sure that you pick it up in the right direction. Although slower and often less direct than the Métro, the bus is an excellent form of transportation in Paris because it lets you take in all the beautiful sights as you travel to your destination.

Taxis are not always as plentiful in Paris as they are in most major American cities, which means that you often have to wait a while to find one. In most instances, you cannot hail a cab from just any street corner. Instead, you have to wait at one of the many taxi stations located throughout the city. Taxis take no more than three people (the front seat is saved for the drivers' dogs!) and the cabbies often charge extra for large bags and packages. The usual tip is 5 to 10 percent of the total fare.

When you leave your hotel, take the following things with you: your passport (for *détaxe* and unexpected money exchanges), a calculator, a map of Paris (from your hotel reception desk, for example, or if you're a real Parisophile, *un plan de Paris*, a book that contains detailed maps of Paris neighborhoods, a complete listing of streets, and other helpful information), a camera (in case you need to photograph a purchase that you're going to ship), and even a tape measure (which comes in handy for measuring tablecloths, furniture, and the like). Of course, don't forget your plastic and your funds, but most of all unleash your spirit of curiosity and remember that shopping and touring through these fascinating and historical showcases is just another wonderful way to experience Paris.

PART TWO

The Districts

2

The Right Bank

THE BIG NAMES

Newcomers to Paris often find it difficult to differentiate between the Left and Right Banks, but once you become familar with the French capital, you'll realize how easy it is to tell the two apart—even if you don't know which side of the Seine you are on. Like the other areas of Paris, the Right Bank (the *rive droite*) touts a very distinct look—chic, elegant, and above all, luxurious. Here are Paris's most beautiful stores, top luxury hotels, and many of the city's best restaurants. Although areas such as place des Victoires, Les Halles, the Marais, the Bastille and République, and the Sixteenth are located on the Right Bank, the term *rive droite* is most often used for the area surrounding the Champs-Elysées as well as that of rue du Faubourg-Saint-Honoré and rue Saint-Honoré.

For more than one hundred years the Right Bank has served as the world's window for designer fashions and, even more precisely, the world of couture—that marvelous French fashion mechanism that, because of its high standards of quality and creation, continues to influence designers and fashion-conscious people worldwide. (The couture houses, along with many of the other big names, have in fact enabled many of France's highly specialized artisans such as milliners or fan makers to survive.) Most of the couture houses are located within the bustling confines of the first and eighth arrondissements, which make up the Right Bank. Today the number of big-name fashion houses (referred to as *couturiers*) that actually put on Haute Couture shows has dwindled considerably; some seasons it may be eight, others even fewer. The word *couture* refers to custom-made fashions, and the origins of Haute Couture date back to 1858, when Charles Frederick Worth created the first Haute Couture house at 7 rue de la Paix.

In order to officially receive the title of Haute Couture (which is unpretentiously called *couture*) by the **Fédération Française de la Couture,** a couture house must fulfill a number of rigid requirements. The costs of producing such a collection and putting on the obligatory show have become prohibitively expensive, which explains why only about eight couture houses, such as Dior, Chanel, Givenchy, and Christian Lacroix, still produce Haute Couture collections.

Each season is kicked off with an Haute Couture fashion show for the international press and buyers, taking place twice a year: in January (spring/summer) and in July (fall/winter). The collections were at one time presented to private clientele within the couture houses' own salons during a month and a half following the press showing, but today videos are most often shown. (These same videos may be shipped to princesses in distant countries so that they may make their selections.) Buyers are mainly interested in purchasing the patterns and the rights to reproduce certain models, whereas the press (at least one thousand French and foreign journalists) represent the couture collections' raison d'être: publicity. The pages of photos and articles that follow each couture presentation create exposure, prestige, and name recognition—all essential to the big names' survival. The bread and butter does not come from selling costly couture fashions, but from the various ready-to-wear, accessories, perfume, cosmetics, and housewares lines that are put out by the house. Licensing agreements only sweeten the pie and, of course, none of this would be possible without the glamour, gloss, and mystique that the couture scene embodies.

Even though most of us can only afford to buy off the rack (there are only about one thousand Haute Couture clients worldwide), there was renewed interest and excitement in the world of couture once Christian Lacroix gave it a brisk new look with the opening of his couture house in the early 1980s. New blood was called in to give life to many of Paris's

first and most respected couture houses; Karl Lagerfeld greatly rejuve-
nated Chanel; John Galliano sensationalized Dior; and other houses such
as Yves Saint Laurent garnered much attention (for a brief moment,
thanks to Tom Ford); but now it seems that some of the bastions of tradition are awaiting the next creative genius to breathe in even more life.
Whether that will come for some of the sleeping giants or not remains
unclear, but there's no doubt that today the emphasis lies much more
with deluxe ready-to-wear and accessories. (Rochas, Nina Ricci, and Céline are examples of houses that have made huge strides toward adopting
a younger, fresher image.) The economic boom experienced by many of
the world's industrialized nations in recent years has further helped to
drive the success of these big names onward and upward. Bernard Ar-
nault, the genius behind one of the most important luxury-goods groups
in the world, LVMH, or Louis Vuitton Moët Hennessy, a holding company that includes Dior, Givenchy, and countless other big names, is
largely responsible for having piloted these renowned French brands to
an even higher stratosphere of worldwide recognition. (Take Dior handbags as an example—they have become all the rage and some of them
cost as much as a small car.)

As such an important fashion reference, the Right Bank has its reasons
for being intimidating and often downright snobbish. If you stand straight
and tall, throw your shoulders back, and assume the same air of authority
as the French, you will have no qualms about crossing the thresholds of
Paris's famous couture houses. Don't leave the city without strolling
along the glorious tree-lined avenue Montaigne, which (along with the
rue François 1er and the avenue George V) makes up the luxury
shop–laden neighborhood called the Golden Triangle. This area became
the hub of Paris's couture houses shortly after Christian Dior opened here
in 1946. Today it is home to most of the Paris *couturiers* even though
the landscape has changed a fair amount over the past fifteen years,
with the addition of other designers or labels that aren't even big name
(French swimwear specialist Eres now has a store here, for example).
Even if you don't intend to buy a $15,000 couture dress, you may want to
take a look at the stores' lovely accessories and more affordable ready-to-
wear lines, much of which is indeed different from what is shown in the

United States. The area is more prestigious than the rue du Faubourg-Saint-Honoré, which has a bit less polish because of the steady stream of tourists and tour buses that flood that part of town.

Look on the other side of the Champs-Elysées. The extensive restoration project that was completed about ten years ago really paid off; the avenue was smartened up considerably, and now many of Paris's big names have opened up magnificent showcases amid the long-established fast food restaurants and movie theaters. Behind les Champs lies the long swath of rue du Faubourg-Saint-Honoré, which later turns into rue Saint-Honoré. (Most people refer to this whole area as Saint-Honoré.) The majority of the couture houses also have shops on the rue du Faubourg-Saint-Honoré and, although the setting varies considerably, the selection of merchandise is quite similar.

One of the most luxurious streets in Paris, rue Royale, runs perpendicular to rue du Faubourg-Saint-Honoré and rue Saint-Honoré. Beginning at place de la Concorde and ending at the Madeleine, this eighteenth-century street harbors many sumptuous establishments, including Maxim's, Lalique, and Paris's most exclusive florist, Lachaume. Farther down rue Saint-Honoré, rue de Castiglione leads into place Vendôme, home of the world's most prominent jewelers. After examining the monumental bronze column made from the melted-down cannons fired at Napoléon's victorious battle of Austerlitz, you'll notice many pristine windows around you showing off their "musts."

Shopping the entire Right Bank could take a month—if not a lifetime. You can find just about anything here, from *the* perfect handbag to a copy of the *New York Times* at William H. Smith! With handbag or paper in hand, stroll over to the Tuileries Gardens, sit down, and contemplate all the beautiful Parisian goods that continue to set the standard for fashion and luxury throughout the world. Then you'll begin to have a greater sense of what shopping in Paris is all about.

Boutiques de Luxe

BALENCIAGA   Frenchman Nicolas Ghesquière has been successfully designing the house's ready-to-wear collection for a number of years now. It's all splendidly displayed in this flagship house in a highly creative, not-to-be-missed contemporary décor. Look for lots of superb volumes and rich textures in both the womenswear and accessories.

10 av George V, 8e; tel.: 01.47.20.21.11; Métro: Alma-Marceau;
Open Monday–Friday 10 A.M.–7 P.M.; Saturday 10 A.M.–1 P.M. and 2:30–7 P.M;
www.balenciaga.com.

BALMAIN Pierre Balmain opened his couture house at this address back in 1945. The ever so elegant spirit of Balmain lives on today in the sleek ready-to-wear collection showcased here. The creamy marble ultraluxurious boutique provides the perfect setting for the graceful silhouettes that have always made up the core of the collection of this celebrated house.

44 rue François 1er, 8e; tel.: 01.47.20.98.79; Métro: Franklin-Roosevelt;
Open Monday–Saturday 10 A.M.–7 P.M; www.balmain.com.

CÉLINE Céline's ready-to-wear and accessories collections for women have become increasingly fresh, vibrantly colored, and fun since American designer Michael Kors took over the helm. Monsieur Kors said *au revoir* to this venerable house in 2004, yet his smart (and sometimes even sassy) look continues to seduce some of the most stylish women in the world. Shop here for high-quality fashions and accessories priced more acceptably than at Hermès and Chanel. Note that although Céline has at least a half dozen boutiques in the United States alone, you can buy here for better selection *and* savings.

36 av Montaigne, 8e; tel.: 01.56.89.07.91; Métro: Franklin-Roosevelt; 58 rue de
Rennes, 6e; tel.: 01.45.48.58.55; Métro: Saint-Germain-des-Prés; 3 av Victor-
Hugo, 16e; tel.: 01.45.01.80.01; Métro: Victor-Hugo; Open Monday–Saturday
10 A.M.–7 P.M.; www.celine.com.

CHANEL Just across from the service entrance of the Ritz Hotel is the site where Mademoiselle Chanel first opened her couture house in 1928. Couture and ready-to-wear designer Karl Lagerfeld perpetuates the Chanel legacy in his updated versions of timeless chic. He has intelligently reworked and reinvented everything from *mademoiselle*'s braid-trimmed box-styled jackets to her long, swingy gold chains, in addition to injecting a huge dose of total fashion innovation into this well-established house. Coco Chanel would indeed be proud since she intelligently revolutionized fashion in numerous ways during her own era. (She added gold chains to her clutch purses, in fact, so that they could be carried more easily.) Now Chanel chic comes in everything from jeans to button-encrusted cuff bracelets.

Go to the Cambon boutique for the biggest selection of ready-to-wear, accessories, makeup, and beauty products (only sold here). Savings are not as fantastic as we all would like. If you benefit from the *détaxe*, you may be able to save about 25 percent on certain items. Chanel's iconic quilted bags ring in between €600 for a teeny tiny one and €1,000 to more than €3,000 for the others. The *détaxe* here will save you another 13 percent. Sorry, men: Ties are the only items Chanel carries for you.

31 rue Cambon, 1er; tel.: 01.42.86.28.00; 21 rue du Faubourg-Saint-Honoré, 8e; Métro for both boutiques: Concorde: Open Monday–Saturday 10 A.M.–7 P.M.; www.chanel.com.

CHLOÉ Looking for something sexy, hip, and beguiling? Chloé has managed to turn out ultrafeminine creations for a good number of years. Stella McCartney helped to revive this long-established French house and, even since her departure, Chloé continues to melt the hearts of many fashion-conscious ladies. Both boutiques sell ready-to-wear and leather bags and shoes.

44 av Montaigne, 8e; tel.: 01.47.23.00.08; Métro: Alma-Marceau or Franklin-Roosevelt; 54–56 rue du Faubourg-Saint-Honoré, 8e; tel.: 01.44.94.33.00; Métro: Concorde; Open Monday–Saturday 10:30 A.M.–6 P.M.; www.chloe.com.

CHRISTIAN LACROIX The world of Christian Lacroix bathes you in sun-drenched harmonies from the couturier's native region, la Camargue, a unique corner of Provence. Terra-cotta tile floors, white and violet walls, and earth-tone accents form a festive backdrop for the folkloric fashions for which he is most famous. Today's look is less Baroque but no less charming.

Chances are you'll be enchanted by Lacroix's eclectic selection of bags, shoes, belts, scarves, and gems. Most are shown in a dazzling array of gypsy-inspired colors and textures, and his costume jewelry is among the best in town. Lesser-priced and more youthful Lacroix frivolities, such as a flamenco-inspired embroidered T-shirt (priced at € 95), may be found in his Jeans lines. You can find Lacroix stateside at Neiman Marcus and Nordstrom, but the selection and prices here are better. A classic purchase would be anything bearing the Provençal cross (the couturier's fetish symbol), hearts, or stars. And for that fairy-tale wedding, take a peek at the bridal gowns.

73 rue du Faubourg-Saint-Honoré, 8e (CL and Jeans); tel.: 01.42.68.79.04;

Métro: Miromesnil or Champs-Elysées-Clémenceau; 2 and 4 place Saint-Sulpice,

6e (CL and Jeans); tel.: 01.46.33.48.95; Métro: Saint Sulpice;

Open Monday–Saturday 10:30 A.M.–7 P.M.; www.christian-lacroix.fr.

COURRÈGES   The sixties wouldn't have been the same without André Courrèges; this is the guy who is responsible for having created mod pantsuits, go-go boots, hip huggers, and for a generation of us baring our midriffs!

Today the futuristic look of Courrèges seems to have the new millennium in mind. Be prepared to be greeted by a go-go-boots-clad saleswoman who looks like she just disembarked from her intergalactic spaceship. Be prepared for new fashion adventures as you try on Courrèges's striking line of clothing. Keep in mind that this is the only Courrèges boutique in the world. (Different collections are sold around the globe through licensing agreements.) So don't miss your opportunity to buy a pair of white vinyl boots or some smart sportswear.

And be sure to take note that there's **Courrèges Café Blanc.** You almost have to wear sunglasses to sit in this blinding white space *(très Courrèges),* but this is one of the best places to stop in this high-priced neighborhood for a low-priced bite to eat. Breakfast, lunch, and snacks are informally served in this little café.

40 rue François 1er, 8e; tel.: 01.53.67.30.00; tel.: 01.53.67.30.13 (café);

Métro: Franklin-Roosevelt; Open Monday–Saturday 10 A.M.–7 P.M.;

www.courreges.com. ✕

DIOR   I'll never forget the first time I visited Christian Dior. It was at least twenty-five years ago, during my junior year abroad, and I had the divine privilege of attending one of their Haute Couture shows, which at the time were presented upstairs in the elegant couture salons. Those private show-ings are practically nonexistent nowadays; instead, Dior's Haute Couture shows are more like Hollywood productions staged outside the house for the likes of celebrities and power-wielding fashion editors.

Those salons are now occasionally used for much smaller viewings, or perhaps for the fitting of a young princess's bridal gown, or as a space for the couturier to practice his talent for divine inspiration. Yet as much as Dior has grown and evolved into probably the most extraordinary fash-ion showcase in Paris, much has remained the same. Most of the ateliers are still here and the fascinating process of creation continues daily just above one of the world's fanciest showcase boutiques.

This is certainly what makes a visit to the House of Dior on avenue Montaigne very different from any stop you might make in another Dior boutique. Truly the flagship, all the beauty and exquisite creative talent behind this name is on view here in full regalia. Mill around, take it all in, watch films of the most recent Dior fashions as if you had a front-row seat. There's no better place (or at least almost) to view couturier John Galliano's saucy creations. It's all very entertaining and lusciously beau-tiful, even if fashion is not your forte.

This is also the only Dior store in the world where you'll discover a stunning collection of home décor and table arts made exclusively for Dior. Favorite items include dishes and *objets* bearing the lily of the valley, Monsieur Dior's preferred flower and his trademark. In addition to all this, the ever-innovative collection of women's ready-to-wear and acces-sories, Baby Dior, and jewelry, you'll also find Dior's men's collections here, one of the most handsome in Paris.

30 av Montaigne, 8e; tel.: 01.40.73.73.73; Métro: Alma-Marceau or Franklin-Roosevelt; 16 rue de l'Abbaye, 6e; tel.: 01.56.24.90.53; Métro: Saint-Germain-des-Près; Open Monday–Saturday, 10 A.M.–7 P.M.; www.dior.com.

EMANUEL UNGARO   A rich palette of colors blooming in a garden-fresh array of prints typifies this designer's two lines: Emanuel Ungaro and Fuchsia. Hot items include brightly colored silk print blouses (€900) and vivid silk shawls in a bouquet of floral prints (€250). The shop also sells women's bags and shoes along with a very refined men's collection.

Prices here tend to run 30 percent less (with *détaxe*) than at the Ungaro boutique in Manhattan.

2 av Montaigne, 8e; tel.: 01.53.57.00.00; Métro: Alma-Marceau;

Open Monday–Saturday 10 A.M.–7 P.M.; www.emanuelungaro.fr.

GIVENCHY I'm sorry to say that it's hard to know if Italian haute couture and womenswear designer Riccardo Tischi will still be on the scene by the time this book is in print. Then again he might be a smash hit. So far, his collections have been a bit spotty and they have not received rave reviews in the press. Let's face it—ever since Hubert de Givenchy retired, life has not been quite the same in this grand old house. Being a part of luxury goods conglomerate LVMH has probably both helped and hindered the creative process.

Do look around, however. I'm sure you'll find at least one item that embodies a bit of the delicious feminine spirit of Audrey Hepburn, Hubert's muse.

3 av George V, 8e (women's ready-to-wear and accessories);

tel.: 01.44.31.51.09; 8 av George V, 8e (women's and men's accessories);

tel.: 01.44.31.49.91; Open Monday–Saturday 10 A.M.–7 P.M.;

Métro for both boutiques: Alma-Marceau; www.givenchy.com.

GUY LAROCHE Hervé Leroux's women's fashions for this esteemed house are constructed but not stiff. The look is sharp and timeless. You can always find a range of classic suits in basic black, grey, and brown, which is why Guy Laroche often caters to well-heeled mother-daughter shopping teams. Sizes range from 36 to 44; a handful of models come in 46.

Count on spending between €2,000 and €2,500 for a cocktail dress; €3,000 to €5,000 for an evening gown.

35 rue François 1er, 8e; tel.: 01.53.23.01.81; Métro: Franklin-Roosevelt;

Open Monday 11 A.M.–7 P.M.; Tuesday–Saturday 10:30 A.M.–7 P.M.

HERMÈS You'll probably notice the beautifully decorated store windows before you even realize that you have arrived chez Hermès ("air-MESS," not hermies). Once you walk inside, you won't be disappointed—Hermès is truly the warmest and most authentic of all the luxury shops on this street.

Hermès began in 1837 as a harness maker, later took up saddle making, and now sells everything from luxury ready-to-wear to arts of the table. (Centuries-old Cristal de Saint-Louis and Puiforcat make up part of their stable of holdings.) Although today they are making only about 450 saddles a year (mostly for American clients), the basic elements in horse-related accoutrement still serve as inspiration for virtually every article in the Hermès store.

Certainly, most Americans come here to buy Hermès's ties, gloves, and, of course, their world-famous silk scarves (priced at €250). The problem is that everyone else wants to buy scarves, too, which creates massive traffic jams. Have an idea of what color scheme you prefer ahead of time (the scarves are divided accordingly) so you won't have to waste much time making your selection. It's also best to go early in the morning, because after noon the crowds are often three deep at the scarf counter. Prices generally run a good amount less than in the United States, and if you benefit from the *détaxe,* your savings are increased by about 10 percent (less here than at other houses). Be sure to ask for the booklet that shows the many glamorous ways to tie a scarf—the salesgirls don't always remember to slip it into your little orange box. Everyone who pops into this exquisite emporium may pick up a complimentary copy of *Le Monde de Hermès,* the glossy lifestyle magazine that this house publishes every year.

If you've planned a larger budget for Hermès, indulge yourself with a piece from their women's ready-to-wear collection. (Jean-Paul Gaultier has once again splendidly unleashed his creativity here.) Many shoppers also flock to their classic leather items. (Grace Kelly immortalized one of their handbags by toting it, and it has been one of the house's signature items ever since.) Much of what is on sale in this house is handmade in its ateliers just outside Paris. These workshops were located upstairs until about ten years ago, when they were relocated because the limited space made it difficult for craftsmen to keep production up with the tremendous success of this celebrated leather-goods emporium. The saddle workshop—the soul of the house—remained. Even with this shift in fabrication, you can be guaranteed that Hermès goods are as superbly handcrafted today as they were in the beginning. Above all, this is a house devoted to quality!

24 rue du Faubourg-Saint-Honoré, 8e; tel.: 01.40.17.47.17; Métro: Concorde or Madeleine; Open Monday 10:30 A.M.–6:30 P.M.; Tuesday–Saturday 10 A.M.–6:30 P.M.; www.hermes.com.

ATTENDING A PARIS FASHION SHOW

Many people dream of attending one of the great Paris fashion shows. Unfortunately, it has become extremely difficult to do unless you're famous or find some other kind of "in." Most of the shows—both Haute Couture and ready-to-wear—are reserved for buyers, press, celebrities, and a handful of the designer's loyal followers.

There was a time when the concierges at the fanciest hotels could occasionally obtain an invitation for their guests, but even that has become a near-impossible feat. The fact that there are fewer and fewer houses presenting Haute Couture collections has narrowed immensely everyone's chances of snatching a coveted little gold chair at one of these prestigious showings. (The number of HC showings has dwindled from about twenty to just slightly more than half a dozen twice a year.) And to me it always seemed as though it was easier to obtain *une place* for a couture show than for a ready-to-wear show.

Having said all this, you can still try, beg, plead, pledge your allegiance to a particular house—whatever approach you feel like taking. Remember that the ready-to-wear collections normally show in October and March; the couture in January and July. The shows last about one week, so if you know you will be traveling to Paris during these times, you can check ahead with the **Chambre Syndicale de la Couture** (tel.: 01.42.66.64.44; www.modeaparis.com) to find out the exact dates of your favorite designer's show and the press contact for that particular house. You can always try to contact the press person—who knows what doors might be opened to you? And if you're feeling nervy, go directly to the show and see if you can elbow your way in. (I've seen it work, believe me, even with their army of security.)

And if all else fails, know that the department stores Galeries Lafayette and Printemps (see pp. 100 and 101) hold weekly fashion shows, and for a much more elegant experience, check with the Hôtel le Bristol (see p. 125).

LANVIN The look of the women's ready-to-wear is still one of unadorned elegance under the creative hand of Israeli designer Alber Elbaz. Many of the pieces, in fact, possess the same sort of modernity as those of the twenties and thirties, when the house was establishing itself. Signature accessories include colorful ballet slippers in satin (€350) and sleek and chic necklaces crafted out of ribbons and beads (€450–€600).

In 1926, Lanvin was the first couturier to launch a line of menswear, which has been considered one of the most elegant in Paris (if not all the world) ever since. Don't be afraid to push open the door and walk inside. Their men's accessories department offers many exquisite gift ideas that would certainly be welcomed by the important man in your life. And for the *nec plus ultra*, go to the top floor to Lanvin Couture to order a custom shirt or suit. (There are more than 16,000 models and loads of luxury fabrics from which to choose.)

At this writing, there are no Lanvin boutiques in the United States.
22 rue du Faubourg-Saint-Honoré, 8e (women's); tel.: 01.44.71.31.73; rue du Faubourg-Saint-Honoré, 8e (men's); tel.: 01.44.71.33.33; Métro for both boutiques: Concorde or Madeleine; Open Monday–Saturday 10 A.M.–6:45 P.M.; www.lanvin.com.

LÉONARD Monsieur Daniel Tribouillard, the creative force behind this celebrated French fashion house, little known to Americans, knows how to make women look good. Vibrant floral prints in the forms of bathing suits, wraps, silk scarves (starting at €195), and dresses are the trademark of Léonard, and the look is always fresh, feminine, and perfect for elegant cruises! The men are not forgotten either, with a bold collection of ties and togs.
48 rue du Faubourg-Saint-Honoré, 8e; tel.: 01.42.65.53.53; Métro: Concorde or Madeleine; Open Monday–Saturday 10 A.M.–7 P.M.; www.leonardparis.com.

LOUIS VUITTON Even those who aren't *très* Vuitton will enjoy looking around this magnificent flagship store on the Champs-Elysées. Here you can truly appreciate the full spectrum of creativity that has exploded over the past fifteen years (thanks largely to American designer Marc Jacobs) in this long-established house, in everything from multicolored LV monogram wallets to gold charm bracelets to a pair of denim mules. And almost everywhere you look there's a nod to the company's origins: the art of travel. (I particularly like the section devoted to travel books and journals.)

I didn't develop an appreciation for Louis Vuitton luggage and bags until I visited the Vuitton home and museum in Asnières, a suburb just north of Paris where many of the Vuitton products are still made. There, I learned about the rich history of this venerated house and, most important, that Louis Vuitton is much more than a name. A former professional packer of traveling gentlefolk's belongings, Louis Vuitton first set up shop in 1854, at a time when many people were just beginning to appreciate the wonders of travel. Thirty-three-year-old Louis revolutionized the industry by introducing more functional, flat-top, canvas-covered trunks that could easily be piled up in baggage compartments. It was Louis's son, Georges, who created the celebrated mustard on chocolate brown LV-stamped canvas in 1896 in an effort to combat counterfeiters. (They had already been copied several times by that year.)

The craftsmanship behind each Vuitton piece is as detail-oriented today as it was in the beginning, producing a quality product that is sure to last forever. People no longer travel the way they used to and, yes, even if you're lucky enough to take the Orient Express from Paris to Venice, chances are that you might take along a piece of luggage more practical than an LV trunk. The trunks, however, are often used as home furnishings—open or closed, standing or lying down, and others might even be customized to fit a certain gentleman's cuff link and watch collection. As for all of the other assorted bags and accessories, you can take them just about anywhere and look chic without appearing too flashy. Virtually each bag was created for a specific purpose: the bag *seau,* for example, a sort of satchel that is probably the most popular of all the Vuitton handbags, was designed to accommodate three bottles of champagne (perhaps for a road trip in a car packed full of Vuitton luggage).

Bon voyage!

101 av des Champs-Elysées, 8e; tel.: 0.810.810.010; Métro: George V; Open Monday–Saturday 10 A.M.–8 P.M.; Sunday 1–7 P.M.; www.louisvuitton.com.

MOTSCH/HERMÈS Milliner Motsch and big-name Hermès formed a blissful marriage a number of years ago, and today the original boutique has been expanded and remodeled in order to accommodate an even bigger representation from the Hermès collection. You won't see as many of the superior quality hats here as before, but this location does serve as a handsome outpost for more Hermès shopping.

42 av George V, 8e; tel.: 01.47.23.79.22; fax: 01.47.20.59.60; Métro: George V; Open Monday 10:15 A.M.–1 P.M. and 2:15–6:30 P.M.; Tuesday–Saturday 10:15 A.M.–6:30 P.M.; www.hermes.com.

NINA RICCI   Subtle hues of creamy beige, grey, and rose surround you in this new, more modern Nina Ricci boutique. (A big change from the frou frou of the past!) Its ready-to-wear line, designed by Lars Nilsson, is still quite feminine, albeit more streamlined and sophisticated than before. Still, you're sure to see a few bows, the perennial NR trademark. Shopping here for accessories and perfumes will leave you feeling like a real lady, and selections from their heavenly lingerie collection will make you feel divine.

39 av Montaigne, 8e; tel.: 01.49.52.59.66; fax: 01.49.52.59.59; Métro: Alma-Marceau or Franklin-Roosevelt; Open Monday–Saturday 10 A.M.–7 P.M.; www.ninaricci.com.

PIERRE CARDIN   Pierre Cardin women's and men's fashions are sold throughout the world, but the collections (including some accessories) featured here are exclusive to this flagship store, just across from the Elysées Palace. Both the women's and men's creations have strong architectural lines and asymmetrical cuts.

59 rue du Faubourg-Saint-Honoré, 8e; tel.: 01.42.66.92.25; Métro: Champs-Elysées-Clémenceau; Open Monday–Saturday 10 A.M.–6:45 P.M.; www.pierrecardin.fr.

ROCHAS   This is the only Rochas boutique in the world. If you're anything like me, you'll enjoy admiring (and smelling) the complete collection of Rochas fragrances, including Femme (€99 for 100 ml of eau de parfum), the fruity, jasmine scent handsomely packaged in a curvaceous bottle patterned after Mae West's hips. The store also headlines leather bags, costume jewelery, scarves, eyeglasses, gloves, shoes, and Rochas's own smart line of women's ready-to-wear, designed by Belgian Olivier Theyskens. The Rochas evening gowns have garnered lots of attention in recent years and have been worn by Naomi Watts, Reese Witherspoon, and Jennifer Lopez, to name a few. These and other parts of their collection are sold at Barney's in the United States, but prices here run about 25 percent lower (including *détaxe*).

33 rue François 1er, 8e; tel.: 01.53.57.22.10; fax: 01.53.57.22.09; Métro: Franklin-Roosevelt; Open Monday–Saturday 10:30 A.M.–7 P.M.; www.rochas.com.

YVES SAINT LAURENT   Innovator, genius, and onetime rebel, this ex-assistant to Christian Dior was the world's first designer to set up a ready-to-wear boutique. He did it on the *rive gauche*, and that store still exists today. Signature Saint Laurent details include superbly cut, elegant silhouettes, sophisticated men's-style tuxedos for women, and vibrant bursts of color in striking combinations. There have been some variations on those themes ever since the grand master retired, but there's no doubt that the creative directors have access to a wealth of Saint Laurent images from which to draw inspiration. (Note that there's no one designer at this writing who is creating a big stir.) Distinguished men shop here, too.

True fashionistas must make a pilgrimage to the former Haute Couture house that is now the home of Fondation Yves Saint Laurent, a vibrant museum where shows on YSL and other artists are exhibited.

38 rue du Faubourg-Saint-Honoré, 8e (women's); tel.: 01.42.65.74.59; 32; rue du Faubourg-Saint-Honoré, 8e (men's); tel.: 01.53.05.80.80; Métro for both boutiques: Concorde; 6 place Saint-Sulpice, 6e (women's); tel.: 01.43.29.43.00; 12 place Saint-Sulpice, 6e (men's); tel.: 01.43.26.84.40; 9 rue de Grenelle, 7e (women's and men's accessories); tel.: 01.45.44.39.01; Métro for these boutiques: Saint-Sulpice or Sèvres-Babylone; Open Monday 11 A.M.–7 P.M. and Tuesday–Saturday 10:30 A.M.–7 P.M; 5 av Marceau, 16e (museum); tel.: 01.44.31.64.00; Métro: Alma-Marceau; Open Tuesday–Sunday 11 A.M.–5:30 P.M.; www.yslonline.com and www.ysl-hautecouture.com for the Foundation.

More Luxe

So you just were invited to a very fancy event in Paris and you have nothing to wear? Of course, virtually all of the *boutiques de luxe* in my book offer some spectacular eveningwear but, ladies, be sure to consider **Loris Azzaro** (65 rue du Faubourg-Saint-Honoré, 8e; tel.: 01.42.66.92.98; www.azzaroparis.com) and **Scherrer** (36 rue du Faubourg-Saint-Honoré,

8e; tel.: 01.42.68.01.77) as well. Cocktail dresses and gowns at Azzaro sizzle with all the sexiness of a sultry Parisian *soirée,* while the approach *chez* Scherrer is one of glitzed-up classicism. Both offer a glittery selection of evening accessories as well. Métro for both boutiques: Concorde.

The male faction may want to access the offerings (for evening and otherwise) back at the golden triangle at **Francesco Smalto** (44 rue François 1er, 8e: tel.: 01.47.20.70.63; Métro: Franklin-Roosevelt; www.smalto.com). The King of Morocco and French celebs such as Jean-Paul Belmondo, Michel Sardou, and rocker Johnny Hallyday have greatly appreciated the Smalto look, so maybe you will, too.

Food and Wine Purveyors

ALBERT MÉNÈS BOUTIQUE   At the beginning of the twentieth century, Albert Ménès sailed the seas as part of France's royal navy. That's how he developed his taste for exotic products from all over the world. By 1921, he began to import spices, teas, coffees, and chocolate from faraway locales, in addition to specialties from England and, later, America. (*Mais oui,* Heinz ketchup became one of the French people's condiments of choice!) Today, fine comestibles bearing the Albert Ménès label may be found in grocery stores and supermarkets throughout France, and they still represent quality. This little shop, chockablock full of Albert Ménès products, is a great place to pick up gifts, since they also sell all kinds of boxes, baskets, jars, and cannisters just waiting to be filled.

41 bd Malesherbes, 8e; tel.: 01.42.66.95.63; fax: 01.40.06.00.61;
Métro: Saint-Augustin; Open Monday 3–7 P.M.; Tuesday–Saturday 10:30 A.M.–2 P.M.
and 3–7 P.M.

BETJEMAN AND BARTON   Tea dealers in Paris since 1919, Betjeman and Barton has not only conquered the tea lovers of Paris but also tea drinkers across the Channel. Founded in France by a Frenchman, Mr. Betjeman, who was later joined by his 100 percent British employee Mr. Barton, the company has so far sold more than three hundred thousand of its distinctive red and green cannisters to Harrod's alone. And the folks here say that ever since he discovered it, Prince Charles drinks only Betjeman and Barton tea. When asked why they've enjoyed such success in England, the boutique's manager once told me that "often the quality of tea is better in France, whereas the English are more about quantity."

Betjeman and Barton goes to great lengths to maintain the quality of their more than two hundred varieties of tea. They developed glossy nylon sachets that are filled with tea leaves and sealed without a staple, which can affect the flavor. (I was told here that most paper sachets around the world are filled with a sort of tea dust rather than leaves.) This kind of detail is nice to know, but I'm sure most people are lured into the Betjeman and Barton boutique by the glowing shopwindows. There, tea cannisters and jam jars vie for attention amid an eclectic collection of teapots. Once inside, the visitor is offered a perfectly brewed cup of Betjeman and Barton tea and left to discover even more teapots—both whimsical and sober—along with a rich selection of teatime accoutrements.

Note: The most distinctive Betjeman and Barton tea is Pouchkine, a tea known for its flavorful Russian-brew taste.

23 bd Malesherbes, 8e; tel.: 01.42.65.86.17; Métro: Saint-Augustin; Open Monday–Saturday 9:30 A.M.–7 P.M.; www.betjemanandbarton.com.

LES CAVES AUGÉ Wine enthusiasts can't come to Paris without stopping here. Les Caves Augé is the oldest wine shop in town, family-run and sure to provide a memorable oenological experience. The décor and goods couldn't be much better, but a large part of the shop's popularity is due to the sommelier, Marc Sibard. An enthusiastic, nice fortysomething guy who may be found in a leather apron most days (if he's not out visiting a vineyard), Marc takes enormous pride in the wines he has selected for his shop and the convivial manner in which he shares them with his clients. There's always a bottle of wine open for *dégustation* (Romanée-Conti tastings, unfortunately, are more formally organized) and plenty of bilingual advice to be dispensed.

And you'd be a fool not to take advantage of the store's recommendations. "We know what's very good before [Robert] Parker or the other big wine critics rate it," Marc recently proclaimed to me. "That's why people should buy what we suggest before the prices go through the roof." Marc further explained that Bordeaux wines aren't much cheaper in France than in the United States, but a wine such as a Châteauneuf-du-Pape from Domaine de la Vieille Julienne (2001 and 2003) can cost 40 percent less here than across the pond.

Try to stop in on a Saturday since that's when Marc organizes tastings (usually twice a month from 11 A.M. to 7 P.M.). They're free and he opens some one hundred bottles per tasting, including many organic wines for which he is well known. There are also spirits to be sampled at different times and, much like the wines, most of these come from small producers rather than the big names. There's much to be discovered in this handsome store that has been delighting customers since 1850.

116 bd Haussmann, 8e; tel.: 01.45.22.16.97; Métro: Saint-Augustin; Open Monday 1–7:30 P.M.; Tuesday–Saturday 9 A.M.–7:30 P.M.; cavesauge@wandoo.fr.

CAVES TAILLEVENT   More like a shrine to the nectar of the gods than a simple wine store, all of the nearly twenty thousand bottles of wine sold here are displayed with the utmost reverence in this modern, Bordeaux-colored setting. You are sure to find numerous bottles of exquisite wines and spirits hard to come by stateside and worth stuffing into your suitcase. (A chablis from the Domaine Raveneau, priced at €28 for a 2003 *premier cru*, appears to be one of the recent favorites among Americans.) Highly convivial tastings are often conducted on Saturdays. In case you're wondering, Caves Taillevent is owned by the Vrinat family, the same people behind Taillevent, one of Paris's high temples of gastronomy, which has existed for more than fifty-five years.

199 rue du Faubourg-Saint-Honoré, 8e; tel.: 01.45.61.14.09; Métro: Ternes; Open Monday 2–8 P.M.; Tuesday–Saturday 9 A.M.–7:30 P.M.; www.taillevent.com.

FAUCHON   Foodie or not, when in Paris every self-respecting visitor should set aside some time to visit Fauchon. Since 1886, Fauchon has paid homage to what the French people like to do most: eat, and not just anything, mind you. From the minute you approach this large, bustling establishment, you see crowds of people, noses pressed up against the store's windows, oohing and aahing over the mouthwatering delicacies and exotic fresh fruits and vegetables on display.

Once you enter the store, if you're anything like me, you might be a bit shocked by the new, trendy look of this venerable old house. Magenta and the starkest of whites dominate this ultramodern décor, which is so up to the minute that perhaps they'll be redoing the store again by the time you read this description. I'm sure many of you will like it, though, since it is kind of fun in a George Jetson sort of way. (Be careful about bumping into the curvilinear counters, since many of them are rather oddly configured.)

Even if you're here just to look, you'll certainly buy at least one of the many tempting treats, which include fancy mustards, jams and jellies, honeys, teas and coffees, frightfully rich foie gras, and any number of extraordinary take-out items, to name a few. You'll also find a tea salon upstairs, a superbly stocked cellar, a wine bar across the street, and a bakery. As you can imagine, it's a treasure trove of gift items.

Main store and tea salon: 26 place de la Madeleine, 8e; wine cellar and wine bar; 30 place de la Madeleine, 8e; tel.: 01.70.39.38.00; Métro for all three establishments: Madeleine; Open Monday Saturday 9 A.M.–8 P.M.; 8 A.M.–7 P.M. for the tea salon; 8 A.M.–9 P.M. for the bakery; www.fauchon.com. ✕

FOUQUET A family-owned business since 1852, Fouquet specializes in handmade sweets that have conquered gourmets around the world. This boutique, established in 1926, began to draw discriminating clients long before the neighboring couture houses set up shop. Their mouthwatering chocolates are only part of the reason for their ongoing success; the shop's hard candies, caramels, nougats, jams, jellies, and honeys maintain great drawing power. If you happen to be in town at Eastertime, you're in luck: their pastel-colored, melt-in-your-mouth *fondants* (creamy sugared sweets) make the prettiest little Easter baskets any bunny would want to deliver. All these goodies are presented in beautiful gift packages, ideal for friends back home. In addition to sweets, Fouquet offers their own exotic collection of mustards, vinegars, spices, nuts, teas, coffees, and many other delectables not sold anywhere else in the world!

22 rue François 1er, 8e; tel.: 01.47.23.30.36; Métro: Alma-Marceau or Franklin-Roosevelt; Open Monday–Saturday 10 A.M.–7:30 P.M..; 36 rue Lafitte, 9e; tel.: 01.47.70.85.00; Métro: Le Peletier; www.fouquet.fr.

HÉDIARD In 1854, Ferdinand Hédiard opened up a shop devoted to the sale of exotic fruits, something quite rare in Paris back in those days. His shop was a real flea market with crates, baskets, and tins spilling forth the bounty of far-off lands. The smell of fresh fruit mingled with the aromas of coffee and tea, vanilla and cinnamon, and many more heady goods. It was a mecca of exoticism, frequented by princes, maharajas, writers, artists, statesmen, and Hollywood stars such as Marlene Dietrich and Charlie Chaplin.

Today's store is far more sophisticated, but the heaps of goods arranged pell-mell throughout still give the impression of precious ship's cargo piled high on the docks. All bear the distinctive red and black Hédiard label, and most of this treasured haul of fine comestibles may be purchased individually or in gift packages. The *pâtes de fruits* (sugared jellies made with real fruit flavorings) are some of Hédiard's best-loved signature treats, but I'm sure you'll also stop short in front of many more delectable items.

If you're looking for a place to dine after your day of shopping, I suggest you flop into one of the animal skin–covered chairs upstairs at **La Table d'Hédiard,** the restaurant here. This soothing and exotic décor provides a refreshing change of scenery indeed. Best to go in the evening to beat the lunchtime crowd, and ask to sit at a table by the windows that overlook the place de la Madeleine.

21 place de la Madeleine, 8e; tel.: 01.43.12.88.88 (boutique) and 01.43.12.88.99 (restaurant); Métro: Madeleine; Open Monday–Saturday 9 A.M.–8 P.M.; 11:30 A.M.–11 P.M. for the restaurant; www.hediard.fr. ✖

MAILLE The French consume an astonishing amount of mustard. It is enjoyed on a variety of dishes from grilled meats to *pot au feu.* The truth is that sharp, flavorful mustards have been a French staple for many years. Maille—probably the most notable mustard house in France—was founded in 1747 in, of course, Dijon, in the province of Burgundy. Stop here to shop for a variety of special mustards, many that you will not find at home. The mustards come in an array of distinctive jars, most of which are made of traditional earthenware.

6 place de la Madeleine, 8e; tel.: 01.40.15.06.00; Métro: Madeleine; Open Monday–Saturday 10 A.M.–7 P.M.; www.maille.com.

LA MAISON DU CHOCOLAT   No trip to Paris is complete without a stop at La Maison du Chocolat. Here you will savor some of the best chocolate in Paris (and all of France, for that matter). Many associate fine chocolate with Belgium or Switzerland, yet the true gourmets know that it is the French who regard it more like a treasured jewel than a candy. From the succulent texture of a mocha ganache to the exquisite gold-embossed box, nowhere else in the world is chocolate so coddled and refined as in Paris.

Monsieur Robert Linxe, a spry, affable man whose enthusiasm for his chocolatey creations is dangerously contagious, is the *génie* behind La Maison du Chocolat. Monsieur Linxe's dedication to quality continues despite his great international success. Monsieur Linxe blends the finest *couverture* (the chocolate maker's raw material) with fresh cream and natural flavorings such as juicy, ripe raspberries or roasted almonds to achieve a candy of unparalleled taste. All the chocolates sold worldwide, as well as the pastries and ice cream (available in the summer), are made by hand at La Maison du Chocolat's *laboratoire* just outside Paris.

The boutique is filled from top to bottom with delectable gift items, including three different types of fixings for making your own hot chocolate, fruit-jelly bonbons, liqueurs from the provinces and, of course, an endless selection of melt-in-your-mouth chocolates—all packaged in elegant chocolate brown boxes (made by the same company that manufacturers Hermès's little orange boxes) that will keep your candies fresh for nearly a month.

It's a treat to come to this location (and the one in the Sixteenth mentioned below) to savor a cup of sinfully rich *chocolat chaud* and/or to relish a chocolatey pastry in this cocoa brown salon. *Bon chocolat!*

52 rue François 1er; tel.: 01.47.23.38.25; Métro: Franklin-Roosevelt; Open Monday–Saturday 10 A.M.–7 P.M. (salon closes at 6 P.M.); 89 av Raymond-Poincaré, 16e; Métro: Victor-Hugo; www.lamaisonduchocolat.com. ✖

LES VINS GEORGES DUBOEUF   Who hasn't heard of Georges Duboeuf? We have him to thank for so much of the Beaujolais *nouveau* that we joyously consume each November and December, and even a bit beyond. Monsieur Duboeuf is certainly the greatest marketer of French wines ever. This store has existed for more than twenty-five years, and in addition to its impressive cache of Georges Duboeuf wines (mostly from Burgundy), it also sells an imperial selection of *grands crus* from Bordeaux as well as some choice spirits.

9 rue Marbeuf, 8e; tel.: 01.47.20.71.23; Métro: Franklin-Roosevelt; Open Tuesday–Saturday 9 A.M.–1 P.M. and 3–7 P.M.; www.duboeuf.com.

More Food and Wine Purveyors

As you wend your way around the place de la Madeleine on your foodie tour, leave some time to take in some of the shops on the rue Vignon. You'll jump into a more down-to-earth, country mode at **La Maison du Miel** (24 rue Vignon, 9e; tel./fax: 01.47.42.26.70; Métro: Madeleine; www.maisondumiel.com), Paris's beloved honey house, where you may choose from more than forty different types of honey from all over France and beyond.

It seems, however, that the French (or perhaps the whole world) are tapping into the therapeutic benefits of chocolate more than honey. Or maybe it has more to do with *luxe*, decadence, and the sheer craving for a piece of chocolate rather than a spoonful of honey. In any event there's no lack of *chocolatiers* in Paris. **Jean-Paul Hévin** (231 rue Saint-Honoré, 1er; tel.: 01.55.35.35.96; www.jphevin.com) and **Michel Cluizel** (201 rue Saint-Honoré, 1er; tel.: 01.42.44.11.66; www.chocolatmichelcluizel.com) are two other chocolate shops worth noting; they're practically next door to each other, which makes comparison shopping all the more fun. Monsieur Hévin has installed a tea/chocolate salon upstairs in his striking royal blue and silver shop. At Chez Michel Cluizel, there's an enormous chocolate fountain at the front of the store to enhance your choco-lovers fantasies tenfold, and that's only the beginning. Métro for both boutiques: Concorde.

If you find yourself on *les grands boulevards*—perhaps on your way to or from Trousselier, one of my favorite shops in Paris (see p. 81), swing by **Au Chat Bleu** (85 bd Haussmann, 8e; tel./fax: 01.42.65.33.18; Métro: Saint-Lazare), a sweet little chocolate shop from the north of France. And, as the name implies, you're sure to see a few blue cats there, too.

Table and Kitchen Arts, Home Décor, and Linens

BERNARDAUD Bernardaud, the whitest and most translucent porcelain of the Limoges family, is also France's best seller. This luminous boutique showcases many of Bernardaud's several hundred patterns and shapes (all are available but not all are on display), along with lots of gift items, amid the soft beige and pale green décor. Some of the patterns, such as the elaborately decorated Empress Eugénie, date back to when the Bernardaud Works first opened its doors in 1863. (Life at the court of Napoleon III was brilliant at that time, and Bernardaud naturally found itself flourishing through furnishing the finest tableware for extraordinary court receptions.)

Other patterns are far more contemporary in color and design, having been created by some of Europe's foremost artists. This same creative genius, both past and present, has also been transferred to jewelry and many delightful little *objets* that are also sold in this boutique. My favorite creations include the *lithophanies,* or votive lights (priced here at €50), little porcelain half globes, which, when placed over a votive candle, illuminate glorious scenes such as the palace and courtyard of Versailles. The actual precursor of the lampshade, these little beauties also show off the magnificent translucence of the Bernardaud porcelain.

If you have a penchant for eighteenth-century porcelain, you will find yourself enraptured by the noble services of the **Ancienne Manufacture Royale de Limoges,** an affiliate of Bernardaud that has been producing china since 1737. They are also exquisitely displayed here.

11 rue Royale, 8e; tel.: 01.47.42.82.66; Métro: Concorde;

Open Monday–Saturday 10 A.M.–7 P.M.; Saturday 10 A.M.–7 P.M.;

www.bernardaud.fr.

CHRISTOFLE In 1830, Charles Christofle patented a process for covering a metal base with a thin sheet of sterling silver. Silverplate was born, instantly making silver more accessible to the middle class. The superior quality of the silverplate chez Christofle has built this company's fine reputation around the globe. Indeed, there are numerous Christofle "pavillons" throughout the world (including about ten in the United States), but here the selection is the best and the atmosphere is grander. Shop carefully: the savings are practically nonexistent on certain items, whereas with other pieces, you may save as much as 25 percent.

9 rue Royale, 8e; tel.: 01.55.27.99.13; Métro: Concorde;

Open Monday–Saturday 10:30 A.M.–7 P.M.; www.christofle.com.

CRISTALLERIES DE SAINT-LOUIS Thanks partly to its affiliation with Hermès, this exquisite crystal maker has finally received in recent years the worldwide recognition it deserves. The company, which obtained its royal name from King Louis IX, was actually founded in 1767 on the site of an old glassworks in Lorraine, dating back to 1586. The Cristalleries de Saint-Louis was the first to produce full lead crystal in France and, today, each piece is still made almost entirely by hand. Prices are considerably lower than in the States.

13 rue Royale, 8e; tel.: 01.40.17.01.74; fax: 01.40.17.03.87; Métro: Concorde or Madeleine; Open Monday–Saturday 10:30 A.M.–6:30 P.M.; closed sometimes between 1 and 2 P.M. for lunch.

D. PORTHAULT Porthault's (pronounced "por-toh") light and airy garden-print cotton percale sheets and heavy hand-embroidered table linens have dressed some of the most famous beds and tables of the world. A family-owned business that prides itself on custom work, the name Porthault is synonymous with quality, durability and, above all, beauty.

Step into this recently opened flagship store to view their superior-quality linens, their new collection of table arts, and dreamy self-indulgences such as nightgowns, serving trays, and the plumpest towels in town. Don't miss their crisp baby clothes in white and pastels, perfect for your most precious little darlings.

Items tend to vary with those sold stateside; here they show mostly the *crème de la crème*—and a lot of it! Paris prices are typically a tad better than in the United States (even more with the *détaxe*), and the bargains are the best if you happen to be here for one of their January sales.

50 av Montaigne, 8e; tel.: 01.47.20.75.25; Métro: Alma-Marceau;
Open Monday–Saturday 10:00 A.M.–6:30 P.M.; closed Monday and Saturday
between 1 and 2 P.M.; www.porthault.fr.

DAUM Founded in the Lorraine province of France in 1887, Daum (pronounced "dome") has enjoyed a renaissance over the past fifteen years. Known largely for its use of *pâte de verre,* a sort of glass paste that may be worked by hand, Daum first gained recognition toward the latter part of the last century for its Art Nouveau creations, artistic reproductions of nature splendidly rendered in this molten medium. Today's *pâte de verre* is more like *pâte de cristal* due to its high lead content (24 percent), which causes the *pâte de verre* to take on even more brilliance and relief. The naturalist tradition so cherished by Daum continues in today's pieces, most of which consist of a perfect union of the sparkling transparency of crystal and the living color of *pâte de verre.*

Classics shine here in this showcase boutique alongside more contemporary creations by artists such as Hilton McConnico. (The house actually commissions six to eight sculptors each year to create special limited edition works.) Most of Daum's pieces, whether jewelry, table arts, or *objets,* are highly sculptural and evoke subjects as wide and varied as sleek panthers to Art Deco–inspired vases. The store's prices run 20 to 30 percent less than U.S. prices, and you may also find pieces from numbered series that are only sold here.

4 rue de la Paix, 2e; tel.: 01.42.61.25.25; Métro: Opéra;
Open Monday 11 A.M.–7 P.M.; Tuesday–Saturday 10 A.M.–7 P.M.; www.daum.fr.

L'ESPRIT ET LE VIN You don't have to be a wine connoisseur to appreciate this interesting boutique close to the delightful Marché Poncelet. Aside from a large selection of wine glasses and carafes, L'Esprit et le Vin features an extensive selection of accoutrements used to enhance the *dégustation* of fine wines: archaic-looking wine-bottle warmers, sophisticated thermometers for determining the best temperatures for consuming select wines, cork tags for displaying noteworthy vintages when using carafes, and more!

81 av des Ternes, 17e; tel.: 01.45.74.80.99; Métro: Ternes; Open
Tuesday–Saturday 10 A.M.–1 P.M. and 2–7 P.M.; www.createdinfrance.com.

GALERIE MAISON ET JARDIN   If I were to recommend only one place in Paris to furnish your home in high-end French style, it would be Galerie Maison et Jardin (no relation to the magazine of the same name). Here, panther couches, lacquered tables, and six-foot-long coffee tables with ball-and-claw feet are paired with simple things in the apotheosis of French style. If you can't pull it together yourself, the gallery is more than equipped to do it for you. In fact, about 50 percent of their business comes from turnkey home décor jobs in L.A. and New York. Most of the gallery's furnishings are artisanally made in its own workshops, and a stunning selection is handsomely displayed in this store's eight show-rooms. An eclectic collection of *objets* and antiques offsets the pieces in a most striking fashion, and surprisingly enough, many of them are within a quite accessible price range. Definitely worth a look-see.

120 rue du Faubourg-Saint-Honoré, 8e; tel.: 01.45.61.93.30; Métro: Saint-Philippe-du-Roule; Open Monday–Friday 10 A.M.–1:30 P.M. and 2:30–6:30 P.M.

GIEN   Gien was founded in 1821 in the town of the same name in the Central Loire region by an Englishman who set out to duplicate the re-fined earthenware produced on the other side of the Channel. It has gained international acclaim for its wide selection of superior-quality French faience based largely on traditional designs. One look at a Gien plate and you'll know it has nothing to do with the inferior-quality earth-enware that we often see from Italy and Portugal.

One of the reasons for the success of Gien is the company's ability to adapt its designs to today's tastes and décor. The majority of their designs are based on classical motifs of fruits and flowers, but more recent additions—such as luncheon plates painted with trompe l'oeil fruit and holly-covered Christmas dishes—have contributed to Gien's wider appeal. One of their more recent collections features an adorable little teddy bear *(ours)*, which I'm sure sells as fast as you can say "Hug me." Most of the pieces in their Faience d'Art collection are based on early nineteenth-century designs and have been painted by hand; the others are not hand-painted, which explains why Gien's prices are less than some of the other high-end faience manufacturers.

If you happen to be in Paris toward the beginning of January or June, try to take in their sales, when much of the faience is marked 30 percent off of regular French retail prices. Some of the pieces are end of series or slightly flawed, but the selection can still be terrific, particularly toward the beginning of the sales.

18 rue de l'Arcade, 8e; tel.: 01.42.66.52.32; Métro: Madeleine; 13 rue Jacob, 6e; tel.: 01.46.33.46.72; Métro: Saint-Germain-des-Prés; Open Tuesday–Friday 10:30 A.M.–7 P.M.; Saturday 11 A.M.–6:30 P.M.; www.gien.com.

LALIQUE Once a master jewelry maker, René Lalique switched to glass making in the early 1900s. From the beginning, Monsieur Lalique received great acclaim for his magnificent sculptural glass pieces, many of which embraced Art Nouveau and Art Deco designs. The few changes that have taken place since the founder's death, in 1945, have only enhanced the basic traditions of this celebrated house. Lalique's satiny masterpieces are now crafted in crystal rather than glass, and some of the pieces are also presented in color (an innovation that Marie-Claude Lalique introduced to the firm).

The boutique on rue Royale is like a fairy tale, from the crystal door handles to the luminous display cases that present the delicate wonders magnificently. You'll discover home décor items, arts of the table, barwear, and jewelry in their frosty splendor. Savings run 20 to 25 percent, and the boutique will gladly handle shipping.

11 rue Royale, 8e; tel.: 01.53.05.12.12; Métro: Concorde; Open Monday–Saturday 10 A.M.–6:30 P.M.; www.cristallalique.fr.

LA MANUFACTURE NATIONALE DE SÈVRES Founded in 1740, La Manufacture de Sèvres was the first porcelain manufacturer in France. Government owned, its production is reserved primarily for the state and for French embassies throughout the world. With each exquisite piece almost entirely crafted by hand, you can understand why the yearly output amounts to only about five thousand works. The good news is that La Manufacture also creates a special collection for sale to the public, all of which is on museumlike display in this small shop. Produced in a limited series, most of these pieces are new editions of seventeenth- and eighteenth-century patterns or contemporary designs by such celebrated artists as Johan Creten, Ettore Sottsass, and Adrian Saxe.

4 place André-Malraux, 1er; tel.: 01.47.03.40.20; Métro: Palais-Royal;
Open Monday 2–7 P.M. and Tuesday–Friday 11 A.M.–7 P.M. and by appointment;
www.manufacturedesevres.fr.

NOUEZ-MOI   You can buy "made in France" embroidered house linens here for a fraction of the price you'd pay at Porthault or Noël. A king-sized sheet set (with pillowcases), for example, costs between €260 and €300 here, whereas at the other houses it would be more like €1,000. The quality is fine; Nouez-Moi has lots of gift ideas; it regularly ships to the United States; and this address is right around the corner from the avenue Montaigne. (The original shop is in the Sixteenth, but of course.)

8 rue Clément Marot, 8e; tel.: 01.47.20.60.26; 27 rue des Sablons, 16e;
tel.: 01.47.27.69.88; Métro: Trocadéro; Open Monday 2–7 P.M.; Tuesday–
Saturday 10:30 A.M.–7 P.M.; www.decofinder.fr.

ODIOT   If you can't drum up the nerve to walk inside, at least take a look at the magnificent display of beautifully crafted silver, gold, and vermeil pieces that adorn the windows of this distinguished boutique. Since 1690, Odiot has responded to the discerning needs of France's aristocracy and, later, the upper upper class by creating patterns personalized with the coat of arms or initials of their families. If you do decide to enter this terribly discreet-looking boutique, you may just discover a few treasures that are very much within your budget—how about a vermeil tumbler for €210?

Some time ago, Odiot acquired Tétard, a company that has been making and selling only sterling silver since 1860. Clients have included the sultan of Brunei, the king of Morocco, and Aristotle Onassis. Truly the temple of the French silversmith trade, the shop's old showcases glisten with silver of the most superior quality and craftsmanship. Tétard had rendered some ten thousand designs into some of the most exquisite table arts in existence, including the Trianon, a very elaborate table service used by Marie Antoinette—not surprisingly the most expensive one here. More titillating items include the same type of salt and pepper shakers—complete with special tops to prevent poisoning—that adorned Louis XIV's table. If you don't run into Bill Gates here, you'll probably bump into a few Parisians seeking to complete sets or services that they inherited from their grandparents! Count on spending between €280 and €330 for a single fork, knife, or spoon. Note that Odiot creates a new product every year.

7 place de la Madeleine, 8e; tel.: 01.42.65.00.95; Métro: Madeleine; Open Tuesday–Saturday 10 A.M.–7 P.M.; www.odiot.com.

PUIFORCAT Slightly off the beaten path lies Puiforcat ("pwee-for-KA"), another distinguished French sterling silver company, which has existed for nearly 180 years. In a luminous décor reminiscent of the Art Deco period (Puiforcat's *grande époque*), clients view tables and display cases set with Puiforcat silver, silverplate, its own brand of Limoges china, and a glittering selection of Saint-Louis crystal.

Be sure to visit the mini museum downstairs, which highlights both original and reproduced works that master silversmith Jean Puiforcat designed in the twenties and thirties, as well as a fascinating collection of antique silver pieces that have served as inspiration for many of the company's creations throughout the years.

If some of the prices seem high chez Puiforcat, remind yourself that all the sterling silver pieces are still made entirely by hand. Puiforcat is sold in a number of high-end department stores in the United States, although it's still smarter price-wise to buy here. The silverplate pieces, of course, won't set you back as much.

2 av Matignon, 8e; tel.: 01.45.63.10.10; 22 rue François 1er; tel.: 01.47.20.74.27; Métro for both boutiques: Franklin-Roosevelt; Open Monday–Saturday 10:15 A.M.–6:30 P.M.

TROUSSELIER At first glance it might seem like an exceptionally beautiful florist, but once you notice the absence of heady smells, you realize that the flowers chez Trousselier are not even real. But it would be inappropriate to use the word *artificial* to describe these exquisite works of art, creations that have attracted Paris's haute bourgeoisie and stylish visitors from all corners of the world for many years.

Trousselier has been "fooling" people with silk, crepe, and cotton imitations of flowers and plants since 1877. Some thirty-five nimble-fingered craftspeople make reproductions that are almost more beautiful than life. (Until about fifteen years ago, the atelier was just behind the boutique; today it is located outside Paris.) One perfectly shaped rose requires at least ninety individually placed petals, and a craftsperson can only make four of them in one day. Prices aren't always staggering either.

In addition to fashion accessories, individual flowers, and floral compositions, the shop sells many artful creations other than *faux fleurs* for the home, including vases and urns turned out of a variety of materials.

73 bd Haussmann, 8e; tel.: 01.42.66.16.16; Métro: Saint-Augustin or Havre-Caumartin; Open Monday–Friday 10:30 A.M.–7 P.M.; Saturday 10:30 A.M.–7:30 P.M.; www.trousselier.com.

More Table and Kitchen Arts, Home Décor, and Linens

As you make your way along the rue Royale (odd-numbered side of the street), I suggest you peek into the galerie Royale and village Royale. Built in the early nineties, the **galerie Royale** (at 9 rue Royale) at first feels a little off-putting due to its austere black marble interior. This imposing space does, however, house many other fine French table arts manufacturers such as **Jean-Louis Coquet** (tel.: 01.53.05.12.20), another highly revered porcelain manufacturer from Limoges. At the other end of the gallery at 8 bis rue Boissy d'Anglas, you'll discover **Ercuis/Raynaud** (tel.: 01.42.66.59.21; www.ercuis-raynaud.com), a fine French silversmith and top porcelain maker that merged. (This company also absorbed the House of Peter of superior quality knife fame; they sell some of their hand-forged beauties here in ebony and stones such as lapis lazuli.) Master box maker **Elie Bleu** (tel.: 01.47.42.12.21; www.eliebleu.fr) will dazzle you with a rich array of boxes (everything from jewelry boxes to humidors), frames, desk sets, and more. Their trademark glossy pieces are made out of beautiful and precious woods including mahogany, sycamore, stainwood, walnut, Macassar ebony, amboyna, palisander and vavona, and thuya burl. Having been stained, many are brightly colored and virtually all are bejeweled with fine inlay. True works of art.

Scoot in at 25 rue Royale to discover the **village Royal**. Once the horse stables of Louis XIII, and then later a conglomeration of charming shops and restaurants, today's version is more of a Disneylike display of storefronts. Fortunately, most of the eighteenth-century architecture has been left intact, and the choice of shops overall is quite in keeping with the neighborhood.

Here is where **Haviland** (tel.: 01.42.66.36.36; www.haviland.fr), probably the most world-renowned porcelain maker in Limoges, chose to open its first store in the French capital. By now you have certainly gathered that Limoges is not a brand name, but rather the name of the city in France where most of the world's finest china is produced. It all originates with the fine kaolin clay from this region, which yields porcelain of great transparency and sheen. The miraculous qualities of this clay were first discovered near Limoges in 1767. Today, Haviland is considered the granddaddy of the porcelain industry in Europe.

Note: You may also enter the galerie Royale and the village Royale on the rue de Boissy d'Anglas side; Métro: Concorde or Madeleine.

Art, Antiques, and Collectibles

ARTCURIAL   A well-established contemporary art gallery, Artcurial offers one of the richest selections of art books and modern prints at its bookstore.
61 av Montaigne, 8e; tel.: 01.42.99.16.16; Métro: Franklin-Roosevelt;
Open Monday–Saturday 10:30 A.M.–7 P.M.; www.artcurial.com.

GALLERY TROUBETZKOY   On any given day, you're apt to discover a priceless Renoir, Delacroix, or Brueghel on the walls of this thirty-year-old gallery. You have to look hard to realize (and even then you need expert eyes) that these superbly rendered works are reproductions. But most clients don't ask for ultracelebrated paintings such as van Gogh's sunflower series; rather, they're more interested in lesser-known works by famous or less-than-famous artists—paintings their friends might take for the real thing. People also often ask for copies to be made once they've sold the original or if there are inheritance issues. (Why not have five copies of that beloved portrait of *grand-père*?) Surprisingly, this is all completely legal, and as long as a work by a renowned artist is hanging in a museum, it's fair game. If you don't find your favorite faux on the wall, consult one of the many binders here. Prices range from €390 to €2,900 depending on the painting's dimensions.

1 av de Messine, 8e; tel.: 01.45.62.66.02; fax: 01.42.25.99.39; Métro: Miromesnil; Open Monday–Friday 10:30 A.M.–1 P.M. and 2–7 P.M.; Saturday 10:30 A.M.–6:30 P.M.; www.gallery-troubetzkoy.com.

L'HEURE BLEUE   In one of the most unassuming, affordable, and tasteful antique shops in Paris, Martine and Vincent Raderscheidt present endearing treasures from the mid-1800s through 1920. "Just like you'd see in a French country house during that period," explains Martine. Their eclectic mix of home décor items works just as well in a country retreat as in a swank Parisian apartment. Vases, lamps, furniture, little paintings, and jewelry are charmingly displayed with a theme such as Summer Garden.

17 rue Saint-Roch, 1er; tel./fax: 01.42.60.23.22; Métro: Tuileries; Open Monday, Tuesday, Thursday, and Friday noon–6:30 P.M.; Saturday 3–6:30 p.m.

MARÉCHAL   Behind a rather unobtrusive shopwindow on this boutique-lined street lies a wonderland of Limoges boxes. This is *the* place in Paris to shop for these little marvels, precious pieces of hand-painted porcelain from central France that have enchanted admirers as far back as the eighteenth century. Downstairs is chock-full of some four thousand boxes on themes as wide and varied as the imaginations of the many artists who created these miniature wonders. Virtually all of life has been immortalized in these precious *boîtes de Limoges* in classic groupings such as fruits, flowers, vegetables, and animals, to more droll subjects such as barbecue grills or stiletto heels. Holiday themes are favorites among the Americans, so the shop is well stocked in Christmas trees, Halloween witches, and other festive symbols. Many of the world's icons, including the Statue of Liberty and Marilyn Monroe, have not been forgotten either. There's a box for every occasion, whether it be a wedding, a birthday, or a bon voyage, to name a few. Maréchal sells darling boxes evocative of France, such as the proverbial *baguette,* the golden croissants, the country French *pique-nique français,* and the bottle of red wine, but the best-selling symbol of France is, of course, the Eiffel Tower. Prices start at €50 and climb to about €3,000 for more elaborate compositions. Most boxes cost €70 to €110 and are consider-

ably less expensive than those of equal quality sold in the United States.
232 rue de Rivoli, 1er; tel.: 01.42.60.71.83; Métro: Tuileries; Open daily 10
A.M.–7 P.M.; www.limogesmarechal.com.

RARISSIME   If you take a close look at this cupboard-sized shop you'll
notice that it was built right into the thick stone walls of the majestic Saint
Roch church. From 1630 until the mid-1970s, this tiny space played host
to some of Paris's best-known coiffeurs, and legend has it that the fellows
on their way to the nearby guillotine were first brought in here for their
last "cut and shave." Fortunately, the extraordinary charm of Rarissime
has remained intact. The shop boasts a small but selective collection of
antiques consisting largely of paintings, prints, ceramics, glass, pewter,
bronzes, and some jewelry (there's not enough floor space for furniture)
from the past couple centuries. Although it may be a bit treacherous, definitely take the narrow stone staircase upstairs to see even more treasures.
18 rue Saint-Roch, 1er; tel.: 01.42.96.30.49; Métro: Tuileries; Open Tuesday–
Saturday noon–7:30 P.M.; closed in August and during certain vacation periods.

*Note: The upper part of the rue du Faubourg-Saint-Honoré abounds with
Paris's leading antiques dealers, offering museum-quality pieces at investment-
level prices. Some of Paris's most prestigious art galleries are located next
door to these same antique shops, which greatly facilitates shopping for
those who are looking to match a contemporary painting with a newly acquired Louis XV armchair.*

LOTS OF ANTIQUING

La Cour aux Antiquaires Located at the end of a sunny courtyard in the middle of
Paris's high-fashion boutiques is this congenial gathering of some fifteen fine-quality antiques shops. The setting is elegant without being a bit pretentious—an excellent way to
take a closer look at some French masterpieces.
54 rue du Faubourg-Saint-Honoré, 8e; Métro: Concorde or Madeleine;
Open Monday 2–6:30 P.M.; Tuesday–Saturday 10:30 A.M.–6:30 P.M.

Le Louvre des Antiquaires Just across from the Musée du Louvre, museum-quality pieces are sold in this modern shopping mall setting. There's no doubt that the antiques at the Louvre des Antiquaires are expensive, but they're not necessarily overpriced. Dealers from all over the world are known to buy here. Even if you're not out to make a major purchase, it's just fun to browse through some of the 250 shops, which sell antiques ranging from Ming Dynasty vases to Napoleon III dining room tables.

2 place du Palais-Royal, 1er; tel.: 01.42.97.27.27; Métro: Palais-Royal; Open Tuesday–Sunday 11 A.M.–7 P.M.; closed Sundays in July and August; www.louvre-antiquaires.com.

SOLD! (OR RATHER, *VENDU!*)

Christie's An edict dating back to Henri II prevented outside auction houses from conducting public auctions in France until recent years. Drouot (France's main auction house) had to finally relinquish part of the marketplace once the heavyweights arrived from across the Channel. Christie's had in fact been present in France since 1968 for diverse auction-related services, but now it officially conducts business from their stunning building on avenue Matignon.

The sales are held in French, although the bids are translated into English.

9 av Matignon, 8e; tel.: 01.40.76.85.85; fax: 01.42.56.26.01; Métro: Franklin-Roosevelt; Open Monday–Friday 9:30 A.M.–5:30 P.M.; www.christies.com.

Drouot Montaigne Part of the long-established Drouot auction house of Paris, Drouot Montaigne conducts the more prestigious sales of antiques and contemporary artwork. See "The Passages" description p. 213 for more on Drouot and their auction process.

15 av Montaigne, 8e; tel.: 01.48.00.20.80; Métro: Alma-Marceau; Open Monday–Friday 9:30 A.M.–1 P.M. and 2–6 P.M.; Most sales take place in the evening, some in the afternoon; www.drouot.fr.

Sotheby's For more than two and a half centuries, Sotheby's has been at the top of the auction world. It entered the world of Paris auctions *toute en élégance* by settling into a sumptuous building, the Galerie Charpentier, that was once the site of countless prestigious auctions and exhibitions in Paris. Now fully renovated, it includes a spectacular ultramodern exhibition space and sales room with seating for 350, a marble staircase, and magnificent Second Empire salons.

The auctions are in French, and items range from French furniture, books and manuscripts, and photographs to old master paintings and drawings, tribal arts, Art Deco, and whatever else reflects the trends of today's fine art and antiques markets.

76 rue du Faubourg-Saint-Honoré, 8e; tel.: 01.53.05.53.05; Métro: Champs-Elysées-Clémenceau; Open Monday–Friday 10 A.M.–6 P.M.; www.sothebys.com.

Note: For both Christie's and Sotheby's, viewings generally take place during the three days prior to the sale (the day of or two days prior for Drouot Montaigne). You can buy catalogs (with some descriptions in English) in person or have one mailed to you.

SPECIAL ANTIQUES SHOWS

Biennale des Antiquaires Indisputably the most prestigious antiques show held in Paris, the Biennale attracts buyers and exhibitors from near and far. The show takes place every other year, typically in September in even years. It recently returned to its first home, the Grand Palais, the premier Beaux Arts exhibition space in Paris, which had been closed for a fourteen-year restoration. The exhibition usually lasts ten days and includes several special events; general admission costs €15. The twenty-fourth showing of this biannual world-class antiques show will take place in 2008.

Tel.: 01.44.51.74.74; www.biennaledesantiquaires.com.

FIAC FIAC is a huge art exhibition that takes place every year in the fall. Artists from all over the world display here, and it's always a happening. It has been held at the Grand Palais and the Louvre recently. General admission costs €20; €10 for art students.

Tel.: 01.41.90.47.47; www.fiacparis.com.

Even More Collectibles

For more artisanal gifts, try **Gault** (206 rue de Rivoli, 1er; tel.: 01.42.60.51.17; www.planetgault.com), where you will discover Jean-Pierre Gault's handmade renditions of typical French houses. Each piece warmly captures the spirit of the many different types of architecture found throughout France.

Jewelry, Shoes, and Accessories

BERLUTI   True connoisseurs of men's footwear must come to Berluti, a Paris bootmaker since 1895. Their shoes and leather goods are distinguished by an unrivaled suppleness that only the finest leathers possess. And if you're a die-hard shoe aficionado who takes shoe polishing seriously, enquire about Berluti's Swann Club, a group of distinguished devotees who gather in prestigious places such as the Hôtel de Crillon to do a sort of group polish. The finest wax, a strip of Venetian linen, and a spot of Dom Perignon do the job very nicely, thank you very much. *Cher, très cher.* You can find Berluti at Barney's in the United States, but it's still better to buy here for selection and price.

26 rue Marbeuf, 8e; tel.: 01.53.93.97.97; Métro: Franklin-Roosevelt;

Open Monday–Saturday 10 A.M.–7 P.M.; www.berluti.com.

DOMINIQUE DENAIVE   Just around the corner from Colette, you'll discover the handsome jewelry creations of Dominique Denaive. Long strands of hefty beads, big chunky rings, and plump drop earrings in a range of colors reminiscent of the desert sky ornament the shopwindow of this tiny boutique. I hadn't seen turquoise like that since my last trip to Santa Fe. The look is ethnic, yet very sophisticated. But this being Paris, there has to be a twist: All of these amazingly real-looking stones are made of resin, a lightweight material that allows you to wear these pieces comfortably.

7 rue du 29 Juillet, 1er; tel.: 01.42.61.78.22; Métro: Tuileries;

Open Tuesday–Saturday 11 A.M.–7 P.M.; www.denaive.com.

GOYARD   One of the most exclusive addresses for travel bags, Goyard offers a blue-chip collection of baggage and accessories in plasticized canvas printed with its famous trademark design of light grey and gold herringbone on black background. An excellent address for the discriminating traveler who does not like to overtly promote signature brands, the house of Goyard has been making superior quality leather goods since 1853. (The founder, François Goyard, started by building trunks out of wood, whereas Louis Vuitton's beginnings were as an expert packer.)

In addition to their more esoteric selection of library trunks and hatboxes, Goyard also offers a handsome choice of handbags and personal items. Their collection of dog accessories is the main draw, however, for stylish pet owners. Imagine collars, leashes, dishes, and blankets, all handmade in Goyard's workshops and customized to fit your privileged pup in size and style. (The process takes a few days.)

233 rue Saint-Honoré, 1er; tel.: 01.42.60.57.04; Métro: Tuileries;
Open Monday–Saturday 10 A.M.–7 P.M.; www.goyard.fr.

HÉLION   The boutique sports a more modern look now, but fortunately not much has changed at Hélion, one of Paris's oldest glove specialists. Opened in 1925 during the height of Paris's *années folles*, or roaring twenties, when women rarely went out without wearing a pair of gloves, Hélion is a family-owned business dedicated to perpetuating the elegant look of Parisian chic. Buttery soft ostrich, kid, cotton, lace, satin, and gold and silver lamé have been cut (often from a single skin, thus necessitating only one seam) into classic and fantasy styles by top-quality glove makers throughout France. The selection for both women and men ranges from sporty to sophisticated and the prices are just as varied. Before you leave, take a peek at Hélion's dreamy collection of hand-embroidered treasures from the Belle Epoque.

22 rue Tronchet, 8e; tel./fax: 01.47.42.26.79; Métro: Madeleine;
Open Monday 1:30–6:45 P.M.; Tuesday–Saturday 10:30 A.M.–6:45 P.M.

LANCEL   Since 1876, the name Lancel has stood for quality and fine French styling. And by the looks of this spectacular new showcase here on the Champs-Elysées (at the former address of the Paris tourist office), its appeal has obviously grown considerably throughout the world. Stop in to take a look at their extraordinary selection of classic leather and faux leather bags, luggage, and personal accessories. Excellent value on most of their goods.

127 av des Champs-Elysées, 8e; tel.: 01.56.89.15.70; Métro: George V; 8 place de l'Opéra, 9e; tel.: 01.47.42.37.29; Métro: Opéra; Open Monday–Saturday 10 A.M.–7:30 P.M.; www.lancel.com.

LONGCHAMP Wow! This well-established French leatherware manufacturer has taken off like a thoroughbred racehorse in recent years. Named after the famous racetrack outside of Paris, the main Longchamp store here sells a grandstand selection of fashionable bags and luggage in leather and plasticized canvas in a kaleidescope of colors and even a few prints.

404 rue Saint-Honoré, 1er; tel.: 01.43.16.00.16; Métro: Concorde; Open Monday–Saturday 10 A.M.–7 P.M.; www.longchamp.com.

PHILIPPE MODEL The place du Marché Saint-Honoré has in the past served as a starting block for many of Paris's most inventive fashion designers. Philippe Model is no exception, and his ingenious millinery talents have won him a reputation as one of Paris's most creative hatmakers. Monsieur Model's high-styled look is further accentuated in his smart collection of gloves, bags, and shoes in such delicious hues as cantaloupe, strawberry, lime, and deep plum. A true colorist indeed.

33 place du Marché Saint-Honoré, 1er; tel.: 01.42.96.89.02; fax: 01.40.20.05.11; Métro: Tuileries; Open Monday–Saturday 10 A.M.–7 P.M.

PIERRE BARBOZA A must for connoisseurs and amateurs of antique jewelry and *objets*, the boutique Pierre Barboza has great prominence on a list of the riches of Paris. You can tell from the antiquated façade that this boutique is among the oldest on the street. It has, in fact, been here since 1934, a little jewel box that provides a dazzling example of how elegant people accessorized themselves in years—if not centuries—past. Monsieur and Madame Gribe have owned this shop for more than fifty years. Depending on how you hit it, let yourself be enchanted by such finery as a Savoy cross from the late eighteenth century or an exquisitely carved snuff bottle from the nineteenth century. Each piece has a story and most of the goods are French.

356 rue Saint-Honoré, 1er; tel.: 01.42.60.67.08; Métro: Palais-Royal;
Open Monday–Friday 10 A.M.–1 P.M. and 2:30–6:30 P.M. and Saturdays in
November and December; closed in August.

RENAUD PELLEGRINO   Like neatly wrapped gifts or candy-colored treats, Renaud Pellegrino's handbags come in many different irresistible shapes, styles, and in recent years, sizes. There's always some feature such as a splash of fanciful embroidery in the shape of a butterfly or a flower that sets them above the ordinary. These charming and delightfully elegant bags have won the hearts of accessory connoisseurs around the world, including Catherine Deneuve and Paloma Picasso. Although less costly than in the United States, the bags fetch prices in the collector's-item range.

14 rue du Faubourg-Saint-Honoré, 1er; tel.: 01.42.65.35.52; Métro: Concorde;
42 rue de Grenelle, 6e; tel.: 01.45.48.36.30; Métro: Sèvres-Babylone;
Open Monday–Saturday 10 A.M.–7 P.M.; www.renaudpellegrino.com.

More Jewelry, Shoes, and Accessories

If you fancy fancy footwear, I'm sure you've heard about Roger Vivier. From the 1930s to the 1970s, Monsieur Vivier created many extraordinary shoes for glamorous women. Today, the house of **Roger Vivier** (29 rue du Faubourg-Saint-Honoré, 8e; tel.: 01.53.43.00.00) is back with another designer in charge, and you can bet the look is still *fabuleux*! Ready-to-wear is at street level; custom-mades are upstairs.

You'll find **Michel Perry** (243 rue Saint-Honoré, 1er; tel.: 01.42.44.10.07) on the other side of rue Royale. Here shoes, boots, booties, and sandals (depending on the season, of course) are displayed on perfectly plump satin pillows ready for the next princess to try. Most of the prices range from €650 to €850, and apparently his creations are taking Paris by storm right now.

La Bagagerie (11 rue du Faubourg-Saint-Honoré, 8e; tel.: 01.47.42.79.13; www.labagagerie.com) has always been a popular address for handbags, luggage, and personal accessories (including umbrellas) for the French and visitors alike. Prices are moderate (by Paris standards), the styles are safe, but as one of my fashion-forward friends said recently, *"Ce n'est pas extraordinaire."* Métro for the above three boutiques: Concorde.

I feel as though I have to mention **John Lobb** (51 rue François 1er, 8e; tel.: 01.45.61.02.55; Métro: Franklin-Roosevelt) the famous English bootmaker here mostly due to their solid association with Hermès in France. Don't, however, expect the selection or the prices to be much different from those in the United States on their exquisitely crafted men's shoes. Do your research. Their ready-to-wears run between €790 and €1,100 and their custom-mades cost about €5,450—yikes!

JEWELS GALORE

Circle around the place Vendôme and continue along the rue de la Paix for one of the most sybaritic shopping experiences of your life. Even the most blasé window shopper can't help but be dazzled by the glittering showings staged by the world-famous jewelers that reside here. The history behind each of these houses is rich, particularly since these purveyors of finery have been welcoming nobility, celebrities, and wealthy industrialists for well over a century. Today, your average guy or gal looking for that incredibly special something for that incredibly special someone can feel at ease shopping here, too, so don't be afraid to push a few doors and step inside. (You might be surprised to find some rather affordable pieces within these hallowed walls.) It's easy to content yourself, however, with window-shopping only, especially if you just want to dream. The following is a list of the majority of the most distinguished jewelers in this area along with their pertinent information:

Boucheron; 26 place Vendôme, 1er; tel.: 01.42.61.58.16; www.boucheron.com.

Cartier; 13 rue de la Paix, 2e; tel.: 01.42.61.58.56; 7 and 23 place Vendôme, 1er; tel.: 01.44.55.32.50; www.cartier.com.

Chanel; 18 place Vendôme, 1er; tel.: 01.55.35.50.05; www.chanel.com.

Chaumet; 12 place Vendôme, 1er; tel.: 01.44.77.24.00; www.chaumet.com.

Mauboussin; 20 place Vendôme, 1er; tel.: 01.44.55.10.00;
www.mauboussin.com.

Mellerio dits Meller; 9 rue de la Paix, 2e; tel.: 01.42.61.57.53;
www.mellerio.fr.

Poiray; 1 rue de la Paix, 2e; tel.: 01.42.61.70.58; www.poiray.com.

Van Cleef & Arpels; 22 place Vendôme, 1er; tel.: 01.53.45.45.45;
www.vca-jewelers.com.

Most of the jewelers are open the following hours: Monday–Friday 9:30 A.M.–
6:45 P.M.; Saturday 10 A.M.–6:45 P.M.; Métro: Opéra.

Womenswear

ALICE CADOLLE Alice Cadolle's custom-made lingerie is as finely
made today as in 1889, when her great-great-grandmother Hermine
Cadolle invented the brassiere (freeing women from the daily pain and
suffering of corsets!). Poupie Cadolle continues this rich legacy today,
providing as much attention and service to women's needs and desires as
her predecessors. The ready-to-wear shop here features some very alluring little numbers, including sensational corsets that would look stunning under a suit or paired with a long skirt for a night out or even a
wedding. Now we can choose when to wear our corsets, by golly!

If it's custom-mades you're contemplating, call ahead for an appointment and plan to have time for at least one fitting. This special salon is located just around the corner at 255 rue Saint-Honoré.

4 rue Cambon, 1er; tel.: 01.42.60.94.22 or 01.42.60.94.94 (for custom-mades);
Métro: Concorde; Open Monday–Saturday 10:00 A.M.– 6:30 P.M.;
www.cadolle.com.

CHANTAL THOMAS Chantal Thomas is one of those boutiques that will
disappear for a while, then reappear with just as much (and sometimes
more) prestige. Now, our lady of lingerie has come in with a real high kicker

on one of the most fashionable streets of Paris. She's no longer showing ready-to-wear but you will find quintessential Chantal Thomas frivolities (that are sometimes necessities, let's face it!) here within the two floors of this small, boudoirlike, pink, satiny boutique. And, as usual, the courtesan theme reigns in everything from a lacey bustier bra, to sexy stockings made to resemble stockings and garter belts, to a frilly little parasol. For inferior versions of Chantal's seduction, look for her pieces chez Victoria's Secret, but once you buy here, it will be hard to settle for less.

211 rue Saint-Honoré, 1er; tel.: 01.42.60.40.56; Métro: Tuileries;
Open Monday–Saturday 11 A.M.–7 P.M.

ERES Opening an avenue Montaigne outpost indicates the success of this well-established swimwear specialist. Clearly Eres knows what a girl wants: bathing suits, cover-ups, assorted tops, and more recently lingerie that is both sexy, sophisticated, *and* comfortable. The secret is in *zee stretch*!

40 av Montaigne, 8e; tel.: 01.47.23.07.26; Métro: Franklin-Roosevelt;
Open Monday–Saturday 10 A.M.–7 P.M.; 4 bis rue du Cherche-Midi, 6e;
tel.: 01.45.44.95.54; Métro: Saint-Sulpice; www.eresparis.com.

JEANETTE MINER If you feel yourself choking at the prices *chez les couturiers,* but long to have a big name–styled frock, check out this little boutique tucked into a courtyard just off the tony avenue Montaigne. A Chanel-inspired suit sells for a fraction of the cost here; count on spending about €8,000 to €13,000 for a complicated tweed chez Chanel, whereas something comparable here rings in at €1,900. Okay, it doesn't say Chanel, but the quality is excellent and all of the pieces are beautifully made. Lighter-weight items for cruise and casual wear also sell here for €500 to €1,100. Know that the sizes run up to 16 and the *détaxe* here is 13 percent.

49 av Montaigne, 8e; tel.: 01.47.20.47.30; Métro: Franklin-Roosevelt;
Open Tuesday–Friday 11 A.M.–5 P.M. and by appointment; www.parisfashions.com.

MARINA RINALDI I'll make an exception here to my predominantly French entries to highlight this Italian designer that specializes in plus-sized fashions for women. You can tell that Italian big-name Max Mara is behind this label, since the quality is *bellissimo*!

265 rue Saint-Honoré, 1er; tel.: 01.42.60.72.73; Métro: Concorde; Open Monday–Saturday 10:30 A.M.–7 P.M.

More Womenswear

If you're looking for well-made womenswear with a distinctly Parisian flair, I suggest you stop in at **Apostrophe** (43 rue du Faubourg-Saint-Honoré; tel.: 01.40.06.91.60; www.apostrope.fr) and **Georges Rech** (273 rue Saint-Honoré, 8e; tel.: 01.42.61.41.14; www.georges-rech.fr). You can count on both classically styled and younger, more fanciful fashions at both of these leading French ready-to-wear manufacturers. The quality is fine at both, and the prices are less than at the big-name designer boutiques. If you're tall, Apostrophe should work well for you.

For modern classic fashions often accented with a bit of lace or embroidery, stop into **Renata** (17 rue Saint-Florentin, 8e; tel.: 01.42.60.11.69). This small boutique features the soft, feminine creations of Renata Benichou.

Métro for the three boutiques above: Concorde.

If you're working with a larger budget and are more oriented toward luxury ready-to-wear (including sportswear and eveningwear), look around at **Jacqueline Perès** (4 rue de Castiglione, 1er; tel.: 01.42.60.67.42; Métro: Tuileries). This chic boutique has been meeting the needs of discriminating women for more than twenty-five years.

Junko Shimada and Corinne Cobson are two womenswear designers—both in very different spectrums—that have been on the scene for a while and are worth mentioning. For a blast of sophistication and true artistic vision, go to **Junko Shimada** (13 rue Saint-Florentin, 8e; tel.: 01.42.60.94.12; Métro: Concorde), the most *parisienne* of all the Japanese designers. She always shows a lot of originality in her knits and leathers. For "street and chic" creations from her daughter, be sure to check out **Junk** toward the back of the courtyard.

Corinne Cobson (6 rue du Marché Saint-Honoré, 1er; tel.: 01.42.60.48.64; Métro: Tuileries) presents a decidedly more casual look. In fact, her latest penchant involves lots of lightweight cotton T-shirts for women and kids. They're all fun and trendy, particularly the children's that sport sayings such as My Mum Is Rich or Born to Be Wild.

For pretty and spirited weekendwear, go to **Chemins Blancs** (177 rue Saint-Honoré, 1er; tel.: 01.42.60.23.35; Métro: Palais-Royal; www .lescheminsblancs.fr). This light and airy French label seems better suited to the Left Bank than the Right amid these high-fashion boutiques, but I guess that just makes the shopping all the more interesting for us.

Women's and Men's Fashions

ALAIN FIGARET If you're on your way to have some shirts made at nearby Charvet, you may want to do some comparative pricing here first. Alain Figaret is one of the leading shirtmakers in France today. The selection is astronomical. Choose from among five different collars, two different sleeve lengths, two different cuffs, and countless styles in several different types of quality cottons (average price is €69)! The women's selection is equally impressive and just as classically styled. The sales staff will readily help you with size equivalents.

21 rue de la Paix, 2e; tel.: 01.42.65.04.99; Métro: Opéra;

Open Monday–Saturday 10 A.M.–7:30 P.M.; 99 rue de Longchamp, 16e;

tel.: 01.47.27.66.81; Métro: Pompe or Trocadéro; www.alainfigaret.fr.

CERRUTI 1881 Much has changed chez Cerruti since Nino sold his fashion house to an Italian group, so don't expect it to be the way it was before. There are no longer custom-mades for men, and the women's collection is more sportswear-oriented. I'll let you peek in and see what you think. This being rue Royale, however, you can count on finding top-notch quality and fine styling in both the men's and women's fashions.

27 rue Royale, 8e; tel.: 01.53.30.18.81; Métro: Madeleine;

Open Monday–Saturday 10 A.M.–7 P.M.

CHARVET *The* place to go for a top-drawer shirt, in both ready-to-wear or custom-made, for men and women. The prices are about the same for men's and women's custom-mades—starting at €370 a shirt—and the workmanship includes such attention to detail as a slightly larger diameter for the left cuff to accommodate your watch. Each shirt usually requires just one fitting and takes four weeks for completion. The most difficult part for you will be choosing from some six hundred fabrics for your *belle chemise*. Keep in mind that some Charvet ready-to-wears or semicustoms are sold in high-end stores outside of France, but you must come here for the custom-mades.

Charvet also offers one of the most distinguished and least expensive gift ideas for men or women that exists in Paris: their braided-knot cuff links (three pairs for €36). These *passementerie* cuff links (free when you buy a French cuff shirt), which come in a fabulously rich range of colors, are a sort of trademark for this nearly 170-year-old French company. They were invented at the beginning of the last century as elegant fasteners for French cuffs.

28 place Vendôme, 1er; tel.: 01.42.60.30.70; Métro: Opéra;
Open Monday–Saturday 10 A.M.–6:30 P.M.

COLETTE   Want to see what's in? I mean what's really *le dernier cri* in terms of beauty products, designer clothing, music, DVDs, books, high-tech gadgets, or even gummy bear candies? If it's put on display in this up-to-the-minute lifestyle boutique, it's considered hot (at least for that brief, shining moment!), whether you agree or not. Clearly, a lot of people come here to check out the scene or to be seen. And everyone here seems to have a look, an attitude, or is it a scowl? I guess it's not cool to smile.

But if you're into the latest digital cameras, iPods, lighters, watches, Lacoste shirts, or any number of other items, many of which were designed exclusively for Colette in a limited series, then this is the place for you. If the loud rap music and heady candles haven't prompted you to leave yet, go upstairs to check out a sparse selection of men's and women's clothing, all of which is displayed in an art gallery–like manner. Downstairs you'll discover a trendy café where you can settle in and focus on your people-watching.

213 rue Saint-Honoré, 1er; tel.: 01.55.35.33.90; Métro: Tuileries or Pyramides;
Open Monday–Saturday 11 A.M.–7 P.M.; www.colette.fr. ✗

HOBBS   Frenchman Patrick Lifshitz is the driving creative force behind this label, prized for its superior quality cashmeres created in a wide range of classic and original styles. The color palette promises to be particularly luscious each collection and typically includes yummy shades such as apple green, berry, pumpkin spice, and lemon drop. If you're looking to make a real fashion statement, choose from one of their more imaginative sweaters emblazoned with an ode to the Beatles, or one embroidered to look like an Indian shirt, or one simply adorned with a magnificent multicolored butterfly. Prices are a bit steep, but they're worth it. And here's the perfect gift for you weary travelers: a soft cashmere throw and pillow that comes in its own cashmere case (priced at €490 before *détaxe*).

45 rue Pierre-Charron, 8e; tel.: 01.47.20.83.22; Métro: Alma-Marceau or Franklin-Roosevelt; Open Monday–Saturday 10 A.M.–7 P.M.

JOHN GALLIANO   Look for the newsprint awnings to find your way to this temple of haute chic. Master Galliano's men's and women's ready-to-wear hangs like works of art in this attention-grabbing space, where elements from many different worlds converge. Louis something furnishings, video monitors spanning two floors pulsating with the designer's latest creations, soft modern music, more newsprint remnants, a sweet-smelling fragrance, and an array of temptingly touchable sexy clothes work together to put all five of your senses on high alert. If you just want to pick up a little something, buy a Diptyque candle (€38) especially created for Monsieur Galliano. Composed of sandalwood, musk, incense, and paper, it is intended to smell like a church and comes gift-wrapped in signature Galliano newsprint.

384–386 rue Saint-Honoré, 1er; tel.: 01.55.35.40.40; Métro: Concorde; Open Monday–Saturday 11 A.M.–7 P.M.; www.johngalliano.com.

LACOSTE   Stop into this store to see what's new in the Lacoste collection of clothing and accessories. You're likely to pay a fair amount more here than in the United States, but some of the products are different and it might be worth it.

It all began with the great French tennis player René Lacoste. The American press called him "the crocodile" during his heyday in the twenties due to his tenacity on the courts. The moniker pleased him so much that he eventually had a bunch of breathable cotton shirts made up for himself, all of which were embroidered with *le crocodile*. They were such a hit within his entourage that he began manufacturing them in 1933 and, as they say, the rest is history.

93–95 av des Champs-Elysées, 8e; tel.: 01.47.23.39.26; Métro: George V; Open Monday–Thursday 10 A.M.–7:30 P.M.; Friday and Saturday 10 A.M.– 8:30 P.M.; www.lacoste.com.

MARIA LUISA   Maria Luisa needs no introduction to most in-the-know fashionistas. She has consistently shown men's and women's fashions and accessories from some of Europe's top *créateurs* for a good number of years. Look around at her mini empire of shops here—all within close proximity to each other—to pick up something new, different, and yes, expensive.

2 rue Cambon (women's), 1er; tel.: 01.47.03.96.15; 19 rue du Mont-Thabor (men's), 1er; tel.: 01.42.60.89.83; 38 rue du Mont-Thabor (women's and men's casual), 1er; tel.: 01.42.96.47.81; Métro for all boutiques: Tuileries; Open Monday–Saturday 10:30 A.M.–7 P.M.

Children's Clothing, Shoes, and Furnishings

PETIT BATEAU   It's been around for more than a century, but this little boat has really sailed onto the scene in recent years. Petit Bateau's children's nightwear and underwear still take up space in many French families' wardrobes, but women are buying here more than ever. Petit Bateau has applied their same formula for soft and cuddly baby and children's clothing to womens' T-shirts, T-shirt dresses, and tanks. As *chez les enfants*, the ladies' look boasts lots of color, quite a few stripes, some more trendy motifs, and—thankfully—more stretch.

If you don't want as much of a crowd, go to the address in the Sixteenth.

116 av des Champs-Elysées, 8e; tel.: 01.40.74.02.03; Métro: George V; Open Monday–Saturday 10 A.M.–7 P.M.; 64 av Victor-Hugo, 16e; tel.: 01.45.00.13.95; Métro: Victor-Hugo; www.petitbateau.com.

Department Stores and Other Biggies

BOUCHARA   French fabrics are among the most beautiful in the world. The Left Bank (near St.-Germain) is particularly well known for its textile showrooms, and a whirl through there is always inspiring for people with a penchant for home décor. You can't always purchase the fabrics directly from the manufacturers unless you're a professional, so you may want to shop here. Bolts and swatches of magnificent *tissus* from some of the most famous French textile houses, including Manuel Canovas and Pierre Frey, fill this large store, located not far from the department stores. If you plan on buying a lot of fabric, check the prices from your suppliers back home first. Overall, fabric costs considerably less in France than in America. You may have to order some of it, but the store will happily ship to the United States.

1–3 rue Lafayette, 9e; tel.: 01.42.80.66.95; Métro: Havre-Caumartin; Open Monday–Saturday 9:45 A.M.–7 P.M.; www.bouchara.com.

CITADIUM   Just behind the Printemps department store, you'll find this monolithic sports emporium where loud music hypes you up to near-Olympic status. Paris really needed a store like this and Citadium clearly delivered in a big, beautiful way. Nowhere else can you find such a selection of gear and attire for virtually every sport imaginable. French highlights include Roland Garros tenniswear, Tour de France fashions and accessories, superwarm sleeping bags from Valandré, Petzel headlamps, every imaginable map and guide on the innumerable hikes of France, extraordinary books on mountains and mountain climbing, lots of hard-to-find French brands, and much more. It's a must!

50–56 rue Caumartin, 9e; tel.: 01.55.31.74.00; Métro: Havre-Caumartin; Open Monday–Saturday 10 A.M.–8 P.M.; Thursday until 9 P.M.; www.citadium.com.

GALERIES LAFAYETTE   Hats off to Galeries Lafayette for **Lafayette Maison,** the stunning table arts and home décor store it recently opened across the street from the main store. They are best known for their up-to-date fashion "boutiques"; but now they've provided even more reasons to shop here, with more than one hundred departments that sell every-thing from dashing hats to creamy soaps. **Lafayette Gourmet** remains my all-time favorite here, though, for munching and food shopping or a little bit of both simultaneously (not very French, but here it works, par-ticularly since there are fifteen eateries at Galeries Lafayette, most of which are in this section). This is where you can find inexpensively priced gift items in great quantities.

For breakfast, lunch, or tea with a nice view overlooking the Opéra, go to the terrace at **Lafayette Café** on the sixth floor. Or you may savor tapas-style plates at **Le Laurier,** a streamlined restaurant in the designer clothes department.

Fashion shows are conducted Fridays year-round at 3 P.M. Call 01.42.82.30.25 to reserve.

35, 38 and 40 bd Haussmann, 9e; tel.: 01.42.82.34.56; Métro: Chausée-d'Antin; Open Monday–Saturday 9:30 A.M.–7:30 P.M.; Thursday until 9 P.M.; www.galerieslafayette.com. ✗

MONOPRIX If you feel like picking up a few trendy items for you or your home, you certainly won't use up too many euros here at this French five-and-ten. You can always find classic items as well, but the quality, of course, won't hold up longer than a few seasons. I've had great luck here with a few odd cosmetics and stockings, particularly the *mi-bas*, or knee-highs that the French do so well in a range of fashionable patterns.

52 av des Champs-Elysées, 8e; tel.: 01.53.77.65.65; Métro: Franklin-Roosevelt; Open Monday–Saturday 9 A.M.–midnight; www.monoprix.com.

PRINTEMPS Printemps department store was recently sold and now this *grand magasin* is more beautiful than ever before. Located right next door to its chief competitor, Galeries Lafayette, Printemps clearly is not allowing itself to be one-upped by its neighbors. Printemps's three distinctly differ-ent stores feature an abundance of goods for you and your home, and more areas are being renovated daily. Their table arts department—now in a glimmering new setting—has always been well known as a favorite bridal registry, so you know there's a large selection of French finery there.

Be sure also to check out their women's shoes and the **Food Hall,** a new section that showcases some of the finest food and wine purveyors of Paris, including La Maison du Chocolat and Caves Taillevent.

Printemps's fashion show is a good way to begin the day, because it starts at 10:30 A.M. on Tuesdays year-round. Reservations are not necessary and there's pretty much always room available.

All of the Printemps restaurants have been redone. An elegant—and most historic—glass cupola may be viewed from their top-floor restaurant, **Brasserie Printemps** (tel.: 01.42.82.58.84), where you may enjoy a lovely lunch in a dashing contemporary setting. There is also a **Ladurée** tea salon (tel.: 01.42.82.40.10; see p. 118) if you can't make it to their famous rue Royale address. There's even a branch of **Be,** Alain Duasse's bakery/food store/café, where you're sure to find many good eats. And for sweeping panoramic views of Paris, go to the self-service restaurant **Deli-cieux** (tel.: 01.42.82.62.76).

64 bd Haussmann, 9e; tel.: 01.42.82.50.00; Métro: Chausée-d'Antin;
Open Monday–Saturday 9:35 A.M.–7 P.M.; Thursday until 10 P.M.;
www.printemps.fr. ✗

Note: Don't forget to ask for your discount shopping card at Galeries Lafayette and Printemps. See "The Essentials" description p. 16 for more information.

PROMOD   Snazzy, inexpensive fashions and accessories for women are the mantra at this large store. This is the kind of place where an elegant French woman might pick up a few tops and accessories to integrate into her high-styled wardrobe. (Think Sharon Stone in a Gap turtleneck at the Oscars.) Expect crowds. Know also that there are many Promods throughout Paris, but this one stays open the latest.

86 av des Champs-Elysées, 8e; tel.: 01.53.53.02.30; Métro: Franklin-Roosevelt;
Open Monday–Saturday 10 A.M.–10 P.M.; www.promod.com.

Discount Shops

ANNA LOWE   This is one of the best discount shops in Paris. The location is convenient, the store is elegant, the 25 to 40 percent (mostly

40!) markdowns are fantastic, the merchandise is nicely presented, both summer and winter fashions are shown year-round, and the saleswomen are lovely—what more could a girl ask for! It's no surprise that the store is run and owned by Suzy, an American woman who has lived in Paris for almost thirty years. Names such as Chanel, Ungaro, Valentino, Galliano, and Gaultier prevail throughout the boutique in everything from fun and funky, prêt-à-porter separates to glamorous, haute couture eveningwear (samples, so they're for the ladies with the figures of runway models). And the good news is, Anna Lowe stocks more and more clothing from the current year. Although limited, Suzy's selection of accessories is also excellent; if you're lucky you will hit upon a medium-sized quilted Chanel bag, priced here at €900 as opposed to the €1,300 price tag at Chanel.

104 rue du Faubourg-Saint-Honoré, 8e; tel.: 01.42.66.11.32; Métro: Miromesnil; Open Monday–Saturday 10 A.M.–7 P.M.; www.annaloweparis.com.

MISS GRIFFES *Griffe* means "mark" or "brand," of which there are many in this small, very neatly organized women's clothing and accessories boutique. Fortunately, not all the *griffes* have been *dégriffés* (this is when the labels have been removed), and you can see for yourself the armloads of fashion-forward designers *(couturiers* and *créateurs)* represented here. From little black dresses to stylish separates, the owner, Madame Marie-Jeanne Vincent (who has been here more than forty years), will certainly be able to outfit you in high style. Count on savings of 30 to 40 percent off retail on prototypes and pieces from current and past collections. Note also that when the dollar isn't very strong, Madame Vincent reduces prices even more and allows you to pay in dollars.

19 rue de Penthièvre; tel./fax: 01.42.65.10.00; Métro: Miromesnil; Open Monday–Friday 11 A.M.–7 P.M.; Saturday noon–7 P.M.

WK By now, you're probably wondering how French women can afford to add the latest styles to their wardrobes every season. Well, many of them actually sell off a lot of their stuff in order to buy even more up-to-the-minute fashions, which is why the selection is so good here at this ultra high-end secondhand store. Most of the big names, including Hermès, Chanel, Prada, Kenzo, and Yves Saint Laurent, are here in great force, all in impeccable condition and nicely organized (some by size, others by label). There are few accessories, but prices are very good on everything.

5 rue du Marché Saint-Honoré, 1er; tel.: 01.40.20.99.76; Métro: Tuileries;

Open Monday–Saturday 11 A.M.–7 P.M.

Books and Music

BRENTANO'S An independently owned bookseller no longer connected with the Brentano's stores in the United States, Brentano's Paris is a lively institution where French, Americans, and people of other nationalities come to shop, browse, and perhaps even meet that special someone. It's very reassuring to come and soak up a bit of the charm of this more than one-hundred-year-old store. Indeed, it's a cozy place that looks quite different from modern bookstores. Today, they are known for their collection of fashion and collecting titles, travel guides, books on crafts, and U.S. and British best sellers. About 30 to 40 percent of their books are in French. The magazine collection is also very international. Oh, and if you're a cat lover (like me!), don't miss the **Cat Gallery,** Brentano's little feline-fetish shop next door.

37 av de l'Opéra, 2e; tel.: 01.42.61.52.50; Métro: Opéra;

Open Monday–Saturday 10 A.M.–7:30 P.M.; www.brentanos.fr.

FNAC FNAC (pronounced "f-KNACK") specializes in all types of electronics ranging from stereos to answering machines. Although this is not the sort of thing you'd want to buy in France, the store's extensive selection of French music and books provides endless gift-giving possibilities at prices that are among the best in town.

74 av des Champs-Elysées, 8e; tel.: 01.53.53.64.64; Métro: George V;

Open Monday–Saturday 10 A.M.–midnight; Sunday noon–midnight; www.fnac.com.

GALIGNANI Considered to be the oldest English-language bookstore in Europe, this two-hundred-year-old, wood-paneled establishment provides a serene setting for perusing a large selection of English, American, and French publications. Occupied by the German general staff during World War II, today Galignani is frequented by tony clients from near and far. The store will gladly obtain long-sought-after books and ship them to you anywhere in the world.

224 rue de Rivoli, 1er; tel.: 01.42.60.76.07; Métro: Tuileries;

Open Monday–Saturday 10 A.M.–7 P.M.; galignani@wanadoo.fr.

HENRI PICARD ET FILS Devoted bibliophiles must stop by this antique bookshop, where three generations of owners have culled the world for some of the most exquisite leather-bound volumes on subjects as varied as horticulture and hunting.

126 rue du Faubourg-Saint-Honoré, 8e; tel.: 01.43.59.28.11; Métro: Concorde;

Open Monday–Saturday 10:00 A.M.–8 P.M.; hepicard@aol.com;

www.abebooks.com.

VIRGIN MEGASTORE Definitely one of the star attractions on the Champs-Elysées, Virgin Megastore is an excellent and fun source for music and books in Paris. You can check out the tunes on one of their many listening stations, grab a bite to eat, or take in a mini concert. Virgin Megastore offers an immense selection of music from its own label as well as from countless other music companies.

52/60 av des Champs-Elysées, 8e; tel.: 01.49.53.50.00; Métro: Franklin-

Roosevelt; Open Monday–Saturday 10 A.M.–midnight; Sunday noon–midnight;

Galerie du Carrousel du Louvre, 99 rue de Rivoli, 1er; tel.: 01.44.50.03.10;

Métro: Palais Royal; www.virginmegastore.fr. 🍴

W. H. SMITH It hardly seems like a visit to Paris is complete for me without stopping into "the English bookshop," W. H. Smith. Their selection of books, videos, maps, and cards is truly excellent, but I think what grabs me the most is the extensive selection of British and American newspapers and magazines, as well as the buzz in the store! Even when you're just browsing, it's not always easy to pass up the Sunday *New York Times*, which arrives here by Monday afternoon (priced at €14). Happy reading.

248 rue de Rivoli, 8e; tel.: 01.44.77.88.99; Métro: Concorde;

Open Monday–Saturday 9 A.M.–7:30 P.M.; Sunday 1–7:30 P.M.;

whsmith.france@wanadoo.fr.

More Specialty Boutiques

CASSEGRAIN   Since 1919, the name Cassegrain has been synonymous with high-quality engraving and paper products. Stop at this fashionable Parisian address to purchase elegant stationery, handsome leather desk accessories, and high-styled writing instruments.

> 422 rue Saint-Honoré, 8e; tel.: 01.42.60.20.08; Métro: Concorde or Madeleine;
> Open Monday–Saturday 10 A.M.–7 P.M.; www.cassegrain.fr.

A LA CIVETTE   It's pretty cool to think you're buying your smokes in the same place that Diderot, Voltaire, and countless other formidable French personalities shopped before you. Purveyors of fine tobacco since 1716, A la Civette is one of those not-to-be-missed places for anyone who enjoys a fine cigar, cigarillo, or cigarette.

Cigar smokers will be particularly thrilled by the shop's selection of top-of-the-line stogies from Belgium, Holland, the Philippines, the Dominican Republic, and of course, Cuba. Cohibas go for about €8 to €30, Punch Double Coronas for around €13.

Shopping for all the cigar smoker's accoutrements is exciting, too, because the shop offers a prime selection of humidors and accessories from France's best suppliers, such as Elie Bleu. This nearly three-centuries-old establishment will also woo you with a rich selection of pipes, lighters, pens, and leather goods.

> 157 rue Saint-Honoré, 1er; tel.: 01.42.96.04.99; Métro: Palais-Royal;
> Open Monday–Saturday 10 A.M.–7 P.M.

MAISON ANTOINE   Monsieur and Madame Antoine arrived in Paris in 1745. In 1767, they were granted the privilege by King Louis XV of renting umbrellas to those unfortunate enough to be caught by intemperate weather—by day or night—without the protection of a simple *parapluie.* Maison Antoine ultimately settled into this address in 1885 and today features one of the most diverse collections of umbrellas, parasols, canes, scarves, gloves, and rain hats in all of Paris.

> 10 av de l'Opéra, 1er; tel.: 01.42.96.01.80; Métro: Palais-Royal;
> Open Monday–Saturday 10 A.M.–6:30 P.M.; www.antoine1745.com.

MAUPIOU Since 1935, fashion-conscious and price-savvy women have been flocking to Maupiou for dressy fabrics, the same sort of textiles used by many Right Bank couture houses. Truly a must for those who like to sew or for those who have an excellent dressmaker back home. This reputable store will seduce you with its luxurious collection of silks from Lyons and Italy, Calais lace, genuine dotted Swiss, and velvet chiffon (also from Lyons), to name a few. Many fabrics also bear the names of famous European designers such as Valentino and Ungaro. Prices range from €30 to €800 per meter (one meter equals approximately one yard).

2 rue de la Paix, 2e; tel.: 01.42.61.08.27; Métro: Opéra; Open Monday–Friday 10:30 A.M.–6:45 P.M.; Saturday 10 A.M.–6:45 P.M.; closed Mondays in August; www.maupiou.com.

MONT BLANC I think there are few things more stylish—or even sexy—than a fountain pen. I started using one shortly after first arriving in France and instantly became hooked. It is an accessory (and an essential tool!) that people are quick to notice, and it instantly makes your handwriting more graceful. You'll find one of the largest collections of *stylos à plumes* and a variety of other writing instruments of the finest quality here at Mont Blanc. Prices range from €230 to €5,000. Note that this is one of the few Mont Blanc stores with a technician on the premises (Tuesday–Saturday) for repairs and engravings.

60 rue du Faubourg-Saint-Honoré, 8e; tel.: 01.40.06.02.93; Métro: Concorde; Open Monday–Saturday 10 A.M.–7 P.M.; www.montblanc.com.

LA PORCELAINE DE PARIS Since 1773, this porcelain maker has been crafting pieces of white gold to adorn the tables of France and, later, beyond. All that has begun to change recently since the company was bought by a *société de sanitaires*. This means that sinks, bathtubs, toilets, and *bidets* now claim center stage, but oh, how lovely they are! Your *salle de bain* will be totally transformed by one of their decorative lavabos. Many Americans have already found this address, so the company is adept at shipping stateside. Whatever your fancy, know that there are twenty-three different décors from which to choose here. Oh, and there are still a few plates to buy as well.

9 rue Pasquier, 8e; tel.: 01.42.65.27.51; Métro: Madeleine;

Open Tuesday–Saturday 10 A.M.–2 P.M. and 3–6 P.M.; www.porcelainedeparis.fr.

REPETTO   Just a few toe steps away from the Opéra Garnier (which now stages primarily ballet performances rather than opera) is Repetto, France's most celebrated dancewear specialist. This is where long, lithe *danseuses* and wide-eyed *petits rats* (the youngest members of the Paris Opera ballet company) come to pick up a fresh leotard or a new pair of ballet shoes. These hand-sewn *ballerines* will set you back between €85 and €155, but they're known to be among the best.

22 rue de la Paix, 2e; tel.: 01.44.71.83.12; Métro: Opéra;

Open Monday–Saturday 10 A.M.–7 P.M.

TERRITOIRE   This is as close as you'll come to a French country store in Paris. Territoire specializes in hobby and leisure merchandise. Here you're apt to unearth just about anything from attractive journals to a sign in French that says "Gone Golfing!" The music of Vivaldi and Mozart fills this large, homey space, rendering Territoire an even more pleasant place for discovering eclectic French gift items.

Next door to the main entrance of Territoire is its children's boutique, which houses a darling collection of French toys and games, many of which are handcrafted.

30 rue Boissy d'Anglas, 8e; tel.: 01.42.66.22.13; Métro: Concorde or

Madeleine; Open Monday–Saturday 10:30 A.M.–7 P.M.; www.territoire.com.

Even More Specialty Boutiques

There's no end to luxury gift ideas in Paris. For those who have elevated smoking to a fine art, stop into **Alfred Dunhill** (15 rue de la Paix, 2e; tel.: 01.42.61.57.58; Métro: Opéra), a long-established British house that set up this Paris branch in 1924. Their collection of menswear and accessories is worthy of note as well.

You may also light your stogies with a Dupont lighter, one of those great symbols of *l'art de vivre*, known for its perfect proportions and streamlined shape. You'll find this handsome *objet* at **S. T. Dupont**

(58 av Montaigne, 8e; tel.: 01.45.61.08.39; Métro: Franklin-Roosevelt; www.st-dupont.com) in a variety of forms along with a collection of men's and women's accessories (only lighters and pens for the ladies) and top-drawer ready-to-wear. The most classic purchase is the *pointe de diamant,* a Dupont lighter whose granular texture makes it look like shimmering diamonds. It has been made for nearly sixty years and comes in gold- or silverplate with prices ranging from €245 to €550, depending on the model.

Markets

You'll have to head outside of the main tourist areas toward place des Ternes (Métro: Ternes) to take in **Marché Poncelet,** one of the most vibrant markets of Paris. Most of the action takes place Tuesday through Saturday from 8 A.M. to 1 P.M. and 4 to 8 P.M. along rue Poncelet, a side street peppered with shops and vendors that sell everything from fresh fish to decorative napkins. This market is largely populated by locals, including many stylish *mères de famille* from the seventeenth arrondissement.

If you are a stamp collector, don't miss the **Marché aux Timbres** (stamp market) set up at the rond-point des Champs Elysées (Métro: Champs-Elysées-Clémenceau) on Thursday, Friday, and Saturday from 10 A.M. to 7 P.M. The pickings are not always extraordinary, but if you know what you're buying, you're sure to walk away with a few finds.

My Special Suggestions

Beauté and *Parfums*

ALAIN DIVERT   The whole mood of this fashionable salon is a reflection of this talented and most charming man: upbeat and smooth, and definitely not snobby. Come here for a great cut and style (or coloring, too, of course), and you won't be disappointed. For an extra treat, ask for one of Monsieur Divert's fresh mint and ginger concoctions, relaxing treatments to revitalize your hair and scalp. A variety of face and body treatments is performed here and there are many interesting products to buy, such as the Alain Divert ginger shampoo.

22 rue des Capucines, 2e; tel: 01.42.66.11.81; Métro: Opéra;
Open Tuesday–Saturday 9:30 A.M.–6:30 P.M. ★ 🛍

ALEXANDRE DE PARIS   For those of you who remember the outrageous hairdos worn by Marissa Berenson and photographed by Richard Avedon in V*ogue* magazines of the sixties and seventies, you may recall that the star coiffeur was Alexandre. Now you no longer have to refer to the pages of magazines to indulge yourself in the illustrious talents of this famed hairdresser.

The Alexandre de Paris boutique, which specializes in luxurious hair accessories, offers just about everything for your curly locks except Alexandre's magical scissors. Beautiful hair ornaments are piled as high as a sixties beehive in the three floors of this boutique. Whether you're looking for headbands, combs, barrettes, scrunchies, clips, or a sophisticated snood, you will find it all here in the most refined styles and materials, including taffeta, satin, leather, suede, velvet, and superior quality *plastique*. Prices range from €12 for a small barrette to €1,000 for a rare piece.

235 rue Saint-Honoré, 1er; tel.: 01.42.61.41.34; Métro: Concorde or Tuileries;
Open Monday–Saturday 10:30 A.M.–7 P.M.; www.alexandredeparis.com.

ALEXANDRE ZOUARI   Most of Paris's top coiffeurs and beauty institutes are located on the Right Bank. Here, this "hairdresser to the stars" occupies two floors of a handsome building with his various salons, all dedicated to the beautification of you from head to toe. It's right on the fringes of the Golden Triangle, so you can always pop in and check out the many Alexandre Zouari products on sale here, and then perhaps line up a time to come by later for some pampering.

1 av du Président Wilson, 16e; tel.: 01.47.23.79.00; Métro: Alma-Marceau;
Open Tuesday–Saturday 10 A.M.–7 P.M.; www.alexandre-zouari.com. ★ 🛍

AMIN KADER   The entrance is so discreet that you might not even notice it. But do push open the wrought iron–gated door to behold the astonishing re-creation of the seventeeth-century chapel of Santa Maria Novella in Florence, right here in the heart of Paris. An abundance of marble, Italian frescoes, and diffused light streaming in from the street cast a near-haloed glow on the Santa Maria Novella fragrances, creams, and potpourris for sale here. Founded in 1612, the original pharmacy where these completely natural products were first made still exists on the piazza Santa Maria Novella, and these luxurious creations continue to be made by hand with centuries-old presses. (No wonder they weren't distributing samples!)

Algerian-born Amin Kader has been delighting women for more than twenty-five years with his sartorial women's fashions of superior quality. Kader's handmade leather bags trimmed with hand-stitched horsehair embellishments in the shape of large floral motifs or Renaissance-inspired patterns have also been big sellers among the Parisians. He has sold Santa Maria Novella products for quite some time, but now he has taken it to a whole new level. Go to Amin Kader's Left Bank boutique to behold a real little chapel, a rarity even in Paris.

1 rue de la Paix, 2e; tel.: 01.42.61.33.25; Métro: Opéra;
Open Monday–Saturday 10 A.M.–7 P.M.; 2 rue Guisarde, 6e;
tel.: 01.43.26.27.37; Métro: Mabillon.

ANNICK GOUTAL Once you enter the cream and gold interior of this music box–like boutique, you will understand why it feels so special to purchase Annick Goutal fragrances in Paris. To me, they embody a perfectly balanced harmony of Parisian refinement and French savoir faire. Former concert pianist Annick Goutal turned her musical virtuosities into the fine-tuned olfactory skill that is required to become a "nose." As does the music world, the perfume industry requires the *parfumeur* to assemble the right notes. Most of these scents, which are blends of natural extracts (as opposed to synthetic), were created by the artist herself on her own *orgue* (or organ, which refers to the organlike arrangement of thousands of bottles of extracts needed in the creation of a new scent). Sadly, this virtuosa passed away in 1999, but the impression she left is indelible. Today, her daughter, Camille, carries on the tradition and now nearly thirty fragrances are sold around the world.

No one knew better than Annick Goutal that people buy fragrances and beauty products as much for the sight as for the smell. Hence, the exquisite packaging. You can wrap yourself in this same ultrafeminine luxury upstairs in a pink satin boudoir where your skin will be buffed and pampered with the finest Annick Goutal products. Prices for facials begin at €20 (for twenty minutes!) and go up to €125 (for *un grand soin* that lasts 75 minutes) and, as always, call or e-mail ahead.

14 rue de Castiglione, 1er; tel.: 01.42.60.52.82; Métro: Tuileries or Concorde; 12 place Saint-Sulpice, 6e; tel.: 01.46.33.03.15; Métro: Saint-Sulpice; 16 rue de Bellechasse, 7e; tel.: 01.45.51.36.13; Métro: Solférino; Open Monday–Saturday 10 A.M.–7 P.M.; castiglione-a.goutal@wanadoo.fr; www.annickgoutal.fr. ★ 🛍

CARITA   The Carita sisters opened their *maison de beauté* here in 1946. The house has been dedicated to making men and women more beautiful—inside and out—ever since. If possible, plan to spend the better part of your day in this venerable institution. (Your face, body, and hair will love you for it!)

Since the beginning, Carita has been known for their high-quality products, and only these special potions and lotions are used throughout the treatments. The *rénovateur* (a combination of roasted sunflower seeds and essential oils) is one such example. Experience its amazing revitalizing properties in a body wrap/massage that will leave your skin toned and glowing. (The cost is €120 for 90 minutes of total renewal.) If you're contemplating a facial, know that Carita's estheticians always make sure to apply a touch of makeup afterward so that you leave your prettiest.

In terms of hair, the stylists chez Carita are equally extraordinary. A big, airy salon just opened upstairs, which seems to attest to their success. The level of expertise here is remarkable, so turn yourself over to their skilled hands and let them give you that new look you've always wanted. I promise, you'll feel like a million bucks when you leave here.

11 rue du Faubourg-Saint-Honoré, 8e; tel.: 01.44.94.11.11; Métro: Concorde or Madeleine; Open Tuesday–Saturday 10 A.M.–6:30 P.M.; Mondays also for the boutique; www.maisondebeautecarita.fr. ★ 🛍

CATHERINE   Thank goodness this long-established *parfumerie* expanded from a tiny boutique to a full-fledged store. This is *the* place to go in Paris (price-wise and otherwise) for perfume, cosmetics, beauty products, and fashion accessories. Their prices even beat out those of Sephora and the department stores! If you purchase a minimum of €175 worth of merchandise, price reductions (including *détaxe*, of course) may run up to 50 percent. Residents of France also benefit from a reduction, so be sure to ask for it if that applies to you. Note that savings on Sisley are the best. Chanel is still a good bargain; Lancôme not at all. Best to do your homework before you arrive in Paris. Ask for information about their mail-order service in case you need to replenish your supply once back home. It's easy to use: fax them what you are looking for, and if their prices appeal to you, place the order.

7 rue de Castiglione, 1er; tel.:01.42.60.48.17; fax: 01.42.61.02.35;
Métro: Tuileries or Concorde; Open Monday–Saturday 9:30 A.M.–7 P.M.

COMPTOIR SUD PACIFIQUE Step into this coastal destination, complete with whitewashed walls, beach cabanas, and exotic wood planking, to enter the world of Comptoir Sud Pacifique. Little known to Americans, this French company specializes in naturally made spicy scents for men and women. Packaged in metal flasks, these heady fragrances may be packed easily for distant trips to exotic ports of call. Their collection of seaside sportswear also floats my boat.

17 rue de la Paix, 2e; tel.: 01.42.61.74.44; Métro: Opéra;
Open Monday–Saturday 10 A.M.–7 P.M.; www.comptoir-sud-pacifique.com.

CREED Making fragrances since 1760, Creed has been purveyor to many important figures over the years, including King George IV, Napoleon III, and Queen Victoria. Having moved to Paris from London in 1854, Creed is the embodiment of British pedigree and French good taste. Many of its fine scents may be used interchangeably by men and women and the names tend to be nearly as exotic as the fragrances themselves: Ambre Cannelle, Santal Impérial, and Fleur de Bulgarie. Today they're hot sellers at high-end department stores such as Barney's, but buy them here in Paris, where the selection and the prices (about 30 percent less with *détaxe*) are the best.

Creed also sells silky creams, fragrant candles (€50), room fresheners

(€48), and soaps (€16), as well as some very classic clothing items, such as silk ties and poplin shirts, which are favorites among the French. Prices range from €65 *(eau de toilette)* to €86 *(eau de parfum)* for 75 ml of fragrance. For a real splurge, consider purchasing a bottle of Eau de Self, your own personal formula that may be created for you at a cost of €700 and up for 1 L of eau de toilette (*eau de parfum* is, of course, more). You must order at least 10 L and make an appointment with Mr. Creed for the consultation. It then takes him one year to concoct it.

38 av Pierre-1er-de-Serbie, 8e; tel.: 01.47.20.58.02; Métro: Alma-Marceau or George V; Open Monday 2:30–6:30 P.M.; Tuesday–Saturday 10:30 A.M.–6:30 P.M.; www.parfumscreed.com.

GUERLAIN Exquisite wrought iron railings and fanciful embellishments distinguish this historic landmark from the rest of the buildings along this busy avenue. Indeed, the Guerlain boutique hearkens back to a time when gloved women spoke in hushed tones when selecting their special fragrance. This sumptuous boutique opened here in 1912, the same year that L'Heure Bleue wooed everyone with the scent of nostalgia and innocence of prewar Paris. The house of Guerlain actually dates back to 1828, when Pierre-François-Pascal Guerlain became an immediate success as a perfumer and purveyor of smelling salts.

Shopping in this marble-clad, crystal-chandelier-illuminated emporium is a must—more so than ever now that the upstairs has been entirely transformed into a spectacular display case for the many, many Guerlain scents. Once you've absorbed the old-fashioned elegance of the main floor, explore the visual and olfactory feast above. Encircled by a glittering gold ribbon made of 350,000 mosaics and illuminated largely by a chandelier the size of a small hot air balloon, the stage has been properly set for the thousands of bottles—in countless shapes, sizes, and motifs—that fill this glowing space. It's all very show-and-tell and, rather surprisingly (for France at least), you're encouraged to test and sniff on your own to your heart's content!

The Institut de Guerlain has also been entirely redone and, from what I observed, it's busier than ever, so do reserve well in advance for a treatment.

68 av des Champs-Elysées, 8e; tel.: 01.45.62.52.57 and 01.45.62.11.21
(Institut); Métro: Franklin-Roosevelt; Open Monday–Saturday 10:30 A.M.–8 P.M.;
Sunday 3–7 P.M.; www.guerlain.com. ★ 🛍

L'INSTITUT LANCÔME Enter the world of Lancôme, an institution that has been at this address since 1936. The whole space was redone in 2001 to promote a totally polysensual experience. Indeed you see, smell, hear, touch, and even taste the many wonders of Lancôme in this highly sophisticated *beauté boutique*.

Few of the Lancôme products sold here are a better bargain than those sold in the United States (where they're made by Cosmair). You will, however, find certain products such as the Blanc Expert (a product to lighten and prevent age spots) and some of the house's original scents sold exclusively here. For those who relish being first, note that new Lancôme products become available here at least three months before their official launch elsewhere.

Call or e-mail at least two weeks in advance to schedule your special Lancôme treatment upstairs. Facials cost between €89 and €120 and men are most welcome.

29 rue du Faubourg-Saint-Honoré, 8e; tel.: 01.42.65.30.74; Métro: Concorde or
Madeleine; Open Monday–Saturday 10 A.M.–7 P.M.; www.lancome.com. ★ 🛍

JEAN PATOU Rue de Castiglione and rue de la Paix form a sort of perfume row. Pop in here to delight in an entirely different atmosphere, one that's like a soft, sophisticated rendition of flower power. All of the fragrances bearing the name of Jean Patou—one of France's greatest couturiers—sell here in this fresh, springlike décor blossoming with white, pink, and fuchsia, the signature colors of this celebrated house. And yes, you may buy Joy, as well as Enjoy (released in 2002), and even inquire about a couture fragrance made especially for you. Enjoy the sniffing in this most beautiful boutique and be sure to ask for samples— they're wonderful!

5 rue de Castiglione, 1er; tel.: 01.42.92.07.27; Métro: Tuileries;
Open Monday–Saturday 10 A.M.–7 P.M.; www.jeanpatou.com.

PARFUMS CARON   The high point of this charming shop is not only Nocturnes de Caron, but also thirty-five perfumes bearing names like French Cancan and Tabac Blond. Most of these scents, created in the first half of the twentieth century, are sold exclusively in this gold-bespeckled boutique. Other heady items include shimmering, silky face powders.

34 av Montaigne, 8e; tel.: 01.47.23.40.82; Métro: Franklin-Roosevelt;
Open Monday–Saturday 10 A.M.–6:30 P.M.

PHARMACIE LECLERC   This may look like an ordinary French pharmacy, but it was here in 1881 that Théophile Leclerc concocted the first Poudre Leclerc, or Leclerc powder, a light, silky face powder that leaves your skin with a healthy glow. The formula remains much the same as the one that first attracted elegant women to this place de la Madeleine emporium: a natural powder made from rice starch, said to be excellent for the skin largely due to its healing qualities. Free of preservatives, the Leclerc powders are also said to help acne and other unsightly imperfections. Most women, however, seem to be drawn to the fact that the powders come in more than twenty shades, perfectly suited for all skin types and hair colors and for use day or night. It used to be that you could only buy the retro-looking silver and gold metallic compacts and containers here. But after becoming the face powder of choice for makeup artists, models, and actresses, Leclerc powders can be found at chic cosmetic counters in thirty different countries. Prices are better here, though (about 25 percent less than what's charged in the United States).

Pharmacie Leclerc is a great source for other French beauty products, particularly those superpowered magnifying mirrors that are hard to find in the United States. The pharmacy also sells medical supplies and medications, both traditional and holistic. If you contact Leclerc by fax, I'm sure you'll be impressed by their kind, expedient service.

10 rue Vignon, 9e; tel.: 01.47.42.04.59; fax: 01.47.42.75.13;
Métro: Madeleine; Open Monday–Friday 8:30 A.M.–7:30 P.M.;
Saturday 9–7:30 P.M.; www.t-leclerc.com.

MORE *BEAUTÉ* AND *PARFUMS*   When you're touring the Champs-Elysées, stop into **Sephora** (70–72 av des Champs-Elysées, 8e; tel.:

01.53.93.22.50; Métro: George V; www.sephora.com), the immense beauty store created by luxury goods behemoth LVMH. It's hard for me to give this star billing, since I'm sure many of you have experienced Sephora in the United States. Prices are better here but, as you've read above, there are other more interesting places to shop for perfumes, cosmetics, and beauty products in Paris.

If you're seeking special pampering for your *cheveux*, consider the hair clinic of **J. F. Lazartigue** (5 rue du Faubourg-Saint-Honoré, 8e; tel.: 01.42.65.29.24; Métro: Concorde; www.jflazartigue.com), *the* place to go in Paris to buy and experience exacting treatments for your locks. They also do hair straightening and provide free hair and scalp analysis.

The French are very big on seaweed-based products and treatments *(soins)*. If this interests you and you don't have time to venture to Brittany, look into **Villa Thalgo** (218–220 rue du Faubourg-Saint-Honoré, 8e; tel.: 01.45.62.00.20; Métro: George V; www.thalgo.fr), one of the few places where you can benefit from thalassotherapy so far from the sea.

Perfect Respites

BE Chef Alain Ducasse has charmed Paris again with another culinary outpost—this one on a much simpler scale. Be *(boulangerie/épicerie)* opened almost five years ago, and like Monsieur Ducasse's other establishments, has garnered much attention from the French. I have a feeling more of this kind of bakery/food store/café will be opening around the capital, but for now come to this part of Paris—not far from the Marché Poncelet—to savor his sandwich creations and a variety of other fine food and wine offerings. Traditional bread made in full view is the star attraction here, and I think one of the best is the *pain aux figues* (fig bread).

73 bd de Courcelles, 8e; tel.: 01.46.22.20.20; Métro: Ternes; Inexpensive; Open Monday–Saturday 7 A.M.–8 P.M.; www.boulangepicier.com.

CAFÉS ET THÉS VERLET Since 1880, this handsome shop has been selling some of the finest coffees in Paris. You can try thirty different ones here along with an equally notable array of teas. Toast, cheesecake, and strudel are served in the morning, and by lunchtime, salad, quiche, and *croque monsieur* (a French sort of grilled cheese and ham sandwich) are added to the menu as well. And, of course, you can still buy nicely packaged coffees and teas, along with an alluring selection of jams, candied fruits, and other sweet and savory items.

256 rue Saint-Honoré, 1er; tel.: 01.42.60.67.39; Métro: Palais Royal or
Pyramides; Inexpensive; Open Monday–Saturday 9:30 A.M.–6:30 P.M. (until 7 P.M.
for the boutique); www.cafesverlet.com. 🛍

DALLOYAU   It's hard to resist the mouthwatering pastries and finger sandwiches that you see in the window chez Dalloyau. Stop in and treat yourself to a little snack from one of Paris's most famous bakers since 1802. They are probably best known for their *macarons*—light and airy cream-filled, cookie-like meringues made from egg whites, sugar, honey, and almond, delicately sandwiched together with a creamy filling and ranging in flavors from chocolate to fennel. These are generally best eaten incredibly fresh. This famed establishment also offers an array of other Elysian delectables that you may either eat on the premises in their sleek restaurant or take out.

All of the following tea salons are open daily; the Bastille address stays open until 11 P.M.

99–101 rue du Faubourg-Saint-Honoré, 8e; tel.: 01.42.99.90.00; Métro: Saint-
Philippe-du-Roule; Open daily 8:30 A.M.–9 P.M. (restaurant closes at 7 P.M.); 2 pl
Edmond-Rostand, 6e (Left Bank tea salon); tel.: 01.43.29.31.10; Métro:
Luxembourg; 5 bd Beaumarchais, 4e (Bastille tea salon); tel.: 01.48.87.89.88;
Métro: Bastille; Moderate to expensive; www.dalloyau.fr. 🛍

LADURÉE   Shopping on rue Royale is not complete without a pause in Paris's most classic tearoom, Ladurée. If you aren't pushed aside by the eager people at the pastry counter to the left as you enter, you'll first notice the rich wood-paneled walls, the Boucher-style ceiling paintings and, above all, the assortment of little round, square, or rectangular wooden tables set up so that most of the clients face out toward the entrance of this distinguished-looking tea parlor. This is, of course, typically French, because no matter where you go or how you are dressed, the French will take note in the most indiscreet manner. This perhaps is why Ladurée is so tremendously popular with Paris's little old ladies. If the waitresses try to hustle you upstairs to their extra salon, see if you can wait for a table on the main level so that you can people-watch, too.

Ladurée's creamy pastries and buttery croissants are among the best in town. Delicious lunches consist of grilled salmon, exotic salads, and finger sandwiches served on silver trays that are as refined as the clientele. Ladurée offers scrumptious take-out goodies as well. They also have two other locations in Paris, but this one is by far the most authentic.

16 rue Royale, 8e; tel.: 01.42.60.21.79; Métro: Concorde or Madeleine; Moderate to expensive; Open Monday–Saturday 8:30 A.M.–7 P.M.; Sunday 10 A.M.–7 P.M.; www.laduree.fr.

MAISON DE LA TRUFFE   Here's something that's distinctly French: truffles. I'm talking about the bumpy ones you find (often with the help of a pig) underground at the foot of an oak tree. France and Italy are the two countries in the world that have coaxed these prized comestibles along throughout the centuries. (None grow in the United States.) And certainly the Maison de la Truffe in Paris is one of the best places on the Continent to taste these little gems.

This warm and homey restaurant offers a perfect respite from the boutique touring here on the place de la Madeleine. The welcome is very friendly, and there's an endless amount of truffle-enhanced dishes from which to choose. I can still taste the subtle, earthy flavor of my *tagliatelles aux truffes noires,* a perfect plate of pasta dressed with paper-thin slices of black truffles and butter. The *omellette aux truffes* appeared to be a popular choice among my fellow diners, so I'm already planning to order that (with a glass of Bordeaux) next time I stop by.

Prices vary wildly depending on what you order. You'll pay a small fortune, for example, for a dish made with *truffes blanches* (white truffles from Italy, available mid-September through December), but a *plat du jour* runs about €18.

19 place de la Madeleine, 8e; tel.: 01.42.65.53.22 and 01.42.66.10.01 (restaurant); Métro: Madeleine; Moderate to expensive; Open Monday–Saturday 9 A.M.–9 P.M.; www.maison-de-la-truffe.com.

MAXIM'S   What is today one of the world's most renowned restaurants began as a simple bar opened in 1893 by Maxim Gaillard, a former *garçon de café*. Maxim's quickly became a sort of club for Paris's golden society and, by the early part of the twentieth century, was frequented by artists such as Sarah Bernhardt and Mistinguett. The magnificent Art Nouveau décor set a splendid stage for all players of the theatrical world and Parisian high society, and it still enraptures restaurant patrons today. Here you dine in a setting composed of creations by the leading artists of this return-to-nature style. Masters such as Majorelle, Prouvé, Gallé, and Guimard (of Paris Métro fame) designed embellishments especially for Maxim's crafted out of bronze, copper, wood, and glass. Foliage and flowers encircle mahogany doors, pillars, and mirrors with a flourish of grace and eloquence typical of Belle Epoque style. From the mural paintings depicting nymphs dancing around lily ponds to the jubilant flora of the stained-glass ceiling, Maxim's offers one of the most sensational settings of all the world's restaurants.

Count on spending about €200 per person for dinner without wine.

You may also experience sumptuous ornamentation at their museum, where Pierre Cardin, owner of Maxim's, re-created the twelve-room apartment of a renowned courtesan. As one would expect, these grand interiors are decorated with the same panache as the restaurant. One-hour visits in English are conducted Wednesday through Sunday at 2 P.M. and the entrance fee is €15.

Don't forget the Maxim's boutique next door. Here you can shop for wines, other gastronomic items, and an assortment of decorative *objets*, all of which bear the jaunty Maxim's de Paris label. This is a good place to pick up Pierre Cardin fragrances and accessories as well.

Restaurant: 3 rue Royale, 8e; tel.: 01.42.65.27.94; Very expensive;
Open Tuesday–Saturday for lunch and dinner. Boutique: 7 rue Royale, 8e;
tel.: 01.47.42.88.46; Open Monday–Saturday 10 A.M.–7 P.M.;
Métro for both: Concorde; www.maxims-de-paris.com.

LE RUBIS   A wine barrel out front to rest your glass on, yellowed walls, and bloodred trim and banquettes confirm the authenticity of this small, rustic-looking wine bar. What a refreshing change of scenery from all the neighboring fashion boutiques! The clientele is a mix of blue-collar workers, local businessmen, and an occasional lady in stilettos.

Omelettes are served in the morning and at lunch, although the locals seem to prefer croissants and *un petit vin blanc* at breakfast. You may also enjoy a piping hot *plat du jour* (lunch only), a fresh cheese platter, or a hearty wedge of *pâté*—all accompanied by a ruby red glass of wine. The ambiance turns especially jolly here during summer evenings, when the crowd tends to spill out onto the street.

10 rue du Marché Saint-Honoré, 1er; tel.: 01.42.61.03.34; Métro: Tuileries; Inexpensive; Open Monday–Friday 7 A.M.–10 P.M.; Saturday 9 A.M.–3 P.M.

SPOON If you're in the mood for a fun, sexy, adventuresome, and delicious dining experience, come to this Alain Ducasse restaurant, which has enjoyed great success since its opening more than eight years ago. It's a must for people who possess a certain *curiosité* about food and wine. The menu proposes all kinds of different possibilities and pairings, so if you let yourself go a little, you'll find yourself titillated by a glorious assortment of flavors and aromas from different parts of the world. It's almost like a supremely delectable tapas experience in a very chichi setting. The staff is lovely—extremely efficient and not a bit prententious. I suggest you let yourself be guided by their recommendations. Depending on how you order, lunch or dinner here can be a bit pricey—but it's worth it. There are also special deals to be had such as a lunch menu at €45.

14 rue de Marignan, 8e; tel.: 01.40.76.34.44; Métro: Franklin-Roosevelt; Moderate to expensive; Closed the week between Christmas and New Year's; Open Monday–Friday noon–2:30 P.M. and 7–10 P.M.; www.spoon.tm.fr.

MORE RESPITES I took a peek at the freshly restored **Café de la Paix** (2 rue Scribe, 9e; tel.: 01.40.07.36.36; Métro: Opéra; www.paris-le-grand.intercontinental.com), and was most impressed by its glorious new-old look. I will definitely take tea there the next time I'm in Paris. I feel as though I have to mention **Angélina,** the popular tearoom at 226 rue de Rivoli (tel.: 01.42.60.82.00; Métro: Tuileries), that I have always felt is overrated. Last time I was there, my hot chocolate was served lukewarm and I found the level of noise and smoking to be insufferable. My cake left me amply satisfied, however. I did enjoy the Old World charm of the room, and I didn't have to go out of my way to go there, so all was not lost. A better choice may have been **Le Café Marly** (93 rue de Rivoli, 1er; tel.: 01.49.26.06.60; Métro: Louvre), a handsome Philippe Starck–designed restaurant that always attracts a stylish crowd. If the weather is nice, sit on one of the canvas-covered banquettes on the terrace facing the brilliant Louvre pyramid, arguably one of the best views of Paris. Prices seem to have gone up a fair amount in recent years (or maybe it's the dollar going down), so make your selection carefully or you may end up paying $25 for a hamburger.

If it's a gorgeous evening and you feel like sitting out on a terrace in the Golden Triangle/Alma Marceau area, check out **Devèz** (5 pl de l'Alma, 8e; tel.: 01.53.67.97.53; Métro: Alma-Marceau; www.devezparis.com). I enjoyed a most memorable meal there one balmy evening at about midnight and it was surprisingly untouristy.

For "making the scene," sneak down to the **Buddha Bar** (8 bis rue Boissy d'Anglas, 8e; tel.: 01.53.05.90.00; Métro: Concorde; www.buddhabar .com), an immense Oriental-theme restaurant/bar that has been a sure bet for a fun night out for a number of years now.

Swishy folks from the fashion world typically gather at **Caviar Kaspia** (17 pl de la Madeleine, 8e; tel.: 01.42.65.33.52; Métro: Madeleine; www.kaspia.fr) or **Davé** (12 rue de Richelieu, 1er; tel.: 01.42.61.49.48; Métro: Pyramides) when they're in town for the collections. Davé is one of my personal favorites that I try to hit whenever I'm in Paris. Definitely some of the freshest Chinese food around—wash it down with a nice rosé de Provence and you'll feel more than satiated.

People are talking about the new look of **Le Drugstore** (133 av des Champs-Elysées, 8e; tel.: 01.44.43.77.64; Métro: Etoile), the giant complex at the Arc de Triomphe end of the Champs-Elysées made up of two restaurants, two movie theaters, boutiques and, yes, a pharmacy. This landmark meeting place was closed for two years for renovations. Its new configuration includes the same glass used for the Pyramide du Louvre and, as you can imagine, features lots of sleek lines and angles. The best part of Le Drugstore is that you can go in the middle of the night or on a Sunday to pick up all kinds of gift items and necessities.

NIGHT MAGIC

You haven't truly seen Paris until you've experienced Paris by night. I'm not talking about the bus trip (which definitely has its own merits). No, I'm talking about the shows, true artistic representations of *la vie française,* or at least the more sensual aspects of French life. **Crazy Horse** and **Lido** offer two entirely different *spectacles*— they're both great and they both have shopping! Le Crazy is intimate, ultrasexy in the most tasteful manner, and highly artistic. Lido tends to be grandiose in a Vegas sort of way, so count on a parade of leggy showgirls and lots of dazzling, eye-popping special effects. You can shop at both places for very nice-quality souvenirs such as pins, baseball caps, bathrobes, and more without even going to the show. Do go if you can, though, since they offer the perfect accompaniment to a few glasses of champagne. Both Crazy Horse (12 av George V, 8e; tel.: 01.47.23.46.46; Métro: Alma-Marceau; www.crazy-horse.fr) and Lido (116 bis av des Champs-Elysées, 8e; tel.: 01.40.76.56.10; Métro: George V; www.lido.fr) are open nightly year-round and shows tend to run about €100 per person (includes champagne). If you don't have that kind of budget, €49 will buy you a seat at the bar at Crazy Horse and two drinks— well worth the price!

Recommended Hotels

CASTILLE   Located on rue Cambon, right next to Chanel between the Concorde and Opéra, this swank hotel is blessed with a great address. When I stayed here many years ago it was lovely, but today you feel a real vibe emanating from everything from the sophisticated décor, to the with-it staff, to the even more with-it clientele. The exquisite frescoes that adorn the walls of the Castille's inner courtyard are probably the only aspect of the hotel that has not changed in recent years. On the patio, you can enjoy a wonderful Mediterranean lunch from **Il Cortille,** the hotel's simply *perfetto* restaurant. Or steal yourself away inside to a more citified décor.

33–37 rue Cambon, 1er; tel.: 01.44.58.44.58; Métro: Concorde; Four-star luxury hotel and part of Star Hotels: Expensive to very expensive; www.starhotels.com.

FOUR SEASONS HÔTEL GEORGE V   From its beginnings in the 1920s, the Hôtel George V was considered a haven of luxury and calm. Today it offers a divine combination of Old World elegance, contemporary flair, and world-class service. From the moment you enter the hotel's lobby, high-styled flower arrangements and precious antiques vie for your attention; I found myself in awe of the sheer beauty of nearly everything that adorns this stunning hotel.

Lunch, tea, or dinner in **La Grand Galerie** is a great way to take in some of the hotel's treasures while doing some people-watching, too—all in an exceptional setting. Here, seated in luxurious armchairs, you're sure to experience a most elegant moment. Piano music begins at three and continues into the dinner hour, which only enhances the romance that reigns here. The hotel's well-known three-star Michelin restaurant, **Le Cinq,** is right next door, but I recommend you dine here: The food is quite exceptional, and it won't break the bank!

Unless you are a die-hard minimalist, you're going to love the **Spa George V**. If Marie Antoinette were around today, this is what she'd want her spa to resemble. Festooned in an array of eighteenth-century fabrics and furnishings, and a trompe l'oeil depicting the gardens of Versailles (located behind the indoor pool), yet fresh as the morning dew, the ambiance of this spa wraps you in cosseted luxury. And you don't have to be a hotel guest to experience its charms, as long as you come for a treatment. So here's my tip for transatlantic travelers: Arrive here directly from the airport and plan on spending a few hours to help you become acclimated to Paris. Often due to early morning arrivals people are not able to check into their hotel rooms right away, so leave your bags here, conquer jet lag with one of the spa's special massages (average price about €150), and then take a short nap behind a veiled curtain in one of their dreamy resting areas. I guarantee that this plan will change the course of your whole stay.

Before you leave, be sure to check out the **Boutique George V,** where you'll find items emblazoned with the hotel's insignia and other irresistible gift ideas such as scarves and shawls from Wolff & Descourtis (see "Place des Victoires" description p. 214 for more information on this label's glamorous offerings).

31 av George V, 8e; tel.: 01.49.52.70.00; Métro: George V or Alma-Marceau; Four-star luxury hotel: Very expensive; www.fourseasons.com. ✂ ★ 🎁

HÔTEL LE BRISTOL I would sometimes feel uncomfortable here back during my shopping service days when I came by to pick up clients. The marble lobby still feels rather cold to me, despite the handsome Gobelins tapestries hanging from the walls. But you must venture beyond this space to discover the real allure of this world-renowned hotel.

The ambiance of the hotel's **Restaurant le Bristol,** for example, furnishes an absolute contrast to what you experience when you walk through the hotel entrance. Here, in this prestigious two-star Michelin restaurant, wrapped in the warmth of sumptuously carved oak paneling, you are sure to rejoice over lunch or dinner. The show is transported to the summer restaurant from May through the end of September, where you may enjoy this fine fare in a lighter, more airy setting. If the terrace is open, by all means go there for the perfect respite, where you will find yourself encircled by impeccable quadrants of grass, cascading roses, lush flowerbeds, and perfect hedges.

The Bristol has come up with a great formula that allows you to experience the fun and flamboyance of a Parisian fashion show while sipping tea and eating cakes in a stately setting. Call the hotel to find out about their Fashion High Teas, held periodically on Saturdays from 3:30 to 5 P.M. in the bar. The latest collections from some of Paris's most famous fashion houses are shown—all for a price of €40 per person.

For spa treatments, know that **Anne Sémonin** is also on the premises. Go to "Place des Victoires/Les Halles" on p. 204 to read more on this progressive beauty institute.

112 rue du Faubourg-Saint-Honoré, 8e; tel.: 01.53.43.43.00; Métro: Champs-Elysées-Clémenceau; Four-star luxury hotel and member of The Leading Hotels of the World: Very expensive; www.hotel-bristol.com. ✗ ★

HÔTEL DE CRILLON Consistently ranked as one of the world's best hotels, the Crillon is an experience relished by precious few. Louis XV commissioned the palace property in 1758, and staying here is like being holed up in a wondrous castle outfitted with today's most prized amenities. (It was the hotel of choice of Lance Armstrong after most of his Tour de France victories.)

Even if you're not planning to spend the night, do stop in for tea, a drink at the bar, or perhaps lunch in one of the hotel's fine restaurants. Better yet, do a little shopping at the **Boutique Crillon,** the hotel's gift shop, just inside the main entrance to your left. They sell bathwear, linens, and knickknacks such as ashtrays bearing the Crillon's crowned *C.* Other tasteful gift items include floral candles and Annick Goutal perfumes, all of which may be purchased 365 days a year!

10 place de la Concorde, 8e; tel.: 01.44.71.15.00 and tel.: 01.44.71.15.92 (boutique); Métro: Concorde; Four-star luxury hotel and part of the Concorde Hotels Group and member of The Leading Hotels of the World: Very expensive; Boutique is open daily 9 A.M.–8 P.M.; www.crillon-paris.com.

HÔTEL LANCASTER   This is as close as many of us will come to staying in a breathtakingly elegant private home in Paris. This historic yet tired landmark hotel was transformed into this privileged enclave a number of years ago, and discriminating travelers have been flocking here ever since. Richly orchestrated colors of saffron, mauve, orange, olive, and chartreuse and abundant antiques create a visual symphony throughout this hotel's sixty well-appointed rooms.

All the Lancaster needed to top it off was an alluring restaurant. And that's exactly what they got when Michelin-starred Michel Troisgros opened **La Table du Lancaster** in March 2004. Keeping in tune with the spirit of the hotel, the cuisine is innovative yet traditional, zesty but not overpowering—just exceptional enough to have earned itself one Michelin star.

7 rue de Berri, 8e; tel.: 01.40.76.40.76; Métro: George V; Four-star luxury hotel: Expensive to very expensive; Restaurant is closed in August except to clients of the hotel; www.hotel-lancaster.fr.

HÔTEL DU LOUVRE   After having been entirely redone awhile back, this hotel emerged as a true gem. With an interior inspired by the hotel's Napoleon III origins, expect a plush assortment of colors and materials throughout. It's not at all over-the-top (as it is at the neighboring Hôtel Costes); instead, the look evokes modern elegance in intense shades of eggplant, topaz, cinnamon, and shimmering beige.

My favorite part of the Hôtel du Louvre, though, is **La Brasserie du**

Louvre. It has been my saving grace several times when I've been out and about alone in this area in the evening—after shopping all afternoon, of course! There are many cafés and restaurants near the rue Saint-Honoré/Palais Royal, but I've found most of them to be too smoky and noisy, or even too hip (that's often hard to take when you're tired). Sometimes you just want to sit in an attractive space, sip a glass of wine, and eat a nice piece of grilled fish without dealing with a lot of fanfare. **La Brasserie du Louvre** opens its terrace in the summer.

place André Malraux, 1er; tel.: 01.44.58.38.38; Métro: Palais Royal; Four-star luxury hotel and part of the Concorde Hotels group: Expensive to very expensive; www.hoteldulouvre.com. ✕

HÔTEL MANSART Named after Jules Hardouin Mansart, one of Louis XIV's great architects and the master designer of the magnificent place Vendôme, the Hôtel Mansart is undoubtedly one of the best bargains in this part of Paris. Located at the corner of the place Vendôme—just a couple of minutes from the Ritz—in an area known throughout the world for its prime real estate, this hotel is a good bet for the money.

5 rue des Capucines, 1er; tel.: 01.42.61.50.28; Métro: Opéra; Three-star hotel and member of Esprit de France Hotels: Moderate to expensive; www.espritfrance.com.

HÔTEL MEURICE Master artisans worked for more than two years on the ambitious restoration of this landmark hotel and the result is *superbe!* Opened in 1835 on the elegant rue de Rivoli by Charles-Augustin Meurice, a most enterprising postmaster, the present-day Meurice sparkles with all of its original opulence and more. The elaborate Louis XVI décor of this palace—most reminiscent of Versailles—has been buffed, polished, and regilded. Dubbed the *Hôtel des Rois* (Hotel of Kings), its hospitality has been enjoyed by many dignitaries and celebrities. If you're lucky, you'll stay in one of the rooms on the rue de Rivoli side, where the views of the Tuileries gardens are perhaps the best in Paris.

Whether you're a hotel guest or not, the **Caudalie Spa** is another reason to come to the Meurice. You don't have to travel all the way to Bordeaux to enjoy the benefits of these renowned wine-based products, specifically formulated in one of France's finest wine regions. At this intimate spa, esthetitians provide treatments such as a Crushed Cabernet Scrub, which features forty-five minutes of sheer relaxation and detoxification, for €94. After this, you can fold yourself into the luxurious leather chairs in the Meurice's **Bar Fontainebleau** to savor your own special nectar. The Meurice Millenium, a champagne cocktail composed of Cointreau, rose liqueur, and pink champagne, will truly complete your *vinothérapie* experience.

If you're just in for breakfast, lunch, tea, or a not-so-fussy dinner, **Le Jardin d'Hiver** (Winter Garden) rates as my favorite. Here amid palm trees and a soft light cast by the century-old Art Nouveau glass roof, you may truly relax, and if it's after 7 P.M., enjoy some swinging jazz as well.

228 rue de Rivoli, 8e; tel.: 01.44.58.10.10; Métro: Tuileries; Four-star luxury hotel and member of the Dorchester Collection: Very expensive; www.meuricehotel.com. ✗ ★

LES PALACES

The French have two words for a palace: *palais* and *château*. Somehow it seemed fitting, however, to adopt the English word *palace* in the early 1900s to describe the glorious grand hotels that were then being built in Paris. What began as a marketing move to attract prominent British tourists soon stuck and, today, when one refers to *les palaces de Paris*, most people know that this includes a select few. Six palatial hotels worthy of being called *palace* exist today in Paris, and once you step into one you will know why. The historical significance of each is remarkable, but it's more likely the profound attention to detail of each fine establishment that puts them head and shoulders above the rest of Paris's splendid hotels. The six include Four Seasons Hôtel George V, Hôtel le Bristol, Hôtel de Crillon, Hôtel Meurice, Hôtel Plaza Athenée Paris, and Hôtel Ritz. Even if you don't plan to spend the night, I wholeheartedly encourage you to stop at one of these bastions of tradition, the *crème de la crème* of all the world's hotels. You may breathe in their allure for the price of *un café* or just a tour around the lobby. Be sure to dress up for the occasion.

HÔTEL PLAZA ATHENÉE PARIS   Truly the *grande dame* of all of the Paris hotels, the Plaza is more luxurious today than ever before after recent renovations. The hotel first opened in 1911 at the same time as the nearby Théâtre des Champs-Elysées and soon became the gathering place for prominent maestros, composers, and performers. By 1936, the hotel was the stomping ground of great celebrities, including Josephine Baker, Rudolph Valentino, and Maurice Chevalier. When Christian Dior opened just down the street, a more fashion-oriented clientele began to flock here, a foxy following that continues to this day. Even if you're not *en résidence* at the hotel, lunch at the Art Deco–style **Le Relais Plaza** is a must: You'll rub elbows with some of the most smartly turned out people in Paris. And, if the weather permits, reserve a table at **La Cour Jardin,** the hotel's court-yard. Here, against a backdrop of creeping green ivy and cascades of red geraniums in clay pots, you can experience the true charm of *un grand hôtel.*

25 av Montaigne, 8e; tel.: 01.53.67.66.65; Métro: Alma-Marceau; Four-star
luxury hotel and member of the Dorchester Collection: Very expensive;
www.plaza-athenee-paris.com. ✖

HÔTEL RÉGINA   Boy, was I glad I brought my red silk pajamas when I stayed here. They were from Victoria's Secret, but still I felt appropri-ately turned out for the regal, crimson-accented furnishings in *ma chambre.* I've stayed here several times, and each time it gets better. Now, after recent renovations, it's truly extraordinary. All of the Régina's Belle Epoque–style interior design has been lovingly restored, from its fabric-covered walls to its ultrarich window treatments.

The Régina's common areas also sparkle; hence, its restaurant and bar have become very alluring gathering places. They, too, possess their own **Cour Jardin,** which is also a delightful place to go during the spring and summer. And here's a hint for you New Year's Eve revelers: The restau-rant and bar offer specials that outdo those of the nearby high-end estab-lishments.

Built on the site of the Royal Stable of the Louvre Palace, the Régina is truly a classic, and its location just across the street from the Louvre is a museumgoer's dream.

2 place des Pyramides, 1er; tel.: 01.42.60.31.10; Métro: Pyramides; Four-star
hotel: Expensive to very expensive; www.regina-hotel.com. ✕

HÔTEL RITZ   Whether you make it up to the rooms or not, this inimitable hotel envelops you in a rich cloak of luxury as soon as you walk
through the door (designed by one of the architects of Versailles). Thank
you, César Ritz, for having opened your "perfect hotel" here in this noble
mansion in 1898. Drinks at the **Bar Hemingway** are always fun, but tea at
the **Bar Vendôme** is my pleasure. Afternoon tea (€35 per person) complete with little sandwiches and cakes is served daily from 4 to 6 P.M. and
it's essential to reserve. A dinner shared with my mom at **L'Espadon,** the
hotel's glorious Rococo-style one-star Michelin restaurant, was one of
the most memorable meals I've ever had.

15 place Vendôme, 1er; tel.: 01.43.16.30.30; Métro: Opéra; Four-star luxury
hotel and member of The Leading Hotels of the World: Very expensive;
www.ritzparis.com. ✕

LA TRÉMOILLE   For an intimate and decidedly urbane hotel experience in Paris, choose La Trémoille, a stylish boutique hotel located in
the heart of the Golden Triangle. You can't beat the location since it is
both within proximity of a lot of goings-on and also tucked into the
rue de la Trémoille, a rather quiet street of Paris, particularly on
weekends.

La Trémoille has been a favorite address since it opened as a hotel in
the late sixties; illustrious folk such as Orson Welles, Duke Ellington, and
Louis Armstrong stayed here back in that day. The hotel closed for more
than a year in 2001, then reopened in 2002, resplendent in a warm,
contemporary-style décor where rich-colored silks, faux fur, and mohair
drapes rule. Today's guests include Richard Gere, Johnny Depp, Ornella
Muti, and lots of not-so-famous people seeking calm, style, and all the
discretion in the world. (So discreet, in fact, that each room is equipped
with a hatch so that meals, laundry, and whatever else you may desire can
be delivered by room service and the housekeeping staff without your
being disturbed.)

If you feel like emerging from your sumptuous seclusion, you can always go down to dinner at **Senso,** a Terence Conran restaurant that serves a refined cuisine against a chic, modern backdrop. The **Senso Bar** is considered to be quite the happening place, so you might just see Johnny after all.

14 rue de la Trémoille, 8e; tel.: 01.56.52.14.00; Métro: Alma-Marceau or
Franklin-Roosevelt; Four-star luxury hotel and member of Preferred Hotels & Resorts
Worldwide: Expensive to very expensive; www.hotel-tremoille.com. ✗

HÔTEL DE VIGNY Imagine feeling as though you were in a country château right in the heart of Paris. Blazing fires, comfy couches, and heavy draperies make this an elegant address, one truly worthy of the Relais & Châteaux mark of excellence. Stop into their restaurant for a drink or light fare even if you are not staying at the hotel.

9–11 rue Balzac, 8e; tel.: 01.42.99.80.80; Métro: George V; Four-star luxury Relais
& Châteaux hotel: Expensive to very expensive; www.hoteldevigny.com. ✗

HÔTEL WESTMINSTER Named after the Duke of Westminster, a most loyal client of the hotel's in 1946, the Hôtel Westminster ranks among Paris's finest hotels. It has been a hotel since 1840, and today's patrons delight in that delicious combination of twenty-first-century amenities in a nineteenth-century setting. Curlicues of wrought iron trim the Baroque facade of this handsome edifice, announcing the elegance that awaits you inside. Like the hotel's lobby, the bathrooms are dressed in marble, a perfect complement to the spacious rooms, recently renovated in a fresh, traditional style. A feeling of intimacy prevails here and, throughout my stay, I felt more like a treasured guest than a nameless client. The best-kept secret, however, lies within the cozy confines of the **Duke's Bar,** redone as a handsome English library—the perfect setting indeed for escaping from the often-hectic rhythm of the big city. Lunch and tea are served here as well.

13 rue de la Paix, 2e; tel.: 01.42.61.57.46; Métro: Opéra; Four-star luxury hotel
and member of Warwick International Hotels: Expensive to very expensive;
www.warwickwestminsteropera.com. ✗

HYATT REGENCY PARIS-MADELEINE Hyatt first stepped onto the Paris hotel scene with this handsome boutique hotel, situated in an area that is both fairly central and a step away from the fray. All of their deluxe, contemporary rooms radiate a good taste and sophistication that is distinctly European. And if you're in search of a space that's truly exceptional, consider suite 706, a slick refuge atop the hotel that also boasts a fabulous terrace and far-reaching views of the city.

I love the ambiance of **La Chinoiserie**, an Oriental-influenced sort of sitting room beneath a huge glass skylight where you can sit on overstuffed red couches to sip champagne, tea, or to enjoy a light bite to eat. A most tranquil interval.

24 bd de la Madeleine, 8e; tel.: 01.55.27.12.34; Métro: Madeleine; Four-star luxury hotel and part of Hyatt International: Expensive to very expensive; www.paris.hyatt.com. ✕

PARK HYATT PARIS-VENDÔME I was nearly stupefied when I stumbled upon this extraordinary hotel. I had read about the opening of the Park Hyatt Paris, but then somehow forgot about it until the day I was hopscotching down the rue de la Paix checking out addresses. It is jaw-droppingly gorgeous, oozing with panache, contemporary, high-stepping design, and poetic artistry. I was in too much of a hurry to experience any of it—not even a drink at their trendy bar, not even a quick stop in their ladies' room (which I'm sure is very hip). Be sure to put it on your list. More to come in my next edition, perhaps...

5 rue de la Paix, 2e; tel.: 01.58.71.12.34; Métro: Opéra; Four-star luxury hotel and part of Hyatt International: Very expensive; www.paris.hyatt.com. ✕

Favorite Tours

GOLDEN TRIANGLE This is the tour you want to take when you're looking and feeling *trés élégant*. Avenue Montaigne, rue François 1er, and avenue George V form this *triangle d'or*, the sacred ground where most of Paris's couture houses and several luxury hotels reside. Strolling down chestnut tree–lined avenue Montaigne always makes me feel like I'm in a very privileged part of Paris, and that's not just due to the proliferation of *luxe*. There's a hush that reigns here, a quiet elegance imbued by these bastions of tradition. Dress your best, enjoy peeking into some of the world's biggest names, and definitely plan to stop for a long, languoring moment at either the Four Seasons George V or the Plaza-Athénée.

CHAMPS-ELYSÉES   Phew! The scene is entirely different over on the Champs-Elysées, where the avenue seems to pulsate with all the excitement of a huge tribe of people that has descended onto an immense outdoor stage. Thank goodness the sidewalks are as oversized as the avenue itself, because the crowds become quite thick here. When I lived in Paris I would only come here to go to the movies. Today, the cinemas still draw a crowd, but so do the many fun and happening stores. I suggest you start toward the top of les Champs at George V Métro and saunter down to the **place de la Concorde.** (This is quite a distance, so be prepared.) The beautiful gardens below (from the rond-point des Champs-Elysées to Concorde) will be your reward. In terms of libations, an *apéritif* outside at Fouquet's is a must for both the lovely setting and the great people-watching.

SAINT-HONORÉ/VENDÔME   I love the almost villagelike feel of the rue du Faubourg-Saint-Honoré and the rue Saint-Honoré. A very fancy village indeed, but the narrowness of these two streets creates an intimate mood that somehow tempers all the glitz and glamor that prevail in this ultrachic shopping district. If it's fashion you're after, this is where you want to be. And best of all, I promise that the window-shopping here is fabulous. (I could spend half a day in front of the Hermès windows alone.) You can pick up rue du Faubourg-Saint-Honoré not far from the rond-point des Champs-Elysées across from the Elysées Palace and work your way all the way down to rue Castiglione or begin farther down toward Tuileries Métro and go in the opposite direction. For even more extraordinary window-shopping (this doesn't mean you can't pop in sometimes!), veer off to the exquisite **place Vendôme** and the adjacent **rue de la Paix,** Paris's high-end jewelry area. Drip, drip, drip go the diamonds, rubies, emeralds, and sapphires so superbly displayed in these windows. A multicolored feast for the eyes indeed. You have no choice now but to duck into one of the neighboring luxurious hotels such as the

Ritz, the Park Hyatt Paris, the Westminster, the Meurice, the Crillon, or the Bristol (at the other end of Faubourg-Saint-Honoré) for a celebratory drink.

ROYALE/MADELEINE Walking the length of rue Royale as far as place de la Madeleine, you'll find all that you need to prepare a proper Parisian feast. First, *la table.* In all my years of entertaining and being entertained in France, I learned that a so-so meal quickly becomes far more interesting when served on fine china. Add some handsome utensils and glistening glasses, and you almost instantly have a first-rate repast. Begin at place de la Concorde and wend your way up to the Madeleine to take in *the* most exceptional table arts houses of France. Stop at **Ladurée** for a leisurely pause or a quick pastry to go, then head up to place de la Madeleine, where you'll be dazzled by two of the world's most alluring food emporiums, **Fauchon** and **Hédiard.** There are also some smaller food and wine purveyors in between such as **Maille,** the **Maison de la Truffe,** and the **Maison du Miel** (on nearby rue Vignon). By now, I'm sure your arms are full of all kinds of provisions and gifts for special loved ones back home. You may pick up the Madeleine Métro here, take a taxi, or fold yourself into the handsome neocolonial décor in the restaurant above Hédiard.

RIVOLI/CARRÉ DU LOUVRE A number of schlocky touristy shops line the stretch of the rue de Rivoli from place de la Concorde to the Louvre, but underneath these nineteenth-century arcades you can find some quality souvenirs to bring home. What might look tasteless amid a jumble of cheesy collectibles might become a most treasured remembrance of Paris to accent your home. The Eiffel Tower decanters continue to sell ad infinitum—small, inexpensive keepsakes that can bring a smile to most people's lips. Tourist shopping takes on a whole different allure when you duck into the **Carré du Louvre** at 99 rue de Rivoli. Not only will this bit of underground exploration allow you to see I. M. Pei's inverted pyramid in the Louvre courtyard (some say it's better than the one up top) but it will also lead you to discover many other beautiful stores. I'm not crazy about the shopping here in what is most certainly one of Paris's most resplendent malls, but you may find it to your liking. Don't miss the Virgin megastore, a storehouse of music and books. You can also buy entrance tickets to the Louvre here, saving you an endless wait in line. (*Ssssh*—don't tell!) Anyone that enjoys fashion and home décor will revel in a visit to the **Musée des Arts Décoratifs** and/or the **Musée de la Mode et du Textile** at 107 rue de Rivoli. Their gift shops rate high as well. The terrace overlooking the Pyramide at Café Marly wins my vote as the best place to stop on this tour.

3

The Left Bank

THE PARISIANS' PARIS

You have not experienced shopping in Paris until you have shopped on the Left Bank. I like to look at the Left Bank as the soul of Paris and the Right Bank as the showcase. The Left Bank is as casual and unpretentious as the Right Bank is formal and cool. There is a sense of free-spiritedness on the Left Bank, or *rive gauche*. Students have always had a stronghold on this area, and it is still considered to be the center of intellectual activity and artistic expression. (L'Ecole des Beaux-Arts is located on the rue des Beaux-Arts, and music from the jazz clubs in the Latin Quarter rings out long into the night.) Compared to the Left Bank, the Right Bank may not have as much tradition deeply embedded into its streets (that's by European standards, remember), but it does have one very solid reputation to uphold: the world's window on designer fashions. Some of this has changed a bit in recent years, but despite the infiltration of many typically Right Bank boutiques across the river, I feel that there is still a noticeable difference between the two sides of the Seine.

The real influx of fashion on the Left Bank began when Yves Saint Laurent went *rive gauche* and moved his collection of high-fashion ready-to-wear here in 1966. Before then, France's best-dressed women wore predominantly couture from the Right Bank houses, so Saint Laurent's trip across the river forced the fashion world to begin to look at the Left Bank and fashion in a different light. Saint Laurent's revolutionary Left

Bank boutique is still there, as well as other big names such as Sonia Rykiel. Most set up shop on the rue de Grenelle, the Left Bank's original prestigious street for designer clothing. Sonia Rykiel moved to the boulevard Saint-Germain in the early nineties, and thereafter the really big names such as Cartier, Armani, Dior, and Louis Vuitton sought out Left Bank outposts for their luxury goods. The economic boom of the past fifteen years further accelerated this influx of high-end boutiques, even though a number of organizations initially tried to prevent such an invasion. This part of Paris, surrounding the Saint-Germain-des-Prés church, has long been considered the literary crossroads of the world. There was a big hullabaloo in an attempt to fend off these stores and save the intellectual character of the area, mainly because so many traditional bookstores and cafés were being bought out and hence, disappearing. (Perhaps in an effort to take away the sting, couture king Karl Lagerfeld opened a bookstore/gallery/boutique on the Left Bank during this contentious period.)

Sadly, many of the old institutions did sell out; nonetheless, I do feel that you'd practically have to bomb the Left Bank for it to lose its unique character. Parts of the Left Bank are still distinctly bohemian; it's not at all unusual to see a writer toiling over a pad and paper in a busy café. And the *rive gauche* has uncontestably remained the Parisians' Paris. Sure, there are a lot of tourists, but not nearly as many as on the rue de Rivoli. Small, quaint hotels replace the need for glitzy palaces but, most of all, these are the streets where many Parisians actually live. The ground floors may be filled with scintillating storefronts, but the rest of the buildings have for the most part remained residential, which means that some of the boutiques' best business comes from their neighbors. Mixed in with all the fashion boutiques are neighborhood grocers, butchers, and bakers, as well as centuries-old antiques shops, interior-decorating showrooms, and art galleries.

There is an abundance of children's clothing boutiques here on the Left Bank. I imagine they popped up to capture the attention of all the *mamans* passing by. Many of the children's stores listed also have Right Bank outposts, but it's much more fun to shop here. And, since many are within close proximity to one another, you can hit several at a time.

Paris's two most famous cafés, café Les Deux Magots (sometimes called the café aux Deux Magots) and its neighbor, Café de Flore, anchor the Left Bank cultural scene. A coffee here might seem a bit steep, but that handful of euros buys you a comfortable seat—sometimes for as long as an hour or more—at one of the world's most stimulating intersections. The sights, sounds, smells, and tastes are well worth the price of a *café crème*.

Food and Wine Purveyors

BARTHÉLEMY The façade of this 150-year-old boutique, the buttery color of a rich *comté,* beautifully frames the appetizing array of cheeses displayed in their shopwindows. Barthélmy is uncontestably the most highly regarded cheese shop of the capital—they even supply the Elysées Palace and many of the embassies. And you never know whom you might run into here: I once found myself rubbing elbows with Catherine Deneuve! Inside, the cheeses are presented with all the reverence expected from an artisanal cheese master. Little goat cheeses, or *petits chèvres*, come in a huge variety of shapes and sizes—hard and soft, covered with herbs, cracked pepper, ashes, or *au naturel*—and are displayed like mini sculptures on milk-white faience trays. Other cheeses look like large hand-cut stones, and many have been laid out on straw mats on a bed made of sprigs of fern. The old tile floor, the marble-faced cupboards, and the barnyard tableau of hens and chickens reinforce the wonderful authenticity of this *fromager.* "We are the defenders of *le cru* (unpasteurized cheese)," Nicole Barthélemy proudly states, and indeed these are the most flavorful of all. The freshest yogurts and creams (do try *crème fraîche*) also sell here, and there's a small but lovely selection of wine. If you're buying cheeses for travel, ask to have them vacuum packed.

51 rue de Grenelle, 7e; tel.: 01.42.22.82.24; fax: 01.45.49.25.16; Métro: rue du Bac; Open Tuesday–Saturday 8 A.M.–1 p.m. and 4–7:15 P.M.; hours vary somewhat in the summer; closed in August.

DEBAUVE & GALLAIS In 1800, chocolate had a somewhat dubious reputation. People debated whether it should be treated as a drug or a sweet. The problem was solved easily enough when a pharmacist and a chocolate maker teamed up to open one of Paris's first chocolate shops, Debauve & Gallais. The myth surrounding the miraculous healing effects of chocolate has since disappeared (or at least diminished), but the regal packages containing flavorful, full-bodied chocolate candies have remained at Debauve & Gallais. The royal blue lettering and *fleur de lis* insignia remind us that this venerable company was indeed purveyor to the kings of France.

30 rue des Saints-Pères, 6e; tel.: 01.45.48.54.67; Métro: Saint-Germain-des-Prés;

33 rue Vivienne, 2e; tel.: 01.40.39.05.50; Métro: Bourse;

Open Monday–Saturday 9 A.M.–7 P.M.; www.debauveandgallais.com.

MARIAGE FRÈRES   This Mariage Frères boutique and tea salon tends to be considerably less crowded than their Marais address. I so prefer this corner boutique at this sleepy intersection, especially since it looks like it was originally a Paris apartment, particularly upstairs, where the tearoom has been installed. Most of the old moldings have been left intact and the wooden floors creak. But the jumble of wooden display cases and palm trees and the heady smell of tea make me feel as though I've just stepped into a divine oasis in the East. Don't miss the cellar, where you'll find a handsome collection of tea crates from faraway lands. The Mariage brothers started as tea merchants in 1854; today you may buy everything from a particularly delicate blend of Darjeeling to tea-scented candles to an Art Deco teapot.

13 rue des Grands-Augustins, 6e; tel.: 01.40.51.82.50; Métro: Saint-Michel;

30–32 rue du Bourg-Tibourg, 4e; tel.: 01.42.72.28.11; Métro: Hôtel de Ville;

Boutique: Open daily year-round 10:30 A.M.–7:30 P.M.; Tearoom: Open daily year-round noon–7 P.M.; www.mariagefreres.com. ✕

PETROSSIAN   The Petrossian brothers were the first to import Russian caviar into France more than a half-century ago. Today, the Petrossian name stands for one of the world's finest caviars. They sell both farmed and wild caviar, so there's a wide variety of this precious roe in an equally broad range of prices. Blue metal boxes of various sizes, painted with Petrossian's famous seascape logo, may be filled with fresh beluga, osetra, or sevruga caviar and are meticulously wrapped for long-distance travel. Aside from Petrossian's handsome selection of gift packages, the shop also sells many other top-quality products including a dazzling array of Russian vodkas.

For an elegant lunch or dinner, consider **Restaurant Petrossian,** which is located just above the boutique. The dining experience here outshines those that take place chez Petrossian in the United States. Here the emphasis is on fine cuisine as well as tastings of their most notable products. Many of the people (predominantly men) who lunch here are from the nearby ministries and embassies, so that alone indicates the quality of this *bonne table*.

18 bd de Latour-Maubourg, 7e; tel.: 01.44.11.32.22; Métro: Latour-Maubourg; Open Monday–Saturday 9:30 A.M.–8 P.M.; Restaurant: tel.: 01.44.11.32.32; Expensive to very expensive; Open Tuesday–Saturday for lunch and dinner; www.petrossian.fr. ✗

POILÂNE The window of Poilâne's bakery resembles one of those marvelous still-life paintings you find at the Louvre. Old-fashioned bread racks are piled high with a variety of rustic breads; bunches of wheat are tucked here and there as gentle reminders of the bounty from which these heavy breads are made. Baskets of *petits pains* (little breads), *sablés* (shortbread cookies), *pains au chocolat*, croissants, and flaky apple tarts complete this wholesome scene.

Pierre Poilâne first opened a *boulangerie* here in this former convent in 1932, and from that time on, the name Poilâne has been synonomous with authentic country bread. The bakery weathered the years after the war when white bread won out in popularity over the heavier, rustic bread made chez Poilâne. During the seventies, Lionel Poilâne developed a network of distributors throughout France and the world. Soon after, Poilâne's dense, traditionally made bread gained a following. It helped that people wanted tastier, more nutritionally sound foods around that time as well.

Each of these brown, flour-dusted round loaves is truly made *à l'ancienne* today as it was in the beginning, from a near-sacred troika of ingredients: flour (with a bit of spelt); a pinch of *sel de Guérande*, the world's most delicious salt, harvested on the western coast of France since the Middle Ages; and leaven. It is this last ingredient that gives Poilâne bread its slightly sharp (often referred to as sourdough) taste and, of course, the manner in which Poilâne produces this ferment represents the best-guarded secret of all. Have a look at all of this during a visit to their bakery downstairs. If you're just one or two persons, there's no need to call ahead (avoid Saturdays, though).

8 rue du Cherche-Midi, 6e; tel.: 01.45.48.42.59; Métro: Saint-Sulpice or Sèvres-Babylone; Open Monday–Saturday 7:15 A.M.–8:15 P.M.; www.poilane.fr.

RICHART Immaculately packaged and presented chocolates are the trademark of this high-quality chocolate maker from Lyon. The Richart chocolates, as well as their boxes, evoke a purity of form that is best appreciated by sophisticated chocolate lovers. Each of the geometrically shaped chocolates is arranged in a glossy white box, complete with pullout drawers for easier consumption.

258 bd Saint-Germain, 7e; tel.: 01.45.55.66.00; Métro: Solférino; Open Monday and Saturday 10 A.M.–7 P.M.; www.richart.com.

RYST-DUPEYRON Eighteenth-century wooden beams and slate-grey floor mosaics represent tradition, and you quickly realize that this is not an ordinary liquor store. Connoisseurs and amateurs alike will be thrilled with the extensive selection of Bordeaux wines and a choice offering of champagne, Portuguese ports, and Scotch whiskies that fill this elegant shop, here for more than thirty years. The main attraction, however, is Monsieur Ryst's own brand of armagnac (from the house of Ryst-Dupeyron, established in 1905): a brandy similar to cognac, differing mainly in its distillation and in its grapes and oak barrels. (Armagnac's grapes and barrels come from the Armagnac region of France, whereas cognac's come from Cognac.)

Hundreds of handsome pear-shaped bottles containing this golden liquid—and dating as far back as the late 1800s—line the left wall. Celebrating an anniversary or birthday with a particular *millésimé* (good year) is an excellent gift idea, and the shop will personalize any of their bottles (port included) with the name and date of your choice. Good news: The people who work in this boutique are as charming as the shop itself. They generally allow you to taste a number of armagnacs, ports, and spirits and are most helpful in advising you on the best years and optimal drinking conditions for the various châteaux wines.

Other tempting items include liquor-soaked fruits, armagnac-filled chocolates, foie gras, gift packages of armagnac, demicrystal glasses, and wooden boxes. For an unusual and incredibly delicious treat, try the chocolates filled with *crème de pruneaux* (cream of prunes) *à l'armagnac*.

79 rue du Bac, 7e; tel.: 01.45.48.80.93; Métro: rue du Bac;

Open Monday 12:30–7:30 P.M.; Tuesday–Saturday 10:30 A.M.–7:30 P.M.;

www.vintageandco.com.

More Food and Wine Purveyors

Even if you're looking for it, you're apt to miss the *patisserie extraordinaire* of **Pierre Hermé** (tel.: 01.43.54.47.77; www.pierreherme.com), tucked in between the fashion boutiques on rue Bonaparte. Step inside at no. 72 to admire the slick and streamlined little jewel-case boutique that contains Monsieur Hermé's precious pastries, chocolates, and ice creams. This is one of the haute couture salons of the pastry world, and his flavors are known to be highly innovative.

You may indulge in the *crème de la crème* of Belgian chocolates not far away at **Pierre Marcolini** (89 rue de Seine, 6e; tel.: 01.44.07.39.07).

The Métro for both of these sleek boutiques is Saint-Sulpice.

Denise Acabou, of A l'Etoile d'Or fame (see "More Stores and Neighborhoods," p. 291), recommended I write about *le chocolatier* **Jean-Charles Rochoux** (16 rue d'Assas, 6e; tel.: 01.42.84.29.45; Métro: Saint-Placide). This is a lady who knows her chocolate, so I had to oblige. Monsieur Rochoux worked for ten years with Michel Chaudin, another legendary French chocolate maker on the Left Bank (149 rue de l'Université, 7e; tel.: 01.47.53.74.40; Métro: Invalides or La Tour Maubourg) I can't wait to taste his chocolates the next time I'm in Paris.

For a more down-to-earth shopping experience, head north of boulevard Saint-Germain to **Huilerie Artisanale** (6 rue Jacob, 6e; tel.: 01.46.34.61.55; Métro: Saint-Germain-des-Prés; www.huile-leblanc.com), a sliver of a shop that showcases a large variety of oils and oil-based products (including soaps), vinegars, mustards, nuts, and more. Just step inside and breathe in that wonderful earthy aroma.

Table and Kitchen Arts, Home Décor, and Linens

CULINARION Culinarion has many boutiques in France specializing in very practical kitchen equipment. Traditional French cooking pans, pie plates, couscous pots, and terrine molds are mixed in with more unusual gadgets like scissors for cutting cheese and rubber gloves to wear when opening oysters—all at fairly reasonable prices.

99 rue de Rennes, 6e; tel.: 01.45.48.94.76; Métro: Rennes;
Open Monday 11:15 A.M.–7 P.M.; Tuesday–Saturday 10:15 A.M.–7 P.M.;
www.culinarion.com.

DESCAMPS A beautiful selection of house linens and bath accessories sells here in lively colors and cheerful prints, all priced less than in America. The saleswomen are particularly helpful in providing you with U.S. size equivalents for bed and table linens. You'll also discover lots of pretty purchases for children (nightclothes, bathwear, and linens) and for the beach, depending on the season. There are Descamps boutiques in almost every district of Paris.

38 rue du Four, 6e; tel.: 01.45.44.22.87; Métro: Saint-Sulpice;
Open Monday–Saturday 11 A.M.–7 P.M.; www.descamps.com.

DÎNERS EN VILLE If you only have time to visit one table arts shop in Paris, I suggest you come here. The crimson red and gold exterior announces the warm and resplendent approach to decorating that seems to be the hallmark of this boutique. The cozy yet luminous interior of this lovely shop makes you feel as though you have just entered a beautiful Parisian home.

Countess Blandine de Mandat Grancey was one of the first people in Paris to set the trend of mixing the old with the new—a fashion that has since become a way of life for most Parisian hostesses. Antique silver is set off against reproductions of old dishes, flatware, and glassware in order to present a look that is both thoroughly charming and affordable.

More modern creations of tableware are shown in the shop as well. Tabletops are king here and most of them are dressed in a burst of colorful prints with 100 percent cotton tablecloths from **Le Jacquard Français** and Beauvillé, two long-established textile companies from eastern France.

89 rue du Bac, 7e; tel.: 01.42.22.78.33; Métro: rue du Bac; Open Monday 2–7 P.M.; Tuesday–Saturday 10:30 A.M.–7 P.M.; www.dinersenville.fr.

EMILIO ROBBA Flowers fashioned out of cotton, silk, and velvet—many of which have been arranged in their own unique vases—are the artistic visions of French decorator/sculptor Emilio Robba. Before creating his tremendously successful collection of decorative items for interiors, Monsieur worked as a florist, developing his sense of composition in forms and colors. Artificial flowers have never been so hyperrealistic and modern. Orchids are his signature flower, and you may find them here in a number of interpretations at prices beginning at €25 (for a small orchid in a shot glass).

The galerie Vivienne address serves primarily as the showroom. You can buy there, but only the large compositions (priced on average €450).

63 rue du Bac, 7e; tel.: 01.45.44.44.03; Métro: rue du Bac; Open Monday–Friday 10:30 A.M.–7 P.M.; Saturday 11 A.M.–7 P.M.; 29 galerie Vivienne, 2e; tel.: 01.42.61.71.43; Métro: Bourse; www.emiliorobba.com.

ESPACE BUFFON Fittingly located just across from the **Jardin des Plantes,** this atelier displays their own plants and flowers in a large "greenhouse." These re-creations of the real thing are sculpted in terracotta. A family affair since 1927, the *famille* Burg perpetuates a tradition that finds its origins in the Renaissance. All their creations are entirely handmade and hand-painted and are, of course, quite ornamental, perfectly suited for a variety of interiors (and some exteriors). Big baskets of flowers (€200 to €500 each) and topiaries are popular themes, and the pieces come in a variety of colors and patinas such as milky white, polychromatic, and verdigris. The atelier, which is right in back, also makes rose-themed candlesticks (priced at €30 to €100), lamps, sconces, and frames, many of which are sold to select high-end stores in the United States.

27 rue Buffon, 5e; tel.: 01.47.07.06.79; Métro: Austerlitz; Open Monday–Friday 9 A.M.–noon and 2–7 P.M.; www.espacebuffon.com.

GENEVIÈVE LETHU More than twenty-five years ago, Geneviève Lethu opened her first store in La Rochelle, a delightful city on the Atlantic coast of France; now she has a boatload of boutiques throughout the world (but not yet in the United States) devoted to the kitchen and the table. Homey-looking, brightly colored dishes ideal for everyday use or festive occasions—attractively displayed with coordinating glassware, cutlery, and table linens—are her strong point. All the current trends and some country French favorites are presented here with great French verve.

95 rue de Rennes, 6e; tel.: 01.45.44.40.35; Métro: Saint-Sulpice or Rennes; Open Monday–Saturday 10:15 A.M.–7 P.M.; www.genevievelethu.com.

JEAN VIER Jean Vier is the leader in Basque linens, fabrics most recognizable by their bold stripes and purity of design. Since the sixteenth century, these stripes have told part of the story of the Basque people. During village gatherings and festivals, the peasants would place a *toile* over their oxen to protect them from the sun and flies. Through the width or color of the stripes, the pattern would also convey information about the wealth and stature of their owners.

These very patterns look stunning when draped over a table for a summer barbecue or made up into a tote for sporty travelers. The fabric quality is supreme and it will wash and wear well for ages.

66 rue de Vaugirard, 6e; tel.: 01.45.44.26.74; Métro: Saint-Sulpice; Open Monday–Saturday 10 A.M.–7 P.M.; Sunday 1–6 P.M.; www.jeanvierparis.com.

MARIE-PIERRE BOITARD Situated on the same resplendent *place* as the Senate, this elegant boutique features finely selected arts of the table by French product designer Marie-Pierre Boitard. Madame Boitard has applied her sense of color, composition, and form to the creation of colorful hand-engraved crystal goblets and vases, hand-embroidered table linens, and specially made patterns of china. These home accessories, as well as a choice selection of antiques, reproductions of antiques, faience, porcelain from Herend, and *petits objets*, are set off against the striking lapis lazuli décor of this exclusive boutique.

9 place du Palais Bourbon, 7e; tel.: 01.47.05.13.30; Métro: Invalides or Chambre des Députés; Open Monday–Friday 10:30 A.M.–7 P.M.; Saturday 10:30 A.M.–6:30 P.M.; www.marie-pierre-boitard.com.

LA MINE D'ARGENT Old sterling silver and silverplate coffee and tea services, hand mirrors, frames, serving dishes, flatware, and teething rings glisten in this reputable boutique. English is spoken, and don't be afraid to bargain.

108 rue du Bac, 7e; tel.: 01.45.48.70.68; fax: 01.45.49.06.55; Métro: Sèvres-Babylone or rue du Bac; Open Monday–Friday 10 A.M.–7 P.M.; Saturday 11 A.M.–6 P.M.

Note: Antique sterling or silverplate is generally priced lower than new.

MISE EN DEMEURE Designed to look like a sophisticated European country house or château, Mise en Demeure presents some very handsome home décor ideas in a variety of themes. The Provençal look is very strong (and so inviting, as usual) but there are also influences from other provinces such as Brittany. Whether you are seeking out a bit of inspiration or that special find, Mise en Demeure supplies many ideas and goods for your house in the country, on the mountain, or by the sea. Provençal pottery and linens from eastern France are just some of the products displayed atop country furniture painted in an array of alluring patinas. Be sure to venture upstairs into the series of old rooms, where amid creaky wooden floors and creamy walls, you'll better appreciate the full warmth of these furnishings and home and table accessories.

27 rue du Cherche-Midi, 6e; tel.: 01.45.48.83.79; Métro: Sèvres-Babylone; Open Monday–Saturday 10 A.M.–7 P.M.; www.miseendemeure.com.

OLIVIER DESFORGES The north of France is well known for its textile makers, and Olivier Desforges has just about the most luxurious touch. This Left Bank store showcases mostly bed linens in a wide range of colors and patterns from this French manufacturer. Some table linens are also sold here, along with a top-drawer collection of nightclothes for men, women, and children. Count on spending about €80 to €85 for a pair of crisp cotton pajamas. Don't miss the Olivier Desforges candles either: fragrant *bougies* wrapped in a taffeta pouch, darling gifts priced at €18 each.

26 bd Raspail, 7e; tel./fax: 01.45.49.19.37; Métro: rue du Bac;

Open Monday 2–7 P.M.; Tuesday–Saturday 10:30 A.M.–7 P.M.

PIERRE FREY ACCESSOIRES Elegant, colorful Pierre Frey fabrics are integrated into breakfast sets, serving trays, pillows, damask tablecloths, silk and wool-blend shawls, and women's and men's canvas traveling bags. If you're looking for a less pricey Pierre Frey gift idea, consider one of their scented candles (€32), called Troene, which will permeate your home with the delightful scent of lily of the valley, the quintessentially French flower that symbolizes happiness. To purchase Pierre Frey fabrics, just go next door.

7 rue Jacob, 6e; tel.: 01.43.26.82.61; 2 rue de Furstemberg, 6e (fabrics); tel.:

01.46.33.73.00; Métro for both boutiques: Saint-Germain-des-Prés;

Open Monday–Saturday 10 A.M.–7 P.M.; closed some of August.

SIÈCLE Whether it be silverware (some twenty patterns), table linens, faience, jewelry, or a variety of other eclectic table accessories and home décor items, the Siècle collection is both whimsical and modern, classic and exotic, a handsome fusion of creative talents and influences. Virtually everything in the store has been designed by Marisa Osorio-Farinha and Philippe Chupin, both graduates of the renowned Ecole du Louvre. Many of the 100 percent linen table linens, for example, have been hand-embroidered in Portugal, a lively nod toward Marisa's roots. (They also embroider linens for Hermès.) And if you like *découpage*, you'll find that, too, in a variety of forms. Prices are steep, but they offer special discounts for Americans—about 5 to 10 percent in addition to the *détaxe*.

24 rue du Bac, 7e; tel.: 01.47.03.48.03; Métro: rue du Bac; Open

Monday–Saturday 10:30 A.M.–7 P.M.; www.siecle-paris.com.

LA TUILE À LOUP   Crafts from nearly every province of France, including Brittany, Savoie, Burgundy, and Provence, fill every nook and cranny of this out-of-the-way boutique. For almost thirty years, discriminating shoppers from all corners of the earth have come to see this handpicked collection of arts and crafts made by artisans drawing from the traditions of their region. The pottery collection is particularly rich, and densely colored plates, bowls, and pitchers are stacked upon and underneath big wooden tables like Christmas presents in Santa's workshop. Baskets from Champagne and Périgord hang from the ceiling along with *bouquets de moisson,* the good-luck bouquets assembled to decorate the harvest wagons. Hand-blown rustic glassware from Auvergne, brightly colored table linens from Alsace and the Basque country, wooden utensils, olive-oil soap, and a wide range of books on the cuisine and local traditions of the provinces round out the abundance of country goods that fill this little shop. Thank goodness they ship all over the world!

35 rue Daubenton, 5e; tel.: 01.47.07.28.90; Métro: Censier-Daubenton;
Open Monday 1–7 P.M.; Tuesday–Saturday 10:30 A.M.–7 P.M.;
www.latuilealoup.com.

More Table and Kitchen Arts, Home Décor, and Linens

If you're looking to do up your home in a bit of a Modern Medieval look—that's to say, with lots of satin and velvet in dark hues and some wrought metal pieces, for example—then stop into **En Attendant les Barbares** (35 rue de Grenelle, 7e; tel.: 01.42.22.65.25; Métro: Sèvres-Babylone; www.barbares.com). Works by design team Garouste & Bonetti are always on show here.

Interested in seeing one of the finest collections of contemporary French furniture in Paris? Even if you have no intention to buy, it's a visual treat to take in the superbly crafted, smooth-as-silk works of **Christian Liaigre,** one of France's foremost designers of our times. (61 rue de Varenne, 7e; tel.: 01.47.53.78.76.42; 42 rue du Bac, 7e; tel.: 01.53.63.33.66; Métro for both boutiques: rue du Bac; www.christianliaigre.fr.).

For considerably less avant-garde home and table decorations in creamy white, ivory, and beige, go directly to **Blanc d'Ivoire** (4 rue Jacob, 6e; tel.: 01.46.33.34.29; Métro: Saint-Germain-des-Prés).

Many home décor shops have congregated on the south side of boulevard Saint-Germain toward Saint-Sulpice. I used to be very excited about much of what I found at **Maison de Famille** (29 rue Saint-Sulpice, 6e; tel.: 01.40.46.97.47), but now it seems much more ordinary. If you're here, take a look around, but I wouldn't make a special trip for it.

If you're sweet on French country with a touch of *la nostalgie,* you'll enjoy shopping at **Comptoire de Famille** (34 rue Saint-Sulpice, 6e; tel.: 01.43.26.22.29; www.comptoir-de-famille.com). I love their big French breakfast bowls in a range of old-fashioned hues. The French actually use them more for their *café, thé,* and *chocolat* than for cereal. They're the perfect size for dunking *tartines* or, I suppose, a glazed donut. Reasonably priced.

For a more sophisticated shopping experience on this street, enter the milky world of **Catherine Memmi** (www.catherinememmi.com). High-end furnishings, including ceramics, are sold at 11 rue Saint-Sulpice, 6e; tel.: 01.44.07.02.02; more gifty items such as scented candles and luxurious linens—most of which are presented in Catherine Memmi's signature cream-colored palette—are featured at 61 rue Bonaparte, 6e; tel.: 01.44.07.22.28.

The Métro for the three boutiques above is Saint-Sulpice.

Art, Antiques, and Collectibles

L'AUTRE JOUR It's worth going out of your way to discover the ever so lovely riches of this shop, particularly if you like Provence. Dorothée d'Orgeval, a tall, elegant Parisian originally from that sun-drenched region of France (and who obviously still spends much time there), has been presenting an exquisite shopwindow of her native land in this tiny Paris boutique for more than thirty years. Antiques are her specialty, and she regularly culls Provence for some of the finest pieces, whether they are faience, textiles, furniture, or little must-haves such as lamps, jelly jars, and mirrors. Her taste is to be envied. She actually works for a number of decorators, particularly many Americans, so maybe she'll give you a few tips here, too.

26 av de la Bourdonnais, 7e; tel.: 01.47.05.36.60; Métro: Ecole Militaire;
Open Monday–Friday 2:30–7 P.M.; closed in August and during certain vacations.

GALERIE ROBERT FOUR   You don't have to own a château to want to buy yourself an Aubusson tapestry. Whether you are in search of an original eighteenth-century treasure or a modern-day reproduction of these world-famous wall coverings, this is the place to go in Paris for the best of Aubusson. Robert Four actually has an atelier in that sleepy little town in the Limousin region of France where this art form took hold about three centuries ago. The atelier—along with a handful of others—restores old works and creates new ones (tapestries *and* rugs) on traditional and contemporary themes. And if petit point isn't your fancy, take a look at their lovely *cartons,* the gouachelike or oil paintings of the original tapestry designs, which sell here for €1,500 to €10,000. The tapestries can run considerably more, but a little pillow may be purchased for €300.

   8 rue des Saints-Pères, 7e; tel.: 01.40.20.44.96; Métro: Saint-Germain-des-Prés; Open Monday 2–7 P.M.; Tuesday–Saturday 10 A.M.–7 P.M.; closed mornings and Mondays during August; www.franceantiq.fr/sna/rfour.

HAGA   This Old World kind of shop provides a refreshing change from the numerous fashion boutiques that line the rue de Grenelle. Feast your eyes on one of the most extensive collections of wooden-spiraled Victorian candlesticks that Paris has to offer, as well as some decorative fish-eye mirrors, silver frames, endearing pictures, and lots of *objets de curiosité.* Their prices are par for the neighborhood—*très cher.*

   22 rue de Grenelle, 7e; tel./fax: 01.42.22.82.40; Métro: Sèvres-Babylone; Open some Mondays and Tuesday–Saturday 11 A.M.–12:45 P.M. and 2:30–7 P.M.; closed in August.

J. C. MARTINEZ   Monsieur Jean-Claude Martinez offers a wide selection of attractive prints and engravings from the sixteenth to nineteenth centuries, classed according to themes (landscapes, horses, hunting, flowers, etc.), regions of France, professions (medicine, law, and the like) and, of course, numerous views of Paris and the provinces. If you can't find what you're looking for here, try Monsieur Martinez's niece's shop at 97 rue de Seine.

21 rue Saint-Sulpice, 6e; tel./fax: 01.43.26.34.53; Métro: Odéon;
Open Monday 10 A.M.–12:30 P.M. and 2:30–7 P.M.; Tuesday–Friday
10 A.M.–7 P.M.; Saturday 10:30 A.M.–7 P.M.; jcmartinez@tiscali.fr.

PIXI & CIE. "You don't play with our figurines, you dream with them," exclaims the daughter of the founder of Pixi & Cie. And as you peer into glass cases neatly lined with these little dream-weavers depicting not only cartoon characters but also figures from our everyday lives (a doctor, a violinist, a magician, a policeman, a painter, each portrayed in its own lifelike setting), you realize that these tiny statuettes do indeed feed the world of the imagination.

All the miniatures are works of art painted by hand in the Pixi & Cie. workshop in Normandy. Their success has been tremendous with both collectors and amateurs alike since 1983, when the store first opened. Their mini-mannequins depicting the Paris Haute Couture designers became a huge rage, but sadly it seems as though most of them were only made in limited editions and are now unavailable. The pieces representing *la vie parisienne* (€9 to €150), however, are also excellent souvenirs of Paris. These lead and resin figurines are some of the most whimsical, packable, and affordable gifts you can buy in Paris.

6 rue de l'Echaudé, 6e; tel.: 01.46.33.88.88; Métro: Mabillon or Odéon;
Open Monday 2:30–7:30 P.M.; Monday–Saturday 11 A.M.–7 P.M.;
closed first two weeks of August; www.pixieshop.com.

AU PLAT D'ETAIN With origins that date back to 1775, this maker of lead soldiers has seen a few wars. All hand-painted with a phenomenal attention to detail, each figurine is more fascinating than the next. There's Emperor Napoleon I, valiant on his horse; an astonishing collection of soldiers—both French and foreign (including Prussians!)—from World War I; and even two shelves of infantry from the American Civil War. Nonmilitary subjects such as circus performers and firemen have also been immortalized here in molten lead. Prices range from €25 to €43.

16 rue Guisarde, 6e; tel.: 01.43.54.32.06; Métro: Saint-Sulpice;
Open Tuesday–Saturday 11 A.M.–12:30 P.M. and 2–7 P.M.;
www.auplatdetain.com.

More Art, Antiques, and Collectibles

I think I first discovered **Schmock Broc** (15 rue Racine, 6e; tel./fax: 01.46.33.79.98) on my way back from the Sorbonne one day during my student years. This Paris classic is loaded with an eccentric collection of objets from the Art Nouveau and Art Deco epochs (and a few repros, too). Its conglomeration of decorative items speaks distinctively of vieux Paris.

LOTS OF ANTIQUING

Le Carré Rive Gauche More than 120 antiques dealers and art galleries make up this prestigious square of the Left Bank. Most establishments open Tuesday through Saturday at 10 or 11 A.M., close at 6:30 P.M., and are located on the following streets: quai Voltaire, rue des Saints-Pères, rue de l'Université, rue du Bac, rue de Lille, rue de Beaune, rue de Verneuil, and rue Allent. The Carré becomes particularly animated over four days in mid May, when each of the locales conducts a *portes ouvertes* (open house), allowing curious onlookers to comfortably browse in their shops well into the evening hours.

The closest Métro stop is rue du Bac. To learn more, go to www.carrerivegauche.com.

Le Village Suisse Although the quality of its antiques is excellent, I think Le Village Suisse is probably the least enchanting place to go antiquing in all of Paris. Some 150 antiques and decorator shops fill this outdoor shopping center–like complex. The selection of goods is as vast as the "village" itself, and the prices, although on the high side, correspond with the going rates for this caliber of merchandise.

54 av de la Motte-Piquet and 78 av de Suffren, 15e; Métro: la Motte-Piquet; Open Thursday–Monday 10:30 A.M.–7 P.M. or by appointment; www.levillagesuisseparis.com.

Note: You may locate a specific item (such as an armoire) or merchant on the Web sites for both Le Carré Rive Gauche and Le Village Suisse. This can be most helpful if you're particularly serious about your antiquing.

Jewelry, Shoes, and Accessories

CAREL Carel is a classic. A good many Frenchwomen have at least one pair of Carel shoes in their closets. I once read about a Frenchwoman who had a collection of about six hundred pairs of Carel shoes, and indeed many of them are referred to as collectibles. The great variety of colors and styles of their charming flats, pumps, and sandals invites you to buy them not just to coordinate with something you already have, but to go out and buy a whole new outfit.

12 rue du Four, 6e; tel.: 01.43.54.11.69; Métro: Mabillon;

Open Monday 11 A.M.–7 P.M.; Tuesday–Saturday 10 A.M.–7 P.M.; www.carel.fr.

FABRICE Fabrice has long been a favorite Paris addresses for sophisticated costume jewelry. Big, chunky bracelets, necklaces, and pins—lots of pins—are fashioned out of copper, silver, gold, resin, lizard, and crocodile. The result is *très mode*, but not at all trendy. All the pieces are made in France especially for Fabrice. Prices range from €50 to €340 for Fabrice's famous brooches.

Their boutique at 33 rue Bonaparte is more roomy and features more of their jewelry, some other accessories, and a collection of chic, ample-cut casual fashions for women in a range of luxurious fabrics. These are the types of fashions I'd imagine a Left Bank art gallery director would wear.

54 rue Bonaparte, 6e; tel.: 01.43.26.09.49; 33 rue Bonaparte, 6e;

tel.: 01.43.26.57.95; Métro for both boutiques: Saint-Germain-des-Prés;

Open Monday–Saturday 11 A.M.–7 P.M.; 54 rue Bonaparte closes in August;

www.bijouxfabrice.com.

HERVÉ CHAPELIER Stop in here to buy one of Hervé Chapelier's sturdy, made-in-France (out of high-resistance nylon) bags. There's one for every purpose, for men, women, and stylish kids. The only hesitation you will have might be which color to choose—they're all so smart. More recent Chapelier creations include cotton bags, jewelry, small leather goods, and beach towels.

1 rue du Vieux Colombier, 6e; tel.: 01.44.07.06.50; Métro: Saint-Sulpice;

Open Monday–Saturday 10 A.M.–7 P.M.; www.hervechapelier.com.

ISADORA   Danielle Poulain is the craftswoman of the Art Deco–inspired costume jewelry that illuminates this shop. Each of her creations is hand-carved in brightly colored Galalith, a hard, synthetic plastic characteristic of the Art Déco era that has been sculpted (as opposed to Bakelite, which is molded). The forms are more simple now than they once were, but the artist's use of color is still striking. The shop also sells many old pieces from the twenties through the seventies that are quite retro and fun! Prices range from €50 to €600 for both the Isadora creations and the vintage pieces.

10 rue du Pré-aux-Clercs, 7e; tel.: 01.42.22.89.63; Métro: Saint-Germain-des-Prés; Open Monday 2–7 P.M.; Tuesday–Friday 1–7 P.M.; Saturday 11 A.M.–7 P.M.; closed in August; isadora75@wanadoo.fr.

J. FENESTRIER   Fenestrier has been handcrafting superb men's shoes since 1895. Not surprisingly, it is also the maker of Robert Clergerie's shoes for women. The men's shoes (much like the women's) are streamlined, stylish versions of the classics. Most men who buy here are young (35 to 40 years old) and prefer Fenestriers to Westons, the other highly regarded French brand. The quality of Fenestrier's shoes is similar to that of the status-symbol Westons, but the styling is a little more *mode*. The average price for a pair of shoes at Fenestrier is about €360, a bit less than chez Weston.

23 rue du Cherche-Midi, 6e; tel./fax: 01.42.22.66.02; Métro: Saint-Sulpice; Open Monday–Friday 11 A.M.–7 P.M.; Saturday 10 A.M.–7 P.M.

MARIE MERCIÉ   "My hats are always based on a story," exclaims the red-haired, effervescent Marie Mercié. And so they are. Whether it's a Moroccan fez or a chic little beanie, each creation looks as though it came from a different place and time, which is, of course, why there is one for everybody's tastes and, most of all, why they are so charming. The notion of humor and simple beauty is present in them all. Sunflowers, plastic fruits, and even nests filled with robin's eggs crown a few hats, while others derive their wit and grace from the artist's choice of color and form. Most of the hats are quite couture, with prices that average

€250 to €350 per *châpeau* (considerably more, of course, for one of Marie's custom-made bridal pieces).

23 rue Saint-Sulpice, 6e; tel.: 01.43.26.45.83; fax: 01.40.26.38.01;

Métro: Saint-Sulpice; Open Monday–Saturday 11 A.M.–7 P.M.

MAUD FRIZON   Anyone who has ever tried to look like a fashion plate has most likely invested in a pair of Maud Frizon's stylish, handmade shoes. The selection here is astounding, and indicative of the wide-ranging realms of this French designer's imagination. Whether this season's look is safari or snakeskin (or some combination of the two), you can count on seeing lots of heels and some good basics, too. Shoes and boots sell for between €300 and €400 a pair, and the saleswomen are particularly friendly for a boutique with such a high-fashion image.

83 rue des Saints-Pères, 6e; tel.: 01.42.22.06.93; fax: 01.45.49.20.59;

Métro: Sèvres-Babylone; Open Monday–Saturday 11 A.M.–7 P.M.

OTHELLO   Here for about thirty-five years, there's no doubt about it—this is *the* shop in Paris for luxurious artisanal jewelry that makes a statement. You might just run into Lauren Bacall or Ralph and Ricky Lauren, or the hottest French actress of the moment—anyone with a bit of style shops here! The window display alone promises a colorful show of what is "in" right now: a bit of chinoiserie, pieces on an animal theme, or streamlined creations in resin. The interior of Othello is like a luxurious den. (There's even a comfy couch for impatient husbands or tired girlfriends to relax upon, and the owner, Annie-Paule Malaval, typically offers her clients tea and orange juice.) About twenty-five different craftspeople create jewelry for Othello, so it's hard to define the style, but overall, the look is big and chunky and full of personality. Some pieces look old, some exotic. Many natural materials such as wood, coral, and ebony make up an integral part of the pieces. Prices range from €100 to €1,000.

21 rue des Saints-Pères, 6e; tel.: 01.42.60.26.24; Métro: Saint-Germain-des-Prés;

Open Monday–Saturday 10:30 A.M.–7:30 P.M.

ROBERT CLERGERIE   Robert Clergerie is to shoes what Yves Saint Laurent is to clothing. Each revolutionized his business in his own way. In 1981, Monsieur Clergerie designed lace-up oxfords for women, inspired by Yves Saint Laurent's tuxedo suits for women. Other innovative designs followed, including raffia sandals and a variety of architectural heels, changing the look of women's footwear forever. After having started out working at Charles Jourdan, Monsieur Clergerie climbed to the top of the fashion-shoe ladder on his own with simple yet original designs. The quality is high, as are the prices, but they are still significantly less than in the United States. Clergerie handbags are sold here as well.

5 rue du Cherche-Midi, 6e; tel.: 01.45.48.75.47; Métro: Saint-Sulpice;
Open Monday–Saturday 10 A.M.–7 P.M.; www.robertclergerie.com.

STÉPHANE KÉLIAN   One of the top names in high-fashion shoe styling, Stéphane Kélian's trademark is his finely woven shoes in the form of pumps, sandals, and loafers. The prices, which are much lower than those charged stateside, fit the caliber of the design and the quality. (Average price of a pair of woman's shoes is €220.) Men's and women's shoes are sold at this boutique along with bags and small leather goods.

13 bis rue de Grenelle, 7e; tel.: 01.42.22.93.03; Métro: Saint-Sulpice; 5 rue du
Faubourg-Saint-Honoré, 8e (women's only); tel.: 01.44.51.64.19; Métro:
Concorde; Open Monday–Saturday 10 A.M.–7 P.M.; www.stephane-kelian.fr.

More Jewelry, Shoes, and Accessories

I could easily devote a whole chapter of this book to women's shoes. Here are a couple of other fashion-forward footwear boutiques that might interest you, but know that there are many more you can discover on your own. For more understated, yet equally hip, women's shoes that pride themselves on fashion *and* comfort, go to **Accessoire** (6 rue du Cherche-Midi, 6e; tel.: 01.45.48.36.08; www.accessoire.fr). Here prices range from €100 to €400, depending on the season and the model. Still looking for that perfect shoe? Try **Charles Kammer** (14 rue de Grenelle, 7e; tel.: 01.42.22.35.13), where there's always a quirky new look featured along with more wearable models.

For ultracomfortable shoes with a certain fashion edge, **Arche** (21 rue du Dragon, 6e; tel.: 01.42.22.54.75; www.arche-shoes.fr) offers a colorful assortment of made-in-France footwear for men and women. Prices here—the average price of a pair of women's shoes is €150—run markedly less than in the States.

And just so you don't think the shoe stores totally outnumber the bag boutiques on the Left Bank, I'd like to mention **Lamarthe** (51 rue Bonaparte; tel.: 01.43.25.13.03) and **Mandarina Duck** (51 rue Bonaparte, 6e; tel.: 01.43.26.68.38). The Web site for both these brands is www. bagage-maroquinerie-paris.fr. They're next door to each other, so you can easily hit them both. Didier Lamarthe originally worked for Mandarina Duck before going out on his own, but there's virtually no similarity between the collections in these stores. You can expect more classics from Lamarthe, whereas Mandarina Duck leans toward *moderne* and, as the name connotes, most of their models tend to be resistant to a driving rain.

Saint-Sulpice is the closest Métro for the above boutiques.

Back on the other side of boulevard Saint-Germain, you may shop for casual looking bags at **Upla** (5 rue Saint-Benoit, 6e; tel.: 01.40.15.10.75; Métro: Saint-Germain-des Prés). They're true French classics, although much less in vogue now than they once were. Their campy design is based on traditional French fishing and hunting bags, closely resembling our Dooney & Burke bags. The prices are excellent, given the quality of their real and faux leather. I had two that I used for many, many years!

Womenswear

CACHAREL   Founded in 1962 in the Provençal city of Nîmes, Cacharel is still going strong. Its name has always been widely associated with darling little Liberty of London prints, seersucker, and women's shirts. You'll almost always find elements from those themes in their women's fashions and accessories, along with a hint of Provence and other more far-reaching influences such as Polynesia. (It all depends on their various designers' inspirations.) Don't miss their children's collection here, which is full of whimsy.

64 rue Bonaparte, 6e; tel.: 01.40.46.00.45; Métro: Saint-Germain-des-Prés; Open Monday–Saturday 10:30 A.M.–7 P.M.; www.cacharel.fr.

CHACOK A certain radiance emanates from the bright reds, yellows, blues, and violets here—all characteristic colors of Chacok's striking women's fashions. The force of Chacok's clothing is their comfort, design, and versatility. Each season introduces another ethnic theme that can be mixed and matched with at least three other items in the shop as well as with clothing from previous years' collections.

18 rue de Grenelle, 7e; tel.: 01.42.22.69.99; Métro: Saint-Sulpice; Open Monday–Saturday 10 A.M.–7 P.M.; www.chacok.com.

FORMES This boutique's maternity clothes are so alluring that you will almost wish you were pregnant just to be able to wear them! Fashionably designed, reasonably priced clothing in fine-quality fabrics (100 percent cotton, wool, linen, and silk) explains the success of this brand, with some ninety shops throughout the world.

5 rue du Vieux-Colombier, 6e; tel./fax: 01.45.49.09.80; Métro: Saint-Sulpice; Open Monday–Saturday 10:30 A.M.–7 P.M.; www.formes.com.

IRIÉ You'll love this boutique for its affordable, up-to-the-minute women's clothing that will most likely still be in fashion next year. Irié creates, out of both natural and synthetic fabrics, modern styles that are just trendy enough to be in this year, and classic enough to bear the test of time. Skirts run €150 to €200, and much of the clothing is washable. The men's collection is across the street at no. 9.

8 rue du Pré-aux-Clercs, 7e; tel.: 01.42.61.18.28; Métro: Saint-Germain-des-Prés; Open Monday–Saturday 10:15 A.M.–7 P.M.; closed in August.

ISABEL MARANT One of the latest French womenswear designers to captivate the fashion press, Isabel Marant has created collections that will resonate with women of any age. Beneath her classic forms and noble fabrics, there's always a touch of gypsy—not at all surprising since she draws inspiration from the four corners of the world. Shop here for that sophisticated French *artiste* look.

1 rue Jacob, 6e; tel.: 01.43.26.04.12; Métro: Saint-Germain-des-Prés; 16 rue Charonne, 11e; tel.: 01.49.29.71.55; Métro: Open Monday–Saturday 10:30 A.M.–7:30 P.M.

JEANNETTE   Any woman can wear French clothing, but it's the way she puts it all together that makes her look French. The not-at-all-intimidating Jeannette Alfandari can show you how to pull it off. She has been in the neighborhood for more than thirty-five years and is well known throughout Paris for finding just the right chic for each woman. Her boutique represents a choice selection of young yet timeless fashions from many of Paris's big names, including Givenchy, Lagerfeld, Gaultier, Lacroix, and Rochas. If you allow Jeannette to "dress" you, you are sure to leave here looking like a true Parisian, not *une femme déguisée* (a disguised woman).

3 rue de Gribeauval, 7e; tel.: 01.45.44.02.04; Métro: rue du Bac;
Open Monday–Saturday 9:30 A.M.–6:30 P.M.; boutiquejeanette@wanadoo.fr.

JOSEPH   Fashionistas should remember this boutique as Kashiyama. For a number of years it has been *the* place to go on the Left Bank for some of the most fashion-forward clothing and accessories of Europe. Kashiyama bought womenswear label Joseph, so now this British designer's creations are showcased here along with show-stopping pieces from the French, Belgian, Italian, and Irish contingencies.

147 bd Saint-Germain, 6e; tel.: 01.55.42.77.55; Métro: Saint-Germain-des-Prés;
Open Monday 11 A.M.–7 P.M.; Tuesday–Friday 10:30 A.M.–7 P.M.; Saturday
11 A.M.–7 P.M.

PRINCESSE TAM-TAM   Princesse Tam-Tam sells cute, mischievous lingerie and swimwear that grown-up girls fall for, too. Many of the skimpy bra and panty sets and pajamas are made of 100 percent cotton. All of their themes are fun, spunky, and very pretty.

53 rue Bonaparte, 6e; tel.: 01.43.29.01.90; Métro: Saint-Sulpice; Open Monday
11 A.M.–7 P.M.; Tuesday–Saturday 10:30 A.M.–7 P.M.; www.princesstam-tam.com.

SABBIA ROSA   Sabbia Rosa is Paris's queen of luxurious lingerie. Madame Rosa fashions satin and silk into beautiful little frivolities that live up to everything you've ever expected out of French lingerie. If you can't find what you're looking for in the shop's *prêt-à-porter* collection, then you may special-order a custom-made item in your favorite color (thirty choices and some prints, too) and style (takes about ten days). The prices are high, but the models are so classic and of such fine quality you'll have them forever, unless, of course, you don't remain the same size—ouch! The ready-to-wear, which is priced considerably less (bras average about €150 each), runs about 20 to 30 percent less than those sold at high-end department stores in the United States.

71–73 rue des Saints-Pères, 6e; tel.: 01.45.48.88.37; Métro: Saint-Sulpice; Open Monday–Saturday 10 A.M.–7 P.M.; closed for two weeks mid-August; sabbia@wanadoo.fr.

VICKY TIEL   Since 1968 American designer Vicky Tiel has been enhancing women's beauty. She began by outfitting some of Hollywood's greatest stars, such as Kim Novak and Ursula Andress, before setting up this Left Bank boutique with the help of Elizabeth Taylor.

She has remained immensely popular over the years, understandably so since her dressy suits, cocktail dresses, and ball gowns are devastatingly glamorous. Her silky creations begin at €2,500 and go up to more than €10,000 (for a more elaborate beaded number), and here you can buy off the rack or have one made up for you. Custom-mades take anywhere from three weeks to three months, depending on the material. (This is a particularly good option for plus-sized women.) Ms. Tiel also specializes in bridal gowns and attendants' dresses, as well as fashions for the mother of the bride and the little flower girls. Prices here are indeed investment-level, but still less than if you were to buy her dresses in the United States.

21 rue Bonaparte, 6e; tel.: 01.44.07.15.99; Métro: Saint-Germain-des-Prés; Open Monday–Friday 10 A.M.–12:30 P.M. and 1:30–6 P.M.; Saturday noon– 6 P.M.; www.vickytiel.com.

Menswear

ARNY'S   A very staid clothing store, specializing in classic fashions for men. Their menswear, however, is not as stuffy as the boutique appears, which is probably why a lot of young, upwardly mobile types shop here for traditional clothing with a flair. Their clothes are expensive, but the quality is so fine that you are sure to get your *kilométrage* out of them.

14 rue de Sèvres, 7e; tel.: 01.45.48.76.99; Métro: Sèvres-Babylone;
Open Monday 10 A.M.–1 P.M. and 2–7 P.M.; Tuesday–Saturday 10 A.M.–7 P.M.;
www.arnysparis.com.

MARCEL LASSANCE One of the best stores in Paris for elegant menswear. French cinema people and politicians shop here for very stylish, somewhat classic clothing. There's not a bit of stodginess in this shop, though, and its success lies in the exquisite wools, cashmeres, and linens selected by Monsieur Lassance, a former textile designer. Dresden blue, malachite green, and terra-cotta red contribute to a modern look; quality fabrics and exclusive styles dictate substantial investment. The shirts are more affordable, priced at about €120.

17 rue du Vieux-Colombier, 6e; tel.: 01.45.48.29.28; Métro: Saint-Sulpice;
Open Monday–Saturday 10:15 A.M.–7:15 P.M.

Women's and Men's Fashions

LAGERFELD GALLERY As you're visiting the antiques shops and art galleries in this neighborhood, do stop into this part of Karl Lagerfeld's world. Part clothing store, part art gallery, part bookstore, this is Lagerfeld's showcase for the supremely cut women's and men's fashions bearing his own label. (No Chanel here!) Each one is displayed like a work of art, and rightfully so. Menswear is downstairs; art books to the back.

40 rue de Seine, 6e; tel: 01.55.42.75.51; Métro: Mabillon or Odéon;
Open Tuesday–Saturday 11 A.M.–7 P.M.; closed in August;
www.lagerfeldgallery.com.

MAC DOUGLAS Since 1947—with the launch of its aviator jacket—Mac Douglas has been the *crème de la crème* of Paris leather outfitters. Every other Parisian dreams of having a Mac Douglas coat or jacket in his or her wardrobe, and throughout these past decades stars such as Brigitte Bardot, Steve McQueen, and Elle McPherson have been photographed sporting Mac Douglas fashions. This highly respected company has also worked with designers including Azzedine Alaïa and Jean Paul Gaultier to confection gorgeous body-hugging fashion statements out of the most supple leather and superior-quality suede.

Whether you're in the market for a leather trench, a travel bag, or a pair of leather sport shoes, this shop features creations for both men and women.

9 rue de Sèvres, 6e; tel.: 01.45.48.14.09; Métro: Sèvres-Babylone or Saint-Sulpice; 20 rue Pierre-Lescot, 1er; tel.: 01.42.36.15.48; Métro: Etienne-Marcel; 27 rue de Passy, 16e; tel.: 01.42.88.96.02; Métro: Passy; Open Monday–Saturday 10 A.M.–7 P.M.; www.mac-douglas.com.

SONIA RYKIEL   Welcome to the Sonia Rykiel kingdom. You may have to hopscotch around a bit, but within a small quadrant of the Left Bank, you can take in all of this designer's many fashions, accessories, and perfumes for men, women, and children. Expect to see lots of knits, stripes, and geometrics in bold colors, black, or very often a striking combination of the two. With a distinctly Parisian look of timeless chic, it's no wonder that Rykiel is so incredibly successful throughout the world. Many of the pieces will stay in your closet for years; others, such as a two-color patent leather peep-toe shoe, are more of a lark. If you are looking for that distinctive Rykiel look in a more dressed-down, affordable version of her leading fashions, go directly to Sonia de Sonia Rykiel on the rue des Saints-Pères.

175 bd Saint-Germain, 6e; tel.: 01.49.54.60.60; 194 bd Saint-Germain, 7e (men's); tel.: 01.45.44.83.19; 61 rue des Saints-Pères, 6e (Sonia de Sonia Rykiel); tel.: 01.49.54.61.00; 6 rue de Grenelle, 7e (women's and men's sportswear); tel.: 01.49.54.66.21; 8 rue de Grenelle, 7e (women's shoes); tel.: 01.49.54.61.15; 4 rue de Grenelle, 6e (children's); tel.: 01.49.54.61.10; Métro for all stores: Saint-Sulpice or Saint-Germain-des-Prés; Open Monday–Saturday 10 A.M.–7 P.M.; www.soniarykiel.com.

More Women's and Men's Fashions

Go to **Et Vous** (69 rue de Rennes, 6e; tel.: 01.40.49.01.64) for fun and youngish-looking fashions and accessories that possess just the right amount of sophistication and classicism for them not to be trendy.

If you have a penchant for quality knitwear with that across-the-Channel flair, stop into **Aux Laines Ecossaises** (181 bd Saint-Germain, 6e; tel.: 01.45.48.53.41) or **Hobbs** (179 bd Saint-Germain, 6e; tel.: 01.45.44.20.00; see "Right Bank," p. 97 for more).

Métro for all three boutiques is Saint-Germain-des-Près.

Children's Clothing

BONPOINT   Bonpoint epitomizes the way children from *bonnes familles* (with *beaucoup de* money) should be dressed. Now, the Bonpoint shopping adventure is more fun than ever in their new flagship store just a skip and a jump away from the Luxembourg Gardens, a magnificent playland for young and old. All their timeless styles are of the finest quality and, needless to say, terribly expensive (although still less costly than stateside). For real treasures, take a look at their vintage collection—the little girls' dresses are so precious.

6 rue de Tournon, 6e; Métro: Odéon; Open Monday–Saturday 10 A.M.–7 P.M.; www.bonpoint.com.

JACADI   Renowned for their magic formula of price, quality, and style, Jacadi is one of the favorite addresses of French mothers for outfitting kiddies aged three months to twelve years. The store's clothing, most of which is made in France, is classic enough that it can be handed down through the years, and the selection is always fresh and neatly presented. A smocked dress here costs about €60—considerably less than at Bonpoint. This is one of many Jacadi boutiques in Paris.

256 bd Saint-Germain, 7e; tel.: 01.42.84.30.40; Métro: Solférino; Open Monday–Saturday 10 A.M.–7 P.M.; www.jacadi-paris.com.

PETIT FAUNE   Petit Faune has created an original style of children's clothing (for ages three months to eight years) for nearly forty years, and it's no surprise that this is a favorite Parisian address for beautifully made children's fashions. The shop uses a lot of color and fanciful prints in its collection, crisp cottons that always create a bright look. Another one of their trademarks is their fine wool (or wool and cotton blend for the summer) knit outfits, which come in a variety of genteel colors for baby. Count on spending about €40 for a little cardigan.

Petit Faune's clothing is as practical as it is beautiful, and all their natural fabrics are made to hold up in the washer. You can also buy a kit at their rue de Rennes outlet and sew or knit up your own creation for considerably less.

33 rue Jacob, 6e; tel./fax: 01.42.60.80.72; 89 rue de Rennes, 6e; tel.: 01.42.22.63.69; Métro for both stores: Saint-Germain-des-Prés; Open Monday–Saturday 10 A.M.–7 P.M.; www.petitfaune.com.

TARTINE ET CHOCOLAT   One nice thing about the French is that they dress their children like children even if the parents themselves sometimes look like fashion victims. Tartine et Chocolat's top quality baby and children's clothes (ages one month to ten years) are classically designed without an inch of froufrou; one of their signature items, *les bloomers* (or rompers), sells here in powder pink or baby blue striped, cuddly soft cotton.

There are four Tartine et Chocolat boutiques in Paris, but I recommend you come here in case you also want to hit nearby Jacadi at the same time. Oh, by the way, *tartine et chocolat* refers to French children's favorite after-school treat: buttered bread with a piece of chocolate stuck in the middle—yum!

266 bd Saint-Germain, 7e; tel.: 01.45.56.10.45; Métro: Solférino; Open Monday–Saturday 10 A.M.–7 P.M.; www.tartineetchocolat.fr.

More Children's Clothing

For more classic children's clothing, know that the very aristocratic **La Châtelaine** (180 bd Saint-Germain, 6e; tel.: 01.45.48.73.31; Métro: Solférino; see "The Sixteenth" description p. 267 for more) opened a boutique here for children three to ten years old. It's much smaller, and offers little for babies, but it will save you a trip to the sixteenth arrondissement. As at Bonpoint, La Châtelaine features a small but select collection of vintage clothing.

If you're working with a smaller budget and prefer more casual, fun-loving togs for your kiddies, check out **Du Pareil au Même** (www.dupareilaumeme.com). Go to 14 rue Saint-Placide (tel.: 01.45.44.04.40) for children, 34 rue Saint-Placide for babies (tel.: 01.42.22.57.50). Métro for both is Saint-Placide.

Department Store

LE BON MARCHÉ Le Bon Marché is Paris's Left Bank department store. The store offers pretty much everything you'd expect to find in a department store in an easy and convenient location. Their gourmet food halls, called **La Grande Epicerie,** remain hands-down the biggest attraction here. A cornucopia of inexpensive gift ideas awaits you, so allow yourself a fair amount of time to take in all of the various food stations and aisles. You may even want to plan to have lunch or tea here—check out **Delicabar** upstairs.

24 rue du Sèvres, 7e; tel.: 01.44.39.80.00; Métro: Sèvres-Babylone; Open Monday–Wednesday and Friday 9:30 A.M.–7 P.M.; Thursday 10 A.M.–9 P.M.; Saturday 9:30 A.M.–8 P.M.; La Grande Epicerie, the food store, is open 8:30 A.M.–9:30 P.M.; www.lebonmarche.fr.

Discount Shops

AFTER Shop here for discounted fashions from Barbara Bui, Chloé, Balenciaga, Costume Nationale, and other alluring French labels. Most of the pieces are last year's, end of series, or vintage, but you'll save about 50 percent (or more with *détaxe*) off of the original price.

35 rue de Grenelle, 7e; tel.: 01.45.44.85.14; Métro: rue du Bac; Open Tuesday–Saturday 11–1:30 P.M. and 2:30–7 P.M.

BONPOINT You can shop for Bonpoint's children's clothing at reduced prices (30 to 50 percent off) not far from the Musée d'Orsay. Their styles are so timeless that it doesn't matter if the articles are a year or two old. Girls may be outfitted here from newborn to age sixteen; boys up through age twelve.

4 rue de l'Université, 7e; tel.: 01.40.20.10.55; Métro: rue du Bac; Open Monday–Saturday 10:30 A.M.–6:30 P.M.; closed one week in mid-August; www.bonpoint.com.

More Discount Shops

Try your luck on **rue Saint-Placide** near where it intersects with rue de Sèvres. You'll find a few discount shops there, but you really have to be a seasoned discount shopper to push through racks and racks of often poorly displayed C-level merchandise.

Books and Music

THE ABBEY BOOKSHOP   Located in the heart of the Latin Quarter, this bookshop features an exquisite seventeenth-century façade. Inside, titles—new and used, in French and in English—from Canada, Ireland, England, and the United States are available here. New and out-of-print books may also be researched and ordered for you. A real nexus of Canadian literature and culture.

29 rue de la Parcheminerie, 5e; tel.: 01.46.33.16.24; Métro: Saint-Michel; Open Monday–Saturday 10 A.M.–7 P.M. (and some Sundays 3–6 P.M. at the whim of owner Brian Spence); www.abbeybookshop.net.

LA CHAMBRE CLAIRE   A must for camera buffs, this is Paris's best-known photography bookstore. The world's greatest photographers are all here: Penn, Avedon, Snowdon, and French celebrities Cartier-Bresson, Dominique Issermann, and Bettina Rheims. Enjoy leafing through the many books in French, English, and German, but research your prices before you decide to buy—the American editions, of course, cost more than in the States. The French publications are a far better buy.

14 rue Saint-Sulpice, 6e; tel.: 01.46.34.04.31; Métro: Odéon; Open Monday 2–7 P.M.; Tuesday–Saturday 10 A.M.–7 P.M.; www.chambreclaire.com.

CHANTELIVRE   It's never too soon to start teaching your child a few key words in French. Chantelivre will provide you with the most extensive and creative selection of books, CDs, posters, and games for children of all ages.

13 rue de Sèvres, 6e; tel. 01.45.48.87.90; Métro: Sèvres-Babylone; Open Monday 1–7:30 P.M.; Tuesday–Saturday 10:30 A.M.–7:30 P.M.; chantelivre@wanadoo.fr.

LA HUNE   Paris's most well-known bookstore for literature, history, and art history books. They're open until midnight (except on Sunday), and even though they don't have many books in English, it is fun just to go and have a look around.

170 bd Saint-Germain, 6e; tel.: 01.45.48.35.85; fax: 01.45.44.49.87;

Métro: Saint-Germain-des-Prés; Open Monday–Saturday 10 A.M.–11:45 P.M.;

Sunday 11 A.M.–7:45 P.M.

REMI FLACHARD   As I entered this shop, the owner, Remi Flachard, peered above the book he was reading to see who had entered his sacrosanct domain of printed material on the history of food and wine. I was delighted to discover a man so passionate about collecting and equally enthusiastic about sharing that passion with others. A rather shy, bookish man, Monsieur Flachard unfortunately does not have much of a command of the English language. But his shop is so beautifully organized, you can find your way around yourself. Most of the books are in French, so if that is a deterrent for you, you may want to turn to Monsieur Flachard's rich collection of menus (€100 to €500) from famous French repasts and restaurants. This is also a good place to go to scout out some of today's most collectible books, many of which are filled with fine illustrations and handsome photography on wine and gastronomy.

9 rue du Bac, 7e; tel./fax.: 01.42.86.86.87; Métro: rue du Bac;

Open Monday–Friday 10:30 A.M.–12:30 P.M. and 3–6:30 P.M.; closed in August.

SHAKESPEARE AND COMPANY   Unquestionably the most colorful of all these booksellers, Shakespeare and Company amuses and bemuses with its down-to-earth business of selling books. In 1951, American George Whitman created a quirky bookshop here in this sixteenth-century house, where clients feel free to rummage and aspiring writers freely flop. Mr. Whitman is in his nineties now and retired, but he still lives above the store. Half the books (British and American publications) are new; the other half, used—so much so, in fact, that you can sometimes unearth some great bargains here. You just may find a rare out-of-print book, too. As with most of the other English-language bookstores, there's always a lot going on here in terms of signings and readings, so try to take in one of those programs as well.

37 rue de la Bûcherie, 5e; tel.: 01.43.25.40.93; Métro: Maubert-Mutualité; Open daily year-round noon to midnight; www.shakespeareco.org.

TEA & TATTERED PAGES Just as the perky name of this shop indicates, you may indeed have tea here and shop for secondhand books. The store boasts thousands of titles, and if they don't have what you're looking for, they'll let you know when it comes in (an expatriate's dream). I promise you bargains and brownies galore.

24 rue Mayet, 6e; tel.: 01.40.65.94.35; Métro: Duroc; Open Monday–Saturday 11 A.M.–7 P.M.; Sundays noon–6 P.M.; www.teaandtatteredpages.com. ✗

THE VILLAGE VOICE Opened in 1982 as a bookstore/café/art gallery, it didn't take long for the books to take over completely and, today, the Village Voice may easily be considered the most literary of all the English-language bookstores in Paris. With some eighteen thousand titles filling this small, two-level shop in this celebrated literary crossroads of Europe—Saint-Germain-des-Prés—the Village Voice takes literature seriously. (There are a few guidebooks, too, thank goodness!) They may no longer be serving up *café*, but the Voice has turned out to be a real hot spot for the many readings it organizes on a regular basis. Toni Morrison, Diane Johnson, Richard Ford, and Edmund White are just a handful of the celebrated authors who have read from their books in this intimate setting.

6 rue Princesse, 6e; tel.: 01.46.33.36.47; Métro: Mabillon; Open Monday 2–7:30 P.M.; Tuesday–Saturday 10 A.M.–7 P.M.; Sunday 1–6 P.M.; www.villagevoicebookshop.com.

More Specialty Boutiques

CAFÉ DE FLORE BOUTIQUE Virtually everything in the famous Café de Flore—and more—is on sale here. The boutique itself, complete with the same mosaic floor found in the café, is a mini replica of this historic Paris landmark. China, coffee services, glasses, tea towels, aprons, refrigerator magnets, ashtrays (€13 each), and other items—many of which bear the emerald green Café de Flore logo—make delightful keepsakes of Paris. The boutique ships all over the world, so you can even buy the Café de Flore table and chairs, too.

26 rue Saint-Benoît, 6e; tel.: 01.45.44.33.40; Métro: Saint-Germain-des Prés; Open Tuesday–Saturday 10 A.M.–2 P.M. and 3:15–7 P.M.; closed first three weeks of August, but you can make purchases directly at Café de Flore at that time; www.cafe-de-flore.com.

AU CAÏD   Who is the sort of person you envision when you imagine a pipe smoker? Perhaps a professor, an intellectual, or a writer? These are exactly the types of people who shop in this old-fashioned shop, located in the middle of the intellectual hub of Paris. Just a puff or two away from the Sorbonne, you can outfit yourself with a fine, artfully made pipe from Saint-Claude, a town in the Jura region of France best known for its pipes. Most of these pipes have been handmade from brier, a heath whose roots are perfectly suited to withstand the slow burn of a smoker's pipe. Other types of pipes are also sold here, along with many more accessories for the smoker's pleasure (no tobacco, though!).

24 bd Saint-Michel, 6e; tel.: 01.43.26.04.01; Métro: Saint-Michel; Open Monday–Saturday 10 A.M.–1 P.M. and 2–7 P.M.; www.aucaid.com.

LES COMPTOIRS DE LA TOUR D'ARGENT   Not too far from Notre Dame is this delightful shop that specializes in handsome gifts from Paris's famous restaurant La Tour d'Argent. Instead of snitching the ashtrays from the restaurant's tables, here you may actually buy them (€25) along with their collection of gift ideas, many of which are emblazoned with the establishment's centuries-old emblem: the silver tower. In addition to a range of gift ideas such as dish towels and aprons that bear the symbol of La Tour d'Argent, you may also bring home some of the restaurant's fine comestibles in the form of jams, coffees, spirits, or melt-in-your-mouth *foie gras de canard*—the same served in the restaurant.

2 rue du Cardinal-Lemoine, 5e; tel.: 01.46.33.45.58; Métro: Cardinal-Lemoine or Maubert-Mutualité; Open Tuesday–Saturday 10 A.M.–midnight; Sunday noon–midnight; www.tourdargent.com.

DEYROLLE Before photography and television, people relied largely on illustrations or preserved specimens to study animal and insect life. Founded in 1831, Deyrolle served a very useful purpose by developing its taxidermy business.

The company started out furnishing schools with specimens of everything from ostriches to Japanese beetles. Today, its clientele is largely made up of decorators or individuals looking to add a certain *je ne sais quoi* to their interiors. Deyrolle also rents its vast collection of specimens for films and special events. And it's almost reassuring to know that, in case you can't bear to lose sight of your beloved pet forever, Deyrolle can preserve him or her, too. But it may be easier to purchase a reproduction of one of their pedagogical posters, first produced for the Ministry of National Education by Deyrolle in 1866.

You may shop for more accessible kinds of gift ideas (mostly garden-oriented) on the ground floor in **Le Prince Jardinier** section of the store. It was, in fact, Prince Louis Albert de Broglie who saved this treasured landmark from extinction (pardon the pun!) when he acquired it a handful of years ago and began renovations. Go to "Passages" p. 219 for more on **Le Prince Jardinier.**

46 rue du Bac, 7e; tel.: 01.42.22.30.07; Métro: rue du Bac; Open Monday 10 A.M.–1 P.M. and 2–7 P.M.; Tuesday–Saturday 10 A.M.–7 P.M.; www.deyrolle.fr.

DIPTYQUE It has been almost twenty years since I first discovered this boutique. Thank goodness, it has not lost any of its original charm despite the fact that its delightful candles have become ubiquitous in so many high-end specialty stores in America. (Diptyque also has boutiques in three U.S. cities.) Not only do the candles have an almost endless variety of fragrances—jasmine, almond, cedar, musk, leather, cinnamon, orange, fig, rose, mimosa, cut hay, tobacco, and the ever-popular honeysuckle, to name a few—the scents are so rich that they can perfume a whole room for hours with their bouquet. Most are presented in very simple little glass jars bearing the ever so recognizable Diptyque label with the name of the scent in a jumbled medieval typeface. Each candle costs €36 (€38 for the dramatic-looking ones in red, black, and green).

They run less than in most specialty stores in the United States, and here you benefit from pretty gift-wrapping. The old wooden display cases also contain a prodigious supply of soaps, room sprays, homemade potpourri, and unique toilet waters, including Vinaigre (vinegar), said to revive and refresh the body, soften the skin, brighten and lightly scent the hair, and even freshen the air in your home.

34 bd Saint-Germain, 5e; tel.: 01.43.26.45.27; Métro: Maubert-Mutualité; Open Monday–Saturday 10 A.M.–7 P.M.; www.diptyqueparis.com.

JEAN LAFONT For real eye-popping fashions, check out Jean Lafont, one of the most recognized Paris boutiques for fashionable eyewear. In most instances, Lafont can craft you a pair of eyeglasses in twenty-four hours, so be sure to travel with your prescription! This one is the largest of all the Lafont boutiques in Paris.

17 bd Raspail, 7e; tel.: 01.45.48.24.23; Métro: Sèvres-Babylone; Open Monday 10–1:30 P.M. and 2:30–7 P.M.; Tuesday–Saturday 10 A.M.–7 P.M; www.lafont-paris.com.

LES OLIVADES Kitty-corner from Souleiado, below, is this lesser-known Provençal fabric manufacturer, Les Olivades. Just like Souleiado, the fabrics here embody all of the vibrancy of Provence with their colors and patterns. The typical paisley motifs of Provençal fabrics have their origins in India. During the eighteenth and nineteenth centuries, light cotton fabrics bearing whimsical designs were imported to Marseilles from India. The French to this day refer to these types of fabrics as *indiennes*. The local Provençals adopted them, since they were particularly well suited to the region's generally warm climate. For special occasions or uses, the fabrics would be topstitched or quilted to add extra embellishment, which is why so many traditional products made from Provençal fabrics today are quilted. After a while, the French started to manufacture their own *indiennes*, which accounts for the many different fabric manufacturers throughout Provence. Les Olivades is one of them, and as for how it compares to Souleiado, I'll let you be the judge. Generally speaking, prices are lower here and, like Souleiado, Les Olivades comes out with a new collection every year. Home décor is right around the corner at 1 rue de Tournon.

95 rue de Seine, 6e; tel.: 01.43.54.14.54; Métro: Mabillon;

Open Monday–Thursday 10 A.M.–1 P.M. and 2–7 P.M.; Friday and Saturday

10 A.M.–7 P.M.; closed two to three weeks in August; www.lesolivades.com.

OLIVIER DE SERCEY Chateaubriand shopped for stationery here. That's quite the claim to fame, and today many other illustrious types, prominent families, grand politicians, and other discerning people consult with Olivier de Sercey for just the right engraved card or paper that will best represent their status. The latest trend is to have your own modest château embossed on your stationery. (Of course, you have to have a château before you can have the letterhead.) Monsieur de Sercey took over a business founded in 1870—that's what you call inheriting a bit of tradition!

96 rue du Bac, 7e; tel.: 01.45.48.21.47; Métro: rue du Bac;

Open Monday–Friday 9 A.M.–7 P.M.; closed in August;

olivierdesercey@wanadoo.fr.

SENNELIER After you've absorbed the mesmerizing beauty of the Impressionist paintings at the Musée d'Orsay, head over here, just a paintbrush-twirl away, to the same shop that furnished so many of the Impressionists with their supplies. Gustave Sennelier opened the doors of the Maison Sennelier in 1887, across the river from the Louvre and around the corner from L'Ecole des Beaux-Arts, Paris's famed fine arts school. The store has remained virtually unchanged since then, with the exception of electric lighting replacing the gaslights.

With the scent of linseed oil hanging in the air and the wood-paneled walls evoking the romance of the nineteenth century, you almost expect to encounter Claude Monet carefully selecting his rich palette of colors. Cézanne, Gauguin, Bonnard, Picasso, Dalí, and countless other artists also shopped here, most of whom came to Sennelier for its extensive range of colors, first in oil, then watercolor, then egg tempera. The colors are no longer ground by hand, but Sennelier still circles the globe to find classic pigments such as cobalts, cadmiums, and

Italian earths. Rare and precious pigments such as genuine cinnabar, lapis lazuli, malachite, verdigris, and bismuth white are the jewels of the Sennelier collection, along with natural herb-derived colorants such as indigo. Today, Sennelier offers more than five hundred colors in both oil paints and pastels, the largest range in the world. Their latest product is an oil stick created in 1991 that allows the painters to apply the paints directly by hand. A full line of special papers is also sold here, and the staff is quite adept at dispensing advice in both French and English. Dominique Sennelier, the grandson of the founder, is often here when he's not off lecturing about colors on another continent. The tradition continues.

There is also a Montparnasse Sennelier boutique that was created in 1936 in response to the local avant-garde movement.

3 quai Voltaire, 7e; tel.: 01.42.60.72.15; Métro: Palais-Royal or Saint-Germain-des Prés; Open Monday 2–6:30 P.M.; Tuesday–Saturday 10–12:45 P.M. and 2–6:30 P.M.; closed Mondays in August; 4 bis rue de la Grande Chaumière, 6e; tel.: 01.46.33.72.39; www.magasinsennelier.com.

SOULEIADO The minute you walk in the door, vivid color tones of warm red, marigold, and *bleu gitane* evoke images of Provence, that sunny region where France meets the Mediterranean. Ever-popular Provençal (many Americans call it French Provincial) prints flourish in a variety of timeless motifs and fashions: bags, table linens, fabrics, bathrobes, gypsy skirts, blouses, and an unlimited supply of cotton, wool, and silk scarves and shawls. Prices range from €11 for a cotton pocket square to €180 for a luxurious shawl. Don't miss the men's French "ranchero-look" shirts (€80) that are also great for women. You'll find that they become even better with age as the cotton softens with washing and the colors fade ever so slightly, as if to show that you've been spending just the right amount of time outdoors.

There are many Souleiado boutiques throughout France, particularly in Provence, and now even about a half dozen in the United States (but prices are better here). This is the main Paris showcase for these beautiful fabrics, and everyone here is quite friendly, speaks English, and is capable of helping out with size equivalents. They also sell a handsome collection of Provençal china and faience and rustic-looking glassware from Biot.

78 rue de Seine, 6e; tel.: 01.43.54.62.25; Métro: Mabillon;

Open Monday–Saturday 10 A.M.–7 P.M.; www.souleiado.com.

Even More Specialty Boutiques

People no longer write letters (or tomes!) like the Marquise de Sévigné, but when we do, we tend to be even more careful about the paper we choose to write them on. **Marie-Papier** (26 rue Vavin, 6e; tel.: 01.43.26.46.44; Métro: Vavin; www.mariepapier.fr) has been supplying Parisians with fine quality, brightly colored papers—for all purposes— since the late seventies, so stock up here.

Colorful displays of another sort beckon you to enter **Cir** (78 rue de Seine, 6e; tel.: 01.43.26.46.50; www.cirier.com), back toward the place Saint-Sulpice. This company has been in the candle business since 1643. Today their wax *(cir)* creations are more fanciful than ever, and perfect Paris souvenirs include lots of Frenchie food items, such as the famed *macarons,* and monument miniatures such as the Eiffel Tower or the Arc de Triomphe.

Aside from all these candles, there's more around the corner that fosters a prayerful mood. You'll notice a few liturgical shops along this most pious stretch of Paris streets where you can buy all sorts of crosses, statues, and images, but the biggest seller is most definitely the *santon* (Provençal for little saint). It became prohibited to use the traditional pieces for the nativity during the French Revolution, so the Provençal people created little figurines depicting the actual people of Provence as a sort of substitute. The most authentic are handmade from terra-cotta and are hand-painted; prices add up fast, so you might not be able to outfit the whole manger all at once! Take a look at **G. Thuillier** (10 place Saint-Sulpice, 6e; tel.: 01.43.26.00.57) and **Au Service de la Liturgie** (8 rue Madame, 6e; tel.: 01.45.48.53.03). The Métro for these shops and Cir is Saint-Sulpice.

Markets

You'll discover an abundance of markets on the Left Bank since this is a far more residential district than the Right Bank. One of the oldest and most famous is the **Marché aux Fleurs** (flower market), open daily until 4 P.M. (Métro: Cité), at place Louis l'Epine. This pleasant market turns into an enchanting **Bird Market** on Sundays from 9 A.M. to 7 P.M. You may, of course, buy flowers at the other markets in addition to an abundance of high-quality food items and assorted other nonfood items. If the weather is inclement, duck into the **Covered Market of Saint-Germain** (4/8 rue Lobineau, 6e; Métro: Mabillon; Open Tuesday–Saturday 8:30 A.M.–1 P.M. and 4–7:30 P.M.; Sunday 8:30 A.M.–1 P.M.). Nearby, the **Marché Raspail** spreads along the boulevard of the same name between rue du Cherche-Midi and rue de Rennes (Métro: Rennes; Open Tuesday–Friday 7 A.M.–2:30 P.M.).

The **Marché Maubert** offers an excellent starting-off place for exploring the shops of the Latin Quarter. Go to place Maubert; Métro: Maubert-Mutualité; Open Tuesday and Thursday 7 A.M.–2:30 P.M.; Saturday 7 A.M.–3 P.M.

And there's always the market street at **rue de Buci** (Métro: Mabillon or Odéon), which I'm sure you'll cross at least once during your boutique touring. Most of the shops here are open Tuesday to Saturday mornings and late afternoons.

My Special Suggestions

Beauté and Parfums

L'ARTISAN PARFUMEUR   Most of the women's and men's fragrances sold here are natural, and all are composed with one idea in mind: re-creating scents that are linked to memories. Thus, Mimosa Pour Moi, a fresh and green fragrance made from the stems, leaves, and little yellow flowers of mimosa trees, recalls images of a weekend spent on the French Riviera during the winter when the mimosas are in full bloom. Other themes include essences that were popular at the Palace of Versailles or during the French Revolution—so distinct that you'll feel as though you had been there!

Take a look at the scented candles, house sprays, and *boules d'ambre*—sculpted terra-cotta balls filled with aromatic vegetable ambergris, just one example of the curious kinds of gifts that the shop likes to feature.

24 bd Raspail, 7e; tel.: 01.42.22.23.32; Métro: rue du Bac;

Open Monday–Saturday 10:30 A.M.–7 P.M.; www.artisanparfumeur.com.

EDITIONS DE PARFUMS FRÉDÉRIC MALLE I love the concept of this store. It offers a glorious way of selecting your own special scent. No cardboard testers here; instead you poke your head through a transclucent door to breathe in each fragrance. Monsieur Malle's staff is well versed in helping you choose which perfume would work best for you. (And you do need direction since, even with the special jet emitters in this *laboratoire*-like boutique, your nose goes into sensory overload after the first few sniffs.) It's no wonder he's such a creative genius—this man comes from good stock. His grandfather founded Parfums Christian Dior and his uncle was Louis Malle, the great film director. After having worked a number of years in the ever so dynamic French perfume industry, Frédéric Malle set out on his own and called upon some of the world's greatest noses (nine so far) to create the fifteen *parfums* sold here at Editions de Parfums Frédéric Malle. Count on spending €120 for 100 ml of perfume; creams, oils, and soaps sell here as well.

37 rue de Grenelle, 7e; tel.: 01.42.22.77.22; Métro: Sèvres-Babylone; 21 rue

Mont-Thabor, 1er; tel.: 01.42.22.77.22; Métro: Tuileries; 140 av Victor-Hugo,

16e; tel.: 01.45.05.39.02; Métro: Victor-Hugo; Open Monday 1–7 P.M. and

Tuesday–Saturday 11 A.M.–7 P.M.; closed one week in mid-August;

www.editionsdeparfums.com.

LA MOSQUÉE Looking for a unique cultural experience? I suggest a visit to Paris's largest mosque. Aside from the devotions practiced here, there is a *hamman* (steam bath), a restaurant, a tea salon, and shopping. This more than eighty-five-year-old landmark gleams inside with vibrant mosaics, one of the marvels of Islamic art. The scene in the *hamman* is not for the timid, however: Partially covered women lounge with the sort of nonchalance that only the French can muster. (Bathing suits are now obligatory, thankfully.) The women's and men's days are separate, but if you haven't grown up with a mess of sisters or spent a lot of time in dormitory bathrooms or locker rooms, you might feel somewhat uncomfortable here. Relax, this is a very safe place, and the baths and treatments are wonderful. (For €38 you may indulge in a bath, *un gommage* [exfoliation], a massage, and a mint tea.) Towels and showers are available, so you just have to show up—although reservations are required for the treatments, so call or fax in advance.

You may sip *thé à la menthe* inside the *hamman* or opt to have it outside with a North African pastry on the little tea salon and patio. More copious feasts such as couscous may be relished inside their moderately priced restaurant. Don't miss the mini souk. This is the place to go for worry beads, djellabas, *babouches*, lanterns, and a variety of other colorful gift ideas.

39 rue Geoffroy-Saint-Hilaire, 5e; tel.: 01.43.31.18.14; fax: 01.43.31.18.14; Métro: Censier-Daubenton; Hamman: Open for women Monday, Wednesday, Thursday, and Saturday 10 A.M.–9 P.M.; Friday 2–9 P.M.; for men Tuesday 2–9 P.M.; Sunday 10 A.M.–7 P.M.; Restaurant, tea salon, and souk: Open daily year-round during the day and in the evening. ✖ 🥄 ★

MORE *BEAUTÉ* AND *PARFUMS* This is a most fragrant neighborhood indeed. Over at 84 bis rue de Grenelle, the boutique **Maître Parfumeur et Gantier** (tel./fax: 01.45.44.61.57; Métro: rue du Bac; www.scentier.com) offers many magical fragrances for people and their homes. Created by Jean-François Laporte, this refined setting re-creates the ambiance of a seventeenth-century "perfume cabinet," where ladies wearing perfumes, hair powder, makeup, *and* perfumed gloves would sit and chat while their order was prepared. (There were 250 perfumers and glovemakers in Paris during that era.)

Au Nom de la Rose (4 rue de Tournon, 6e; tel.: 01.46.34.10.64; Métro: Odéon; www.aunomdelarose.fr) boutiques blossomed in Paris a number of years back, just like the roses in the Bois de Boulogne during the month of June. It's a delightful little shop that carries a gorgeous supply of fresh roses and other rose-scented gift ideas such as candles and room fresheners.

Perfect Respites

LES BOUQUINISTES   This stylish restaurant is one of the baby bistrots of the renowned Paris chef Guy Savoy, and also a perennial favorite among American visitors to Paris. The look is contemporary, the cuisine superlative, and the views extraordinary. Call ahead (sure, they speak English) and ask for the corner table that furnishes memorable views overlooking the Seine, the *bouquinistes* (Paris booksellers), and the Palais de la Justice. If you want to be really French, come for lunch and you'll find yourself in the company of distinguished types from the neighboring publishing houses. If you're here on vacation you won't have to feel guilty about delighting in a long, leisurely lunch and frittering away the rest of the afternoon strolling through the nearby galleries and antiques shops. More Americans show in the evening, which is reassuring to some, but makes me feel like more of a tourist.

53 quai des Grands-Augustins, 6e; tel.: 01.43.25.45.94; Métro: Saint-Michel; Moderate to expensive; Open Monday–Friday for lunch; Monday–Saturday for dinner; www.guysavoy.com.

CAFE DE FLORE   Jean-Paul Sartre once said, "One feels more intelligent here." This may be part of the reason that Café de Flore became such an important gathering place for writers and artists during the Occupation and the years following. It's a perfect place to while away some time in front with a café, or a glass of wine, or an outstanding hot chocolate. The surroundings are as attractive as the people. The coffee is served to you with grace. And the eggs, for which they are quite renowned, are farm fresh and served up with large quantities of butter. It can be quite pricey, but Café de Flore is not your average café.

172 bd Saint-Germain, 6e; tel.: 01.45.48.55.26; Métro: Saint-Germain-des-Prés; Moderate to expensive; Open daily 7:30 A.M.–1:30 A.M.; www.cafe-de-flore.com.

CAFÉ DE LA MAIRIE   I first came to this café the very day I arrived in Paris with the intention to stay a few years. Well, I ended up staying eleven years in all, and I can't help thinking that the feelings that welled up inside me during my first visit to this café had something to do with it.

Like the *grands cafés* of the boulevard Saint-Germain, this one is frequented by literary types and people from the nearby publishing houses. There are many more students, however, and a sandwich here costs about what a coffee costs at the more tony cafés. There aren't so many tourists either. The view is great, since all chairs face the sun and the splendid Saint-Sulpice church and fountain. The terrace is here most days, except when it's terribly cold; if that's the case, be prepared for a bit of a smoke-out inside—it's all part of the ambiance. Very inexpensive.

8 place Saint-Sulpice, 6e; tel.: 01.43.26.67.82; Métro: Saint-Sulpice;

Open Monday–Saturday 7–midnight or 1 or 2 A.M. (depending on the crowd);

Sunday 9 A.M.–9 P.M.

LES DEUX MAGOTS   Like its famous neighbor, Le Flore, Les Deux Magots has been firmly planted here since the latter part of the nineteenth century. Jean-Paul Sartre, Simone de Beauvoir, and other existentialists lingered here (Sartre, in fact, lived upstairs with his mother), and Ernest Hemingway came here to write. Today, the crowd is more glossy than intellectual, but this being the Left Bank, there's always a little of everything. The most outstanding feature of Les Deux Magots is its terrace, which seems to grow as the days become longer. The café encompasses the whole corner of the boulevard Saint-Germain and rue Bonaparte, just across from the Saint-Germain-des-Prés church, so it's pretty hard to have a bad view. They also have a boutique on the premises where you may buy china, glassware, and other gift items from this celebrated café.

190 bd Saint-Germain, 6e; tel.: 01.45.48.55.25; Métro: Saint-Germain-des-

Prés; Moderate to expensive; Open daily 7:30 A.M.–1 A.M.;

www.lesdeuxmagots.com.

LES NUITS DES THÉS   Stop in here before or after you explore the neighborhood's antique shops. Located in an old *boulangerie* (bakery), this nostalgic salon has pink marble floors, white lacquered chairs, salads and quiches, and of course, gooey desserts. Their chocolate cake will set you just right, I promise. Owner Jacqueline Cédelle has been welcoming locals and visitors alike here for more than twenty years.

22 rue de Beaune, 7e; tel.: 01.47.03.92.07; Métro: rue du Bac; Moderate;
Open daily noon–7 P.M.; closed Sundays during June and July, all of August;
www.lesnuitsdesthes.com.

LA PALETTE   Truly a must, La Palette ranks as one of the most authentic gathering places in all of Paris. Many of the people who congregate here are regulars, a good number are from the nearby Ecole des Beaux-Arts and even more are art dealers. (If you can eavesdrop in French, you'll certainly hear about what's hot and what's not.) La Palette has, in fact, been the rendezvous of artists since the days of Picasso and Vasarely, who not only gathered here but often paid their bills with paintings as well. Some of those works and a jumble of many more in a variety of media hang on the walls of this rustic café, along with some thickly encrusted artists' palettes. The terrace here is great, too.

43 rue de Seine, 6e; tel.: 01.43.26.68.15; Métro: Odéon; Inexpensive;
Open Monday–Saturday 8 A.M.–2 A.M.; closed for three weeks in August.

LA ROTISSERIE D'EN FACE   Thanks to chef Jacques Cagna, there's one more lovely place to lunch in this boutique-filled part of Saint-Germain-des-Prés. For lunch *or* dinner, La Rotisserie d'en Face is a civilized and handsome restaurant where you are sure to eat very well. The specialties come from the rotisserie, and here I reveled in the most tender and tasty golden breast of chicken that I have ever eaten. Served up with a creamy potato purée and a puddle of *jus,* this is the sort of deceptively simple French cooking that is always so appreciated during trips to France. *Bon appétit!*

2 rue Christine, 6e; tel.: 01.43.26.40.98; Métro: Odéon; Open Monday–Friday
for lunch and dinner; Saturday for dinner only; www.jacquescagna.com.

AU SAUVIGNON   It may seem like an ordinary café, but if you look around, you'll notice that this is one of the liveliest *bistrots à vin* in Paris. During the warm months, this popular wine bar more than doubles its crowd size, making it a fun place for people-watching. Sit down and sip a glass of Puligny-Montrachet and watch the world go by. Delicious smoked ham, rillettes, pâté, and cantal sandwiches, served on Poîlane bread, make for a light, tasty snack at any hour.

80 rue des Saints-Pères, 7e; tel.: 01.45.48.49.02; Métro: Sèvres-Babylone; Inexpensive; Open daily 8 A.M.–10 P.M.; closed in August.

THE TEA CADDY Just across from the oldest and most intimate church in Paris, Saint-Julien-le-Pauvre, sits this darling little English tearoom. This Paris landmark was opened in 1928 by a British woman, and then sold thirty years later to a Frenchwoman, along with all the recipes for crumbles and scones. I particularly like to seek refuge here on a dreary, drizzly day, since the interior is so cozy. Oak beams and paneling, stained glass, demure wooden chairs, and blue and white porcelain cups create a perfect setting for a moment of contemplation over a cuppa and a slice of apple pie.

14 rue Saint-Julien-le-Pauvre, 5e; tel.: 01.43.54.15.56; Métro: Saint-Michel; Inexpensive; Open Wednesday–Monday noon–7 P.M.; closed in August and on Christmas; www.the-tea-caddy.com.

MORE PERFECT RESPITES I can't sign off here without mentioning Hélène Darroze, the young (obviously female!) chef that half of Paris seems to be admiring. If you are looking to line up a special lunch or dinner, you might want to try to reserve a table here at **Restaurant Hélène Darroze** (4 rue d'Assas; tel.: 01.42.22.00.11; Métro: Saint-Placide; www.relaischateaux.com).

And don't forget about the already long-established *grand chef* Christian Constant. He has a boutique just next door to his restaurant, **Le Violin d'Ingres** (133 rue Saint-Dominique, 7e; tel.: 01.45.55.64.67; Métro: Ecole Militaire; www.violindingres.com or www.christianconstant.com). See what he carries in specialized cooking utensils, condiments, spices, and deluxe take-out.

Recommended Hotels

HÔTEL LUTETIA I arrived in my room just in time to see the big, red, fiery sun setting next to the Eiffel Tower and to admire the glistening gold dome of Les Invalides. The view was nothing less than spectacular, a view that may be appreciated from a good number of the rooms in this fine hotel. The Lutetia is the only grand hotel of tradition on the Left Bank. You can almost count them on every other street corner on the Right Bank, but not so on this side of the Seine. The hotel poses a perfect solution for visitors who want to be on the Left Bank but who don't want to be squeezed into a smallish hotel room with their two tons of baggage.

The Lutetia is most *agréable* for a good number of other reasons as well. You may take a break from your shopping and enjoy a delightful lunch in their **Brasserie Lutetia**. Fresh seafood platters (available September through May) are their specialty, so why not share one of those with your traveling companion along with some perfectly chilled Sancerre? Or you may want to end your day with a drink wrapped in the ruby red décor of the **Bar Lutèce,** where you may enjoy piano music every evening once the boutiques close at 7 P.M. Jazz trios play here Wednesday through Saturday (except in August) beginning at 10:15 P.M. The Left Bank is, after all, the heart of the music scene in Paris.

45 bd Raspail, 6e; tel.: 01.49.54.46.46; Métro: Sèvres-Babylone; Four-star hotel and member of the Concorde Hotels group: Expensive to very expensive; www.concorde-hotels.com. ✗

HÔTEL LE MADISON Situated at the core of the lively Saint-Germain-des-Prés district is Le Madison, a charming hotel just a skip across the street from this revered Paris church. Be sure to ask for a room with a view and you'll be able to gaze upon the glorious structure and its abbey for hours. Like most other Left Bank hotels, the rooms are a bit small here, but each is freshly decorated in traditional French fabrics of rich hues. Luxurious bathrooms more than make up for any shortcomings of room size; they can be counted among the French capital's most delightful *salles de bain*!

143 bd Saint-Germain, 6e; tel.: 01.40.51.60.00; Métro: Saint-Germain-des-Prés; Three-star hotel: Moderate; www.hotel-madison.com.

HÔTEL MONTALEMBERT If you didn't make it to Christian Liaigre's design shops, stop in instead for a drink here, one of the Left Bank's most stylish, yet discreet, establishments. Indeed, Paris's top interior designer set the tone of this sleek, seductive hotel, its popular bar, and restaurant; but it's the staff that carries it off with true panache. (I have to admit that before I actually came here I had imagined a rather pretentious place, but that could not be further from the truth.)

The location—beautifully tucked away on the rue de Montalembert, a quiet street just off the boulevard Saint-Germain—also makes the Montalembert particularly alluring. Their comfy terrace and guest rooms are the biggest benefits of this tranquil address. If you do decide to stay here, be sure to specify whether you prefer a classic or contemporary-style room.

3 rue de Montalembert, 7e; tel.: 01.45.49.68.68; Métro: rue du Bac; Four-star hotel and member of Preferred Hotels & Resorts Worldwide: Expensive to very expensive; www.montalembert.com. ✕

HÔTEL D'ORSAY As the name indicates, this hotel is located steps away from the Musée d'Orsay and just a short walk across the Seine to the Tuileries Gardens. After a recent refurbishment, it's more endearing than ever and truly a terrific Left Bank address.

93 rue de Lille, 7e; tel.: 01.47.05.85.54; Métro: Solférino; Three-star hotel and member of Esprit de France hotel organization: Moderate; www.espritdefrance.com.

HÔTEL LE SAINTE-BEUVE Not far from those glorious Luxembourg Gardens, you can lay your head on the pillow of one of the friendliest and most alluring hotels in Paris. Jean-Pierre Egurreguy is both the owner and director of Le Sainte-Beuve and there's no doubt that he and his staff are committed to making guests feel very much at home. Englishman David Hicks decorated the twenty-some rooms, and the result is an inviting display of warm, sunbathed colors punctuated by French antiques. Famous people are said to have resided here, too (I'm not giving any names since the hotel prides itself on its discretion), and visitors looking for a dose of French charm and quiet clearly feel good at Le Sainte-Beuve as well.

9 rue Sainte-Beuve, 6e; tel.: 01.45.48.20.07; Métro: Vavin; Three-star hotel: Moderate; www.hotel-sainte-beuve.fr.

HÔTEL LE SAINT-GRÉGOIRE   It has been twenty years since I first discovered this boutique hotel and I'm happy to report that it is still a little gem. The Saint-Grégoire has everything you would expect from a Left Bank hotel: It is quaint, intimate, ideally located, and the service is quite personable. The rooms are attractively decorated, all carefully accented with antiques and rich draperies. But the real showpiece is the breakfast room, a centuries-old vaulted cellar! Book ahead here since it is much in demand. If by any chance they can't accommodate you, consider staying at their sister property, the **Hôtel le Lavoisier**, on the Right Bank.

43 rue de l'Abbé-Grégoire, 6e; tel.: 01.45.48.23.23 or 01.53.30.06.06 (for the Hôtel le Lavoisier); Métro: Saint-Placide; Four-star hotel and member of Epoque Hotels: Moderate to expensive; www.hotelsaintgregoire.com; www.paris-hotel-lavoisier.com.

HÔTEL LE TOURVILLE   This delightful little hotel is located right in the middle of the "executive quarter," the part of Paris where most of the consulates and ministries have taken residence. If you're looking to remove yourself from the typically noisy tourist hotels and neighborhoods, this is the place to stay. The area is quiet, and the grand avenues (as well as the nearby Champs de Mars) offer ideal spaces for long walks or a quick run. As for the hotel itself, most of the rooms are quite spacious (by Left Bank standards), very luminous, and handsomely decorated in warm hues of golden yellow, sand, and rosy pink.

16 av de Tourville, 7e; tel.: 01.47.05.62.62; Métro: Ecole Militaire; Four-star hotel: Moderate to expensive; www.hoteltourville.com.

Favorite Tours
RUE DU BAC   Whatever you do, make sure you walk the stretch of rue du Bac from the rue du Bac Métro to the rue de Grenelle. This is one of the most enticing areas of Paris because here, fancy fruit and fish sellers are lined up cheek by jowl to fashionable boutiques (two of my all-time favorites reside here), and the clientele is made up largely of very attractive Parisians. Enjoy the smell of roast chickens and the rattle of dishes from the cafés—these are the scents and sounds of the city of Paris.

LEFT BANK FASHION AXIS   I refer to the area made up of rue Saint-Sulpice, rue Bonaparte, place de la Croix Rouge, rue de Grenelle, rue du Dragon, rue des Saints-Pères, and most of the other streets within their vicinity as the Left Bank Fashion Axis. There are also a good number of home décor and specialty shops located within this broad area, but the fashion boutiques definitely dominate the scene. If you're looking for a pair of shoes, for example, go directly to the **place de la Croix Rouge** and pick just about any street that radiates from this centrally located intersection. The rue de Grenelle is especially nice to stroll down since it's not as busy as some of the adjacent streets. Vehicular traffic becomes quite jammed up on the stretch of rue des Saints-Pères from boulevard Saint-Germain to rue de Sèvres, but that shouldn't bother you much if you are on foot. No wonder one of the best wine bars in Paris, **Au Sauvignon,** is so popular here—you're likely to need wine after all this fashion foraging.

SAINT-GERMAIN AND RENNES   The rue de Rennes and the boulevard Saint-Germain are the two main thoroughfares of the Left Bank, and also probably the two most densely concentrated streets from a shopping standpoint on this side of the Seine. One could consider this the "downtown" area of the Left Bank, even though that sort of configuration of streets doesn't truly exist in Paris. I can't say that touring the length of these streets is my favorite thing to do, but it's a good idea to follow them and nip into the more charming side streets from time to time. No matter which direction you pick, don't miss the **Saint-Germain-des-Prés church,** Paris's second oldest and one of the finest examples of Romanesque architecture.

CAFÉ QUARTER AND BUCI-FURSTEMBERG   I'm sure you've gathered by now that the area north of the boulevard Saint-Germain is prime for antiquing and gallery-going. There's also a large concentration of interior decoration showrooms here as well as a good number of other types of boutiques mixed in with all this art. You may start at the two big cafés, **Café de Flore** and **Les Deux Magots** at Métro Saint-Germain and head north on rue Bonaparte toward the Seine. Be sure not to miss the lovely **place de Furstemberg,** a good place to steal away a bit of calm just steps away from all the cacophony. Wander along the rue Jacob, one of my favorite streets in this area. I like the ambiance throughout this whole quadrant; the weave of narrow streets takes me back in time, which is something I can't easily experience elsewhere. Forego **Mariage Frères** in the Marais and plan a pause at their tea salon in this neighborhood. For more antiquing, head west toward the Carré Rive Gauche (see p. 152).

LATIN QUARTER As I mentioned above, I recommend that you begin your Latin Quarter tour at the **Marché Maubert;** once you've taken in this marvelous market, amble off through the oldest streets of Paris. Be sure to pay particular attention to each edifice and always look up to take in the whole building. Don't miss the English-language booksellers: You'll love their spirit and particular sense of tradition. Plan to have lunch or tea at **The Tea Caddy** and be sure to peek into the tiny gem of a church, **Saint-Julien-le-Pauvre.** Walk a bit up the rue Saint-Jacques, the oldest street in Paris, from which pilgrims walked to Santiago de la Compostela in Spain. (The scallop shell was used to symbolize the completion of the pilgrimage and was brought back to France as a souvenir.) Rue Saint-Jacques will take you up to the Sorbonne and near the Panthéon; here you can cut across, stroll through the **Luxembourg Gardens,** then head back out onto boulevard Saint-Michel. Most of the shops here cater to the student crowd, so it's a good place to go for young, trendy fashions at affordable prices. Here you can end your tour at the **Musée de Cluny,** a precious little museum devoted to Roman and medieval history. If you choose to head east from Maubert, you'll be able to take in some of my favorite shops, including Diptyque, Les Comptoirs de la Tour d'Argent, and La Tuile au Loup. They're rather spread out but well worth the walk.

SEINE SIDE The shopping along the *quais* (the riverbanks) can be pretty touristy, but if you walk on the Seine side of the street, you'll find yourself next to some of the world's greatest peddlers, the *bouquinistes*. Here, in makeshift wooden storefronts, you'll meet salesmen as interesting as their eclectic assortment of goods: dusty old nineteenth-century novels by Flaubert; past issues of *Paris-Match* magazine; turn-of-the-twentieth-century postcards of Paris; engravings of Napoléon, France's greatest leader; and much, much more. If you grow tired of looking at old bric-a-brac, just look toward the banks of the Seine for one of the world's most magnificent views!

4

Place des Victoires and Les Halles

ON THE EDGE OF FOOD AND FASHION

Once the Left Bank gained a strong foothold in the Paris shopping world, the place des Victoires and Les Halles began to take over as fashion hubs. This district has experienced many ebbs and flows shopping-wise and right now I'd say it's holding steady. (It's not a super hot spot, but it still has much to offer.)

To me, the glorious nineteenth-century place des Victoires and the surrounding area remain an attractive place to shop without the crowds you often encounter on the Left Bank. The original anchors of the place, Victoire and Kenzo, continue to draw sophisticated shoppers, although for the complete Kenzo experience, I recommend you go to the flagship store, located on the edge of this district.

Rue Etienne-Marcel is the main thoroughfare here, and also perhaps the street that has seen more boutiques open and close in the past twenty years. It saw the New Wave and its whole deconstruction of Western clothes brought on by Japanese designers come and go. (The exception is Yohji Yamamoto, who still serves as a veritable magnet for alternative types dressed all in black.) And now, with the proliferation of jeans stores and trendy boutiques, the shopping scene skips to a different beat. When the luxury baby-clothes store Bonpoint opened here a number of years ago, it confirmed that the rue Etienne-Marcel had mellowed. But, the overall spirit is by no means pedestrian.

Unlike the Place des Victoires, the Les Halles area underwent drastic transformations, and in some ways it seems as though its identity is still adrift today. After harboring Paris's major wholesale food market for hundreds of years, Les Halles became a hole in the ground in the seventies, and later developed into France's largest shopping mall in the early eighties. Now, some two hundred stores, fast food restaurants, and cinemas make up the Forum des Halles, the mammoth underground complex that has been such a source of controversy and change for the entire Les Halles neighborhood. The various kitchen supply stores that are clustered in Les Halles are the remnants of this bustling area that Zola once called "the belly of Paris." The major food markets were displaced outside the capital to Rungis, near Orly airport.

I don't think the Forum des Halles is worth your time at all. In fact, this dull and smelly underground shopping mall has been such a failure that plans are in the works to somehow improve upon it. (Can't wait to see how!) What is probably France's (and maybe even Europe's) biggest subway and commuter train (RER) interchange is located underneath the Forum. This, of course, means the area is packed with suburbanites and is a perpetual hangout for drifters, making it one of the most dangerous stations in Paris and also one of the most confusing. When possible, I have suggested alternative Métro stations.

Having said all this, there are still many lively places to shop and tour within this area. My "Favorite Tours" will point you in the right direction, and as you read on through this chapter, I'm sure you'll find a number of establishments you'll be eager to check out.

Food and Wine Purveyor

STOHRER Here's a bit of history for you: When the Polish princess Marie Leszczynska married King Louis XV, she brought her father's pastry chef, a certain Mr. Stohrer, with her. He remained in Versailles five years, during which time he created the rum baba, a delicious cake soaked in rum and often topped with pastry or whipped cream (or both!). In 1730, he opened a boutique at 51 rue Montorgueil, next to the city marketplace. The business is still thriving today, and thirty-some pastry chefs are said to bake the *babas au rhum* from the original eighteenth-century recipes. Don't miss the interior of the shop, which was sumptuously decorated in 1864 by Paul Baudry, the decorator of the Garnier Opera. The queen of England also stopped here on a recent visit to Paris.

51 rue Montorgueil, 2e; tel.: 01.42.33.38.20; Métro: Etienne-Marcel; Open daily year-round 7:30 A.M.–8:30 P.M.; closed first two weeks of August; www.stohrer.fr.

For more food and wine purveyors, see "Markets" description on p. 203.

Table and Kitchen Arts, Home Décor, and Linens

A. SIMON   I love this kitchen supply store for the strangest reasons: not for its infinite selection of cooking accessories and tableware, but for all the very ordinary items that it sells wholesale to Paris cafés and restaurants. You can find some of the most typically French gift ideas in this store at prices that won't blow your budget. All the dishes, demitasse cups, wine pitchers, condiment sets, crockery, and those oh-so-kitsch signs that read CRUDITÉS, CAMEMBERT ASSIETTE, QUICHE, SAUCISSON, AND OEUFS SUR LE PLAT—the same ones that you find in every neighborhood café in France—are sold here. These intrinsically French everyday items become real novelties back home!

48 Montmartre, 2e; tel.: 01.42.33.71.65; Métro: Etienne-Marcel; Open Monday 1:30–6:30 P.M.; Tuesday–Saturday 9 A.M.-6:30 P.M.; www.simon-a.com.

DECLERCQ PASSEMENTIERS   There's no question that the French believe that fabrics—like outfits—require accessorizing. And there is no better way to do it than with sumptuous *passementeries,* or trimmings. Fringes, braids, tiebacks, tassels, and a variety of other accoutrements are crafted by this venerable house for the embellishment of curtains, furniture, bedspreads, and even theater décors. Declercq Passementiers began in 1852 with a little workshop not far from its current location; today their production takes place outside Paris, but 80 percent of it is still done by hand. A family business for six generations, it is a delight to visit here not only to see (and buy!) their handsome trimmings but also to visit the museum downstairs. Here you'll see a rich collection of old passementeries and one-of-a-kind works.

15 rue Etienne-Marcel, 1er; tel.: 01.44.76.90.70; Métro: Etienne-Marcel;
Open Monday–Friday 9:30 A.M.–6 P.M.; www.declercqpassementiers.fr.

DEHILLERIN   Since 1820, great European chefs have outfitted themselves at this Aladdin's cave of traditional cookware and kitchen utensils. The dimly lit interior of this warehouse of a store hasn't changed much in a good number of years, either. As you stand there looking down the rows of amply stocked shelves and at the hundreds of goods hanging from the ceiling, you can't help but feel the extraordinary authenticity of this shop.

Every inch of Dehillerin is covered with kitchen equipment for both professional and home use. Their pots and pans come in a stupendous variety of sizes and shapes (some so big you could sit inside of them) and materials, including stainless steel, cast iron, and copper (Dehillerin will even repair and re-tin your old ones). Other typically French items include wooden butter molds, madeleine tins, terrine molds, and those marvelous aluminum seafood platters and pedestals found at every brasserie in France.

18 and 20 rue Coquillière, 1er; tel.: 01.42.36.53.13; Métro: Les Halles or
Louvre; Open Monday 9 A.M.–12:30 P.M. and 2–6 P.M.; Tuesday–Saturday
9 A.M.–6 P.M.; www.e-dehillerin.fr.

DUTHILLEUL & MINART   After you've purchased everything you need to become a true French chef at one of the cookware shops in the neighborhood, stop in here for the clothing that will enable you to look the part. Uniforms for everyone from café waiter to maître d'hôtel are sold here to both professionals and the general public. Sporting a soufflélike toque (chef's hat), a pastry-maker's heavy cotton jacket, or a *tour de cou* (the white dishtowel-like scarf that French cooks wear around their necks) will help friends take your culinary talents more seriously at your next dinner party. *Bleus de travail*, the royal blue work clothes that are worn by laborers throughout France, are also sold here, and if you dress them up with a wide belt and some showy jewelry they could be a hot addition to your wardrobe back home. *Pourquoi pas?*

14 rue de Turbigo, 1er; tel./fax.: 01.42.33.44.36; Métro: Etienne-Marcel;
Open Monday–Saturday 10 A.M.–7 P.M.; afternoons only in August.

GALERIE LAGUIOLE I had the pleasure of visiting the town of
Laguiole in the Aveyron *département* (in south-central France) when I
was researching *The Riches of France*. Going there helped me to better
understand the Laguiole (pronounced "lie-YULL") knife, the instrument that has appeared on many of the best tables in recent years.
Laguiole is probably the most rural place I've visited in France, and I've
seen a lot of this country. The wonderfully rich and rugged terrain there
explains why herdsmen developed a special knife in the nineteenth century to help them with their labors. And like many utilitarian objects in
France, this knife seemed to be designed to be beautiful as well. The
sweet curvilinear shape of the handle begs to be caressed; to cut with
such a flawless piece makes all other blades seem like butter knives.

Although the Laguiole knife originated in this remote area, it came to
be manufactured elsewhere in France (and even in places such as Tai-
wan). Laguiole, in fact, has come to refer to the shape, not necessarily
where the knife has been made. The best ones, of course, are made in
Laguiole today, and this is one of the top makers. Prices can be high depending on the choice of model and handle (many of which have been
made from exotic woods, horn, or bone), but never as high as in the
United States.

1 place Sainte-Opportune, 1er; tel.: 01.40.28.09.42; Métro: Châtelet;
Open Tuesday–Saturday 10:30 A.M.–1P.M. and 2–7 P.M.;
www.forge-de-laguiole.com.

QUIMPER FAÏENCE What a contrast! Here, tucked in amid the hub-
bub of Les Halles, is this bright little boutique that showcases faience
from one of France's oldest makers. What a breath of fresh air! What a
taste of French country!

This cheerful faience has been sold by HB Henriot in the town of
Quimper in Brittany (the province that juts out into the Atlantic) since
1690. Each piece is hand-painted and is easily identified by the feathery

brushstrokes in a range of primary colors and by the little folkloric designs of Breton people or flowers. Buying it here is second best to buying it at the source in Quimper. And in case you're wondering, yes, prices are less at this store than in the United States. Here's a great gift item: traditional bowls for cereal, café, tea, or hot chocolate that may be personalized with someone's name; they cost €25 and may be shipped in two weeks—terrific for baby.

84 rue Saint-Martin, 4e; tel./fax: 01.42.71.93.03; Métro: Châtelet;

Open Monday–Saturday 11 A.M.–7 P.M.; closed one week mid-August;

www.quimperfaience.com.

More Table and Kitchen Arts, Home Décor, and Linens

As you meander in and out of these old streets, you will certainly discover more food-related stores than those I've listed. Back up toward the place des Victoires, you can shop for cookware in a more spick-and-span setting at **Kitchen Bazaar** (50 rue Croix-des-Petits-Champs, 1er; tel.: 01.40.15.03.11; Métro: Bourse or Palais-Royal; www.kitchenbazaar.fr). Members of the old guard, however, will probably want to outfit themselves at two other kitchen specialists in Les Halles, both of which have existed longer than most Parisians can remember: **La Bovida** (36 rue Montmartre, 1er; tel.: 01.42.36.09.99; www.bovida.com) and **MORA** (13 rue Montmartre, 1er; tel.: 01.45.08.19.24; www.mora.fr). Métro for both boutiques is Etienne-Marcel.

If you're contemplating doing up your home château style, stop into **Tassinari et Chatel** (10 rue du Mail, 2e; tel.: 01.42.33.17.22), one of the most reputable silk houses of Lyon, which has woven exquisite silk upholstery fabrics for the past two centuries. Prices may seem a bit extravagant to cover all four walls of your living room with one of their silken fabrics. However, if you are only interested in upholstering a favorite armchair or two, you will be pleasantly surprised with how affordable these superb fabrics can be. For more handsome French upholstery fabrics, go to **Lievre** next door at 13 rue du Mail, 2e; tel.: 01.42.16.88.00. The Métro for both is Sentier; the Web site for both is www.lelievre.tm.fr.

Art, Antiques, and Collectibles

LOTS OF ANTIQUING

Le Village Saint-Honoré Only a few of the shops in this small complex are truly worthy of close attention, but if you are touring Les Halles, the village Saint-Honoré is just a short walk away.

91 rue Saint-Honoré, 1er; tel.: 01.42.33.23.74; Métro: Châtelet;

Open Monday–Saturday noon–7 P.M.

Note that for cutting-edge artwork, you may want to cruise the galleries around Beaubourg.

Jewelry, Shoes, and Accessories

ANTHONY PETO   Mr. Peto is to fedoras as Marie Mercié is to picture hats and, in fact, his connection doesn't end there. Being a Briton, it's only normal that Mr. Peto has an innate skill for putting just the right spin on these classic men's hats, most of which are of his own creation (average price €130). The shop also sells the classic Basque beret fashioned out of felted wool with a leather band around the inside (to prevent any scratchiness, *n'est-ce pas?*). Women shop here, too, and not just for their men!

56 rue Tiquetonne, 2e; tel.: 01.40.26.60.68; fax: 01.40.26.38.01;

Métro: Etienne-Marcel; Open Monday–Saturday 11 A.M.–7 P.M.; closed one week mid-August.

FREE LANCE   French shoe manufacturer Free Lance wows fashionistas each season with its superbly styled, high-quality women's footwear. The look is indeed constantly changing according to current trends, but one thing is for sure: You'll always find the most cutting-edge shoe designs, the kind that will make you look instantly cool.

54 rue Montmartre, 1er; 01.40.26.61.00; Métro: Etienne-Marcel; 30 rue du Four, 6e; tel.: 01.45.48.14.78; Métro: Mabillon; Open Monday–Friday 10 A.M.–7 P.M.; Saturday 10 A.M.–7:30 P.M.; www.freelance.fr.

GAS Just one look at the exotic costume jewelry sold here clues you in to this season's trends. Depending on when you hit it, the look might be barbaric, Baroque, or somewhere in between! The good news is that the pieces here never really go out of fashion since Monsieur Gas and his team of designers draw inspiration from Africa, India, the Far East, and Santa Fe. Count on spending about €85 for a pair of earrings, noticeably less than chez Gas in the United States.

Next door features fun and funky accessories and clothing from Gas and a variety of European labels that correspond perfectly with the Gas look of the moment.

44 rue Etienne-Marcel, 2e; tel.: 01.45.08.49.46; fax: 01.42.33.36.17; Métro: Etienne-Marcel; Open Monday–Saturday 10:30 A.M.–7 P.M.; closed one week mid-August.

More Jewelry, Shoes, and Accessories

You'll discover a decent number of shoe boutiques within this district, but if you're looking for truly classy fashion-forward footwear for women, be sure to visit **La Boutique** (46 rue Croix-des-Petits-Champs, 1er; tel.: 01.42.61.49.24; Métro: Palais-Royal), just off the place des Victoires. This was previously Robert Clergerie, but now the shop features Clergerie and a few other high-stepping lines.

Womenswear

BARBARA BUI Part French, part Vietnamese, it seems as though womenswear designer Barbara Bui has found the right balance of yin and yang. Her success has escalated worldwide ever since she opened her first boutique here on rue Etienne-Marcel. Her look is feminine and modern with just the right amount of edge and ethnicity to give it attitude. The quality of the fabrics is fine, and most are shown in muted colors and cut into fluid forms. Prices run 30 percent less here than in the United States with the *détaxe*.

Relax in the **Barbara Bui Café** with a coffee or a sandwich before you continue on your fashion foray.

23 rue Etienne-Marcel, 1er; tel.: 01.40.26.43.65; Métro: Etienne-Marcel;
Open Monday–Saturday 10:30 A.M.–7:30 P.M.; Café stays open a bit later;
This store closes for three weeks in August; 50 av Montaigne, 8e;
tel: 01.42.25.05.25; www.barbarabui.com. ✗

CLAUDIE PIERLOT Femininity without frills is the Claudie Pierlot look. Her clothing is worn by both young and mature women (small sizes) who prefer a neat, subtle approach to a more sophisticated fashion statement. Claudie Pierlot's clothing is somewhat similar to Agnès b.'s; however, its quality and prices tend to be better.

1 rue Montmartre, 1er; tel.: 01.42.21.38.38; Métro: Les Halles; 1 rue du 29
Juillet, 1er; tel.: 01.42.60.01.19; 23 rue du Vieux-Colombier, 6e; tel.:
01.45.48.11.96; Métro: Saint-Sulpice; Open Monday–Friday 10:30 A.M.–7P.M.;
Saturday 10:30 A.M.–7:30 P.M.; www.claudiepierlot.com.

SCOOTER One of the best places to go in Paris to dress or accessorize a teenaged girl, Scooter sizzles with all the current trends raging through the capital. It's a fun shop, too, because the music is upbeat, and the costume jewelry, clothes, shoes, and bags are zestily displayed. Hey, maybe Mom can get in the groove, too.

10 rue de Turbigo, 1er; tel.: 01.45.08.50.54; Métro: Etienne-Marcel;
Open Monday 2–7 P.M.; Tuesday–Saturday 10 A.M.–7 P.M.; closed all of August;
www.scooter.fr.

VENTILO I've always liked Ventilo's chic, ethnic-inspired fashions for women, but one of the best parts of this large store is its tearoom. Even on the greyest of Paris days, light streams in through the tall windows that look out onto the rue du Louvre. Ventilo offers an unbeatable formula all around: good food and fashion in an attractive setting, all at reasonable prices.

27 bis rue du Louvre, 2e; tel.: 01.44.76.83.00; Métro: Etienne-Marcel;
Open Monday–Saturday 10:30 A.M.–7 P.M.; tearoom Monday–Friday 10:30 A.M.–
5 P.M.; www.ventilo.fr. ✗

VICTOIRE If someone (your husband, for example) told you that you could go to only one women's clothing store in all of Paris, this might be a good one to try. Victoire is the Paris showcase for up-to-the minute elegant womenswear from many of Europe's hottest (or soon-to-be-hot) designer labels. They have their own label, but it's best known as a multi-brand store. One of the original retailers of the place, Victoire has thrived in Paris for almost forty years. It is Parisian in every sense of the word, which means that the sales staff is particularly skilled in helping you pull together just the right look. (Take advantage of it!) You'll need them, too, since the merchandise is arranged in a seemingly haphazard way, another real Parisian trait. This is apparently done so that you won't be tempted to put together a too-coordinated look. (I think the biggest identifying characteristic of a well-dressed Frenchwoman is that she can pull to-gether several different pieces from several different designers with great flair.) This might be a little confusing to orderly types, but relax: You can always ask the staff for assistance.

10 and 12 place des Victoires, 2e; tel.: 01.42.61.68.71; Métro: Palais-Royal or Etienne-Marcel; Open Monday 11:30 A.M.–7 P.M.; Tuesday–Saturday 10:30 A.M.–7 P.M.; 4 rue Duphot, 1er; tel.: 01.55.35.95.05; Métro: Madeleine; 1 rue Madame, 6e; tel.: 01.45.44.28.14; Métro: Saint-Sulpice; 16 rue de Passy, 16e; tel.: 01.42.88.20.84; Métro: Passy or Muette; www.victoire-paris.com.

More Womenswear

For fashionable and quite affordable Parisian knits for women, check out **Plück** (18 rue Pierre-Lescot, 1er; tel.: 01.45.08.10.40; Métro: Châtelet), a French knitwear company that has been in business for about thirty years.

There's nothing like a crisp white shirt, though, and you can find many, along with a few cream-colored and even some black ones, at **Anne Fontaine** (50 rue Etienne-Marcel, 1er; tel.: 01.40.41.08.32; www .annefontaine.com). Most are made of cotton, some organdy; all are made in France, and they're great fashion basics.

Still looking for something for your hard-to-please teenaged daugh-ter? **Naf Naf** (63 rue Etienne-Marcel, 1er; tel.: 01.42.36.15.28; Métro: Etienne-Marcel; www.nafnaf.fr), the great success story from the Sentier,

Paris's garment district, is a sure bet. Tweens and twentysomethings shop here, too.

Métro for both of the above boutiques is Etienne-Marcel.

Menswear

VICTOIRE HOMMES   Down the street from place des Victoires at the corner of rue Croix-des-Petits-Champs is the Victoire men's boutique. The concept here is similar to the women's boutique, so you can imagine this shop turns out many smartly dressed men.

10–12 rue du Colonel-Driant, 1er; tel./fax: 01.42.97.44.87; Métro: Palais-Royal;

15 rue du Vieux-Colombier, 6e; tel.: 01.45.44.28.02; Métro: Saint-Sulpice;

Open Monday–Saturday 10:30 A.M.–7 P.M.; www.victoire-paris.com.

THIERRY MUGLER   Sliding glass doors part the dramatic, dimly lighted interior of this ultra *"fa-shun"* boutique. Thierry Mugler's sharp, angular look didn't seem to adapt to this new millennium for women; but for men, it appears to be hitting all the right chords, particularly for metrosexual types with a bit of an edge.

54 rue Etienne-Marcel, 2e; tel.: 01.42.81.57.23; Métro: Etienne-Marcel;

Open Monday–Saturday 10:30 A.M.–7 P.M.; www.thierrymugler.com.

Women's and Men's Fashions

AGNÈS B.   Agnès de Fleurieu is the creative talent behind Agnès b. (The *b* stands for Bourgois, the name of her first husband.) She opened her first small boutique on rue du Jour about three and a half decades ago in a former butcher shop. Now the street looks more like her turf, counting numerous boutiques that feature fashions and accessories for women, men, children, gifts for the home, and an art gallery! She, in fact, has more than a hundred boutiques throughout the world.

The success of Agnès b. is largely due to the timelessness of the fashions—nothing is so trendy that you have to get rid of it with the onslaught of the next season. This form of low-key elegance is, of course, inherently French. The clothes here may best be described as more stylish versions of French preppy BCBG *(bon chic, bon genre)*; simple cuts in soft jerseys and crisp cottons give way to a tasteful way of dressing that is never too flashy or too boring.

If you want to bring home one of her signature fashions, take a look at her little Crayola-colored pearl-snap cardigans made out of a light sweat-shirtlike material, priced at about €380. They now come in three different models.

2 rue du Jour, 1er (children's); tel.: 01.40.39.96.88; 3 rue du Jour, 1er (men's); tel.: 01.42.33.04.13; 6 rue du Jour, 1er (women's); tel.: 01.45.08.56.56; 10 rue du Jour, 1er (bags and luggage); tel.: 01.45.08.49.89; 19 rue du Jour, 1er (gifts); tel.: 01.42.33.27.34; 44 rue Quincampoix, 4e (art gallery); tel.: 01.44.54.55.90; Métro for the above boutiques: Les Halles; Open Monday–Saturday 10 A.M.–7:30 P.M. except for the art gallery, which is closed on Mondays; www.agnesb.fr.

JEAN-CHARLES DE CASTELBAJAC Probably Paris's most witty *créateur,* Jean-Charles de Castelbajac designs fashions and home accessories for people who have a sense of humor and who like to show it. After having roosted on the Right Bank, then the Left Bank, this location here in Les Halles is his latest incarnation. His creations are still very bright and colorful, and a friend of mine actually called them "kids' clothing for adults." Be sure to check out his knits for men and women; he has a contract with Rossignol, so they're made out of high-tech breathable materials. His quirky humor appears in his own form of camouflage, bubbles, and *mode* on his porcelain plates and cups. Do take a look.

10 rue Vauvilliers, 1er; tel.: 01.55.34.10; Métro: Les Halles or Bourse; Open Monday–Saturday 11 A.M.–7 P.M.; www.jccastelbajac.com.

KENZO Kenzo, France's leading designer from the land of the rising sun, has received worldwide recognition for more than thirty years for his vibrant and florid fashions that conjure up images of faraway lands and storybook characters. Enchanting motifs, such as bold flowers and paisleys, and whimsical themes based on folkloric costumes from all corners of the earth, are fashioned into clothing that is both timeless and up-to-date. The men's fashions are less dreamy but equally colorful and well proportioned. And now that Monsieur Kenzo Takeda has come out of retirement, the Kenzo collections are more fabulous than in recent years. Kenzo is part of LVMH so, not surprisingly, the Kenzo kingdom has gained an even stronger foothold in Paris and beyond.

Here at the Pont Neuf address, you'll discover men's fashions on the ground floor; women's on the first; more womenswear, accessories, and children's fashions on the second; and **La Bulle Kenzo** on the fourth. I've yet to experience the fourth floor since the waiting list for a massage is about four to five months. (The special *bulles,* or bubbles, that serve as treatment rooms, are apparently the big attraction.) You may go here, however, to sample and buy Kenzo beauty products and fragrances of this eternally blooming big name.

1 rue Pont Neuf, 1er; tel.: 01.73.04.20.00 and 01.73.04.20.04 (La Bulle reservations taken by phone only); Métro: Pont Neuf; Open Monday–Saturday 10 A.M.–8 P.M.; www.kenzo.com and www.labullekenzo.com. ★

MARITHÉ & FRANÇOIS GIRBAUD Funky music blares, and luminous yellow lighting sets the upbeat mood of the three levels of this loft-like space. Inside, many of the creations are greyish blue, the color of stonewashed denim: the very thing that made Marithé & François Girbaud famous in the seventies, and it's just as strong today. Denim originated in the French town of Nîmes (de Nîmes), and although jeans are considered inherently American, denim has come full circle with the countless innovations of the French label Girbaud. Girbaud invented stonewashing, and is also credited with having started the trends of bell-bottom jeans, baggies, and cargo pockets. The Girbaud design team continues to invent, seeking inspiration from today's street culture and exotic lands. A recent trip here revealed jeans that were scrunched, embroidered, grommeted, and tassled. Leather jackets, flouncy blouses, hip belts, and many more happening fashions round out the Girbaud collection.

38 rue Etienne-Marcel, 2e; tel.: 01.53.40.74.20; Métro: Etienne-Marcel; Open Monday 11:30 A.M.–7 P.M.; Tuesday–Saturday 10 A.M.–7 P.M.; www.girbaud.com.

More Women's and Men's Fashions

Les Halles has long been known for its *fripe,* or secondhand clothing, most especially hip, chic, and cool stuff for the young crowd. Fashion-conscious folks have always flocked here for vintage jeans, shirts, and leather jackets. Kiliwatch has gone uptown, you might say, since this ultra-trendy boutique moved from the center of Les Halles to this more high-styled address on rue Etienne-Marcel. And now **Espace Kiliwatch** (64 rue Tiquetonne, 2; tel.: 01.42.21.17.37; eureka.kiliwatch@wanadoo.fr) looks like the most popular kid on the block; with a bevy of motorcycles parked out front and a high-energy beat inside, the scene here on a typical Saturday afternoon seems like a primer for the night's clubbing crowd. You'll find lots of different vintage from books to groovy duds.

Shop for women's and men's fashions to the beat of techno music in a loftlike décor at **Torn** (44 rue Etienne-Marcel, 2e; tel.: 01.42.33.66.47; www.billtornade.com). Here, too, you're sure to pick up something with just enough edge to turn a few heads.

Paul & Joe boutiques have been popping up around Paris in recent years. And it's no wonder—their fashions are trendy enough to generate a certain buzz season after season, yet they're also timeless enough to hold up in your closet for a number of years. Women rejoice, for the look chez *les femmes* is most definitely feminine. Rather girly-girl, actually, so sophisticated types need not apply. If you do come by here, though, take the silver staircase up to the store's large womenswear department (46 rue Etienne-Marcel, 2e; tel.: 01.40.28.03.34; www.pauland-joe.com).

Yohji Yamamoto is intrinsically linked to his two favorite urban centers—Tokyo and Paris. Many view him as an artist more than as a fashion designer. He was one of the first designers to have established rue Etienne-Marcel as a major axis of avant-garde fashions. For his men's collection, go to 47 rue Etienne-Marcel, 1er; tel.: 01.45.08.82.45; women's fashions are displayed at 25 rue du Louvre; tel.: 01.42.21.42.93.

Métro for the above boutiques is Louvre or Etienne-Marcel.

Children's Clothing, Shoes, and Furnishings

See also Agnès b. description above.

POM D'API   Pom d'Api sells the most inventive shoes for children (ages three months to fourteen years) in all of Paris. Although Pom d'Api carries a classic line, most people come to the shop for its ever-so-fun creations. Prices vary with the creativity, the more outlandish, the more you'll have to pay.

13 rue du Jour, 1er; tel.: 01.42.36.08.87; Métro: Les Halles; 28 rue du Four, 6e; tel.: 01.45.48.39.31; Métro: Mabillon; 140 av Victor-Hugo, 16e; tel.: 01.47.27.22.00; Métro: Victor-Hugo; Open Monday–Saturday 10 A.M.–7 P.M.; www.pomdapi.fr.

Department Stores and Other Biggies

BHV   The BHV is your typical French family-style department store: no frills, no glamour, just a whole lot of utilitarian items to keep you and your home looking shipshape. The highlight of the BHV is its world-famous basement, which looks like a handyman's dream; aside from an astronomical selection of screws, bolts, and nuts in every imaginable size, you will also find Louis XVI–style door handles, wine bottle caddies, Belle Epoque bathroom fixtures, weather vanes from the provinces, and more. You can also enjoy a snack in the **Café BHV**, which not surprisingly resembles a workshop.

52 rue de Rivoli, 4e; tel.: 01.42.74.90.00; Métro: Hôtel-de-Ville; Open Monday–Saturday 9:30 A.M.–7:30 P.M. (until 10 P.M. on Wednesday); www.bhv.fr. ✕

Discount Shop

ET VOUS   You can't beat the savings on the men's and women's fashions and accessories at this popular French label's outlet. Prices have been slashed as much as 70 to 80 percent on articles from last year's collections; and if you come by well enough into the current season, you're likely to unearth some real finds from this year's collection for as much as 50 percent off. See "Left Bank" description p. 162 for more on Et Vous.

17 rue de Turbigo, 2e; tel.: 01.40.13.04.12; Métro: Etienne-Marcel;

Open Monday noon–7 P.M.; Tuesday–Saturday 10:30 A.M.–7 P.M.

Specialty Boutique

LA DROGUERIE   This shop has everything you need to stimulate your creative juices: rows and rows of yarn in glossy silk, nubby cotton, and fluffy angora; jar after jar of candy-colored beads and buttons in every imaginable shape and size; and strands of sparkling gold chains, silken cord, and iridescent threads—all in a marvelous panorama of colors. It's enough to make you want to go home and start knitting, making jewelry, or just sewing on those missing buttons. And there's always *un nouveauté*—the latest one is yarn made out of bamboo, which, so I've heard, is delightful.

9 rue du Jour, 1er; tel.: 01.45.08.93.27; Métro: Les Halles; Open Monday

2–6:45 P.M.; Tuesday–Saturday 10:30 A.M.–6:45 P.M.; www.ladroguerie.com.

Markets

Since this was once the epicenter of all the food distribution of Paris, one would think that this area would be stocked solid with all kinds of markets. That's no longer the case, but there are enough food and wine purveyors to pique your interest.

The **Rue Montorgueil** is here and it is arguably one of the most vibrant market streets in Paris. Truly a remnant of Les Halles, this is where fishmongers, butchers, and a host of other purveyors have hawked their goods for centuries. The celebrated *patisserie/traiteur* Stohrer also resides here along with some nonfood-related boutiques that have been able to encroach upon this near-sacred epicurean terrain. Most of the shops open Tuesday through Saturday from 8 A.M. to 1 P.M. and 4 to 8 P.M.; some on Sundays, too; Métro: Etienne-Marcel.

If you're over by the Place des Victoires/Bourse area, you may go to the **Bourse Market,** which takes place on place de la Bourse Tuesday through Friday 12:30 to 8 P.M.; Métro: Bourse.

My Special Suggestions

Beauté and Parfums

ANNE SÉMONIN   Anne Sémonin opened her first boutique here on place des Victoires more than twenty years ago. Today her skin-care products are sold throughout the world. Here you may shop for some of these made-to-measure, completely natural creams, potions, and lotions in this beautifully streamlined boutique. Best to do so after you've experienced one of the Sémonin signature treatments such as the Jet-Lag, a totally destressing session consisting of a restorative mud mask and foot and back massages (€75 for 40 minutes of decompression). Best to reserve (by telephone) at least one week in advance. Oh, and in case you miss them at the boutique, be sure to ask about the Anne Sémonin oral cosmetics so that you may enjoy a completely holistic approach to beauty and well-being. Anne Sémonin is known to be revolutionary—she was one of the first to introduce aromatherapy into today's products and spa treatments.

2 rue des Petits-Champs; tel.: 01.42.60.94.66; Métro: Bourse;

Open Tuesday–Saturday 10 A.M.–7 P.M.; www.annesemonin.com. ★

Perfect Respites

LA CLOCHE DES HALLES   Situated between the place des Victoires/galerie Vivienne area and Les Halles is this superfriendly, very French wine bar. Only the freshest foods such as country ham, pâté, whole-milk cheeses, green salads, Poîlane bread, and home-baked tarts make their way to the little tables of this convivial spot. Order a glass or two of Chiroubles to accompany this good, hearty fare, and you'll feel total bliss, French style. If you're in town for the Beaujolais nouveau launch, the third Thursday of November, come by here, where the *fête* ranks among the best of Paris.

18 rue Coquillière, 1er; tel.: 01.42.36.93.89; Métro: Les Halles; Inexpensive;

Open Monday–Friday for lunch and dinner; Saturday for lunch only.

LINA'S SANDWICHES   This type of deli/sandwich shop is not inherently French, but Parisians have taken to it like New Yorkers to pastrami on rye. It's a great place to go to fill a hungry shopper's stomach without taking a lengthy lunch in a smoke-filled café!

50 rue Etienne-Marcel, 1er; tel.: 01.42.21.16.14;. Métro: Etienne-Marcel;

Inexpensive; Open Monday–Saturday 9 A.M.–6 P.M.; www.linascafe.fr.

AU PIED DE COCHON   One of the last important vestiges from the golden era of Les Halles, Au Pied de Cochon is one of the city's great institutions. It is so symbolic of Paris, in fact, that this popular restaurant was meticulously re-created in Atlanta and Mexico City. Au Pied de Cochon is indeed one of the best places to go for a bite to eat in the middle of the night (particularly for its famous *soupe à l'oignon gratinée*). This was always the tradition of Les Halles—there were many places where the market people could grab a good meal in the wee hours of the morning, but few remain today. This beautifully restored brasserie remains open year-round twenty-four hours a day, serving as a marvelous meeting place for all kinds of people from the sports and entertainment worlds. Jet-lagged tourists, late-night partyers, and other night owls often have the good fortune of crossing paths with international celebrities. I've been told, in fact, that the ambiance here becomes especially jocular around 4 A.M.

Remember, too, that Au Pied de Cochon sets up a wonderful terrace in the summer. Their specialties include superfresh seafood, grilled meats, and of course, pig's feet! Moderately priced. You also may purchase some of their little pink pigs as souvenirs—just ask your waiter.

6 rue Coquillière, 1er; tel.: 01.40.13.77.00; Métro: Les Halles or Louvre;

Moderate; Open year-round 24 hours a day; www.pieddecochon.com.

WILLI'S WINE BAR   Many Englishmen have made it their mission to become more than adequately informed about wines. Mark Williamson, owner of this fashionable wine bar, has taken that propensity quite seriously. So much so, in fact, that Willi's has become an institution. Plan to stop here if you feel like rubbing elbows with Paris's upwardly mobile types from the neighboring financial district and with glamour girls from the nearby fashion boutiques. The ambiance is as glossy as the clientele, making it a perfect place to stop for a bite to eat, a glass of wine, or even a long, leisurely dinner. Menus are priced at €25 and €19.50 for lunch; €34 for dinner, not including wine. Totally nonsmoking establishment; best to reserve.

And there's shopping here, too, particularly if you're a collector of wine bottle art. For more than twenty-five years, Mark Williamson has commissioned an artist to create an image for the ongoing Willi's Bottle Art Collection. These works are also available in limited-edition posters. Inquire here or on the Web site to learn more.

13 rue des Petits-Champs, 1er; tel.: 01.42.61.05.09; Métro: Bourse or Palais-Royal; Moderate to expensive; Open Monday–Saturday for lunch and dinner and in between for glasses of wine; www.williswinebar.com.

MORE PERFECT RESPITES Although I'm not a big fan of getting caught up in too much of the riffraff on the rue Pierre-Lescot side of Les Halles, there are some cafés and little restaurants that can be a lot of fun. **Au Père Tranquille** at 16 rue Pierre-Lescot (tel.: 01.45.08.00.34) is one of the best places to sit and people-watch. For an extraordinary view in a contemporary setting, breeze on over to **Georges** (tel.: 01.44.78.47.99), the Pompidou Center's top-floor restaurant and café. If you feel like going American, you'll discover the greatest concentration of American bars and restaurants in Les Halles. My all-time favorite is **Joe Allen** at 30 rue Pierre-Lescot (tel.: 01.42.36.70.13; www.joeallenparis.com). *Vive l'Amérique!*

Favorite Tours

VICTOIRES For a more elegant shopping experience, begin your tour at place des Victoires. You can combine this tour with the galerie Vivienne or even the gardens of Palais-Royal, as described on p. 227 in "The Passages" chapter. Bourse and Palais-Royal are your closest Métros. From here you may head down rue Etienne-Marcel, and if you're feeling energetic hit some of the places of interest that are more toward Les Halles. Your best bet might be to take a right onto rue Montmartre (as you're walking away from place des Victoires) and amble down toward the fashion boutiques of rue du Jour. If you're all shopped out and need a bit of cultural stimulation, try popping into the **Saint-Eustache church,** where, if you're lucky enough, you'll hear one of the most sonorous pipe organs in Paris.

LES HALLES   I suggest you begin toward Métro Etienne-Marcel. From here, you may make your way up the rue Etienne-Marcel as you zigzag in and out of the side streets such as rue Montorgueil and rue Tiquetonne. Take a left onto rue Montmartre (if you don't want to go all the way up to the place des Victoires), hit rue du Jour, rue Coquillière and Au Pied de Cochon (for lunch, anytime!), **Saint-Eustache** church, and then circle back toward the very animated area around Les Halles, toward the rue Saint-Denis and rue Pierre-Lescot. The street culture is certainly the most varied and demonstrative that Paris has to offer, and the eclectic shops reflect the latest trends. You can sit for hours in the cafés (I suggest Au Père Tranquille) watching the world go by, or wander about and take in the many different forms of free street entertainment: mimes, rock music, clowns, and fire-eaters. From here you may head off toward the Marais to take in the **Georges Pompidou Center,** Paris's museum of contemporary art. Or, for more shopping for the table, go to Quimper Faience and Galerie Laguiole, both found within close proximity of each other not far from Métros Châtelet and Hôtel-de-Ville.

5

The Passages

PARIS'S NINETEENTH-CENTURY SHOPPING MALLS

It was a romantic era, and Paris's *grands boulevards* were in full swing. Balzac, Zola, and Alexandre Dumas held court in local cafés while crowds packed the nearby theaters and dance halls. Money flowed freely during these pre–Industrial Revolution days, and now that shop merchants had acquired a more respectable stature, commercial expansion was imminent.

The early part of the nineteenth century experienced a building boom and gave birth to a new type of architectural development—the covered passage—throughout most of the big European cities and America. Also known as arcades or galleries, these passages, which usually cut through or alongside buildings, provided shortcuts the length of city blocks. Glass roofs, hand-carved woodwork, and tile floors typify most of the thoroughfares that became precious commercial space for shop owners.

In Paris, the increasingly important *haute bourgeoisie* could stroll through the brightly lit passages—away from the already congested streets of Paris—free from rain, mud, and dust. In these protected passageways, boutique storefronts shimmered with a variety of goods displaying everything from walking sticks to freshly baked bread.

Nearly all of Paris's passages are located on the Right Bank, north of the rue Saint-Honoré. The chic part of town throughout most of the nineteenth century, it proved to be the ideal neighborhood for setting up luxury boutiques. Proximity to a theater, a ballroom, or later a train station was also part of the criteria in choosing the right location for a passage.

The popularity of the *grands boulevards* grew, and Paris's earliest department stores, or *grands magasins,* were established here toward the end of the nineteenth century. The success of these *grands magasins* led to the demise of the passages and eventually the luxury boutiques were forced to move out. Craftspeople and more specialized boutiques, such as stamp collectors, sure of a loyal following, moved into these beautiful spaces. As time went on, the upkeep of the passages proved too burdensome, and many of them fell to near ruin. Fortunately, renewed interest in their future restored some of the passages to their original splendor, and the hollow echo of footsteps on tile floors can once again be heard resounding from within.

Food and Wine Purveyors

LUCIEN LEGRAND FILLES & FILS The main entrance of this reputable establishment is around the corner at 1 rue de la Banque; here you'll discover a beautiful old *épicerie* (food store) that is now best known for its selection of fine wines and spirits. The boutique is filled from cork-covered ceiling to tile floor with an extensive choice of wines and spirits—many from lesser-known producers—as well as many different kinds of pâtés, jams, coffees, teas, candies, and even chilled champagne (a rarity in Paris). The wine accessory collection is near stupendous, too, and I was told that they sell about one hundred different corkscrews alone. The look is decidedly more modern on the galerie Vivienne side. An old stockroom (still used today) serves as the backdrop for the sleek bar and tasting room that garners much attention in this space. Stop here for lunch, tea, or a toast to the town.

1 rue de la Banque, 2e; tel.: 01.42.60.07.12; Métro: Bourse; Open Monday 11 A.M.–7 P.M.; Tuesday–Friday 10 A.M.–7:30 P.M., Saturday 10 A.M.–7 P.M.; wine bar open daily noon to 7 P.M.; www.caves-legrand.com. ✖

A LA MÈRE DE FAMILLE The old-fashioned gold lettering on the bottle-green façade of this store is by no means a *répro*. A la Mère de

Famille has, in fact, existed since 1761—that's before the French Revolution! Today, this boutique is as alluring inside as it is outside, and most people are happy to discover its handsome wood-framed glass showcases brimming with sugary confections, wines and spirits, and other favorite comestibles from all corners of France. The mosaic floor has withstood the passage of many connoisseurs both big and small. Children love this boutique—it's like an old candy store. But to me, one of the most interesting features of A la Mère de Famille is the amusing glass-enclosed booth reserved for the cashier.

35 rue du Faubourg-Montmartre, 9e; tel.: 01.47.70.83.69;

Métro: Richelieu–Drouot; Open Monday–Saturday 9:30 A.M.–8 P.M.;

Sunday 10 A.M.–1 P.M.; www.lameredefamille.com.

Table and Kitchen Arts, Home Décor, and Linens

CASA LOPEZ   Casa Lopez's 100 percent wool needlepoint rugs have been admired in the French decorating world for a good number of years. The rugs, which are priced between €500 and €1,000, boast colorful designs in both figurative and abstract patterns that work well with both modern and classic décors. Their needlepoint kits (average price €80) for making pillows, chair cushions, and small tapestries have also helped to bring this venerable art form back into fashion.

39 galerie Vivienne, 2e; tel.: 01.42.60.46.85; Métro: Bourse;

Open Monday–Saturday 11 A.M.–7 P.M.; www.casa-lopez.com.

JOYCE PONS DE VIER   Also in galerie Vivienne, be sure to admire the little home décor showplace of Madame Pons de Vier, a decorator of excellent taste. Perfectly placed amid all her wallpaper and fabric books are armloads of gift ideas—old and new—such as tiny mother-of-pearl spoons for caviar or sugar, lamps, candlesticks, books, pottery, little footstools and tables—whatever suits Madame's fancy. *Très parisien.*

64 galerie Vivienne, 2e; tel.: 01.42.96.32.18; fax: 01.40.20.00.62;

Métro: Bourse; Open Monday–Friday 11 A.M.–7 P.M; Saturday 11 A.M.–7 p.m.

during November and December or you may call for an appointment;

closed in August.

More Table and Kitchen Arts, Home Décor, and Linens

And while you're in galerie Vivienne, stop into **Emilio Robba** to look around at his stunning faux floral compositions. If it's the weekend, you'll just have to content yourself with peering in the window. Only the major pieces are for sale here, however, so you may also want to take in his Left Bank boutique for smaller gift items. See "Left Bank" description p. 144 for more on Emilio Robba.

Art, Antiques, and Collectibles

CINÉDOC   Just looking in the window tells you that this shop is a must for serious cinema aficionados—I once counted fourteen different books on Marilyn Monroe! Its selection of photos, posters, books, magazines, and postcards has been covering the world of cinema from a to z for more than twenty years. Unlimited unusual gift ideas—why not bring home a poster for your teenager that advertises a Bollywood film?

45 passage Jouffroy, 9e; tel.: 01.48.24.71.36; Métro: Grands Boulevards;
Open Monday–Saturday 10 A.M.–7 P.M.; www.cine-doc.fr.

GALERIE 34   You feel as though you have just stepped back in time once you enter the cozy, red-velvet interior of this small shop entirely devoted to antique canes. If you don't already have a cane collection, this boutique will inspire you to start one. You have probably never seen such a vast variety. There are five-foot-tall wooden theater canes, glass and Baccarat crystal canes, and an array of sculpted knobs in almost every material imaginable: ivory, wood, stone, ceramic, porcelain, silver, and brass.

34 passage Jouffroy, 9e; tel.: 01.47.70.89.65; Métro: Grands Boulevards;
Open Monday–Saturday noon–6:30 P.M.; closed in August; www.canesegas.com.

GALERIE MARTINE MOISAN   How lovely to find an art gallery in the magnificent galerie Vivienne. Stop in to see the current exhibition. Madame Moisan has been here for more than twenty years and features works in a variety of media from mostly French artists. Those interested in learning a thing or two from a real professional should inquire about Martine's Saturday morning drawing classes/Paris tour for children and adults (English spoken).

6 galerie Vivienne, 2e; tel./fax: 01.42.97.46.65; Métro: Bourse;

Open Monday–Friday noon–7 P.M.; Saturday 2–7 P.M.; martine-moisan@wanadoo.fr.

PHOTO VERDEAU   Did you know that photography was invented in France in 1839? Louis Daguerre created the first photographic image, which was called the daguerreotype. No wonder Paris is big on photography! And this boutique reminds us of *leur passion*. Regis Besse, the shop's owner, has assembled an interesting collection of photographs from the nineteenth century through today. A great place to poke around.

14 passage Verdeau, 9e; tel./fax: 01.47.70.51.91; Métro: rue Montmartre;

Open Monday–Friday 10:30 A.M.– 7 P.M.; Saturday noon–7 P.M.;

verdeau@club-internet.fr.

SERGE PLANTUREUX   Monsieur Plantureux caters to a large international clientele of collectors in search of old photos from around the world. Everything from African warriors, to a Visconti filming of Sophia Loren, to photos by Man Ray, may be unearthed among his collection of rare and obscure works. And if it's not here, he'll do his best to find it for you.

4 galerie Vivienne, 2e; tel.: 01.53.29.92.00; fax: 01.47.03.08.85; Métro:

Bourse; Open Tuesday–Saturday 1–6 P.M.; www.galerie-vivienne.com.

LOTS OF ANTIQUING

Quartier Drouot Some sixty antiques dealers and gallery owners are gathered around Paris's major auction house, the Hôtel Drouot. All of this is enough to bring out the hunter-gatherer in even the most timid collectors!

Around rue de la Grange-Batelière, rue Drouot, rue de Provence, and rue Lafayette, 9e; tel.: 01.47.70.41.73; Métro: Richelieu-Drouot or Le Peletier; Most are open Monday–Friday 10 A.M.–6:30 P.M.; some on Saturday; most are closed in August; www.quartierdrouot.com.

SOLD! (OR RATHER, *VENDU!*)

Hôtel Drouot The hardest part about Drouot for a foreigner is pronouncing the name of this highly reputable auction house. It actually is quite easy—just say "drew-OH." If you enjoy antiquing (even just to look!), the pickings inside represent some of the best antiques buys to be had in town. Much of the bidding is done by dealers, but if you're confident enough, you can easily join in on the fun as well. If you just want to admire some beautiful things or take in another colorful aspect of French life, walk in off the street. If you're interested in buying, here are a few tips on how you should proceed:

Buy *La Gazette de l'Hôtel Drouot,* a weekly publication sold at newsstands, or go online at www.gazette-drouot.com to find out about upcoming sales at Drouot and at other auctions in and outside Paris. You may also pick up a catalog on the main floor at Drouot, which will help you keep track of the numerous sales and exhibitions that go on throughout the day.

Go to www.drouot.fr to find out how to buy (or even sell) at Drouot. This information is in English, but if you don't speak French fluently, you're at a great disadvantage during the sales because the bidding goes very fast. If you don't have a French-speaking friend to accompany you to the sale, you may arrange to have one of the auctioneer's assistants bid for you.

Be quick with your calculator in order to know exactly how much money you're talking about in dollars. Remember that you have to pay a 10.754 percent commission to the house, and if it's a large item, you'll also have to pay shipping expenses. Additional storage fees will be charged if the purchase is not shipped out right away. The shipping department at Drouot can make arrangements to have your purchase transported overseas (sometimes via another shipping agent).

All of this may sound confusing to you, but it's not as complicated as you think. One more reassuring factor about buying at Drouot is that the French auctioneers run a tight ship, and it's rare that something will be represented as anything more than it really is. In other words, if they claim that the item up for sale was a part of Marie Antoinette's trousseau, it probably was!

9 rue Drouot, 9e; tel.: 01.48.00.20.20; fax: 01.48.00.20.33;

Métro: Richelieu–Drouot or Le Peletier; Open Monday–Saturday 11 A.M.–6 P.M.;

Exhibitions: 11 A.M.–6 P.M. day before the sale; 11 A.M.–noon day of the sale;

214 | THE PASSAGES

Sales generally begin at 2 P.M., however, certain sales may take place in the mornings, evenings, or even Sundays; closed in August; www.drouot.fr.

See "Right Bank" description p. 86 for information on **Drouot Montaigne,** Drouot's most prominent satellite house.

Jewelry, Shoes, and Accessories

CHRISTIAN LOUBOUTIN   Shoe fetishists take note: If master shoe designer Christian Louboutin can't satisfy your vagaries, then you must be a near-hopeless case. Monsieur Louboutin's creative scope has captured the hearts of high-stepping ladies including the likes of Princess Caroline of Monaco and Sarah Jessica Parker, and countless die-hard shoe *devotées* in between. The collection is ever-changing, since this former landscape designer seems to be constantly dipping into his wellspring of creativity. Expect lots of heels, a fair amount of peep-toes, and even a petal or two. Prices range from €220 to €2,000 with €450 being the average; models shown here are sometimes different from those sold in the United States.

19 rue Jean-Jacques Rousseau, 1er; tel.: 01.42.36.05.31; Métro: Palais-Royal; 38–40 rue de Grenelle, 7e; tel.: 01.42.22.33.07; Open Monday–Saturday 10:30 A.M.–7 P.M.; www.christianlouboutin.fr.

WOLFF & DESCOURTIS   Absolutely one of my favorite boutiques in Paris—and it's not just because of Victoria Wolff, the lovely Botticelli blonde who runs it. I have ruined myself on the purchase of many beautiful scarves and shawls from this store, but I have no regrets, since I've worn them all frequently and know they will be part of my wardrobe forever. Like works of art displayed in a gallery, a different selection of kaleidoscope-colored scarves and shawls hangs in the window each new season. Creaky floors and big wooden tables make you feel as though you have just stumbled upon a nineteenth-century fabric store. And in many respects you have; Wolff & Descourtis was founded by a certain Monsieur Wolff back in 1875.

Today, Victoria spends much of her time poring over old textile documents in order to re-create what will become Paris's next best thing in scarves and shawls. Whether the motif is an artistic interpretation of an elephant (symbol of abundance and *la force tranquille*) or more traditional flowers, the end result is always captured in the finest weaves of silk, wool, cashmere, velvet, or a blend of any two. Victoria works with ateliers in Lyons and Como to achieve these superior quality fabrics, which are later cut into the quintessential French accessory—a scarf or a shawl. Prices begin at €180 for a fine wool-and-silk blend challis shawl and escalate to €800 for a hand-painted jewel-colored velvet creation.

Looking for a totally outrageous and divinely coquette accessory for you or your home? How about a handbag in the form of a Folies Bergères–type *bustier*? Each piece is entirely handmade and a unique work of art (priced at €2,000 and up). You could wear it on your wrist or pose it on your dresser as a jewelry case.

And there's something for men here, too. As a nod to her British mum, Victoria decided to showcase London's celebrated fragrances from the 250-year-old house of Floris. The soaps are so glorious that they will perfume your bathroom for weeks (€22 for three). Other delightful Floris products sold here include highly concentrated bath salts, shower gels, *eaux de parfum,* and *eaux de toilette* (even No. 89, which was created for James Bond in 1955). But I found their *parfums de bouche,* or mouth perfumes, to be the most intriguing; Prince Charles prefers the rose mouthwash.

18 galerie Vivienne, 2e; tel.: 01.42.61.80.84; fax: 01.40.46.95.88; Métro: Bourse; Open Monday–Friday 11 A.M.–7 P.M.; Saturday 2–7 P.M.; www.galerie-vivienne.com.

Womenswear

DIDIER LUDOT   Didier Ludot is a near legend in Palais Royal—if not in all of Paris. His neatly arranged shop presents particular treasures from days gone by: secondhand Hermès bags, Chanel jewelry and suits, Pierre Cardin *minis,* and crocodile luggage, to name a few. Truly collector quality, Monsieur Ludot's finds have captured the attention of some of the most fashionable ladies of the world. If you can't make it here, write, since Monsieur Ludot is quite accustomed to filling even the most eso-teric requests for vintage women's fashions by mail.

And if it's a little black dress you're after, be sure to visit Didier Ludot's more recently opened boutique, which specializes in *la petite robe noire*, on the other side of Palais Royal. Here you will find an abundance of these classic sheaths, many of which have been reproduced from some of the fashion world's most famous little black numbers. Prices range from €500 to €2,000 for these dresses; although still pricey, the vintage frocks may be considered a bargain compared to the price of to-day's big-name fashions.

24 galerie de Montpensier, 1er; tel./fax: 01.42.96.06.56; 125 galerie de Valois, 1er (La Petite Robe Noire); tel./fax: 01.40.15.01.04; Métro: Palais-Royal; Open Monday–Saturday 10:30 A.M.–6:30 P.M.; www.didierludot.com.

More Womenswear

One of the newcomers to Les Jardins du Palais Royal, **Jerome l'Huillier,** presents his high-styled, up-to-the minute women's fashions here in an art gallery–like setting (27 rue de Valois, 1er; tel.: 01.49.26.91.61; Métro: Palais-Royal).

Japanese designer **Yuki Torii** (38–40 galerie Vivienne, 2e; tel.: 01.42.96.64.66) represents the Asian contingent with her beguiling women's fashions. The prices are rather steep, but you just might fall for them. More *exotisme,* mostly in the form of colorful and eclectic acces-sories for you and your home, await you at **Catherine Vernoux** (26 ga-lerie Vivienne, 2e; tel.: 01.42.61.31.60). Métro for both boutiques: Bourse.

Women's and Men's Fashions

JEAN PAUL GAULTIER   Jean Paul Gaultier continues to captivate the fashion world as well as complete neophytes with his level of creativity. His clothes are indeed remarkable. He is a master at deconstruction: His cuts are classic, though the unique way in which they are assembled is not. Although the prices are rather high on his women's ready-to-wear, they still represent good value for such *créations.* You can buy more affordable Gaultier fashion from his Jeans line here. Don't forget that Jean Paul

Gaultier is one of the few designers who produces an Haute Couture collection on a fairly regular basis; he has also been wildly applauded for the ready-to-wear collection he designs for Hermès.

And I'm sure you'll love the Hollywood glam décor of his showcase boutique. French interior designer Philippe Starck transformed this already superb space a few years ago into an oversized boudoir. As with many of the boutiques in Paris these days, you'll discover a sparkling array of mirrors, glass, and crystal (à la Swarovksi) in everything from the display cases to the chairs. Cream-colored quilted walls and an abundance of puffy padding throughout soften the scene—very seductive, indeed. Accessories are sold here as well; men's fashions may be found upstairs.

6 rue Vivienne, 2e, at the entrance to galerie Vivienne; tel.: 01.42.86.05.05; Métro: Bourse; 44 av George V, 8e; tel.: 01.44.43.00.44; Métro; George V; Open Monday–Friday 10:30 A.M.–7 P.M.; Saturday 11 A.M.–7 P.M.; www.galeriegaultier.com.

More Women's and Men's Fashions

Over in the Palais Royal Gardens, the tiny shop **L'Escalier d'Argent** (42 galerie Montpensier, 1er; tel.: 01.40.20.05.33; Métro: Palais-Royal; www.escalierdargent.com) charms you with adornments reminiscent of the king's court. The real draw here lies in the handmade vests for men and women, handsome additions to any jaunty dandy's wardrobe. Owner Madame Danou Jacquard is a direct descendant of the Jacquard family, the very people who invented the Jacquard weaving loom. Madame Jacquard's heritage is not at all lost on these creations, for each of the silk brocade, damask, and ottoman fabrics boasts florid and flamboyant designs, all reproduced from seventeenth- and eighteenth-century textile archives. Average price of each vest is about €300; the men's ties look distinctly French as well.

Discount Shop

LA MARELLE One of the long-standing boutiques of this picturesque passageway, La Marelle ranks among the best of Paris's many second-hand shops. Everything is sold in excellent condition (many items are still covered, in fact, in plastic bags from the dry cleaners). Most of the women's clothing and accessories bear quite recognizable labels from major French brands. If it's Saturday, expect a flurry of activity.

21 and 25 galerie Vivienne, 2e; tel.: 01.42.60.08.19; Métro: Bourse; Open Monday–Friday 10:30 A.M.–6:30 P.M.; Saturday 12:30–6 P.M.; closed one week mid-August.

Bookstores

LIBRAIRIE JOUSSEAUME   Having been here since 1826, when galerie Vivienne first opened, this bookstore has changed hands a few times, of course, but the current shop has been in the same family for the past four generations. Oak woodwork and windowpanes form the walls of this shop, which sells both old and new books and once catered almost entirely to a clientele of *haut luxe*. Consult with François Jousseaume for your favorite French (and some English) literary finds.

45–47 galerie Vivienne, 2e; tel./fax: 01.42.96.06.24; Métro: Bourse; Open Monday–Saturday 11 A.M.–7 P.M.; jousseaume-books@wanadoo.fr; www.galerie-vivienne.com.

LA LIBRAIRIE DU PASSAGE   You practically trip over this bookstore, whose clutter of new and secondhand fine arts books spills out into the passageway. Handle them carefully: Each one contains its own history.

50 passage Jouffroy, 9e; tel.: 01.56.03.94.10; Métro: Grands Boulevards; Open Monday–Saturday noon–7 P.M.

LIBRAIRIE PAUL GRIBAUDO   Do you have a fascination for old maps? This little boutique at the entrance to the galerie Vivienne specializes in old books. But I was most taken by Monsieur Gribaudo's extraordinary collection of maps from the sixteenth through the nineteenth centuries, from all over the world.

6 rue Vivienne, 2e; tel.: 01.42.61.16.40; Métro: Bourse; Open Monday–Saturday 2:30–7 P.M.

More Specialty Boutiques

LE BONHEUR DES DAMES What a crafter's paradise—needlepoint, cross-stitch, and embroidery kits, ribbons, and other assorted trimmings fill this little shop, truly creating *le bonheur des dames*, or "ladies' happiness" (also the title of one of Zola's novels). Good news: The instructions for the kits are translated into English. Prices range from €30 to €150, and once you complete them they're sure to make lovely adornments for your walls.

8 passage Verdeau, 9e; tel.: 01.45.23.06.11; Métro: Grands Boulevards; Open Monday–Saturday 10:30 A.M.–2 P.M. and 2:30–7 P.M.; www.bonheurdesdames.com.

Pain d'Epices

Pain d'Epice means gingerbread, one of French childrens' best-loved snacks, and I'm sure the store Pain d'Epices must be one of their favorites as well. It looks like an old country store jammed with the sort of toys that delight any child and that adults will enjoy giving. All kinds of marionettes hang from the ceiling, and, in a corner, you'll find porcelain-faced dolls whose glass eyes beg you to take them home. But the strong point of this boutique is its miniatures; at least a hundred cubbyholes display mini kitchen accessories, straw baskets, French furniture, and the world's smallest games (chess, backgammon, and poker), to name a few. You'll also find mini, mini foods such as cheese platters, baguettes, bottles of red wine, and a plate full of peel-and-eat shrimp! Upstairs you'll find a pastel-colored collection of soft, huggable dolls, stuffed animals, and numerous other gifts for baby.

29 passage Jouffroy, 9e; tel.: 01.47.70.82.65; Métro: Grands Boulevards; Open Monday 12:30–7 P.M.; Tuesday–Saturday 10 A.M.–7 P.M.; Thursday until 9 P.M.; www.paindepices.fr.

LE PRINCE JARDINIER How appropriate to have such a lovely garden shop amid these beautiful gardens. Stand inside this boutique for a moment and admire the view outside through its tall windows. Here you'll find a most sophisticated version of Smith & Hawken. This is a one-of-a-kind shop, and just the place for poking around and snatching up a few typically French garden-themed gifts. Be sure to take the old wrought iron staircase upstairs to explore the library and cabinet of curiosities. For a bit on the gardener prince behind this house, see p. 170.

37 rue de Valois, 1er; tel.: 01.42.60.37.13; Métro: Palais-Royal;

Open Monday–Saturday 11 A.M.–7 P.M.; www.princejardinier.fr.

SI TU VEUX   This quaint little shop is brimming with a ton of inexpensive toys and games for children aged newborn to twelve. It appears that the French are doing up birthdays in a big way, just like their friends across the Atlantic. You'll create quite a stir if you tell the other kids' moms that you bought your party supplies in Paris!

68 galerie Vivienne, 2e; tel.: 01.42.60.59.97; Métro: Bourse;

Open Monday–Saturday 10:30 A.M.–7 P.M.; closed in August; www

.galerie-vivienne.com.

TRACTION OPTICIEN   After having taken one look at this boutique and the eyeglasses and sunglasses it sells, I thought it was a new arrival on the Paris fashion scene. Not really. Traction, in fact, has been making glasses since 1872. That gives them the advantage of having an archive of old models, many of which have been reproduced here as vintage pieces (and are so "in" today). Let yourself be dazzled as well by their large collection of colorful eyeglass cases and pouches, and by their *portes-lunettes*, or eyeglass chains, which make fabulous eye-catching accessories.

56 galerie Vivienne, 2e; tel.: 01.44.50.58.88; Métro: Bourse; Open Monday,

Tuesday, Thursday, and Friday 11 A.M.–6:30 P.M.; Wednesday 11 A.M.–6 P.M.;

Saturday 11 A.M.–7 P.M.; www.traction-prodlunettes.com.

Even More Specialty Boutiques

Serious (or even not-so-serious) artists may want to visit Passage Choiseul (42 rue des Petits-Champs and 25 rue Saint-Augustin, 2e; Métro: 4-Septembre) near galerie Vivienne, that houses **Lavrut** (tel.: 01.42.96.95.54; www.lavrut.com), one of Paris's most reputable suppliers of graphic, technical, and fine-arts materials since 1922. Thousands of brightly colored pencils, hundreds of paintbrushes in every imaginable shape and size, French and Dutch oil paints, and even a box with 525 different kinds of pastels answer every whim of amateur and professional artists.

Collectors will be thrilled by the handful of shops devoted to old and new civilian and military medals and lead soldiers in the Palais Royal Gardens. **A Marie-Stuart** (3–5 galerie de Montpensier, 1er; tel.: 01.42.96.28.25; fax: 01.43.80.37.40), named after a queen widowed three times, was founded more than two hundred years ago by a jeweler who specialized in the black gemstones that ladies in mourning wore. Today you can revel in all the pageantry of the French military and other civil institutions through the shop's brilliant collection of beribboned medals. Nearby (and next door to the renowned Comédie Française), **Les Drapeaux de la France** (place Colette, 1er; tel.: 01.40.20.00.11; drapeaux@freesurf.fr) has been saluting *la France* and other foreign lands since the fifties with vast armies of lead soldiers. Métro for both boutiques is Palais-Royal.

Back up at 47 passage des Panoramas, I encourage you to look in at **Stern** (tel.: 01.45.08.86.45; fax: 01.42.36.94.48), engravers since 1840, and also the oldest boutique here. Sober, dark wood paneling bespeaks a staid and traditional firm, which is *comme il faut* when your client base reads more like the guest list for an emperor's coronation. All the engraving is carried out by hand, a skill that Stern's artisans deftly apply to invitations to embassy receptions, calling cards, and letterheads.

Across the street at passage Jouffroy, you can shop for a houseful of country French gift items at **Comptoir de Famille** (35 passage Jouffroy, 9e; tel.: 01.47.70.51.12; www.comptoir-de-famille.com. See Left Bank description p. 149 for more.

If you haven't found just the right miniature for your special dollhouse at Pain d'Epice, you may also pop into **La Boîte à Joujoux** (41 passage Jouffroy, 9e; tel.: 01.48.24.58.37; www.joujoux.com) to see what they have to offer. Lovers of French cartoon characters will rejoice in this shop's collection of *bandes dessinées* collectibles such as Tin Tin and Astérix.

The Métro for the above three boutiques is Grands Boulevards.

FAIRY FINGERS

During the golden days of *les grands boulevards,* two ateliers devoted to the art of *la broderie,* or embroidery, established themselves here. If you've ever admired the sumptuously embroidered couture creations featured in fashion spreads, you have most likely been gazing at the exquisite work of **Lesage,** a house that has specialized in high-styled embroidery for more than 135 years. I once had the good fortune of visiting the Lesage workshops here, where I witnessed nimble fingers hard at work over creations that would later be swishing down the runways of famous couturiers. I would have called the setting Dickensian if it were not for the fact that virtually every nook and cranny of this little labyrinth of modest rooms was jammed with pearls, beads, sequins, silky threads, ribbons, lace, feathers—all the materials necessary to the adornment trade. The atelier is not open to the public, but you can take a tour if you sign up for one of their courses at the **Ecole Lesage: Atelier de Broderie.** A great variety of programs is offered for both short (a few hours) and extended sessions. Lessons are in French, English, and Japanese.

13 rue de la Grange-Batelière, 9e (end of the courtyard, stairway B, fourth floor); tel.: 01.44.79.00.88; answering machine/fax: 01.44.79.01.94; Métro: Richelieu-Drouot; www.lesage-paris.com.

In 1860 the Malbranche family founded the hand embroidery workshop of **Maison Malbranche.** Madame van de Velde, a descendant, carries on the legacy today. Here, luxurious table and bed linens are meticulously embellished with both traditional and modern designs using a variety of specialized techniques. You can learn some (or all!) of those stitches by signing up for lessons. As chez Lesage, class length has a lot of flexibility; here, for example, you may devote as few as two or as many as sixteen hours (or more) to this unique art form. The classes, however, are only in French, but as Madame van de Velde said, "that's not a problem since we learn better by showing and doing than by talking."

17 rue Drouot, 9e; tel./fax: 01.47.70.03.77.

Métro for both is Richelieu-Drouot.

***Note: Both of these schools are open* by appointment only.**

Market

See "Place des Victoires and Les Halles" description p. 203 for the Bourse Market.

My Special Suggestions

Beauté and Parfums

DETAILLE If you visit passages Jouffroy and Verdeau, and meander up rue du Faubourg-Montmartre (stopping off at A la Mère de Famille along the way), you'll come upon this quaint *parfumeur.* With its old wooden drawers, desk, and mirrors showcasing old-fashioned bottles of potions, lotions, and fragrances, the shop looks as though it has seen many years of service; indeed, the shop appears locked in time. Detaille has been patronized by many of Europe's elite since 1905 for a special protective skin cream called le Baume Automobile de la Comtesse. In 1900, after having discovered that joyriding in her dashing convertible resulted in terribly dry skin, the Comtesse de Presle consulted with a chemist friend to create a remedy for her condition. A healing balm concocted from egg whites and plants was born, the same that sells today at Detaille. Other natural-based products are also sold here, including silky lotions for the hands and feet, and the ubiquitous scented candles.

10 rue Saint-Lazare, 9e; tel.: 01.48.78.68.50; Métro: Notre-Dame-de-la-Lorette; Open Monday 3–7 P.M.; Tuesday–Friday 10 A.M.–7 P.M.; Saturday 11 A.M.–4 P.M.; closed part of August; www.detaille.com.

LES SALONS DU PALAIS ROYAL Step into this rich, velvety boutique to penetrate the exclusive world of Serge Lutens perfumes. Monsieur Lutens worked for a number of years as the artistic director of Christian Dior Cosmetics before teaming up with Shiseido. For Shiseido, he has created twenty perfumes (€100 for 75 ml), sold exclusively here and on their Web site. From the looks of this astrologically inspired plum and mauve jewel box—and from a whiff of his fragrances—Monsieur Lutens knows a thing or two about what women like.

...lois, 1er; tel.: 01.49.27.09.09; Métro: Palais-Royal;
...nday–Saturday 10 A.M.–7 P.M.; www.salons-shiseido.com.

Perfect Respites

LE GRAND COLBERT   A rich décor resplendent with palm trees and polished brass, mahogany, globe lamps, and wall panels with Neoclassic motifs of olive branches and garlands defines this lively brasserie, Le Grand Colbert. At lunchtime, the restaurant is a popular place for nearby financial whizzes to meet and strike up deals; late in the evening it fills up with the local theater crowd. Jack Nicholson, Diane Keaton, and Keanu Reeves dined here in the movie *Something's Gotta Give*, and many Americans have been coming here ever since. It's a great place to celebrate a birthday, because—in typical brasserie style—the waiters will make quite a fuss when it comes to delivering your special dessert. Specialities include sole meunière, grilled meats, crème caramel, and more, all at reasonable prices. You may also stop in either for a *café* or an afternoon cup of tea (from 3 to 6 P.M.) to mull over your purchases and admire the sumptuous décor. There are two entrances to this establishment: one in the galerie Colbert, the other on rue Vivienne.

2–4 rue Vivienne, 2e; tel.: 01.42.86.87.88; fax: 01.42.86.82.65;
Métro: Bourse; Open daily year-round noon–1 A.M.

LE GRAND VÉFOUR   There has been a restaurant here since before the French Revolution. French illuminaries—Bonaparte, Victor Hugo, Colette—have dined here. You may as well dine in the same polished, eighteenth-century décor that they admired. Today, Le Grand Véfour still boasts a distinguished and tony clientele, a fascinating mix of French and foreigners who come for the outstanding cuisine of Guy Martin. No wonder Michelin gave him three stars.

17 rue de Beaujolais, 1er; tel.: 01.42.96.56.27; Métro: Palais-Royal or Bourse;
Very expensive; Open Monday–Friday 12:30–1:30 P.M. and Monday–Thursday
8–9:30 P.M.; Closed the week between Christmas and New Year's, Easter week,
and all of August; www.relaischateaux.com/vefour.

A PRIORI THÉ   The galerie Vivienne wouldn't be nearly as lovely today without this delightful tea salon. A Priori Thé has been a fashionable gathering spot since it opened some twenty years ago. The light, airy feeling of the galerie is enhanced by the flow of tables and chairs that pour out into the passageway. Relax and enjoy a nice hot pot of Darjeeling with one of the famous brownies. (The owner is American!) They serve breakfast, lunch, and, of course, it's teatime all day long; but depending on the day and hour, you might just be in for a wait.

35 galerie Vivienne, 2e; tel.: 01.42.97.48.75; Métro: Bourse;
Open Monday–Friday 9 A.M.–6 P.M.; Saturday 9 A.M.–6:30 p.m.; Sunday noon–
6:30 P.M.; www.galerie-vivienne.com.

Recommended Hotel

HÔTEL CONCORDE SAINT-LAZARE   Just a few steps away from the Gare Saint-Lazare, the train station Monet so eloquently depicted on eleven different canvases, and on the fringes of *The Passages* district, you will discover this grand hotel, welcoming travel-weary voyagers for well over a century. A historic monument, the hotel's entrance and massive lobby woo you with large columns of cream and pink marble, heavenly paintings and sculptures of angels, and Baroque chandeliers in bronze and crystal. It is a setting unequaled in this part of Paris. (Gustave Eiffel designed this extraordinary space, in fact.) I insist you stop in here for a look around or, even better, for a refreshment in the **Golden Black Bar** or lunch at the **Café Terminus.**

If you decide to make the Hôtel Concorde Saint-Lazare your base while in Paris, know that their rooms are decorated in a classic yet colorful style, and that the location is actually quite convenient to many places of interest. And in terms of service and hospitality, this hotel is truly interested in meeting the needs of its clients.

108 rue Saint-Lazare, 8e; tel.: 01.40.08.44.44; Métro: Saint-Lazare; Four-star
luxury hotel and member of the Concorde Hotels Group: Expensive to very
expensive; www.concordestlazare-paris.com. ✗

Favorite Tours

THE BIG TOUR   I conducted walking tours for a while in Paris, and the Passages tour was always the most popular. The one I'm going to outline here takes half a day, walking at a leisurely pace and browsing here and there along the way. If you think you'd like to spend more time in the boutiques, or stop for lunch and tea, allow yourself the full day. I highly recommend this tour for anyone who is particularly interested in architecture and history. (You can easily do just a part of this tour as well.)

Start at **passage Jouffroy** (12 bd Montmartre, 9e; Métro: rue Montmartre or Richelieu-Drouot), one of the most colorful passages on the walk, featuring an eclectic mix of shops. Probably the busiest of the passages, the passage Jouffroy attracts many different types of people coming from the nearby *grands boulevards* and the neighboring **Musée Grévin** (Paris's wax museum, tel.: 01.47.70.85.05). Once you have come to the end of passage Jouffroy, cross the street, and you will arrive at the entrance to **passage Verdeau** (6 rue de la Grange-Batelière, 9e; Métro: Grands Boulevards or Richelieu-Drouot). This passage is not as lively as the passage Jouffroy, but I still find it interesting.

From here you can continue to head north to investigate some of the antiques shops around Drouot (or even go to an auction) and also venture off to A la Mère de Famille, Detaille, the Hôtel Concorde Saint-Lazare (for an elegant lunch, perhaps), and even the department stores as described on pp. 15 to 17 of "The Essentials" and pp. 100–102 of "The Right Bank." Or, you may turn around, trace your steps back out through passages Verdeau and Jouffroy, and carefully cross the boulevard Montmartre to arrive at **passages des Panoramas** (11 bd Montmartre, 2e; Métro: Grands Boulevards or Richelieu-Drouot). This is Paris's oldest passageway, dating back to 1800. Probably the most interesting passage from a historical point of view, the shopping is more lackluster than it once was when Jean-Marie Farina (now Roget-Gallet) peddled his special blend of eau de cologne, and Marquis sold their chocolates to some of the most famous and wealthy people of Paris. The trompe l'oeil panoramas, Paris's first gaslights, and the Turkish embassy are long gone, but despite the neon lights and so-so restaurants, the original charm has remained. Stroll through and breathe in a bit of the nostalgic past as you stumble upon several philatelic boutiques and the backstage entrance to the Théatre des Variétés.

As you exit passage des Panoramas, take a right onto rue Feydeau and then a left onto rue Vivienne. Walk down past la Bourse (the stock market) to the entrance of **galerie Vivienne** (6 rue Vivienne, 2e; Métro: Bourse). Built in 1823 on what once were the stables of the Duc d'Orléans, galerie Vivienne is a superb example of Neoclassic architecture. The galerie is now restored to its original splendor and is once again a very fashionable place to shop. In fact, the boutiques that you find here are the most chic of all of those on this tour.

Just next door to galerie Vivienne is **galerie Colbert** (6 rue des Petits-Champs, 2e; Métro: Bourse). This galerie has also been magnificently restored; the elegant rotunda, stately arcades, and trompe l'oeil marble columns remind us of a time when the passages were among the most majestic places in Paris.

From here, head toward place des Victoires, taking a left onto rue des Petits-Champs. You may either pick up part of the Victoires/Les Halles tour here or walk down rue Croix des Petits-Champs to **galerie Véro-Dodat** (2 rue du Bouloi, 1er; Métro: Palais-Royal). Somber woodwork and bronze window frames give a jewel box–like quality to this narrow passageway, which was opened in 1826 by two *charcutiers* (delicatessen salesmen). It is in remarkable condition considering that this ancient thoroughfare has not undergone much renovation over the years. The serenity of galerie Véro-Dodat contributes to the privileged feeling the visitor experiences when strolling through this fine example of architecture from the Restoration period. Most of the shops here exude a nostalgic quality that almost convinces you that you'll come across a corsetted woman peering into the next shopwindow. I'll let you experience the boutiques on your own. Please write to me if you find anything particularly memorable.

PALAIS-ROYAL/VIVIENNE It seems that the fashionable set these days begins by strolling through the **Palais-Royal Gardens,** then settles into a chic lunch at Le Grand Véfour, then saunters on toward galerie Vivienne. Although not officially considered a passage, the arcades at the

Palais-Royal were precursors to the nearby galleries that were constructed a short time later. Originally made of wood, these arcades were built in 1786 (a few years before the revolution) so that newly installed merchants could generate some extra funds for the aristocratic Orléans family (the occupants of the Royal Palace at the time). The passageways within the Palais-Royal have experienced a real renaissance in recent years and, now, in addition to strolling through this most picturesque cityscape, you may also visit some of Paris's more interesting and stylish boutiques. (American designer Marc Jacobs opened his first European boutique here.) Best to begin at Palais-Royal (Métro: Palais-Royal) to follow the flow up toward the galerie Vivienne/place des Victoires area.

OTHER PASSAGES

Nineteen different Paris passages remain today, most of which are experiencing some sort of rebirth, partly due to the rising prices of retail space in the French capital. The six mentioned in this tour are considered to be the most attractive; others have not quite survived a century or more of dilapidation. Keep your eyes open whenever you are near the *grands boulevards*, since you may just discover another passageway that will tickle your fancy.

If you like poking around the Sentier, Paris's garment district, then stop into **passage du Caire** (2 place du Caire or 33 rue d'Alexandrie, 2e; Métro: Sentier), which has been taken over almost entirely by wholesalers. Most of these prêt-à-porter boutiques claim not to sell retail, but if you push the right doors and use a savvy approach, you may get lucky.

If you're near the Saint-Lazare district, you may want to breeze through **passage du Havre** (69 rue Caumartin or 109 rue Saint-Lazare, 9e; Métro: Havre-Caumartin), the most glitzed-up passage of Paris. More like a modern shopping mall containing forty boutiques on two levels, this passage has added much life to this neighborhood and boasts a wide range of patrons from laborers to bankers—a true reflection of the colors of Saint-Lazare.

6

The Marais

THE QUARTIER OF CONTRASTS

The Old World charm of the Marais usually promises a refreshing contrast to the frenetic pace that you experience in other parts of the French capital. A labyrinth of small and narrow streets intimates a time when this area resembled a peaceful seventeenth-century village.

This is a neighborhood to explore on foot. A walking tour of the Marais not only provides you with countless hours of treasure-hunting, but also enables you to catch a glimpse of some of the nearly one hundred *hôtels particuliers* (private mansions) that have made this quartier one of the most historic neighborhoods of Paris. The Marais was the fashionable place to live during the seventeenth century, and these mansions attest to the elegance and grandeur of that era. In the eighteenth century, these magnificent homes fell out of glory; small industries moved in, setting up heavy machinery in the salons that once housed Paris's aristocrats. Years of destruction and impoverishment followed until 1962, when France's minister of culture, André Malraux, called for the renovation of this depressed area. Now virtually all of the mansions have been fully restored and converted into office space, luxury apartments, and a few museums—a complete turnabout that has made the Marais one of the priciest and most fashionable places to live in Paris.

The fashion world caught on fast, too, as the whole neighborhood began to change. In the early eighties, designers on the rise like Lolita Lempicka (who has sinced moved to the Sixteenth) and Popy Moreni started buying up old run-down shops and converting them into alluring fashion show-cases. More boutiques followed with the idea that an off-the-beaten-path location would provide a more exclusive address for their clientele. And the face of the Marais became transformed, as well. As you look at some of the façades of certain boutiques, you may even notice that they were once bakeries or butcher shops. The most decorative exteriors are, in many instances, in *verre eglouisé* (glass gliding) and have fortunately remained totally intact.

This movement spurred a whole new trend, which made the Marais a big fashion hub during the late eighties and early nineties. You'll still find many wonderful fashion boutiques here, but a Marais address does not have quite as much cachet as it once did. There are more trendy fashion boutiques here than ever before, but fortunately they have not entirely edged out all the quaint little curiosity shops that have existed for years. This creates an intermingling of old and new, which makes for surprising contrasts.

The Marais has also become increasingly popular with the homosexual community; toward the west side of this district you'll actually find a few cafés and restaurants that are favorite gathering spots for gays. This, of course, has made the shopping scene here even more fashion-forward!

Many of the shops remain open on Sundays in the Marais. This was a good thing in the beginning, but with the increasing popularity of the neighborhood, the Sunday crowds have become almost unbearable. You may want to plan a visit *en semaine* (during the week). The good news is that much of the Sunday mob scene is in the street; it's actually surprisingly calm inside the majority of the boutiques, so maybe Sundays could work for you, too.

The highlight of a visit to the Marais is most definitely the place des Vosges, a glorious plaza symmetrically surrounded by rosy brick town houses (actually most are faux bricks because bricklayers were a scarcity in Paris at the time). Built in 1605 by Henri IV, with two such town houses at opposite ends once intended for the king and queen, the place des Vosges is also Paris's oldest public square, and in my opinion, the most eloquent. Take time out from your shopping and touring to sit here and take in all this beauty.

Food and Wine Purveyors

A L'OLIVIER Almost at the corner of rue du Pont-Louis-Philippe, you'll be able to spot this store by the olive trees in huge planters outside. A real house of tradition since 1822, this homey shop sells many different types of olives, olive oil, vinegars flavored with raspberry, tarragon, and sherry, and cooking oils made from hazelnut, walnut, and palm. Lots of inexpensive gifts for the chefs back home.

23 rue de Rivoli, 4e; tel./fax: 01.48.04.86.59; Métro: Saint-Paul; Open Monday 2–7 P.M. and Tuesday–Saturday 10 A.M.–7 P.M.; www.olivier-on-line.com.

More Food and Wine Purveyors

If you're craving sugar, go directly to the west end of the Marais. Not only is **Mariage Frères** located here, where you can either sit and have a pastry or buy some sweets to go (see "Left Bank" description p. 139 for more), but you'll also discover a few *chocolatiers,* two worth mentioning. I would first go to **Chocolats Mussy,** a quaint shop that is the showcase for the chocolates of *Maître Chocolatier* Sylvain Mussy. He's best known for his *chocolats à la casse,* big bars of chocolate chock full of almonds, pistachios, and dried fruits that the salesperson will break off for you. Monsieur Mussy also sells honeys made by his brother, as well as honey-flavored caramels. Oh, I can hardly stand it!

In the time it takes you to savor a few chocolates, you will have arrived at **Cacao et Chocolat,** a considerably more glossy boutique known for its imaginative chocolates, many of which have a hint of exotic flavors such as cayenne pepper or ginger. Go to 36 rue Vieille-du-Temple, 4e; tel.: 01.42.71.50.06; www.cacaoetchocolat.com), and be grateful that I'm encouraging such taste comparisons.

Métros for the above boutiques are Hôtel-de-Ville or Saint-Paul.

Table and Kitchen Arts, Home Décor, and Linens

ARGENTERIE DE TURENNE As soon as you push open the door, you're almost knocked over by the pungent smell of tarnished silver. The scent only adds to the charm and authenticity of the boutique, which is considered one of Paris's best shops for buying antique silver and silver-plated items.

Much of what is sold here comes from hotels that have gone out of business, estates, and, occasionally, old cruise ships. Mixed patterns of silver-plated flatware are sold by the kilo (about €60 per kilo or about €5 per piece; a kilo equals nearly fifteen pieces). The walls are lined from top to bottom with shelves that contain hundreds of silver teapots, frames, platters, champagne buckets, and more unusual items such as silver egg cups, wine tasters, and toast holders (which you can also use for your mail!).

19 rue de Turenne, 4e; tel.: 01.42.72.04.00; fax: 01.42.72.08.24; Métro: Saint-Paul; Tuesday–Saturday 10:30 A.M.–7 P.M.; closed the first three weeks of August.

More Home Décor

Looking for an unusual *objet* for your home? You're likely to find a unique treasure such as a Baroque candlestick or a curious statuette at **Les Mille Feuilles** (2 rue Rambuteau, 4e; tel.: 01.42.78.32.93; Métro: Rambuteau; www.lesmillefeuilles.com).

Art, Antiques, and Collectibles

LA CALINIÈRE If you're in the market for antique lamps or lighting fixtures, but don't have time to hit the flea markets, you may want to have a look around at La Calinière. Like *les puces,* this boutique offers a charming collection of knickknacks and *objets* from days gone by, which makes it interesting just to browse around even if you're not looking to buy. Its forte is a great and varied collection of every imaginable type of illumination from the Art Nouveau and Art Deco periods, all of which can easily be adapted to plug in stateside.

68 rue Vieille-du-Temple, 3e; tel.: 01.42.77.40.46; Métro: Saint-Paul; Open Monday–Saturday 11 A.M.–7:30 P.M. and some Sundays.

MEUBLES PEINTS Monsieur Jean-Pierre Besenval ferrets out eighteenth- and nineteenth-century Alsatian armoires and little commodes that have fallen to ruin and restores them, inside and out, to their original glory. Each piece is stripped, treated, and painted in the tiny workshop behind this boutique. All the egg tempera paintings are bright, colorful, and highly decorative; most of the images are folkloric paintings of fruit and flowers, typical of the eastern part of France; others bear Renaissance-inspired landscapes in the trompe l'oeil technique. Count on spending €4,800 to €15,500 for an armoire; about €3,500 for a diptych.

Monsieur Besenval also gives courses (in English) so that you, too, can learn this masterful art. Inquire here or consult his Web site for information on those programs.

32 rue de Sévigné, 4e; tel.: 01.42.77.54.60; Métro: Saint-Paul;
Open Tuesday–Saturday noon–7 P.M.; Sunday 2–7 P.M.; www.meublespeints.com.

LOTS OF ANTIQUING

Le Village Saint-Paul Probably the most countrylike and charming of all of the Paris antiques complexes, the village Saint-Paul consists of a courtyard (surrounded by a refurbished grouping of seventeenth-century town houses) populated by antiques dealers and *brocanteurs* selling a variety of antiques and secondhand goods. They're in somewhat of a period of transition now, so some boutiques have opened and closed, but it's still worth a look. You may enter the village at 19 rue Saint-Paul.

Métro: Saint-Paul, Sully-Morland, Pont-Marie; Open every day except Tuesday and Wednesday 11 A.M.–7 P.M.

SOLD! (OR RATHER, *VENDU!*)

Crédit Municipal de Paris Folded into an elegant *hôtel particulier* in the Marais is the Crédit Municipal de Paris, one of the most modern and intimate auction houses of Europe. All the action takes place in one movie theater–like hall where bidders sit comfortably on red velvet seats as the show unveils before them. Two to three auctions a week are conducted here, and nearly all consist of jewelry, silver, art objects, and furs that have been pawned off by once well-to-do Parisians. The rules are similar to those at Drouot, and the sales are also announced in *La Gazette de l'Hôtel Drouot*. Viewing takes place mostly the morning of the afternoon sale, sometimes the day before. Best to find someone to translate for you if you don't understand French.

55 rue des Francs-Bourgeois, 4e; tel.: 01.44.61.65.00; fax: 01.44.61.65.32; Métro: Rambuteau; Open Monday–Friday 9 A.M.–4:30 P.M.; www.creditmunicipal.fr.

Jewelry, Shoes, and Accessories

BABYLONE Pay attention or you might walk right by this sliver of a boutique. Babylone sells its own brand of costume jewelry, all of which is handmade in its Paris workshops, and reasonably priced from €15 to €200. The value is excellent, particularly since many of these stylish pieces sell for quite a bit more at high-end department stores in the United States. I love the look—classic, yet fun and candy-colored.

11 rue des Francs-Bourgeois, 4e; tel.: 01.44.54.03.84; Métro: Saint-Paul; Open Monday 11:30 A.M.–7:30 P.M.; Tuesday 12:30–7:30 P.M.; Wednesday–Saturday 11:30 A.M.–7:30 P.M.; Sunday noon–7:30 P.M.; closed sometimes at lunch and one week mid-August; www.babyloneparis.com.

JEAN-BAPTISTE RAUTUREAU This is the "it" place for men's shoes. The same makers as Free Lance shoes for women bring you the tops in men's shoes and boots. Prices aren't cheap (average €400 for a pair of shoes) but that doesn't seem to slow the shoppers down any here.

16 rue du Bourg-Tibourg, 43; tel.: 01.42.77.01.55; Métro: Hôtel-de-Ville; Open Monday–Saturday 11 A.M.–1 P.M. and 2–8 P.M.; Sunday 2–8 P.M.; 24 rue de Grenelle, 7e; tel.: 01.45.49.95.83; Métro: Sèvres-Babylone; www .rautureau-appleshoes.fr.

K. JACQUES A stop here in the summer instantly transports you to Saint-Tropez, that sizzling spot in the sun on the French Riviera. Sun, of course, means sandals, this shop's forte. Here, you will find them in a range of colors and materials, from Mediterranean blue to sensuous snakeskin. But the real *sandale de Saint-Tropez* has always been fashioned from plain beige leather. To some, this version might seem a bit dull, but they become far more interesting when you learn that they were first introduced to Saint-Tropez in 1920 after one of the city's native sons happened to see a statue in Rome ceremoniously clad in this footwear. The look caught on, most likely for comfort first, then as a fashion statement, and today as a classic. Prices range from €120 to €140.

Other types of sandals and moccasin-style shoes for men, women, and children round out the collection. And, as you can imagine, the look changes considerably in the winter, when the shop features lots of stylish yet practical footwear, hats, and scarves.

16 rue Pavée, 4e; tel.: 01.40.27.03.57; Métro: Saint-Paul;

Open Monday–Saturday 10 A.M.–8 P.M.; Sunday 2–8 P.M.; www.kjacques.com.

LOUISE GELINAS Truly one of the most extraordinary jewelry and accessory shops of Paris, anything you buy at Louise Gelinas may be considered a fashion statement. Each piece—whether it be a string of old glass beads, a cocktail ring, a handwoven scarf, an embroidered bag, or even a silk jacket—stands alone. Many things (particularly the jewelery) are oversized and are clearly made with a sophisticated woman in mind. Owner Louise Gelinas—a demure Annie Lennox look-alike—displays exquisite taste in her choice of pieces. Most are from France, some are from Italy, but all exude timeless chic with a hint or more of ethnicity.

19 rue Pavée, 4; tel.: 01.42.74.26.02; Métro: Saint-Paul;

Open Tuesday–Saturday 11:30 A.M.–7:30 P.M.; Sunday 3–7 P.M.

MI AMOR/SIC AMOR Two terrific boutiques glisten with a gold mine of creations from Paris's most exciting costume jewelry designers of the moment. Philippe, one of the owners and a designer himself, has all the right connections in obtaining much-in-demand treasures from Paris's most persnickety designers (they don't sell to just anybody)—all at lower than normal prices. Magically luminous resin, featherweight metal, brightly colored plastics, and iridescent glass have been molded, sculpted, and blown into countless different unconventional shapes—such a realm of creation that you know you've come across a real find!

You'll find mostly jewelry at no. 20; other fashion accessories at no. 10. 10 & 20 rue du Pont-Louis-Philippe, 4e; tel.: 01.42.71.79.29 and 01.42.76.02.37; Métro for both stores: Saint-Paul, Hôtel-de-Ville, or Pont Marie; Open daily 11 A.M.–7 P.M.; www.mi-amor.com.

More Jewelry, Shoes, and Accessories

Paper *and* costume jewelry vie for your attention over on rue du Pont-Louis-Philippe. **Laurent Guillot** is the newcomer on the block at no. 22 (tel.: 01.48.87.87.69; www.laurentguillot.com), but he has another boutique in the Marais at 48 rue de Turenne (tel.: 01.42.77.37.21) that has existed for almost ten years. You'll see that most of his pieces have been crafted out of gold leaf–backed Plexiglas—quite striking.

More (faux) gold is on view at **Cécile & Jeanne,** a very popular costume jewelry maker that boasts boutiques all over the world. It's a good thing that the dove is this designer's emblem. I bought a pair of her swingy dove earrings at least ten years ago that I often grab from my jewelry box. And I recently saw former secretary of state Madeleine Albright wearing Cécile & Jeanne dove earrings and a dove brooch when she appeared on *The Daily Show* with Jon Stewart. Now *that's* a good way to promote world peace. Way to go, Cécile & Jeanne (12 rue des Francs-Bourgeois, 3e; tel.: 01.42.71.21.93; www.cecilejeanne.com).

The Métro for the above boutiques is Saint-Paul.

Womenswear

AZZEDINE ALAÏA This tiny man from Tunisia certainly knows how to show off a woman's body properly. How does he do it? Slinky body-hugging clothes, expertly stitched together in the most body-forgiving shapes. Amazingly enough, even the most curvaceous women look smashing when slithering around in an Alaïa dress, proving the theory that his tight fits are designed to hold you in, rather than out! Best known for his leather and knit creations, Alaïa offers a bit of both here—along with some *très* sexy shoes—no matter what the season.

This is the only Alaïa boutique in the world, aside from the Alaïa discount shop just around the corner.

7 rue de Moussy, 4e; tel.: 01.40.27.85.58; fax: 01.42.76.08.48; Métro: Hôtel-de-Ville; Open Monday–Saturday 10 A.M.–7 P.M.

POPY MORENI After having spent a number of years designing womenswear for various designers, including Nino Cerruti, Popy Moreni took the plunge and set up her own boutique in the Marais. She is Italian inside and out, which explains the commedia dell'arte side to all her creations. Popy Moreni feels that the street is the theater and her clothes set the stage. Her sophisticated fashions are bought by the most eccentric of women, and she is best known for her glittery collection of eveningwear.

Good news: large-sized women will find certain models available in sizes 38 to 50.

13 place des Vosges; 4e; tel.: 01.42.77.09.96; Métro: Saint-Paul; Open Monday–Saturday 10 A.M.–6:30 P.M.; closed in August.

More Womenswear

Poised on the elegant place des Vosges is the Paris showplace of Japanese designer **Issey Miyake.** Here, Monsieur Miyake has created a gallery to showcase his most artistic women's fashions (3 place des Vosges; tel.: 01.48.87.01.86; www.isseymiyake.com).

Paule Ka, purveyor of elegant sixties-inspired silhouettes, first set up shop here in the Marais and continues today at 20 rue Mahler; tel.: 01.40.29.96.03; www.pauleka.com. The knitted twinsets here will give you the shape of a lovely pinup from that era. This designer's shoes, bags, and hats—most of which match the suits to a T—will most definitely charm you if the clothes don't.

Animale (26 rue de Sévigné, 4e; tel.: 01.42.71.91.59) is a midrange brand that has a lot of success with the *parisiennes.* It's very creative, slightly wild (as the name indicates), and good for *femmes rondes,* or large-sized women. (The French language is so beautiful—we should say round women, as well!)

Métro for the above boutiques is Saint-Paul.

The western end of the Marais offers many unexpected discoveries, such as **Madame Zaza of Marseille** (18 rue Sainte-Croix de la Bretonnerie;

tel.: 01.48.04.76.03; Métro: Hôtel-de-Ville), a women's clothing boutique filled with the *exotisme* of that colorful city. Reasonably priced, too.

Women's and Men's Fashions

L'ECLAIREUR L'Eclaireur has been a fixture in the Marais for a good number of years. Now, they have locations on the Right Bank and place des Victoires district as well. I'm sending you here, though, since this is where it all began (and where they're the best represented). They excel in fashions (and, of course, lots of accessories!) from many of Europe's hottest designers. Whatever is sold here is considered the newest, greatest thing. I made the mistake of coming here once at the end of fashion week and was overwhelmed by the crowds of fashion editors from all over the world.

To view their very select collection of table arts—including many fabulous trays from Fornasetti—go to L'Eclaireur's new address in Galerie Royale, *the* kingdom of high-end table arts.

3 ter rue des Rosiers, 4e (women's); tel.: 01.48.87.10.22; 12 rue Malher, 4e (men's); tel.: 01.44.54.22.11; Métro: Saint-Paul; 8 rue Boissy d'Anglas; 8e (men's, women's, and table); tel.: 01.53.43.03.70; Métro: Concorde or Madeleine; Open Monday–Saturday 11 A.M.–7 P.M.; closed Mondays in August; www.leclaireur.com.

ZADIG & VOLTAIRE Zadig & Voltaire stores have popped up all over Paris and are rapidly spreading throughout the world. (There's one in West Hollywood at this writing.) The look is best described as Parisian grunge, so don't expect anything too shabby. You will find lots of jeans for men and women (priced at €180 on average) and fun tops and jackets to set them off.

42 rue des Francs-Bourgeois, 4e; tel.: 01.44.54.00.60; Métro: Saint-Paul; Open Monday 1–7:30 P.M.; Tuesday–Saturday 10:30 A.M.–7:30 P.M.; Sunday 1:30–7:30 P.M.; closed Mondays in August; 1 and 3 rue du Vieux-Colombier, 6e; tel.: 01.43.29.18.29 and 01.45.48.39.37; Métro: Saint-Sulpice; www.zadig-et-voltaire.com.

More Women's and Men's Fashions

Autour du Monde (12 rue des Francs-Bourgeois, 4e; tel.: 01.42.77.16.18; Métro: Saint-Paul; www.autourdumonde.com) appeals to more conservative tastes with just the right amount of flair. Call it the French version of Banana Republic.

Discount Shops

Shop for **Azzedine Alaïa's** sexy womenswear at about 50 percent off at 18 rue de la Verrerie, 4e; tel.: 01.42.72.83.19. Savings can be even more if the piece is from a collection more than a year old. A pair of killer shoes, for example, rings in at €100.

For reduced-price women's and men's fashions of a whole other genre, go to the discount shop of **Zadig & Voltaire** at 22 rue Bourg-Tibourg, 4e; tel.: 01.44.59.39.61. Their young and loose weekend wear from mostly past collections sells here at nearly half off.

Métro for both boutiques is Hôtel-de-Ville.

Books and Music

THE RED WHEELBARROW BOOKSTORE   This well-stocked English-language bookstore will give you a good reason to venture over to the less tourist-trod side of the Marais. (You can also enjoy antiquing on this street and at the nearby Village Saint-Paul.) Its staff favorites section is of particular note, and you'll also want to inquire about its special events.

22 rue Saint-Paul, 4e; tel.: 01.48.04.75.08; Métro: Saint-Paul;

Open Monday–Saturday 10 A.M.–7 P.M.; Sunday 2–6 P.M.;

www.theredwheelbarrow.com.

A LA BELLE HORTENSE   Stop in for a peek at literary life, French style. The combination coffeehouse/bookstore comes as no surprise, but wine bar/bookstore is decidedly more novel. You can actually still enjoy *un café* as well in this handsome space devoted to books and gab.

31 rue Vieille-du-Temple, 3; tel.: 01.48.04.71.60; Métro: Saint-Paul or Hôtel-de-Ville ✗ .

Specialty Boutiques

A LA BONNE RENOMMÉE Late-nineteenth-century dark wood floors, paneling, and showcases create a warm and handsome setting for the luxuriously rich patchworks sold in this shop. This is exactly the sort of boutique that most visitors yearn to stumble upon during a Parisian shopping excursion, and I'm thrilled that little has changed here over the years.

Patchwork is decidedly chic at this store. Their assortment of ready-to-wear and accessories is made up of rather Slavic-looking patchworks composed of the finest jacquards, satins, velvets, paisleys, flower prints and especially the most extraordinary ribbons that the town of Lyons has to offer. The attraction of these folkloric designs lies in their unusual mixture of materials, textures, and colors. Each creation is finished off with a fanciful touch of tassel or fringe.

Many of the shapes used in the women's apparel and bags are as heart-warming as the patchworks: amply cut jackets, shirts, and vests, soft and floppy drawstring pouches, and Gothic-shaped handbags conjure images of Eastern European lands. Belts, change purses, eyeglass cases, and pins make up some of the more traditional items that are both affordable and easy to bring home as gifts.

26 rue Vieille-du-Temple, 4e; tel.: 01.42.72.03.86; Métro: Saint-Paul or Hôtel-de-Ville; Open Monday–Saturday 11 A.M.–7 P.M.; Sunday 2–7 P.M.; www.labonnerenommee.com.

PAPIER+ Papier+ blends modernity with elegance in its sober yet vibrantly colored collection of fine stationery and paper articles. Blank notebooks, photo albums, guest registers, artists' portfolios, and more, bound in heavy canvas, have been neatly arranged in piles that form a rich temple of hues at this long-established address.

The size range on most of their products is outstanding. And the various papers have been carefully selected for different purposes: a certain paper for books destined for writing, another for drawing, and so on. (The white paper is, of course, acid-free; the black is not.) There is much attention paid to detail, which explains the devoted following of artists, architects, illustrators, and nonprofessionals it has from all corners of the world. Caution: If you're anything like me, you'll become hooked on their photo albums, and you'll want to buy nothing but these. They may require a little extra effort to paste in the photos (none of those cheesy plastic sheaths here), but the end result is a keepsake that you and your heirs will cherish forever.

9 rue du Pont-Louis-Philippe, 4e; tel.: 01.42.77.70.49; Métro: Saint-Paul; Expensive; Open Monday–Saturday noon–7 P.M.; www.papierplus.com.

More Specialty Boutiques

Rue du Pont-Louis-Philippe is indisputably Paris's paper street. Aficionados of fine-quality paper products and well-designed desktop accessories are sure to be enchanted by the eclectic offerings on this little street. **Mélodies Graphiques** (10 rue du Pont-Louis-Philippe, 4e; tel.: 01.42.74.57.68; fax: 01.42.74.30.01) is a must for indefatigable admirers of Florentine papers, those attractive marbleized papers that, although invented by the bookbinder of Louis XIII during the seventh century, have flourished under the Italians over the past few hundred years.

The shop **Calligrane** (4–6 rue du Pont-Louis-Philippe, 4e; tel.: 01.48.04.31.89; fax: 01.40.27.84.08) offers papers and desk accessories of a decidedly more contemporary style in three separate boutiques. They also feature Italian papers, sleek sheets from Fabriano, the oldest mill in Europe that crafts artfully made papers. Other stationery samples sport textures as rich and diverse as the countries from which they originate: Japan, China, Brazil, India, Thailand, and even a few handmade offerings from Auvergne in the heart of France. Calligrane's selection of desk accessories consists of lots of leather these days, so there's no reason not to feel cozy at your desk if you outfit yourself here.

If you're looking for sleek office accessories, go to **L'Art du Bureau** (47 rue des Francs-Bourgeois, 4e; tel.: 01.48.87.57.97; fax: 01.42.78.66.77), back on the main thoroughfare of the Marais.

Bathing aficionados should be sure to stop into **Bains-Plus** (51 rue des Francs-Bourgeois, 4e; tel.: 01.48.87.83.07), a long-standing boutique of the Marais that specializes in the art of the bath. I think you'll like their selection of robes and pajamas, too.

Down the street, **Entrée des Fournisseurs** (8 rue des Francs-Bourgeois, 4e; tel.: 01.48.87.58.98; www.entreedesfournisseurs.com) sells all the buttons and bows, fancy frogs and fun beads that you'll ever need to zip up your own couture creations. I also love their kits for making cross-stitch samplers in perfect French.

Métro for all of the above boutiques is Saint-Paul.

Market

So you like the idea of doing your food shopping at the end of the day? The **Baudoyer Market,** located at place Baudoyer in the Fourth, is a rarity in that it allows you that opportunity on Wednesdays when it's open 3 to 8:30 P.M. also Saturday 7 A.M. to 3 P.M.; Métro: Hôtel-de-Ville.

My Special Suggestions

Beauté and Parfums

LES BAINS DU MARAIS I had the most skin-sational experience of my life at these baths. In fact, after a few hours of being bathed, buffed, and polished here, I vowed to myself that I would return to this amazing place every trip I make to Paris. Why are these baths so extraordinary? First of all, going to a bathhouse is a Marais thing to do, and all different types of people have made this part of their weekly ritual for many years. But the main reason is that this is by no means your average bathhouse—it's more of a luxurious spa that emphasizes many of the marvelous therapeutic practices of the Orient.

As you pass through the discreet entrance to Les Bains du Marais on this narrow, winding street of the rue des Blancs-Manteaux, you enter an old warehouse space that is quietly humming with people padding about in bathrobes and a staff working to respond to everyone's needs. Exposed stone walls and an old glass roof provide the perfect setting for the hip hair salon and restaurant/tea salon on the main level, but it's downstairs where you'll really experience the greatest range of sensations. You'll want to begin by sweating out all of your body's impurities in the marble-clad hamman, and as you build up your resistance to the heat, you can try to sweat it out even more in the hotter eucalyptus room. The ultimate experience, however, is the Oriental massage, an extremely vigorous treatment that is a combination of an intense exfoliation and deep penetrating massage. It is not for the faint of heart or for those uncomfortable with baring their bodies to members of the opposite sex. (The young Moroccan men give the most vigorous massages!) The whole idea behind this manipulation is to eliminate all the dead skin so that your whole body may finally breathe more easily. It is also said to improve circulation and rid you of toxins, stress, and bad energy. In North Africa, most women undergo this sort of treatment every two weeks.

After all this, you feel delightfully exhausted. Go rest in the *salle de repos,* a dimly lit room where you sip mint tea on Oriental-style daybeds and then slumber. You won't be ready for dancing after this, but the relaxation and therapeutic benefits will most certainly be felt the next day and several thereafter.

Access to the hamman, sauna, and resting room (bathrobes, towels, and slippers are provided) is €35; add an additional €35 for the Oriental massage. Be sure to bring your bathing suit on coed days; and don't worry, the baths, and all the rest of this beautiful facility, are whistle clean.

31–33 rue des Blancs-Manteaux, 4e; tel.: 01.44.61.02.02; Métro: Rambuteau; Open Monday 11 A.M.–8 P.M., Tuesday 11 A.M.–11 P.M., and Wednesday 10 A.M.– 7 P.M. for women only; Thursday 10 A.M.–11 P.M., Friday 10 A.M.–8 P.M., and Saturday 11 A.M.–8 P.M. for men only; Wednesday 7–9 P.M.; Saturday 10 A.M.–8 P.M. and Sunday 11 A.M.–11 P.M. mixed; www.lesbainsdumarais.com. ✕ ★ 🕮

MORE *BEAUTÉ* AND *PARFUMS* If you fancy fragrances (mostly for your home) and flowers, don't miss **Hervé Gambs** (9 bis rue des Blancs-Manteaux, 4e; tel.: 01.44.59.88.88; Métro: Rambuteau; www.hervegambs.fr), a pretty little shop that sells Monsieur Gambs's creations, the majority of which are composed of preserved flowers.

Perfect Respites
LE LOIR DANS LA THÉIÈRE The décor in this popular tearoom is as unpretentious as its delicious assortment of homemade quiches, terrines, pies, and cakes. An odd selection of oversized chairs and round, wobbly

tables (local garage sale–type furnishings) provide a laid-back setting for those interested in a quick, tasty bite at an honest price. Weekends are very busy. Inexpensive.

3 rue des Rosiers, 4e; tel.: 01.42.72.90.61; Métro: Saint-Paul; Open daily year-round 10 A.M.–7 P.M.

MA BOURGOGNE No trip to the Marais (especially your first one) is complete without stopping in this often-busy café, not necessarily for the food, but for the view of the magnificent place des Vosges, Paris's most stately square. Rain or shine, you may sit at one of the tables underneath the arcades and order up *un plat du jour, un café noir,* or a chilled glass of Beaujolais. Inexpensively priced, but credit cards aren't accepted.

19 place des Vosges, 4e; tel.: 01.42.78.44.64; Métro: Saint-Paul; Inexpensive to moderate; Open daily year-round 8 A.M.–1 A.M.

MORE PERFECT RESPITES **Mariage Frères** see "Left Bank" description p. 139. And for a real taste of the Jewish heritage here, go to **Jo Goldenberg** (7 rue des Rosiers, 4e; tel.: 01.42.77.67.74; Métro: Saint-Paul).

Recommended Hotel

HÔTEL PAVILLON DE LA REINE Staying at this hotel is a particular treat, and lots of people know it, so do book ahead, particularly on weekends if you want to experience the romance and extraordinary history of one of the oldest residences of Paris. It's like visiting the provinces of France while benefiting from all the advantages of being in the heart of Paris. The only four-star hotel in this inimitable part of town, this discreet establishment seduces you with its country-manor charms and regal touches. Low ceilings and exposed wood beams, many of which date back to the house's seventeenth-century origins, create a distinctly cottagelike feeling, but quiet luxury abounds in the tasteful use of fabrics of both traditional and contemporary design. (You may actually choose to have a room either *classique* or *moderne.*) Solid and unyielding Renaissance-style furnishings fill virtually every nook and cranny of the hotel, along with many period paintings—a constant visual reminder that this edifice (as with most of the other splendid *hôtels particuliers* in the neighborhood) was erected with royalty in mind.

28 place des Vosges, 3e; tel.: 01.40.29.19.19; Métro: Saint-Paul; Four-star hotel: Expensive to very expensive; www.pavillon-de-la-reine.fr.

Favorite Tours

SAINT-PAUL You've probably noticed by now that the Métro most often indicated is Saint-Paul. I usually get off at Saint-Paul and begin to burrow my way into the Marais via rue Pavée. This will lead you directly onto the rue des Francs-Bourgeois, the main thoroughfare of the Marais, where you'll find the greatest concentration of shops. Be sure to check out the side streets within this whole area, and don't hesitate to push a few doors to peek inside the inner courtyards. (There's usually a button on the doorframe to the right that will unlock it for you—this is totally okay.) I highly recommend you go to the **Musée Carnavalet** (the museum of the city of Paris at 23 rue de Sévigné; tel.: 01.44.59.58.58). There's also the **Musée Picasso** (5 rue de Thorigny; tel.: 01.42.71.25.21;), which is also housed in a *hôtel particulier*. I think both of their museum shops are quite nice, too. If you have extra time, you may want to visit the **Maison de Victor Hugo** (6 place des Vosges; tel.: 01.42.72.10.16) for a glimpse at how this major French literary figure lived. (It also allows you to see the interior of one of these town houses.)

HÔTEL-DE-VILLE Begin near the Hôtel-de-Ville; pick up rue de la Verrerie, then turn left onto rue du Bourg-Tibourg and start to work your way into the Marais. Here on the west side you can hit the sweet shops and even Mariage Frères if it's not too crowded. Look around rue Vieille-du-Temple, one of my favorite streets here, then cut through the Jewish quarter on the rue des Rosiers and the rue du Roi-de-Siècle. This area has been a vibrant part of Paris since the thirteenth century. Synagogues are scattered among Jewish bakeries, delicatessens, Turkish baths, and Greek cafés—more unexpected contrasts of the wonderful Marais district of Paris. The rue des Rosiers will take you to some of the top fashion boutiques of the Marais. From there you can either head back into the district on rue Pavée, pick up the Métro at Saint-Paul, or cross rue Saint-Antoine to rue Saint-Paul to go antiquing.

7

Bastille and République

PARIS EST

A good number of changes have taken place in this eastern part of Paris over the past two decades but, thankfully, the fabric of the neighborhoods that make up this area has by no means become threadbare. Toward the late eighties and through much of the nineties, the Bastille became really hot. After a good run attracting people to its happening *restos,* boutiques, and art galleries, the real buzz turned toward rue Oberkampf. But then on Oberkampf restaurants and boutiques ended up closing nearly as fast as they opened. Now, the Canal Saint-Martin/rue Beaurepaire area generates the most excitement as the latest "in" place of the capital. All kinds of trendy restaurants and fashion boutiques are emerging here faster than the time it takes to get a boat through a lock. Some popular international brands such as Agnès b. and American Apparel have even moved in, although if this part of town is anything like Oberkampf, some may be on their way out by the time this book hits the shelves. Thank goodness that with all of this, much stays the same. The one continuous thread on this east side of town is that it remains genuine for the most part, thanks to the people who live here, an interesting mix of working-class types, immigrants and, in recent years, artists, writers, architects, photographers, and graphic designers in search of more affordable living and working spaces.

As much as there have been ebbs and flows in the Bastille district recently, there has also been continuity. Since the seventeenth century, artisans have populated the crooked little streets and courtyards typical of this area, and today—even with the so-called gentrification of the Bastille—many of these artisans and small-tradespeople have managed to remain in their ateliers. As you explore this area, walk into some of the courtyards (don't be afraid to push open a few doors as you go along) and you'll discover craftspeople carrying out *les vieux métiers* (the old trades) such as cabinetmaking, gild work, and hand varnishing.

The furniture-making industry was once big business here; now most of the craftspeople carry out highly specialized jobs for some of Paris's most prestigious antiques dealers and flea market merchants. Paris's renowned furniture street, the glitzy rue du Faubourg-Saint-Antoine, sells many tacky living- and dining-room sets, ostentatious enough to make you think that this was where Liberace did his shopping. Nevertheless, I have indicated many long-established houses of Elysian quality in this industry, which are located around here and are very much worth your attention.

The volume is cranked up in the Bastille at night, so if you feel like making the scene, you might want to come here to check it out after you've explored the shops earlier in the day.

To me, a tour around the Canal Saint-Martin area is the perfect antidote to the often frenetic pace of the big city. Perhaps it's the quaintness of this stretch along the water that is so calming. The lapping of the water against the canal soothes, and yes, the whole area has a villagelike appearance, particularly in fair weather when people lounge along the banks of the canal, setting up planned or impromptu picnics as though they were on the shores of a beautiful lake.

All in all, the east side of Paris has much to offer. I've indicated some of the key addresses here, but I know you'll discover more on your own, perhaps some that will have just opened!

Food and Wine Purveyors

LA BAGUE DE KENZA   For a true taste of the sweetness of the neighborhood surrounding the Canal Saint-Martin, stop into this bakery shop/tea salon for a bit of *pâtisserie orientale,* accompanied by a sugary mint tea. When this bakery opened more than fifteen years ago, its clientele was predominantly North African, the very people who live and work in this part of town. Now that this area has become so hip, there's been a huge shift—so much so, in fact, that the North African patrons are now in the minority. It's actually become very chic to bring a box of B.K.'s mouthwatering cookies to a hostess as a gift, so I'm sure they would be very well received on the other side of the Atlantic as well. You'll spend about €15 for a box (ten pieces) of their *ghribia,* a buttery, melt-in-your mouth cookie that stands up to a good strong cup of coffee.

106 rue Saint-Maur, 11e; tel.: 01.43.14.93.15; Métro: Parmentier; Inexpensive; Open daily except Friday 9 A.M.–10 P.M.; Friday 2:30–10 P.M. ✗

BRULERIE DAVAL   Step inside the passageway at 12 rue Daval to discover this specialty coffee roaster on your left. The Brulerie Daval is an example of the type of *petit commerçant* concealed within the inner courtyards of this district. Look around here—you'll see lots of workshops that have been recently redone.

As you push open the door at this favorite neighborhood shop, you are greeted with the aroma of freshly roasted 100 percent arabica and the smile of Madame D'Amico, a most amiable shop owner. Look around and see if there's not a special coffee, tea, or jam that you can purchase from this lovely lady.

12 rue Daval, 11e; tel.: 01.48.05.29.46; Métro: Bastille; Open Tuesday–Saturday 10 A.M.–1 P.M. and 3–7:30 P.M.; sometimes on Sunday; closed from mid-July through the end of August.

MAISON ANDRAUD   Just a few steps from the place de la Bastille, you'll discover one of the oldest shops in the neighborhood, a *confiserie* (candy store) founded in 1903. The décor is Art Deco from the thirties, a most elegant showcase for the display of some of France's best-loved sweets. Homemade chocolates and candies fill the dark wood shelves that line the walls of this handsome boutique, along with many specialty items from the provinces, including various fine cognacs and spirits, jams, honey, and cookies.

12 rue de la Roquette, 11e; tel.: 01.47.00.59.07; Métro: Bastille;

Open Tuesday–Saturday 10 A.M.–6:45 P.M.; closed July and August.

DU PAIN ET DES IDÉES Christophe Vasseur made the leap from the world of fashion to the art of making bread, and from the look of his scrumptious array of breads, pastries, and other confections, he's intent on making his goods very good *and* beautiful. He took over this superb old bakery (classified an historic monument) in 2002 and ever since, his philosophy has been that "a bakery is a beacon in a neighborhood. It's a place for exchanges and encounters." Christophe also says, "In this bread, there's love *and* friendship." Ponder that as you bite into a piece of his bread filled with reblochon or feta while you picnic nearby along the lovely Canal Saint-Martin.

34 rue Yves-Toudic, 10e; tel.: 01.42.40.44.52; Métro: République;

Open Monday–Friday 8 A.M.–6 P.M.

Table and Kitchen Arts, Home Décor, and Linens

HOULÈS And what would furniture be without its trimmings? Houlès has been offering all the necessary—and frivolous—embellishments since the beginning of the twentieth century. For more than one hundred years, the Houlès market has extended well past the nearby furniture makers of the Faubourg, and today you'll find their trimmings in the smartest interior décor studios of the world. The pom-poms here are indeed pricey, but still less than in the United States. And what a difference a bit of color-coordinated braid or fringe can make to a throw pillow or two. This immense showroom sells to both individuals and members of the trade.

18 rue Saint-Nicolas, 12e; tel.: 01.43.44.65.19; Métro: Ledru-Rollin;

Open Monday–Friday 8:45.–12:30 A.M. and 1:30–6:30 P.M.; variations in hours during August; www.houles.com.

LES JARDINS DU ROI SOLEIL The name of this store means "the gardens of the Sun King." If you've been to Versailles, you have a clue about how the Sun King's gardens looked. Probably one of the most memorable features of these vast expanses of royal gardens are the square tubs that were used to hold Louis XIV's orange trees. This store offers exact replicas of these planters in a variety of sizes and colors, all carefully crafted out of solid oak and cast iron. Perfect for elegant gardens, terraces, or interiors and, of course, they ship.

32 bd de la Bastille, 12e; tel.: 01.43.44.44.31; Métro: Bastille;

Open Monday–Friday 10 A.M.–6 P.M.; closed in August; www.jardinsroisoleil.com.

RINCK Any mention of Versailles reminds me of all those treasures of the three Louis (XIV, XV, and XVI) that were destroyed during the revolution. And the few that were saved have mostly ended up in museums. So how do you procure your own exquisite piece of French patrimony, or something close? In comes Rinck, probably the most important furniture maker in all of France. Founded in 1841, Rinck has continued the furniture-making tradition of the Faubourg-Saint-Antoine. Here, they are within close proximity to the many skilled craftsmen whose talents they rely on to perfectly sculpt, gild, varnish, adorn, or polish a certain piece of furniture, a certain work of art. As you can imagine, most of their works are special orders (many for high-profile types). Rinck also works a lot with decorators such as Charlotte Moss and Christian Liaigre on both sides of the Atlantic. It's best to call for an appointment.

8 passage de la Bonne-Graine (enter 115 rue du Faubourg-Saint-Antoine), 11e;

tel.: 01.47.00.42.67; Métro: Ledru-Rollin; Open Monday–Friday 8 A.M.–7 P.M.;

Closed sometimes for lunch; www.rinck.fr.

ZUBER & CIE. The Alsace region in eastern France has been known for centuries for its handsome wallpapers and textiles. The house of Zuber was founded there in 1797, and since then, its wallpaper has been crafted with little change to the process—there's no hint of the Industrial Revolution ever having taken place. Nearly a forestful of pearwood blocks is used in the printing of each exquisite wallpaper panel—as many as eighty for the more intricate prints. Most of the scenes are trompe l'oeil, a technique that allowed nineteenth-century travelers to sojourn in far-off lands without ever leaving their living rooms. Even Jackie Kennedy was conquered by the lifelike marvels of Zuber when she acquired the thirty-two-panel panorama *Vues d'Amérique* for the White House during her stint there.

Today Zuber's grand salons and showrooms testify to the fact that these entirely handcrafted wallpapers are still very much in demand. The woodblock method is still used, and most of the collection is based on the company's rich archives. In 1984, the company reintroduced the textile designs that Zuber had discontinued more than a century ago. The selection today is stupendous, at prices that reflect the craftsmanship involved with each design. Consider the collection of accent papers for more affordable Zuber creations. A border cannot begin to rival a panorama in price or effect, but it's easier on your wallet.

5 bd des Filles-du-Calvaire, 3e; tel.: 01.42.77.95.91; Métro: Filles-du-Calvaire;
Open Monday–Friday 10 A.M.–6 P.M.; Closed two weeks mid-August;
www.zuber.fr.

Art, Antiques, and Collectibles

VERREGLASS A marvelous rainbow of colors radiates within this small shop. Inside you discover superb pieces of glassware as old as the nineteenth century and as recent as from the 1960s. After many years working at the flea markets, Claudius Breig opened his glass showcase in the then up-and-coming neighborhood of the Bastille. His reputation grew, and now collectors and antiques dealers from all over the world call for his most select pieces of European glassware, the majority of which are from the twentieth century. Monsieur Brieg also sells wrought iron pieces, mostly in verdigris from the late thirties, crafted into candlesticks, sconces, and the like, all reasonably priced from €10 to €500.

32 rue de Charonne, 11e; tel./fax: 01.48.05.78.43; Métro: Ledru-Rollin;
Open Tuesday–Saturday noon–7 P.M.

More Art

If it's contemporary you're after, find your way to the **Galerie Pierre Passebon** (5 passage Charles Dallery, 11e; tel.: 01.48.06.00.22; Métro:

Voltaire) to admire works from some of today's most happening photographers, artists, and artisans.

Remember to check out the funky art galleries throughout the Bastille.

And if you happen to be in Paris in October, you are really in luck; this is when the **Génie de la Bastille** (www.legeniedelabastille.net) usually takes place, an open house held by the local artists and art galleries that allows you to take a peek behind closed doors until midnight every day for almost a week!

Jewelry, Shoes, and Accessories

DUELLE   You're apt to walk right past this boutique because it's no bigger than a shoebox, but don't, or you'll miss the area's best selection of avant-garde costume jewelry. Here, plastic, resin, and fabric have been worked, molded, and sewn into a variety of forms. The shop has been here for more than twenty years and the jewelry and accessories are just as kooky as ever.

21 rue Daval, 11e; tel.: 01.47.00.93.72; Métro: Bastille;
Open Tuesday–Saturday 11:30 A.M.–7:30 P.M.

Womenswear

STELLA CADENTE   Enter the modern dollhouselike interior of this lavender-colored boutique to discover the delightfully feminine creations of Stella Cadente. (The name is Italian for shooting star; the Ukranian designer's name behind this label is more of a mouthful.) Amid the ruffles, feathers, sequins, and embroidery, there's enough sophistication here to render these fashions and accessories exceedingly desirable. (Count on spending €190 on average for a skirt; €255 for a dress.) Miss Me, the signature fragrance of Stella Cadente, perfectly embodies the spirit of nostalgia and romance of this label; its hints of sugar and almond remind you of the smell of Grandmother's kitchen.

93 quai de Valmy, 10e; tel.: 01.42.09.66.60; Open daily 11 A.M.–7:30 P.M.;
www.stella-cadente.com.

Women's and Men's Fashions

ANTOINE & LILI Pepto pink, apple green, and sunshine yellow store-fronts signal that you've arrived at *le village* of Antoine & Lili on the banks of the Canal Saint-Martin. This always colorful, sometimes zany French label is responsible for the rebirth of this neighborhood, and it's no surprise: The eclectic collection of "stuff" sold here, in addition to the store's own men's, women's, and children's fashions, reflects the multicultural influences of this part of Paris. Their clothes should make you feel happy when you wear them and, of course, there's often a playful twist such as mixing flowers with polka dots on a shirt or skirt. (Average price of a skirt is €95.) You can always find some good basics here, too. As for the home décor boutique, anything goes, particularly if it's kaleidoscope-colored and very kitsch. Few are original creations; most have been culled from around the world.

> 95 quai Valmy, 10e; tel.: 01.40.37.41.55 (men's and women's clothing and
> accessories); 01.40.37.58.14 (home décor); 01.40.37.34.86 (children's);
> Open Monday 11 A.M.–7 P.M.; Tuesday–Friday 11 A.M.–8 P.M.;
> Saturday 10 A.M.–8 P.M.; Sunday noon–7 P.M.; www.antoineetlili.com.

Métro stations for the above quai Valmy addresses are J. Bonsergent or République.

More Women's and Men's Fashions

You'll find casual, outback-ready togs here at the multibrand store **Comptoir du Desert** (72–74 rue de la Roquette, 11e; tel.: 01.47.00.57.80; Métro: Bastille). A far more conservative outpost for men's and women's fashions than elsewhere in the area.

Specialty Boutiques

ANNE HOGUET There once was a time when Paris boasted fifteen workshops that made fans—today only one is left, Anne Hoguet, a fourth-generation fanmaker. Her patrons include Christian Lacroix, Karl Lagerfeld, the Opéra de Paris, and other discriminating people in search of a bit of repair for one of their treasured fans or perhaps the purchase of a new little wonder. You can buy a fan here for as much as several hundred euros or as little as €6. You may also visit the **Musée de l'Eventail** (Fan Museum), a converted part of Madame Hoguet's atelier that displays historic creations made from antique papers, feathers, lace, chamois, and even Plexiglas.

2 bd de Strasbourg, 10e; tel.: 01.42.08.19.89; fax: 01.42.08.30.91; Métro: Strasbourg-Saint-Denis; Boutique open Monday–Friday 9 A.M.–12:30 P.M. (except Thursday, when lunch begins at noon) and 2–6 P.M.; Museum open Monday–Wednesday 2–6 P.M.

BASTILLE OPTIC   Looking for a pair of loony *lunettes* (eyeglasses) or some specs with just a bit of zip? Whether you're an artist, a gallery owner, an architect, or just someone out to modernize his or her image, Bastille Optic will provide you with one of Paris's best selections of contemporary eyewear from *créateurs* such as Anne et Valentin.

38 rue de la Roquette, 11e; tel.: 01.48.06.87.00; Métro: Bastille; Open Monday 2:30–7 P.M.; Tuesday–Saturday 10 A.M.–7:30 P.M.; bastilleoptic@noos.fr.

CYCLES LAURENT   Anyone who knows a hoot about cycling knows that this sport is big in Europe, particularly in France. If you want to outfit yourself like a pro, stop into Cycles Laurent, probably the best-known shop in Paris for high-end racing bikes. Most of the major French brands are represented here, including Mavic (wheels) and Look (carbon frames and pedals). An elite address for both track and road bikes, the shop prides itself on its custom sizing of frames, a job that can be done with great precision whether you make it to this small old-school store or call in your measurements. The day I was here they were shipping two frames to the United States for individuals who had phoned in their measurements. And if you're considering bringing your bike over to perhaps trace the Tour de France route, their full-service bike shop can reassemble it for you after your flight.

9 bd Voltaire, 11e; tel.: 01.47.00.27.47; Métro: République or Oberkampf; Open Monday–Saturday 10 A.M.–6:45 P.M.; www.cycleslaurent.com.

GEORGES KRIVOSHEY   Argentinean Georges Krivoshey perpetuates the near-forgotten art of silk painting—a craft popular in France during the eighteenth century—in his considerably off-the-beaten-path (actually rather hidden) atelier on the second floor of this building. Make an appointment to avoid disturbing the artist at work, and once you find your way in, you'll be enraptured by the exquisite beauty of his creations. Most of Monsieur Krivoshey's classic fruits, flowers, and birds have been deftly painted onto deeply colored velvets; others grace more delicate pieces of taffeta and silk. His works have nothing to do with the paintings of Elvis, moonrises, and the like plastered on velvet that you see at roadside stands in rural America—Monsieur Krivoshey's masterpieces are rendered with far more finesse and subtlety. In fact, he worked on the restoration of the painted velvet furnishings of the Château de Fontainebleau and is often in demand by Paris's top couture houses. Whether you are shopping for a signature piece in the form of a pillow, a throw, a bedspread, a painting (€500 to €3,500), or a sumptuous bustier perfect for a romantic evening (about €500), you will be acquiring a veritable work of art.

46 rue Albert-Thomas, 10e; tel./fax: 01.40.40.04.35; Métro: J. Bonsergent; By appointment only; www.atelierkrivoshey.com.

VIADUC DES ARTS

A destination in itself—particularly for lovers of arts and crafts—the Viaduc des Arts houses nearly fifty craft shops and ateliers in a half-mile stretch of the twelfth arrondissement along the avenue du Daumesnil, near Bastille and République. Officially opened in 1998, it took ten years to transform these mid-nineteenth-century arches, which served as a railroad viaduct, into an arts center of quality and broad appeal. Many of the artisans have come here from the provinces. Probably the best known and most interesting are those from the **Ateliers du Cuivre et de l'Argent** (113 av Daumesnil, 12e; tel. 01.43.40.20.20; www.atelier-du-cuivre.com), a transplant from Villedieu-les-Poêles (God's Town of Frying Pans), a bastion of tradition in Normandy long known for its copperware. Stop by **Maison Fey** (15 av Daumesnil, 12e; tel.: 01.43.41.22.22), a workshop originally from Paris that showcases superbly crafted boxes that look like stacks of leather-bound books—the perfect volumes for hiding prized possessions!

The house of **Guillet** (1 bis av Daumesnil, 12e; tel.: 01.43.40.80.00; www .guillet-fleurs.fr) has been handcrafting exquisite silk, cotton, and leather flowers in their Paris workshops since 1896. They've kept the couture houses blooming with garden-fresh *faux fleurs* for many years. The fact that they moved their Left Bank boutique here is a testament to the good shopping that the Viaduc offers. Many of their pieces are quite affordable, too, and each one would make a stunning *souvenir de Paris* pinned on your lapel, hats, evening bag, or waist once you're back home.

Le Viaduc Café (43 av Daumesnil, 12e; tel.: 01.44.74.70.70) is a good place to go for a little respite, but to recharge your batteries, I suggest you take a brisk walk upstairs along the beautiful expanse of the viaduct.

Most of the shops at the Viaduc des Arts are open Monday–Saturday 10 A.M.–7 P.M., although some close during lunch; some are open Sunday afternoons; many close in August. The closest Métro is near 109-113 av Daumesnil: Gare de Lyon, exit rue de Challon.

Markets

The covered and outdoor markets at the place d'Aligre (Métro: Ledru-Rollin) provide one of the greatest spectacles of all the markets: Here the ambiance is not unlike that of North African souks. Open Tuesday to Sunday 8:30 a.m.–1:30 p.m., the **Marché Aligre** also touts a large and often interesting selection of *fripes* (antique clothing) and *brocantes* (secondhand items).

You may also swing by the **Bastille Market** on boulevard Richard Lenoir between rue Amelot and rue Saint-Sabin; Métro: Bastille; Open Thursday 1 A.M.–2:30 P.M and Sunday 7 A.M.–3 P.M.

Note that the east side of Paris—known to be predominantly working-class—boasts a significant number of markets (in addition to the two above), many of which have existed for centuries.

My Special Suggestions

Perfect Respites

CHEZ PAUL   A traditional bistrot with a New Wave twist. The clientele, an eclectic mix of Paris's avant-garde artists, writers, and theater people, crowds this restaurant for all the right reasons: It is conveniently located to their lofts; the help is hip and particularly friendly; and, most of all, the food is delicious. A good handful of tourists arrives on any given day or night, but this hardly detracts from the genuine flavor of this quirky gathering place. Thick, juicy steaks and succulent *confit de canard* (duck preserved in its own fat) are served up with golden-brown fried potatoes and washed down with generous amounts of Bordeaux wine. It's best to reserve a table for dinner.

13 rue de Charonne, 11e; tel.: 01.47.00.34.57; fax: 01.48.07.02.00;
Métro: Bastille; Moderate; Open daily year-round for lunch and dinner.

HÔTEL DU NORD This landmark establishment—made famous in the 1938 film of the same name starring the renowned French actress Arletty—has been impeccably restored and now gleams with the same sparkle reverberating throughout the Canal Saint-Martin neighborhood. Stop in here for a respite—big or small—to soak up the warm and cozy ambiance of the hotel's bar and restaurant, which has been made to resemble a large living room/library. Oh, and don't ask about the room rates (like I did!). Hôtel du Nord is a totally fictional hotel, made for the movies.

102 quai de Jemmapes, 9e; tel.: 01.40.40.78.78; Métro: J. Bonsergent,
République, or Goncourt; Open daily 9:30 A.M.–1:30 A.M.

PAUSE CAFÉ BASTILLE A favorite hangout for artists (and for those pretending to be artists), the Pause Café also offers a bona fide glimpse of local color. Savor its homemade quiche and *plats du jours,* or munch on *une salade à l'italienne* in this laid-back setting, worthy of its following.

41 rue de Charonne, 11e; tel.: 01.48.06.80.33; Métro: Ledru-Rollin; Inexpensive;
Open Monday–Saturday 7:30 A.M.–2 A.M.; Sunday 9 A.M.–8 P.M.

MORE PERFECT RESPITES A ton of restaurants have been opening up around the Canal Saint-Martin area these past few years, so you definitely have a lot to choose from. There's not one, however, that inspires me to say you must go there. The views from the terrace of **Chez Prune** (71 quai de Valmy, 10e; tel.: 01.42.41.30.47) are particularly enjoyable; but if you can't sit outside, you'll have to contend with a lot of smoke inside this popular restaurant. For a much quieter lunch or tea (and perhaps a better meal), go nearby to **Le Repère** (29 rue Beaurepaire, 10e; tel.: 01.42.01.41.20).

Back toward the other end of quai Valmy, **Le Sporting** (3 rue des Récollets, 10e; tel.: 01.46.07.02.00; www.lesporting.com) presents a more sophisticated dining experience that I'm anxious to try.

Nearby, you'll find a more intimate setting at **Le Verre Volé** (67 rue de Lancry, 10e; tel.: 01.48.03.17.34). Here, surrounded by a wine collection the envy of any *sommelier,* you can lunch in this cubbyhole of a wine bar, then shop for a good bottle or two before you go.

Métro stations for the above restaurants are J. Bonsergent or République. Over by the Bastille area, there are many restaurants and bars going off at night. (Some are actually open for lunch as well.) If you really want to make the scene and groove to some loud Latin music, cha-cha on over to **Barrio Latino** (46 rue du Faubourg-Saint-Antoine; tel.: 01.55.78.84.75; Métro: Bastille; www.buddha-bar.com), a great place to dine, dance, and take in the feverishly exciting Cuban décor.

Recommended Hotel

HÔTEL CROIX DE MALTE In keeping with the vibrant spirit of the neighborhood, this hotel is awash with colorful prints and lively murals. It doesn't have the amenities of the grander hotels, but the service is most friendly. The rooms are clean and bright and very reasonably priced. And the location is more in fashion than ever!

5 rue de Malte, 11e; tel.: 01.48.05.09.36; fax: 01.43.57.02.54;

Métro: République; Two-star hotel; Inexpensive; www.croixdemalte-paris-hotel.com.

Favorite Tours

BASTILLE It only takes a bit of poking around to delight in the innumerable riches of the Bastille. From fancy furniture to funky frippery, this neighborhood enjoys a happy balance of tradition and the offbeat.

I suggest you start at the beginning of the rue de la Rocquette at the place de la Bastille (note that the restaurant La Tour d'Argent is not the famous one) and work your way in. The best Métro stop for the Bastille tour is Bastille. Don't forget about **boutique of the Opéra** de la Bastille either, located at the foot of the Opéra, which gives star billing to many opera-related gift items.

CANAL SAINT-MARTIN/BEAUREPAIRE I think your best bet is to begin at Métro République, exit toward the boulevard Magenta, and take rue Beaurepaire up toward the Canal. As always, look down the cross streets as you go and don't be afraid to get a little lost. Work your way north toward the Canal Saint-Martin and plan to spend awhile leisurely strolling and browsing until you've found just the right charming bistrot to sit down in for an hour or more.

Note that if you'd like to explore more of this side of town, you could seek out **Bercy-Village,** east of the Parc de Bercy sports complex in the Twelfth; Métro: Cour Saint-Emilion. Here, old wine warehouses have been converted into twenty stores and lots of restaurants (mostly chain-type); Open daily 11 A.M.–9 P.M.; restaurants until 2 A.M. You can even catch a film in one of their new cinemas. I find it a little too Disneyland-like for my taste, but it does provide another nice distraction, so maybe it will be just the thing for you.

8

The Sixteenth

PARISIAN PREPPY

The Sixteenth is not only a Paris arrondissement but a way of life as well. To be *seizième* (Sixteenth) is to be BCBG *(bon chic, bon genre)*, the French equivalent of preppy. French preppies lead lives amazingly similar to those of their American counterparts. As in the United States, BCBGs are found at the heads of major corporations; BCBGs work at the Bourse (stock market) and hold top-level positions at the most reputable banks; and BCBG moms make sure that household activities and family obligations run like clockwork.

The differences? Only the real BCBGs know how to properly pull off a *baisemain* (hand kiss)—which is actually more of a gesture toward kissing the hand rather than a real kiss—stay in and play bridge on Saturday nights, or organize suitable *rallyes* for their daughters (soirées intended to expose young women to a potentially good catch). In France, class is far more entrenched than in the United States and it creates a different set of rules that dictate how one is to live and act, whether young or old.

All the stately nineteenth- and early twentieth-century buildings along the elegant, tree-lined streets of the sixteenth arrondissement provide *des très bonnes adresses* (excellent addresses) for France's upper crust. Although the rents here are among the highest of the capital, the Sixteenth is one of the most residential areas in Paris. Like many other European cities, the wealthy are settled in the western part of the French capital or in the western suburbs, where they evade pollution blown east by the prevailing westerly winds. (Factories are located to the north and east of most European metropolises.)

Not too many major tourist attractions are found in the Sixteenth, either, which makes the streets and the shopping areas less crowded and more devoted to the local clientele.

You'll notice that I haven't indicated any charming tearooms for a stop-off during these three tours. In the Sixteenth, it is more widely accepted to invite friends over for tea or to go to Ladurée, the genteel tea parlor on rue Royale (see "Right Bank" description, p. 118). Throughout, you will recognize the true BCBGs by their Chanel suits, Hermès scarves, pearl necklaces, tweed jackets, oxford shirts, Westons, Burberry trench coats and, nowadays, Docksiders and Ralph Lauren polo shirts. The men are often accompanied by their faithful Labradors (good for those traditional weekend hunts); the women carry well-groomed and extremely well-behaved Chihuahuas in their arms.

Food and Wine Purveyors

LENÔTRE This is one of many Lenôtre boutiques in Paris, all temples to French gastronomy made possible by the highly developed culinary skills of Gaston Lenôtre, a Frenchman from the provinces who opened his first pastry shop in the capital in 1947. Call it haute take-out. Here you can buy all the essential components of a primo gourmet picnic or a complete dinner at home for eight. (Believe it or not, this is what many of the people from this neighborhood do.) From roasted quail to chocolate éclairs to a cornucopia of gourmet gift items, Lenôtre has what it takes to put your taste buds in overdrive. No wonder Lenôtre has expanded throughout the world; there's even a boutique in Las Vegas at the prestigious Paris-Las Vegas (where else?).

48 av Victor-Hugo, 16e; tel.: 01.45.02.21.21; fax: 01.45.00.34.63;

Métro: Victor-Hugo; Expensive; Open Monday–Thursday 9:30 A.M.–9 P.M.;

Friday–Sunday 9 A.M.–9 P.M.

Table Arts, Home Décor, and Linens

BACCARAT *Hou la la!* This is *the* place that wowed me the most during my research for this book. Crystal aficionado or not, you absolutely must plan a visit to this extraordinary house of Baccarat. It embodies all the luxe, innovation and, most of all, *création* for which this almost 250-year-old company is renowned.

Baccarat moved its headquarters here in 2003 from the dreary rue de Paradis, after transforming the private mansion of Viscountess Marie-Laure de Noailles into one of the world's most exceptional showcases. French designer Philippe Starck morphed this already grand residence into a dramatic space that marries tradition with modernity, highbrow sophistication with street culture, and history with sensory sensations in the most seductive way. A crimson carpet trimmed with little fiber optics (reminiscent of glittering crystal) leads you through the dimly lit interior of this striking establishment to the boutique, gallery-museum, and restaurant.

The Cristalleries de Baccarat were founded in 1764 by the Bishop of Metz during the reign of Louis XV. Baccarat crystal has often been referred to as "the crystal of kings," and its degree of purity has granted it a place at the world's most eminent tables. The crystal in the main art de vivre room is so magnificently displayed that it wasn't until I spotted very discreet prices that I realized that it was also for sale. The bishop would certainly be proud today.

More subdued lighting surrounds you in the jewelry and accessories rooms, which resemble the kinds of private nooks you find at fancy jewelers. (Baccarat, in fact, collaborates with place Vendôme jewelers for some of their jewelry creations priced here between €80 and €1 million.) But just when you think that this looks way over the top, Starck whips you back to reality by leaving the walls rough, their only embellishment the faded script of old building notes (scribbled notations made by the original architects and builders).

Probably the biggest hit of this whole enterprise has been the **Crystal Room,** the former dining room of the mistress of the house, which was converted into a luxurious restaurant where you dine off of fine china and sip wine from ruby red Baccarat crystal glasses. As of this writing, the waiting list is still one to two months long; however, light lunches are served at a few tables in the hallway, also referred to as *la galerie*. It's not nearly as divine, but here there shouldn't be much of a wait. You may also have afternoon tea in the Crystal Room, which is a lovely alternative. If you have a special event to celebrate—particularly one that takes place during the summer—reserve the boudoir room, which can accommodate eight to eleven diners. There's no extra charge for this privileged enclave and you also benefit from a grand terrace. The lunch menu at the Crystal Room is priced at €75 per person; dinner rings in at €120.

You may take an audio tour of the museum (about 45 minutes long) that is included in the €7 admission price.

11 place des Etats-Unis, 16e; tel.: 01.40.22.11.00 and 01.40.22.11.10 (restaurant); fax: 01.40.22.11.99 (restaurant); Open Monday–Saturday 10 A.M.–7 P.M.; Restaurant open same days for lunch, tea, and dinner; Métro: Boissière; www.baccarat.fr. ✗

NOËL No, Noël does not specialize in Christmas decorations, but it does sell luxury linens for the home, fine enough to have dressed Mrs. Henry Ford's table, and to have swaddled Prince Charles. It all began in 1883 with Madame Noël selling exquisite Alençon and Venetian embroideries in her Left Bank boutique. The business was later taken over by her son, who revived a style of embroidery that had been in vogue during the eighteenth century. Famous for its more than thirteen thousand hand-embroidered or hand-guided embroidery designs, Noël showcases its many grand creations in a light and airy boutique that has become the destination for linens connoisseurs worldwide. Only the most precious fabrics are used, including long-fiber cotton, linen batiste, voile, and organdy on all their tablecloths, bed linens, terry cloth robes and towels, linens for baby, and accessories. You may buy finished items from the store's collection, purchase a do-it-yourself embroidery kit, or splurge on a custom-made piece. Prices, overall, befit the heirloom quality of the products.

1 av Pierre-1er-de-Serbie, 16e; tel.: 01.40.70.14.63; Métro: Iéna; Open
Monday–Saturday 10:30 A.M.–7 P.M.; www.noel-paris.com.

VERRERIE CRISTALLERIE D'ARQUES The same company that produces most of the glassware used in bistrots and restaurants throughout
France also prides itself on a sparkling collection of crystal lovely enough
to grace the world's most stylish tables. Both handblown and pressed
glass techniques are employed in the making of this crystal, all of which
contains a lead content of more than 24 percent. Reasonably priced.

6 place des Etats-Unis, 16e; tel.: 01.47.23.31.34; Métro: Boissière;
Open Monday–Saturday 10 A.M.–6:30 P.M.; www.arcdecoration.com.

Jewelry, Shoes, and Accessories

J. M. WESTON Located on the other side of the place Victor-Hugo is
French shoemaker Weston. These superbly crafted French men's and
women's shoes have people coming to this boutique in droves. The prices
are so steep, averaging between €380 and €570, it's a wonder they have so
much appeal, but a pair of Westons will almost never wear out. The styles
and colors are all very classic, and there is a wide assortment from which
to choose. Don't be surprised if you see a lot of young people in the boutique; Westons are just as popular with French high-schoolers as with
high-level executives.

97 av Victor-Hugo, 16e; tel.: 01.47.04.23.75; Métro: Victor-Hugo;
Open Monday–Saturday 10 A.M.–7 P.M.; www.jmweston.com.

Womenswear

LOLITA LEMPICKA The Lempicka look—feminine and classic with a
coquettish touch of fantasy—distinguishes Lolita from the rest of Parisian designers. Playful trimmings of lace and cutwork embroidery are
often used to take the seriousness out of more traditional styles.

Her evening dresses and bridal gowns are real showstoppers and, for
the most part, sensationally seductive. They are the sort of dresses that can

instantly make you feel gorgeous when the fit is right. I have a luscious three-quarter-length dress with matching bolero jacket, all in a heavy chartreuse silk trimmed with lavender lace. It makes me feel like a million bucks whenever I put it on—and I've had it for ages!

46 av Victor-Hugo, 16e; tel.: 01.45.02.14.46; Métro: Victor-Hugo; Open Tuesday–Saturday 11 A.M.–6:45 P.M.; closed in August.

MAUD DEFOSSEZ Maud and her daughter keep women chic in a classic French way. Maud Defossez creations have always looked quite couture, but nowadays as at *chez les grandes maisons,* the look is not as dressy as it once was; instead there's a greater emphasis on comfort and packability. Their big sellers of late are washable fashions made from *microfibre.* Today's woman travels more than ever before but that doesn't mean she wants to look any less elegant. All French-made in a variety of stylish colors, the quality and the cuts are excellent (either in 100 percent cotton or wool depending on the season), and prices range from €190 for a top to €650 for a jacket. Sizes run up to 46, higher for a special order. No wonder Maud dresses so many of the ambassadors' wives.

33 rue des Sablons, 16e; tel.: 01.47.27.34.33; fax: 01.56.28.18.46; Métro: Trocadéro; Open Monday–Saturday 10:30 A.M.–1 P.M. and 2–7 P.M.; closed in August.

Women's and Men's Fashions

HERVÉ CHAPELIER Stop in here if you missed Monsieur Chapelier's basic-looking nylon bags and knapsacks, which come in a variety of expressive colors, in his Left Bank shop. Here the selection is not nearly as vast, but this will also give you a chance to see the biggest assortment of Hervé Chapelier sweaters. Shetland, lamb's wool, cashmere, camel hair, wool and angora blend, merino, and wool from sheep in Geelong, Australia, are fashioned into classic sweaters and scarves expressly for this boutique by the finest knitting mills across the English Channel. Count on spending about €140 for a wool and angora blend V-neck, €180 for a downy Geelong sweater.

13 rue Gustave-Courbet, 16e; tel.: 01.47.27.83.66; Métro: Pompe or Victor-Hugo; Open Monday 2–7 P.M.; Tuesday–Saturday 10:15 A.M.–1:30 P.M. and 2:30–7 P.M.; www.hervechapelier.com.

More Women's and Men's Fashions

The abundance of classic clothing stores in the Sixteenth—particularly in the triangle of rue de la Pompe, rue Longchamp, and rue Gustave-Courbet—makes the area look like a shopper's paradise for men's and women's traditionally styled fashions. Don't let the words *classic* and *tradition* throw you, though, because this being France, you can bet that most of the fashions have a certain zip to them that make them anything but boring. I like shopping here not only because I prefer classic styles, but also because the prices in these shops tend to be quite reasonable. On the rue de la Pompe, look in at **Harrison** (no. 130, tel.: 01.47.27.96.62), **Phist** (no. 130, tel.: 01.47.27.47.41), and **John Demersay** (no. 133, tel.: 01.45.53.05.15). **Renoma** (no. 129 bis, tel.: 01.44.05.38.25) corners the more sophisticated market with its fashions and accessories, many of which have been sported by certain French celebs. For shirts, men's pajamas, and accessories, swing by **Fil à Fil** (140 av Victor-Hugo; tel.: 01.47.04.55.74). Two shops on the rue Gustave-Courbet further delineate this area as a classic-clothing enclave: **Curling** (no. 6 and no. 8, tel.: 01.47.27.64.75 or 01.47.27.76.80; www.curling.fr) and **Axxon Marcus** (no. 10, tel.: 01.47.27.00.49). And if you haven't found what you're looking for yet, you can also try **Atelson** (93 rue de Longchamp tel.: 01.45.53.91.28). All these shops cater to both men and women.

Métro for all the above boutiques is Pompe, Victor-Hugo, or Trocadéro.

Children's Clothing, Shoes, and Furnishings

BONNICHON For more than one hundred years, Bonnichon has crafted fine-quality baby furniture and baby buggies for France's most pampered *bébés*. Cradles, cribs, beds, changing tables, and rockers are attractively displayed in pretty pastels and pure white. Each set is enhanced with Bonnichon's coordinating sheets, dust ruffles, and curtains, most of which have been hand-embroidered.

Its traditional-style prams are also quite grand, and in addition to its own brand, Bonnichon sells England's Silver-Cross, the Rolls Royce of baby carriages. The selection of baby outfits is just as prim and proper. The store will even create a custom-made trousseau for baby from its exquisite selection of fabrics, ribbons, and frills. Prices are high. If you aren't able to cart it home with you, Bonnichon will take care of shipping.

7 av Victor-Hugo, 16e; tel.: 01.45.01.70.17; Métro: Etoile;

Open Monday–Saturday 10–7 P.M.; www.bonnichoncreations.com.

LA CHÂTELAINE   This is where the ladies from the Sixteenth come to buy superior quality babies' gifts that guarantee a distinctively BCBG look as early as the cradle. La Châtelaine (the mistress of the château) features layette, smock dresses, and little boys' trousers of heirloom quality that only the elite (or the most extravagant) can afford. The store's baby furniture and trousseau-caliber house linens are equally luxurious and exclusive. And if you're a sentimental type, you're likely to swoon over La Petite Châtelaine, their "vintage" collection for girls and boys.

170 av Victor-Hugo, 16e; tel.: 01.47.27.44.07; fax: 01.47.27.19.85;

Métro: Pompe; Open Monday–Saturday 10 A.M.–7 P.M.; closed two weeks in August.

CHIPIE   Good old apple-pie American fashion with a French twist. The French certainly know how to turn our basics, like blue jeans, football sweaters, and knapsacks, into incredibly chic and fun pieces. Chipie does exactly that with its clothing and accessories for kids of all ages. The look for the adults is very *junior,* as the French would say, so you're probably better off focusing on the kids and teens in your entourage. And, remember, Chipie comes from the word *chiper* (to take or borrow), so that automatically implies sharing—even between boys and girls.

129 rue de la Pompe, 16e (children and adults); tel./fax: 01.47.27.60.01;

Métro: Pompe; Open Monday 11 A.M.–7 P.M.; Tuesday–Saturday 10 A.M.–1 P.M. and 2–7 P.M.; www.chipie.fr.

More Children's Clothing
PETIT BATEAU   (64 av Victor-Hugo, 16e; See "Right Bank" description p. 99)

Department Stores and Other Biggies

ETAM *"Fantastique!"* That's exactly what a particularly fashion-conscious friend says about this clothing and accessories store entirely devoted to *les femmes*. Etam's selection of bags and shoes is sure to strike you as particularly creative, and the prices are so low you'll probably want to buy a number of items. Lingerie and swimwear (in the summer) also take center stage, so you might just want to shop here before you hit the high-priced fashion houses. There are many Etam stores throughout Paris, but I like this location the best. Plus, you can check out the other stores on the street (mentioned below) at the same time.

67 rue de Passy, 16e; tel.: 01.55.74.00.74; Métro: La Muette;
Open Monday–Saturday 10 A.M.–7:30 P.M.; www.etam.com.

FRANCK ET FILS This large almost-department-type store caters to women in a big way. They've spiffed up their look in recent years so now you can enjoy shopping for stylish women's fashions and accessories here more than ever. Franck et Fils belongs to Le Bon Marché group, which is partly why their restaurant/tea salon is called **Café de la Grande Epicerie**. They serve and sell many of the same products found in the food halls of La Grande Epicerie, albeit on a very small scale.

80 rue de Passy, 16e; tel.: 01.44.14.38.00; fax: 01.44.14.38.99;
Métro: Muette; Open Monday–Friday 10 A.M.–7 P.M.; Saturday 10 A.M.–
7:30 P.M. ✕

PRISUNIC Like Monoprix, Prisunic is France's answer to Woolworth's. Amid much of the junky stuff of this Printemps-owned five-and-ten, you will definitely be able to unearth some typically French (and cheap) gift ideas that will make a hit back home. It's particularly fun to do this kind of shopping in an affluent neighborhood like the Sixteenth!

22 bis rue des Belles-Feuilles, 16e; tel.: 01.45.53.32.03; Métro: Pompe;
Open Monday–Saturday 9 A.M.–10 P.M.

PROMOD
76 rue de Passy, 16e; See "Right Bank" description p. 102.

Discount Shops

RÉCIPROQUE   I'm not much on buying secondhand clothing, but if you love wearing creations by Paris's top designers but can't afford the prices, then this *dépôt-vente* (consignment store) is for you. The men's and women's clothing, accessories, and gift items here are in excellent condition, clean, and best of all, up-to-date.

The women's store is particularly rich in big-name merchandise, since many of Paris's most fashionable women put their used clothing up for sale at Réciproque. Most of these women are slaves to fashion, which means that they change their wardrobes about every three months. That, of course, only makes Réciproque's stores all the more interesting! The display racks are clearly marked, mostly according to designer, and if you're a seasoned shopper, you'll do great here. Most of their goods are priced 30 to 70 percent below their original cost.

88, 92, 93, 95, 97 and 101 rue de la Pompe, 16e; tel.: 01.47.04.30.28;
Métro: Pompe; Open Tuesday–Friday 11 A.M.–7 P.M.; Saturday 10:30 A.M.–
7:30 P.M.; www.reciproque.fr.

Specialty Boutiques

L'ENTREPÔT   The entrance to this store is small and unassuming, but if you follow the stairs up to the first floor, you will enter a huge *entrepôt* (warehouse) lined with metal shelves displaying an incredibly wide and fun range of inexpensive gift ideas. Different sections of this loftlike space are filled with cards, bath products, T-shirts, kitchen accessories, dishes, useless but decorative gadgets, house linens, ready-to-wear, flashy boxer shorts, children's birthday party supplies, and much, much more.

50 rue de Passy, 16e; tel.: 01.45.25.64.17; fax: 01.40.50.89.82;
Métro: Muette; Open Monday–Saturday 10:30 A.M.–7 P.M.

KLOCYCLE   As you amble around Paris, particularly in the sixteenth arrondissement, you're sure to notice people zipping around on little scooters. The quintessence of the French scooter is the Solex, a light motorbike that you start by pedaling. It was introduced in the thirties, but the classic Solex really had its heyday in the sixties (think of Brigitte Bardot and Saint-Tropez). They almost died out for a while, but later reemerged. Today they are made in Hungary. Roland Kloeti, owner of this store, sells both the brand-spanking-new models and the vintage ones, completely reworked and presented here in mint condition (count on spending €700 to €900 for a model from the sixties and expect to wait about three months—the time to restore it—for delivery). They also sell some other French and European scooters and will readily ship abroad. Klocycle also plans to begin renting bikes and scooters (including Solex) soon—yippee!

104 rue Lauriston, 16e; tel./fax: 01.45.53.27.67; Métro: Boissière;
Open Monday 2–6 P.M.; Tuesday–Friday 8:30 A.M.–noon and 1:30–6 P.M.;
Saturday 9 A.M.–noon; klocycle@aol.com.

More Specialty Boutiques

For a little distraction from the many clothing boutiques of this area, check out **Bathroom Graffiti** at 98 rue de Longchamp (tel.: 01.47.04.23.12; Métro: Trocadéro), a fun-loving shop filled with lots of catchy gift ideas.

Shopping for cigars and/or luxury gift items in the sixteenth arrondissement? Go directly to avenue Victor-Hugo toward the Arc de Triomphe. Here you'll find two long-established boutiques sure to help you in your search: **Lemaire** (no. 59; tel.: 01.45.00.75.63) and **Boutique 22** (no. 22; tel.: 01.45.01.81.41). Métro for both is Etoile.

Markets

One of my favorite markets is the roving market on the avenue **President Wilson** (between place d'Iéna and rue Debrousse; Métro: Iéna or Alma-Marceau; Wednesdays and Saturdays 7 A.M.–2.30 P.M. This is where the chic ladies of the Sixteenth shop in search of prime foods for their families and evening entertaining.

If it's raining, you might want to go to the **Passy Covered Market** (place de Passy; Métro: Muette; Open Tuesday-Saturday 8:30 A.M.–1P.M. and 4–7:30 P.M.; Sunday 8:30 A.M.–1 P.M.)

My Special Suggestions

Beauté and Parfums

P. DE NICOLAÏ Because she grew up in the Guerlain family, developing a keen sense of smell became second nature to Patricia de Nicolaï, founder of this little-known perfume emporium. All the fragrances sold here have been created by this young woman in the laboratory located behind a glass window at the back of the boutique. This in itself provides you with the rare opportunity of seeing the workplace of the *parfumeur*, made up of hundreds of meticulously arranged vials and one small scale. Here, infintesimal doses of extracts are measured in order to achieve a perfectly balanced mixture of scents (highly complex perfumes may be composed of some one hundred extracts).

You may either purchase one of P. de Nicolaï's fragrances in its own distinguished *flacon*, or buy it separately and choose from the luxurious collection of handblown glass and crystal bottles sold in the boutique. Heavenly bath and body products are also sold here.

69 av Raymond-Poincaré, 16e; tel.: 01.47.55.90.44; Métro: Victor-Hugo; Open Monday–Friday 10 A.M.–7 P.M.; Saturday 10 A.M.–1 P.M. and 2–7 P.M.; www.parfumnicolai.com.

Perfect Respites

LA BUTTE CHAILLOT Elegance has no limits in this part of Paris, comfortably poised on the rim of the Right Bank within the Sixteenth. This "baby bistrot" of renowned chef Guy Savoy is not at all babyish in appearance. Expect to enjoy a superb meal in a sleek, sophisticated décor—a perfect ending to a lovely day spent in this part of town.

110 bis, av Kléber, 16e; tel.: 01.47.27.88.88; Métro: Open daily except Saturday lunch; closed three weeks in August; www.buttechaillot.com.

G.R. 5 Avid walkers and hikers who have done a bit of trekking through France know that the G.R. in G.R. 5 stands for *grande randonnée*, or "big hike." There are G.R.s across this Gallic land, and if you've spent any time on them, you know that you need to fill yourself with hearty meals along the way. Shopping and touring can work up an appetite, too, so even if you have not just climbed Mont Blanc, I strongly urge you to plan a meal here to enjoy some delicious mountain cuisine. This is one of my favorite addresses in Paris, and I've enjoyed many memorable meals here in this rustic setting with red and white checked tablecloths, savoring their specialty raclettes and fondues. Raclette, incidentally, refers to the cheese that is scraped *(raclé)* from the wheel once it has been grilled to desired doneness. This, served up with some smoked ham and sausages, potatoes, and little pearl onions and pickles, is what you'd call a bit of alpine delight in the heart of Paris.

19 rue Gustave-Courbet, 16e; tel.: 01.47.27.09.84; Métro: Pompe or Victor-Hugo; Moderate; Open Monday–Saturday for lunch and dinner.

MORE PERFECT RESPITES **Brasserie Stella,** *the* classic brasserie of the Sixteenth, was refurbished not too long ago. Like most of the fine brasseries in Paris, this is where you can stop for lunch and dinner as well as for tea or a drink. Situated in the BCBG area at 133 avenue Victor-Hugo; tel.: 01.47.17.60.54; Métro: Victor Hugo. You're sure to see some quintessential *dames du seizième* here as well.

If you haven't noticed by now, I'm big on views and ambiance. **Café de l'Homme** (17 pl du Trocadéro, 16e; tel.: 01.44.05.30.15; Métro: Trocadéro; www.cafedelhomme.com), the restaurant at Trocadéro, has both, plus an extraordinary terrace that looks out on the Eiffel Tower. Come in the evening for a razzmatazz light show of France's best-known symbol.

Recommended Hotel

HÔTEL RAPHAEL Located on the edge of the eighth arrondissement but in the Sixteenth nonetheless is this intimate hotel that exudes all the elegance of *la vieille France.* It's a favorite among businesspeople—both for a stay or to delight in a fine meal—but it also can provide a most agreeable sojourn for leisure travelers. Its terrace restaurant, **Les Jardins Plein Ciel,** however, is nothing short of *formidable!* You'll marvel at some of the best panoramas of Paris up on their seventh floor, but you may also experience a superior culinary moment in this unparalled setting amid flowers, topiaries, and teak garden furniture. Menus are priced at €70 for lunch; €90 for dinner. Good news: You may also stop by for a refreshment outside of lunch or dinner times. The terrace restaurant is only open during fair weather, but it's best not to choose a windy day.

17 av Kléber, 16e; tel.: 01.53.64.32.00; Métro: Etoile; Restaurants open Monday–Friday for lunch and dinner; Terrace restaurant also open Saturday night for dinner and daily 3:15–10:30 P.M. for a drink or tea; Four-star hotel and member of the Leading Small Hotels of the World: Expensive to very expensive; www.raphael-hotel.com. ✕

Favorite Tours

VICTOR HUGO From L'Etoile to the first part of the avenue Victor-Hugo, you'll still find a few big names, such as Céline, that have opened up for the ladies of the Sixteenth, who have a hard time making it over to the nearby eighth arrondissement. Many of the people who live in this part of town never shop elsewhere, which explains why the shopping here is so good. ("If they won't come to us, we'll go to them" seems to be the philosophy of the store owners in this neighborhood.) The fashion designers in this part of town tend to feature the more classic side of their collections, unlike what is shown on avenue Montaigne or rue du Faubourg-Saint-Honoré. To me, the biggest reason for venturing to this section of avenue Victor-Hugo is to go to womenswear designer Lolita Lempicka, particularly since this is now her only boutique in Paris. Métro: Etoile, Kléber, or Victor-Hugo.

BCBG The Pompe/Longchamp/Gustave-Courbet triangle is flush with men's and women's clothing shops that feature classic (but by no means old and fusty!) fashions. Most of the boutiques have been heavily anglicized, as demonstrated by both their names and their selection of merchandise. You can actually walk here from the Victor-Hugo tour— just stroll down the avenue, stopping at Lenôtre and perhaps Weston along the way. Definitely plan a thorough investigation of the Réciproque shops on rue de la Pompe, where you're sure to find some killer bargains. If you want to begin near the BCBG triangle, rue de la Pompe is the closest Métro. If you start at place Victor-Hugo, the Métro is Victor-Hugo. Keep in mind that this area is fairly close to the **Musée du Vin** (Wine

Museum) at 5 square Charles-Dickens, tel.: 01.45.25.63.26; Métro: Passy or Trocadéro. Here you may enjoy lunch (best to reserve) and visit some vaulted cellars that date back to the Middle Ages. If you feel like being more of a tourist, the Eiffel Tower—and the many sun-filled cafés at the place du Trocadéro—are just a short distance away.

PASSY   The area around Passy is considerably more commercial, which means loads of shops, most of which I described in the Right Bank and Left Bank districts, that have branches here as well. If you want to start with culture, begin by viewing the extensive collection of Monet paintings and medieval manuscripts in the **Musée Marmottan** (2 rue Louis-Boilly; tel.: 01.44.96.50.33; www.marmottan.com). It is not only one of the most intimate museums in Paris, but also one of the least crowded, plus, it has recently been renovated. Then you could go to Franck et Fils for lunch and have a full afternoon to tour the rue de Passy. Métro for the museum and rue de Passy is Muette.

Note: You may incorporate a visit to Baccarat (see p. 262) fairly easily from any one of these tours, and I strongly suggest you do so!

9

Neuilly

SUBURB CHIC

Every large city has its chic suburb, or *banlieue chic*, but Neuilly (short for Neuilly-sur-Seine) is even more noteworthy because it's only a Métro station away from Paris. An extension of the Sixteenth, style-wise, for me an ideal day here would begin by going to the market at the place du Marché (open Sunday, Wednesday, and Friday 8 A.M. to 1 P.M.; Métro: Sablons). After marketing along with the well-turned-out dowagers and stylish ladies of the neighborhood, you could poke around some of the boutiques concentrated around place Parmentier on the rue de Chartres and rue Sablonville. Now you're ready for the real reason for venturing to Neuilly: superb beauty treatments. Clearly that's why the women here look so good!

Note: If you're here toward the end of May, you should attend the three-day show La Braderie de Neuilly, which draws some 750 antiques dealers to this tony suburb.

Womenswear

FRED LANSAC   For a bit of beautification of your wardrobe, go to Fred Lansac, a veritable institution for more than thirty-five years, now carried on by Monsieur Lansac's son. This shop is responsible for dressing some of the most fashionable ladies of Neuilly, the sixteenth, the seventeenth, and the seventh arrondissements—all very traditional neighborhoods. This is a particularly good place to come if you are in search of a dressy suit, a cocktail dress, or other suitable frocks for an out-of-the-ordinary occasion. Count on spending between €1,150 and €1,300 for a suit or a dress. Other more casual knit and synthetic ensembles are priced less and work well for travel. Many of the silhouettes have been designed for mothers of the bride or for large women. The overall look is French classic: Some may call it dowdy, but as Monsieur Lansac once stated, "I know how to cater to my clientele." Hats and accessories also sell here, *bien entendu.*

35 av du Roule, 92200 Neuilly-sur-Seine; tel.: 01.46.24.60.36;

fax: 01.47.22.04.20; Métro: Porte Maillot; Open Tuesday–Friday

9:30 A.M.–7 P.M.; closed the last week in July and all of August.

My Special Suggestions

Beauté and Parfums

CARLOTA Carlota is *the* place to go for a real French manicure. The only thing is that French manicures are not really French: They originated in the United States, in fact. Originally, a Frenchwoman tried to introduce them in her native land, but when the French stuck up their fine aquiline noses to her enterprise, she trotted it off to America. The manicures caught on big there so, in typical French fashion, the French decided to adopt them. A French manicure involves applying an opaque "liner" on the outer rim of the nail, then topcoating the whole surface with a more transparent polish. The result looks prettiest with combinations of pink and white or beige and cream. This and other nail and hand treatments are available at Carlota. And its technicians are real experts. Plan on spending €39 for a treatment that will leave you with some of the silkiest hands and exquisite nails imaginable. Face and body treatments are also available.

15 rue de Sablonville, 92200 Neuilly-sur-Seine; tel.: 01.47.47.12.12;

fax: 01.47.47.99.01; Métro: Porte Maillot; 16 av Hoche, 8e; tel.: 01.42.89.42.89;

fax: 01.42.89.46.86; Métro: Etoile; Open Tuesday–Saturday 10 A.M.–7 P.M.; closed one week mid-August; www.carlota.com. ★ 👜

INSTITUT CLARINS As early as 1954, long before aromatherapy became a buzzword, Jacques Courtin-Clarins was creating skin-care products with scents that completely enhanced your whole state of well-being. In fact, I know many people (including myself) that have become totally hooked on the fragrances of these all-natural products. When they see the results these seemingly magical creams, oils, and tonics have on their skin, they're smitten for life! Clearly, the plants and essential oils that make up these predominantly plant-based products promote external and internal healing in sometimes surprising ways.

Clarins sun creams (and self-tanners) are among the best-selling in the world, since Clarins is totally committed to taking care of people's skin and sunscreen is the best place to start. A visit to the Institut Clarins in Neuilly further confirms this commitment to excellent skin care. Here, skilled estheticians carry out a variety of specialized treatments designed to promote better vitality for your face, body, and spirit. Breathe in the glorious meadow of Clarins scents. That's where the healing begins.

You'll find the whole range of Clarins products at this luminous red and white boutique, including their best seller in France, Eau Dynamisante, a deliciously perfumed toilet water that you can spray all over yourself to make you feel instantly invigorated. For a considerably heavier scent, choose Par Amour, a sensual fragrance composed of roses, sandalwood, and other heady ingredients.

Treatments range in price from €62 to €75 and it's best to reserve (by phone or fax) one month in advance. Men are most welcome here, too, and, in fact, there's an extensive skin-care line for them.

4 rue Berteaux-Dumas, 92200 Neuilly-sur-Seine; tel.: 01.46.41.94.14.; fax: 01.46.41.94.16; Métro: Sablons; Open Monday–Friday 8:45 A.M.–7 P.M.; www.clarins.com. ★ 👜

Perfect Respite

DURAND DUPONT DRUGSTORE Plan to have lunch here at this large, happening restaurant amid a colorful tropical décor accented with teak furniture and palm trees. If the weather is nice, ask to be seated on their interior patio. The menu offers both traditional and more exotic entrées.

14 pl du Marché, 92200 Neuilly-sur-Seine; tel.: 01.41.92.93.00; Métro: Sablons; Moderate; Open daily 8 A.M.–2 A.M.

PART THREE

More Shopping

10

Flea Markets

PORTE DE CLIGNANCOURT/SAINT-OUEN   Parisians like to do a lot of grumbling about the fact that there are no longer any bargains *aux puces,* but the flea markets today still rank among their favorite places to go in search of the rare, the antiquated, and the extraordinary. Of course, the chances of paying next to nothing for a porcelain figurine that you later discover is worth a small fortune on the rue du Faubourg-Saint-Honoré are one in a million. An excursion to the flea markets should not be made solely with the intention of striking a deal, but more with the idea of experiencing the most fabulous buying and selling place on earth for antiques. (Some 120,000 to 150,000 people come here each weekend.)

Prices have been driven up at Clignancourt because antiques dealers come from all corners of the world in search of France's most treasured *antiquités.* Dealers usually come on Friday, when the crack of dawn sees the arrival of trucks, vans, and station wagons unloading the week's take from the provinces, producing goods tempting enough to whet the appetite of even the most blasé Madison Avenue antiques dealer. If you have enough gumption, you too may mingle among the collectors on Friday mornings in search of that rare find that would cost four times as much back home. If you can't quite get up the nerve to go on a Friday, Saturday mornings aren't bad, either. Start out early, stop at **Le Restaurant Paul-Bert** (20 rue Paul-Bert; tel.: 01.40.11.90.28) while the croissants are still warm at the counter, and then begin to *chine* (search) with the rest of Paris's antique buffs.

The flea markets at Clignancourt comprise over a dozen different markets. Each has its own personality and each is made up of countless stalls or shops (actually more than two thousand dealers in all) that sell an assortment of goods in all price ranges. Don't limit yourself to looking at the best and the most beautiful markets, because the true spirit of *les puces* lives in the shabbier stalls that sell secondhand goods and assorted tchotchkes that have not yet regained their polish of earlier years. As you stroll through the endless series of alleys filled with nineteenth-century curiosity items, turn-of-the-century memorabilia, and rusted metal parts, you'll have a greater sense of the feeble beginnings of this massive market, which was formed well over a century ago by Paris's most affluent ragpickers.

The **Marché Jule-Vallès** is probably the most typical example of this sort of lower-end marketplace. Often the best deals are found here, and it is not uncommon for Paris antique dealers to buy from Vallès, do a little fixing up, and resell the same goods for a hefty profit. The **Marché Paul-Bert** is somewhat similar to Vallès with considerably more charm because of its open-air stalls. The ambiance is quite villagelike; at lunchtime the dealers set their tables with red and white checked tablecloths and sit down to a crusty loaf of bread, cheese, and a bottle of wine. The antiques that are sold in these two markets are for the most part *brocantes,* "secondhand items" that are of less importance and value than full-fledged antiques.

The most handsome markets at Clignancourt are **Vernaison, Biron, Cambo,** and **Serpette.** Opened in 1920, Vernaison is the granddaddy of them all and to this day continues to be the biggest and most eclectic of the Clignancourt markets. Biron and Cambo are among the slickest, and haggling in these markets is best reserved for true pros. The **Marché Serpette**, which opened more than twenty-five years ago, is the dealers' favorite stomping ground because everything here is sold in mint condition. One of the more recent markets, the **Marché Malassis** (named after the field where the first traders set up their wares, which also happens to mean "poorly seated") houses more than one hundred exclusive boutiques in a pastel-colored castle reminiscent of the Mediterranean.

Part of a day at the flea markets should include a stop in one of the informal restaurants that have played an important role in the history of *les puces*. Traditional meals include *moules frites* (mussels in wine with French fries) or *boeuf gros sel* (tender pot roast) and can be found at **La Chope des Puces** (122 rue des Rosiers; tel.: 01.40.11.02.49), where you will be serenaded with *la chanson française* on weekends. There are more tasty meals and Yves Montand and Edith Piaf tunes served up with *l'accordéon* **Chez Louisette** (tel.: 01.40.12.10.14) at Marché Vernaison.

If you're going to the flea markets by Métro, you have to walk a good ten to fifteen minutes toward the outskirts of Paris from the porte de Clignancourt station. Often people make the mistake of getting caught up in the **Marché Malik** (one of the first markets, which used to specialize solely in *fripes*, or "used clothing") and become so turned off by the series of tacky clothing shops that they turn around and head back. You have to pass through part of this market to arrive at the good ones. Once you're on the rue des Rosiers (the main drag), all the other markets are clearly marked. If you're traveling by car, you're better off coming very early in the morning because the parking space is limited.

Antiquing at the flea markets is not unlike other antiquing in Paris, but here you will probably feel more comfortable with dickering down the prices. Although many of the dealers (especially at Biron and Cambo) now accept credit cards, it is best to come well supplied in cash (preferably euros). Cash also increases bargaining power, and if you're clever enough, you may be able to drive the price down by 25 to 35 percent. You have to know your limits, though, because some dealers are less flexible than others. There is no *détaxe* on items that are one hundred years old or more, and if you want to ship, that can be arranged at most of the stalls. The prices can be exorbitant; however, it may very well be worth it, considering all the money you have just saved by buying your French antiques in France.

Good luck and enjoy the *atmosphère*!

Métro: porte de Clignancourt; Open Saturday, Sunday, and Monday 7:30 A.M.– 7 P.M.; www.parispuces.com.

PORTE DE MONTREUIL   Certainly the most exotic of all of the Paris flea markets, porte de Montreuil is overrun with dime-store peddlers and *brocanteurs* that sell collectibles of mostly mediocre quality. Not for the skittish, but it can be very fun.

av de porte de Montreuil; Métro: porte de Montreuil; Open Saturday, Sunday, and Monday 8 A.M.–7 P.M.

PORTE DE VANVES   The flea market at porte de Vanves consists mainly of *brocanteurs* selling secondhand items. It is much smaller than Clignancourt and certainly less animated, but nonetheless can prove to be very amusing for the adventuresome antiques enthusiast. The first part of the market overflows with merchants selling new and cheap merchandise; you have to go at least halfway down before you find the good stuff.

porte de Vanves, porte Didot, av Georges Lafenestre, rue Marc Sangnier, 14e; Métro: porte de Vanves; Open Saturday and Sunday 7 A.M.–7:30 P.M.

Note: Hours for the above markets are approximate. Also remember that there's a flea market at the Marché Aligre; see "Bastille and République" description on p. 256 for more.

And There's More

For more antiquing, look in the local papers or check with your concierge for news about shows and exhibitions taking place during your stay. The magazine *Aladin* (www.aladinmag.com) is an excellent source of information. In the spring and fall, shows called *foires* or *brocantes* are often held in Paris at the place de la Bastille, Piscine Deligny, and Batignolles. On the fringes of the city, shows take place periodically at Vincennes, Chatou, and Le Bourget.

11

More Neighborhoods

All the establishments in this chapter are located outside the more tourist-oriented districts of Paris. In all instances, there's at least one particular boutique that I want to draw your attention to, and in some cases I've expanded the information to include other highlights in that neighborhood.

Fifteenth Arrondissement

LE CORDON BLEU BOUTIQUE This world-renowned culinary institution, founded in 1895, has developed an extensive line of gourmet foods, culinary accessories, books and videotapes, chef's wear, and tableware, most of which sells here in LeCordon Bleu's distinctive cobalt blue packaging. Some people are lucky enough to sign themselves up for a course or two at Le Cordon Bleu, but if you can't do that, try a little shopping!

8 rue Léon-Delhomme, 15e; tel.: 01.53.68.22.50; Métro: Vaugirard;
Open Monday–Friday 8 A.M.–7 P.M.; Saturday 8 A.M.–4 P.M.; www.cordonbleu.net.

Eighteenth Arrondissement

KUBE Expect the offbeat if you choose to stay in this hotel, located in a rough and remote part of Paris. But if you're looking to broaden your

286 | MORE NEIGHBORHOODS

horizons, this is just the place for you. Kube is cooler than cool and it's a luxury boutique hotel to boot! By the time you read this, chic fashion boutiques will probably be moving into what were once the neighborhood's Turkish cafés and Indian restaurants. And Kube boasts Paris's first icehouse bar, the **Ice Cube.** Yes, just like in the Great North. Don't worry: they supply the parkas, but do reserve.

1–5 passage Ruelle, 18e; tel.: 01.42.05.20.00; Métro: La Chapelle; Four-star hotel: Expensive; www.kubehotel.com. ✗

TATI The slogan of this almost sixty-year-old bargain basement bonanza is "*les plus bas prix*" ("the lowest prices"). That's exactly what you'll find in this Frenchified souk of sorts along with the masses from this colorful neighborhood. The store's pink and white checked bags—originally the carrying bag of choice for immigrants—today have achieved icon status as a cheeky fashion statement, so you must buy something, whether it's a T-shirt or a wedding dress.

4 bd Rochechouart, 18e; tel.: 01.55.29.50.00; Métro: Barbès;
Open Monday–Friday 10 A.M.–7 P.M.; Saturday 9:15 A.M.–7 P.M.; www.tati.fr.

Note: Marché Saint-Pierre, the fabric market at the foot of Montmartre (Métro: Anvers), is equidistant between this area and Pigalle (see p. 290). Here, housewives and struggling young designers ferret out every imaginable type of fabric at prices that are the best in Paris. You could very well take in part of the Eighteenth, Marché Saint-Pierre and Montmartre, and Pigalle in half a day or so.

Denfert/Daguerre/Alesia

LA BOUTIQUE DE L'ARTISANAT MONASTIQUE There is no big flashing sign that indicates this boutique, but once you find it, you'll wend your way down to an immense cellar devoted to the sale of the many arts and crafts and comestibles produced by the nuns and monks of France. You'll find lots of quality gift ideas here at competitive prices, such as hand-painted Limoges china, wooden toys, Provençal prints, the requisite cakes and liqueurs, lavender sachets, and embroidered table linens.

68 bis av Denfert-Rochereau, 14e; tel.: 01.43.35.15.76; Métro: Port-Royal;
Open Monday–Friday noon–6:30 P.M.; Saturday 2–7 P.M.; closed in August;
www.artisanat-monastique.com.

PARIS ACCORDÉON If you try to think of a musical instrument that
evokes all the nostalgia of France, chances are the accordion will first
come to mind. Invented in Austria in the early part of the nineteenth
century for the ladies of the court, where the fanlike appearance of this
instrument contributed to its success, it soon became very popular in
France. According to the owner of Paris Accordéon, Patrick Quichaud,
"Today, the accordion is found in virtually all types of music"—from the
traditional *musette* style to more jazzy tunes. And Monsieur Quichard
should know: He started taking lessons at this boutique when he was
seven. He and his wife, Lydie, own and operate this unique shop now, the
only store in France entirely devoted to *l'accordéon*. You can buy old or
new accordions (and you just might, when you take a look up close at the
many gleaming instruments on display here) or bring in your own to be
restored. They also sell books about accordions, CDs, and sheet music in
all genres with favorite accordion accompaniments, but you can also sign
up for lessons (in English) or arrange to hire an accordionist for your own
personal serenade. The shop's brightly painted yellow and red façade—
in the happy spirit of the accordion—is hard to miss.

80 rue Daguerre, 14e; tel.: 01.43.22.13.48; Métro: Denfert-Rochereau;
Open Tuesday–Friday 9 A.M.–noon and 1–7 P.M.; Saturday 9 A.M.–noon and
1–6 p.m.; www.parisaccordeon.com.

More Daguerre

I fell in love with the rue Daguerre—uncontestably the most animated street of the fourteenth arrondissement—when I spent my junior
year of college here quite some time ago. Being a market street, the rue
Daguerre is always animated, but particularly when the merchants are
open Tuesday through Saturday from 8 A.M. to 1 P.M. and 4 to 8 P.M. For a
sweet and flaky *chausson aux pommes* (apple turnover), go to the bakery **Le
Moulin de la Vierge** (82 rue Daguerre, 14e; tel.: 01.43.22.50.55), where
I would pick up many an afternoon snack—and it's still just as good.

Many shops on rue Daguerre are of interest, but certainly the milliner **Divine** (39 rue Daguerre, 14e; tel.: 01.43.22.28.10) wins the award for the most quintessentially Parisian establishment. Stop in here to select a *châpeau* for a man or a woman—or perhaps a piece of retro costume jewelry—all of which will bestow upon you a distinctly Parisian air.

The Métro for the rue Daguerre is Denfert-Rochereau.

RUE D'ALÉSIA You can easily walk down to this discount alley from rue Daguerre and Denfert-Rochereau. Most of the shops are pretty mainstream and virtually all of the merchandise is last year's, but still, the savings are consistently good, about 50 percent off retail across the board. Just don't expect any really big names, except for **Sonia Rykiel,** which is worth the trip: 110–112 rue d'Alésia, 14e (women's and children's); tel.: 01.45.43.80.86 and at no. 64 (men's and Sonia de Sonia Rykiel); tel.: 01.43.95.06.13. **Cacharel Stock** (no. 114; tel.: 01.45.42.53.04) is one of my favorites for men, women, and children. **Dorotennis Stock** (no. 74; tel.: 01.45.42.40.49) is good for athletic types. They sell mostly womenswear and are big on ski outfits. I'll leave you to explore the rest of rue d'Alésia on your own. The closest Métro is Alésia; most of the stores are open Monday afternoons and Tuesday through Saturday from 10 A.M. to 7 P.M.

Paradise Street (rue de Paradis)

A quiet residential street for princely Parisians during the eighteenth century, the rue de Paradis began to change in 1831 when the Cristalleries de Baccarat moved in. Just a few streets away from the Gare de l'Est (the train station of the east), the rue de Paradis proved to be an ideal address for setting up the Paris showrooms of France's great crystal makers, all of whom were (and still are) located in the eastern part of France, mostly in Lorraine, and a few in Alsace and Champagne. Cristalleries de Saint-Louis followed Baccarat, and by the end of the nineteenth century, the great porcelain manufacturers of Limoges moved into the newly budding district as well.

Today, much has changed since Baccarat moved to the Sixteenth, which prompted the headquarters of other important French table arts companies to pull up stakes as well. This is still the place to shop if you are looking to invest in an entire table service, or if you just want to add a couple of place settings to an existing one, or even if you're looking for a better price on that stunning vase you saw in a rue Royale boutique. The prices here are the best in Paris because shop owners offer reductions from 15 to 20 percent, depending on the amount you purchase. This does not apply to hundred-dollar knickknacks, of course.

Here are the types of savings you can expect to encounter on rue de Paradis, as well as in numerous other Paris boutiques:

Note: The comparisons below are made to regular retail prices in the United States.

- Lalique, Daum, and Saint-Louis crystal costs 25 to 35 percent less; savings on Baccarat are about 30 percent.
- Buying Christofle and Ercuis/Raynaud silver-plated pieces in France saves you about 25 percent.
- Most brands of Limoges china cost about 30 to 40 percent less.
- Other European brands such as Wedgwood, Rosenthal, and Villeroy & Boch run about 25 percent less in France.

The approximate 15 percent savings from *détaxe* cancels out the shipping, insurance, and customs expenses incurred to send your merchandise home; any additional discounts that the boutique gives you only sweeten the pot. However, these savings may vary depending on the rate of the dollar.

Also, these savings depend largely on the prices practiced in your favorite stores back home. For example, in the United States, stores offer so many different types of promotions that it is often possible to purchase Baccarat crystal on sale (Lalique prices are more consistent), which means that it is always smart to check the prices at home before you go on a wild shopping spree in Paris.

The boutiques I've listed below carry a huge selection of table arts from France's top manufacturers. (And what they don't have in the store, they can usually order for you.) Nearly all the boutiques on the rue de

Paradis ship and accept orders by phone, fax, or e-mail from overseas. Most of these boutiques do a large amount of their business in export, so you won't have any problems finding salespeople who speak English.

AURELIA PARADIS
21 bis rue de Paradis, 10e; tel.: 01.42.47.07.00; fax: 01.48.00.92.85; www.aureliaparadis.com.

LIMOGES-UNIC/MADRONET The Madronet family has owned and operated some of the oldest and most respected establishments on the street since 1932.
34 rue de Paradis, 10e; tel.: 01.47.70.54.49; fax: 01.45.23.18.56; www.limoges-unic-madronet.com.

LUMICRISTAL The boutique, which marks the site where the first table arts retailer opened on the rue de Paradis 135 years ago, is located in the same building where Camille Corot, the great nineteenth-century landscape painter, was born and died.
22 bis rue de Paradis, 10e; tel.: 01.47.70.27.97; fax: 01.45.23.23.75; www.lumicristal.com.

The closest Métro stop for the rue de Paradis is Château d'Eau or Cadet; most of the stores here are open Monday through Friday from 10 A.M. to 7 P.M.; some are also open on Saturday; some close for a couple of weeks in August.

Note: The Canal Saint-Martin/Beaurepaire tour is just a short distance away, so why not do both neighborhoods at once?

Pigalle

ARCHI-NOIRE Located near Pigalle, an area known chiefly for its overabundance of seedy sex shops and world-renowned music stores, is Archi-Noire, a boutique worth the detour. Madame Renault devotes most of her free time to combing the antiques shows outside Paris in search of streamlined *objets*—including lots of jewelry—from the thirties, fifties, sixties, and seventies, and a few other rare collectibles.

19 rue Victor-Massé, 9e; tel.: 01.48.78.01.82; Métro: Pigalle;

Open Tuesday–Saturday 1–7:30 P.M.; closed first two weeks of August.

A L'ETOILE D'OR The first time I came here I found Denise Acabou exuberantly lecturing about the many virtues of chocolate to a group of some twenty chocolate aficionados who were crowded into her handsome Art Nouveau–decorated boutique. The old woodwork and marble counters leave no doubt that this little shop has been a *confiserie*, or "candy store," since 1904. But I would guess that it is within the past thirty years— ever since Madame Acabou took charge—that the shop has earned its legendary status. Madame Acabou is indeed *un personnage* (a personality or a character), for her passion for both chocolate and this neighborhood is undeniably contagious. Her blond braids, wool plaid skirt, and navy cardigan make her look like a Swiss miss of *un certain age*, but her approach is 100 percent French. Chocolate makers throughout France send her samples with the hope that she may select their sweets for her renowned showcase. Most have been refused, since Madame Acabou is, of course, quite discriminating. Those sweets that she has chosen are truly some of the best of France and include chocolates from Bernachon of Lyons and Weiss in Saint-Etienne, and salted butter caramels from Quiberon, to name a few. Her quality control is exemplary, too, for not only are the chocolates properly preserved, but Madame Acabou claims that if they don't sell within a week, they are marked down. Now, that's my kind of discount shopping!

30 rue Pierre-Fontaine, 9e; tel.: 01.48.74.59.55; fax: 01.45.96.01.71;

Métro: Blanche; Open Monday 3–7:30 P.M.; Tuesday–Saturday 11 A.M.–7:30 P.M.;

closed August through early September.

PAMP'LUNE Looking for a change from the classically styled children's clothing for which the French are best known? You're sure to find it here at Pamp'lune where most of the togs (for ages newborn to ten years) have been patterned after the fashions of Mom and Dad. Expect lots of color and fun.

4, bis rue Piemontesi, 18e; tel.: 01.46.06.50.23; Métro: Pigalle;
Open Monday–Friday 10 A.M.–6:30 P.M.; Saturday 11 A.M.–7:30 P.M.;
closed two weeks in August; www.lescreateursdesabbesses.com.

NIGHT MAGIC

Pigalle is in its prime at night, of course, and the most celebrated haunt is the Moulin
Rouge, right here at the foot of Montmartre. Having opened in 1889, the **Moulin Rouge**
is the oldest cabaret in the world, and although the show continues to evolve, its world-
famous French cancan has thankfully remained as high-spirited and raucous (or at least
almost) as in the beginning. The room where the audience sips champagne and watches
the *spectacle* is a sight to behold, a scene set with a sea of tables illuminated by little red-
shaded lamps—truly a vision from a Toulouse-Lautrec painting were it not for the people
clad in modern-day clothing.

And, of course, you'll want to bring home a souvenir. If you attend the show, you
can shop here in their mini boutique, or in the gift shop near the main entrance. All of
their gifty items bear the Moulin Rouge logo, but my favorite purchases are found in
their collections of postcards and posters, all of which depict suggestive images from the
Moulin's most famous revues. Many of these were created by the French illustrator
Gruau, and they are simply *formidable!*

82 bd de Clichy, 18e; tel.: 01.53.09.82.82; 11 rue Lepic, 18e (boutique);
Métro: Pigalle; Admission price ranges from €87 to €97 (includes half bottle of
champagne); two shows a night; mini boutique opens at 7 P.M. daily year-round for
clients; main gift shop Tuesday–Saturday 10 A.M.–7 P.M.; www.moulin-rouge.com.

*Note: Don't tell anyone I told you, but you can also visit the Musée de
l'Erotisme (and its gift shop!) while you're here. It's located at 72 bd de
Clichy, 18e; tel.: 01.42.58.28.73; Métro: Blanche; Open daily from 10 A.M. to
2 A.M. Go to www.musee-erotisme.com for a preview.*

Rue Louise-Weiss

I've saved the latest most happening place for last. It's no surprise that
this gallery-laden street is situated in the east of Paris, *the* side of town

that has seen the greatest number of transplants over the past two decades from the more gentrified parts of the capital. Check out the jumble of art galleries here in this section of the thirteenth arrondissement, which figure among the most cutting-edge in all of France. Be sure also to browse around in **Images Modernes** at no. 11 (tel.: 01.45.70.74.20; www.imagesmodernes.com), a bookstore that many consider to be the heart and soul of the neighborhood, and that features rich fine-arts books. It's a twenty-minute Métro ride here from la Madeleine on the supersleek no. 14 line. You'll want to hop off at Bibliothèque, named after the **Bibliothèque Nationale,** the frighteningly modern behemoth of a library, which partly explains the rebirth of this part of the city. Here you can also take in the **MK2 Bibliothèque** (128–162 av de France, 13; www.mk2.com), an equally contemporary-style complex that houses a fourteen-screen cinemaplex, several restaurants, and a lounge. And as with any "in" neighborhood, there are often a lot of events and gallery openings taking place here on rue Louise-Weiss. Go to www.louise13.com or www.louise13.fr to find out about the avant-garde exhibitions that you can attend.

Shopping Glossary

accessoires de cheveux—hair accessories

accessoires de cuisine—kitchen accessories

accessoires de maison—home accessories

accessoires de mode—fashion accessories

achats—purchases

acheter—to buy

antiquités—antiques

arts de la table—table arts

boutique—shop or store

boutique de luxe—luxury-goods store

boutique à réduction—reduced-price store

brocante—secondhand goods

cadeau—gift

carte de crédit—credit card

céramiques—ceramics

chaussures—shoes

cher, pas cher—expensive, not expensive

chèque, travelers—check, traveler's check

cosmétiques—cosmetics

couleur—color

couture—sewing (as in by hand)

couturier—couture designer

créateur/créatrice—male or female creator/designer

cristal—crystal

dégriffé—unlabeled designer clothing

délai—time limit

détaxe—tax refund

directeur/directrice de la boutique—shop manager

directeur/directrice du magasin—store manager

échange—exchange

espèce—cash

faïence—faience or refined earthenware

faire du shopping—go shopping

fin de séries—end of series, remnants

grand—big

grand magasin—department store

griffe—label

heures d'ouverture—store hours

linge de maison—house linen

linge de table—table linen

lingerie—lingerie, underwear

livraison—delivery

magasin—store

mannequin—fashion model

marché—market

meubles—furniture

la mode—fashion

modèle—model

paiement—payment

parfum—perfume

petit—small

porcelaine—porcelain or china

poterie—pottery

prix—price

prix à réduction—reduced prices, discount

produits—goods or products

produits de beauté—beauty products

produits de luxe—luxury goods

propriétaire de la boutique—boutique owner

propriétaire du magasin—store owner

les puces—flea market

retouche, retouches—alteration, alterations

retoucheur/retoucheuse—man or woman who does alterations

soldes—discount sales

style—style

styliste—designer

T.V.A.—V.A.T., or value-added tax

taille—size

tissu—fabric

vaisselle—dish or dishware

vendre—to sell

vendeur/vendeuse—salesman/ saleswoman

vente—sale

vente aux enchères—auction

verrerie—glassware

vêtements d'enfant—children's clothing

vêtements de femme—women's clothing

vêtements d'homme—men's clothing

vitrine—store window

For more shopping-oriented vocabulary, consult a phrase book.

Quick Reference

Do you have only a few days to spend in Paris? Are you looking to visit some of the most quintessentially Parisian establishments? Have you wondered where I tell my best friends to go when they're in Paris? If you've answered yes to even one of these questions, this Quick Reference is for you.

I'm writing this with a certain amount of reservation since, of course, I think everything in this new edition of *The Riches of Paris* is worth the visit. I wouldn't have put them in the book if I didn't think they were special! This Quick Reference should help you to get started, though. It is not a "best of" list, although some of the establishments below would definitely qualify. It is, however, a mix of addresses sure to provide you with an experience that is positively Parisian.

ART AND ANTIQUES Argenterie de Turenne p. 231, L'Autre Jour p. 149, La Calinièrè p. 232, L'Heure Bleue p. 84, Maréchal p. 84

ARTS AND CRAFTS Le Bonheur des Dames p. 219, Entrée des Fournisseurs p. 242, Papier+ p. 240, Lavrut p. 220, Sennelier p. 172

BAGS, LUGGAGE, AND ACCESSORIES Goyard p. 89, Hervé Chapelier pp. 153 and 265, Longchamp p. 90, and, of course, all the big names including Chanel, Dior, Hermès, and Louis Vuitton!

BEAUTIFUL BARS   Bar Fontainebleau at Hôtel Meurice p. 127, Bar Hemingway at Hôtel Ritz p. 130, Duke's Bar at Hôtel Westminster p. 131, Golden Black Bar at Hôtel Concorde Saint-Lazare p. 225, Willi's Wine Bar p. 205

BEAUTY INSTITUTES AND SPAS   Les Bains du Marais p. 242, Carita p. 112, Guerlain p. 114, Institut Clarins p. 277, Spa George V at Four Seasons Hôtel George V p. 124

BOOKS AND MUSIC   Brentano's p. 104, FNAC p. 104, Shakespeare and Company p. 167, the Village Voice p. 168, Virgin p. 105

CAFÉS AND INEXPENSIVE EATS   Les Deux Magots p. 179, Café de Flore p. 178, Café de la Mairie p. 178, La Cloche des Halles p. 204, La Palette p. 180

CHILDREN (INCLUDING TOYS AND GAMES)   Bonpoint p. 163, La Châtelaine p. 164, Pain d' Epices p. 219, Petit Bateau p. 99, Territoire p. 108

CHOCOLATE   Debauve & Gallais p. 138, A l'Etoile d'Or p. 291, Fouquet p. 71, La Maison du Chocolat (mostly for their chocolate salon!) p. 73, Richart p. 141

DISCOUNT CLOTHING AND ACCESSORIES AND FIVE-AND-TENS   Anna Lowe p. 102, Etam p. 268, Miss Griffes p. 103, Monoprix p. 101, Réciproque p. 269

EXCEPTIONAL DINING EXPERIENCES   La Cour Jardin at Hôtel Plaza Athenée p. 129, Crystal Room at Baccarat p. 262, Le Grand Véfour p. 224, Les Jardins Plein Ciel at Hôtel Raphael p. 272, Spoon p. 121

FABRICS, NOTIONS, AND TRIMMINGS   Bouchara p. 100, La Droguerie p. 203, Entrée des Fournisseurs p. 242, Houlès p. 249, Maupiou p. 107

FAVORITE MARKETS   Marché Aligre p. 256, Marché Maubert p. 175, Marché Raspail p. 175, Marché Poncelet p. 109, Marché aux Puces Saint-Ouen p. 281

FOOD SHOPS   Barthélemy p. 138, Hédiard p. 72, A l'Olivier p. 231, Poilâne p. 140, Stohrer p. 189

FRAGRANCES AND BEAUTY PRODUCTS   Catherine p. 112, Creed p. 113, Les Editions de Parfums Frédéric Malle p. 176, Guerlain p. 114, Les Salons du Palais Royal p. 223

FRENCH COUNTRY CHARM   Les Olivades p. 171, Le Prince Jardinier p. 219, Quimper Faience p. 192, Souleiado p. 173, Territoire p. 108, La Tuile à Loup p. 148

FUN FOR THE WHOLE FASHION EXPERIENCE   Antoine & Lili p. 253, A la Bonne Renommé p. 240, Colette p. 97, L'Eclaireur p. 238, Espace Kiliwatch p. 201 and, of course, the big names!

GOOD GIFT SHOPS   Café de Flore Boutique p. 168, Les Comptoirs de La Tour d'Argent p. 169, Diptyque p. 170, L'Entrepôt p. 269, Pierre Frey Accessoires p. 47

HAIR SALONS AND ACCESSORIES   Alain Divert p. 109, Alexandre de Paris p. 110, Alexandre Zouari p. 110, Carita p. 112, F. Lazartigue p. 117

HATS AND GLOVES   Anthony Peto p. 194, Hélion p. 89, Hermès p. 61, Marie Mercier p. 154, Philippe Model p. 90

HOME DÉCOR AND LINENS   D. Porthault p. 77, Descamps p. 143, Dior p. 59, Jean Vier p. 145, Mise en Demeure p. 146

JEWELRY   Fabrice p. 153, Louise Gelinas p. 235, Mi Amor/Sic Amor p. 235, Othello p. 155, Pierre Barboza p. 90

KITCHEN AND CHEFS' WEAR A. Simon p. 190, Culinarion p. 143, Dehillerin p. 191, Duthilleul & Minart p. 191, Kitchen Bazaar p. 193

LINGERIE Alice Cadolle p. 93, Chantal Thomas p. 93, Nina Ricci p. 66, Princess Tam-Tam p. 159, Sabbia Rosa p. 159

MEN'S SHOES Berluti p. 88, J. Fenestrier p. 154, J. M. Weston p. 264, Jean-Baptiste Rautureau p. 234, Stéphane Kelian p. 156

MENSWEAR Arny's p. 160, Curling p. 266, Dior p. 59, Lanvin p. 63, Marcel Lassance p. 161

MODERATELY PRICED DINING La Brasserie du Louvre at Hôtel du Louvre p. 127, Chez Paul p. 256, G.R. 5 p. 271, Le Grand Colbert p. 224, La Table d'Hédiard p. 72

MUCH-LOVED HOTELS Hôtel Lutetia p. 181, Hôtel Meurice p. 127, Hôtel d'Orsay p. 183, Hôtel Pavillon de la Reine p. 244, Hôtel Régina p. 129

SCARVES AND SHAWLS Christian Lacroix p. 58, Dior p. 59, Hermès p. 61, Léonard p. 67, Wolff & Descourtis p. 214

SMOKE SHOPS AND MEN'S ACCESSORIES Alfred Dunhill p. 108, Au Caïd p. 169, A la Civette p. 106, Hermès p. 61, S. T. Dupont p. 108

STATIONERY AND WRITING INSTRUMENTS Calligrane p. 241, Cassegrain p. 106, Marie-Papier p. 174, Mont Blanc p. 107, Papier+ p. 240

SWEATERS AND OTHER KNITWEAR Hervé Chapelier pp. 153 and 265, Hobbs p. 97, Jean-Charles de Castelbajac p. 199, Aux Laines Ecossaises p. 163, Sonia Rykiel p. 162

TABLETOP SHOPS Baccarat p. 262, Bernardaud p. 75, Dîners en Ville p. 143, Marie-Pierre Boitard p. 145, Siècle p. 147

TEA SALONS La Bague de Kenza p. 247, Ladurée p. 118, Mariage Frères p. 139, A Priori Thé p. 225, the Tea Caddy p. 181

WINE AND SPIRITS SHOPS Les Caves Augé p. 69, Caves Taillevent p. 70, Fauchon p. 70, Lucien Legrand Filles & Fils p. 209, Ryst-Dupeyron p. 141

WOMEN'S AND MEN'S FASHIONS Agnès b. p. 198, Jean Paul Gaultier p. 216, Kenzo p. 199, Marithé & François Girbaud p. 200, Paul & Joe p. 201, and, of course, the big names!

WOMEN'S SHOES Christian Louboutin p. 214, Free Lance p. 194, Maud Frizon p. 155, Michel Perry p. 91, Robert Clergerie p. 156

WOMENSWEAR Chacok p. 158, Irié p. 158, Jeanette Miner p. 94, Maud Defossez p. 265, Stella Cadente p. 252, and, of course, the big names!

YOUNG LOOKS Et Vous p. 162, Chipie p. 267, Naf Naf p. 197, Princesse Tam-Tam p. 159, Scooter p. 196

Index

I n this general index, places and establishments beginning with articles have been alphabetized both with and without the articles that make up their names. For example, "La Bagagerie" is listed under both *L* and *B*. Page numbers in boldface indicate the page(s) where the entry is most fully described.

Maps

Map 1: Paris Overview and Arrondissements

1 Cimetière de Montmartre
2 Sacré Coeur Basilica
3 Parc La Villette
4 Parc des Buttes Chaumont
5 Jardins du Trocadero
6 Palais Chaillot
7 Cimetière de Passy
8 American Embassy
9 British Embassy
10 Petit Palais
11 Grand Palais
12 Arc de Triomphe
13 Madeleine
14 Gare St-Lazare
15 Parc Monceau
16 Palais de la Découverte
17 Opéra Garnier
18 Galeries Lafayette
19 Printemps
20 Gare du Nord
21 Gare de l'Est
22 Opéra Bastille
23 Palais Omnisports de Bercy
24 Ministère des Finances
25 Gare de Lyon
26 Parc de Montsouris
27 Cité Universitaire
28 Cimetière Montparnasse

Bois
de Boulogne

THE RIGHT BANK

THE SIXTEENTH

THE LEFT BANK

29 Gare Montparnasse
30 Bureau des Objets Trouvés (Lost and Found)
31 Louvre
32 Palais Royale
33 Forum des Halles
34 Musée de l'Orangerie
35 Central Post Office
36 Bourse
37 Bibliothèque Nationale
38 Ecole des Arts et Métiers
39 Archives Nationales
40 Musée Camavalet
41 Musée Picasso
42 Centre George Pompidou
43 place des Vosges
44 Musée Victor Hugo
45 Notre Dame
46 Mémorial de la Déportation

47 Université de Paris
48 (Sorbonne)
49 Ecole Normal Supérieure
50 Musée de Cluny
   Museum Nationale d'Histoire
51 Naturelle
52 Panthéon
53 Eglise St-Etienne du Mont
54 La Mosquée
55 Jardin des Plantes
56 Jardins du Luxembourg
57 Eglise St-Sulpice
58 Théâtre Nationale de l'Odéon

59 Eiffel Tower
60 Champs de Mars
61 Ecole Militaire
62 UNESCO
63 Hôtel des Invalides
64 Assemblée Nationale

bd. Ney   18e   bd. Ney   rue de la Chapelle   bd. Macdonald   Canal de l'Ourcq

rue Championnet   rue d'Aubervilliers   r. Corentin Cariou   av. Jean Lolive

rue Ordener   Marcadet   Caulaincourt   2   rue Custine   rue de Clignancourt   rue des Poissonniers   r. l'Evangile   rue de Flandre   rue Archereau   rue de l'Ourcq   Canal de l'Ourcq   av. Jean Lolive   bd. Sérurier   bd. Indochine   bd. d'Algérie

bd. de Clichy   Pl. PIGALLE   bd. de Rochechouart   bd. de la   Chapelle   Pl. DE STALINGRAD   Bassin de la Villette   av. Jean   Jaurès   19e   r. Armand Carel   r. David d'Angiers

9e   av. Trudaine   rue de Châteaudun   La Fayette   Poissonnière   21   Canal St-Martin   av. Secrétan   4   PL. DU COLONEL FABIEN   PL. DU COLONEL FABIEN

THE PASSAGES   Montmartre   bd. des Italiens   du 4 Sept.   r. d. Petit Champs   2e   37   36   r. Réaumur   St-Denis   blvd. St-Martin   rue du Fbg.   du Temple   rue des Pyrénées   PL. GAMBETTA   bd. Mortier   bd. Gambetta

PL. DES VICTOIRES   LES HALLES   32   31   r. St-Honoré   rue de Rivoli   35   33   Louvre   Pont Neuf   42   RER   3e   rue de Turbigo   38   rue du Temple   rue des Archives   39   rue St-Martin   40   41   11e   la République   av. de la République   av. Gambetta   20e   65

6e   THE MARAIS   Ile de la Cité   45   46   RER   4e   rue St-Antoine   43   44   BASTILLE AND RÉPUBLIQUE   rue du Chemin Vert   rue de la Roquette   av. Philippe Auguste   rue de Charonne   bd. Davout

St-Germain   St-Germain   57   56   MICHEL   RER   49   Ile St-Louis   bd. Henri IV   rue du Faubourg   22   rue de Montreuil   St-Antoine   NATION   RER   Cours de   Vincennes   av. du Dr. Arnold Netter

LUXEMBOURG   MAUBERT   Pont de Sully   47   av. Ledru Rollin   Pont d'Austerlitz   bd. Diderot   PL. DE LA NATION   bd. Picpus   12e

35   RER   L'Observatoire   DENFERT   51   52   PL. DE LA CONTRESCARPE   5e   rue Monge   rue Buffon   Seine   25   RER   av. Daumesnil   PL. FÉLIX ÉBOUÉ   rue de Charenton   av. Daumesnil   bd. Soult   Parc Zoologique

PORT ROYAL   RER   48   rue Mouffetard   54   53   rue Censier   50   GARE D'AUSTERLITZ   24   23   bd. de Bercy   de Bercy   quai   Pont de Bercy   Pont de Tolbiac   de Bercy   bd. Poniatowski   Bois de Vincennes

bd. St-Jacques   bd. de Port Royal   bd. Arago   av. des Gobelins   bd. St-Marcel   rue de la Gare   rue du   PL. D'ALESIA   rue de Jeanne d'Arc   rue de Tolbiac   Pont National   rue de Paris

6   DENFERT ROCHEREAU   rue d'Alésia   13e   rue de Tolbiac   bd. A. Blanqui   av. de Choisy   av. d'Ivry   rue National   rue Regnault   Chevaleret   RER   BD. MASSÉNA

26   RER   CITÉ UNIVERSITAIRE   27   Jourdan   bd. Kellerman   bd. de Masséna

0   1 mile
0   1 km

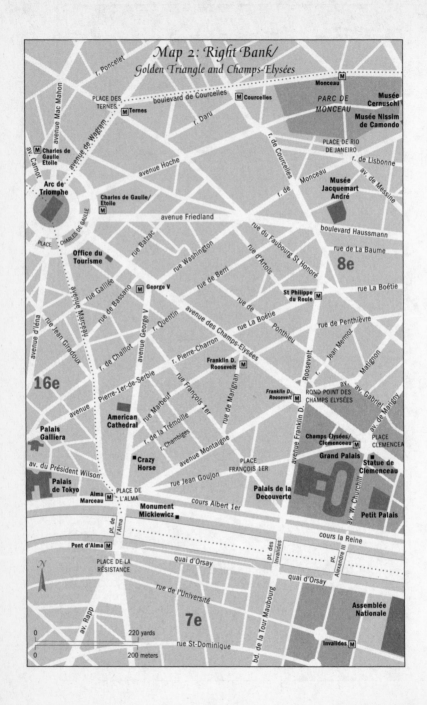

Map 2: Right Bank/
Golden Triangle and Champs-Elysées

r. Poncelet

PLACE DES
TERNES

boulevard de Courcelles

M Courcelles

M Ternes

r. Daru

Monceau M

PARC DE
MONCEAU

Musée
Cernuschi

Musée Nissim
de Camondo

avenue Mac Mahon

avenue de Wagram

avenue Hoche

r. de Courcelles

PLACE DE RIO
DE JANEIRO

r. de Lisbonne

av. Carnot

M Charles de
Gaulle
Etoile

Charles de Gaulle
Etoile

r. de
Monceau

r. de Messine

Musée
Jacquemart
André

Arc de
Triomphe

Charles de Gaulle/
Etoile
M

avenue Friedland

boulevard Haussmann

PLACE
CHARLES DE GAULLE

rue de La Baume

Office du
Tourisme

rue Balzac

rue du Faubourg St Honoré

8e

avenue d'Iéna

avenue Marceau

rue Galilée

rue de Bassano

George V

rue Washington

rue de Berri

rue d'Artois

rue de La Boétie

St Philippe
du Roule M

rue La Boétie

rue de
Ponthieu

rue de Penthièvre

avenue George V

St Quentin

avenue des Champs-Elysées

Roosevelt

r. Jean Mermoz

16e

rue Jean Giraudoux

r. de Challlot

r. Pierre-Charron

Franklin D.
Roosevelt M

Franklin D.
Roosevelt M

ROND POINT DES
CHAMPS ELYSEES

av. Gabriel

Matignon

Pierre-1er-de-Serbie

rue François 1er

rue de Marignan

av.

av. de Marigny

Palais
Galliera

American
Cathedral

rue Marbeuf

r. de la Trémoille

r. Chamblges

avenue Montaigne

PLACE
FRANÇOIS 1ER

Champs Élysées/
Clemenceau M

PLACE
CLEMENCEA

av. du Président Wilson

Crazy
Horse

rue Jean Goujon

Palais de la
Decouverte

Grand Palais

Statue de
Clemenceau

Palais
de Tokyo

Alma
Marceau M

PLACE DE
L'ALMA

Monument
Mickiewicz

cours Albert 1er

avenue Franklin D.

av. W. Churchill

Petit Palais

pt. de
l'Alma

Pont d'Alma M

cours la Reine

N

PLACE DE LA
RÉSISTANCE

quai d'Orsay

pt. des Invalides

pt. Alexandre III

quai d'Orsay

rue de l'Université

bd. de la Tour Maubourg

Assemblée
Nationale

av. Rapp

7e

0   220 yards

0   200 meters

rue St-Dominique

Invalides M

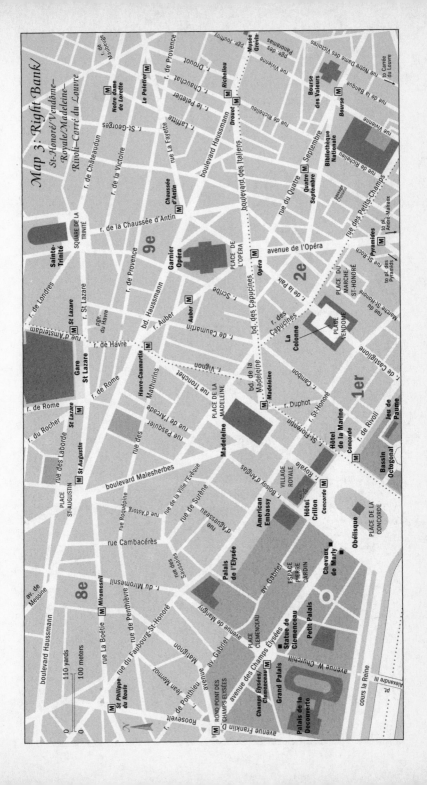

Map 3: Right Bank/
St-Honoré/Vendôme–
Royale/Madeleine–
Rivoli–Carré du Louvre

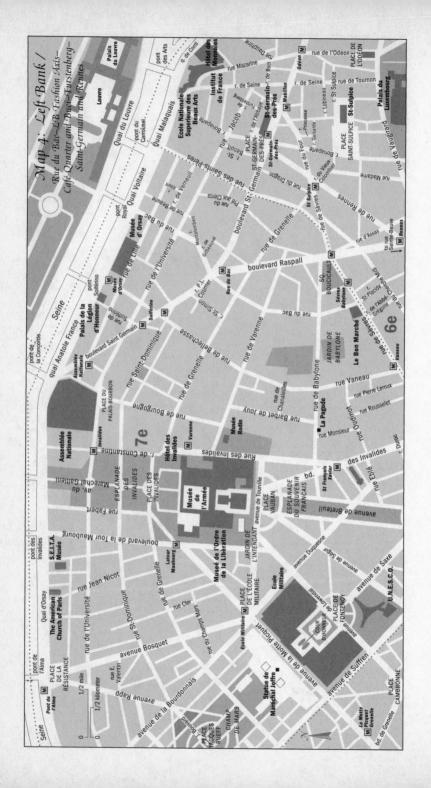

Map 4: Left Bank /
Rue du Bac—LB Fashion Axis—
Café Quarter and Buci-Furstenberg—
Saint-Germain and Rennes

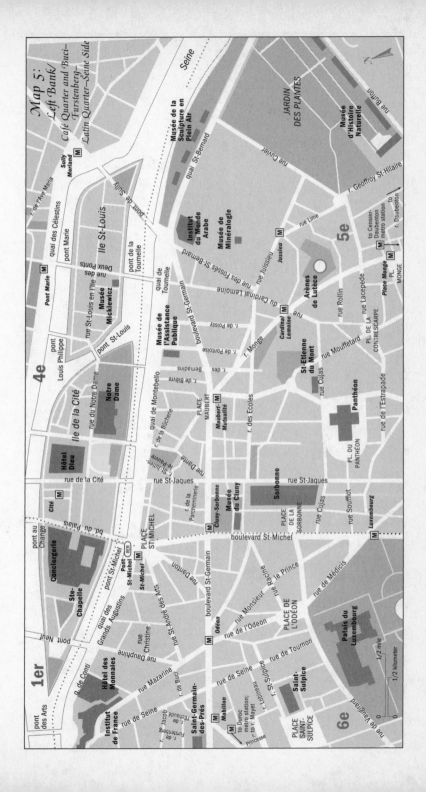

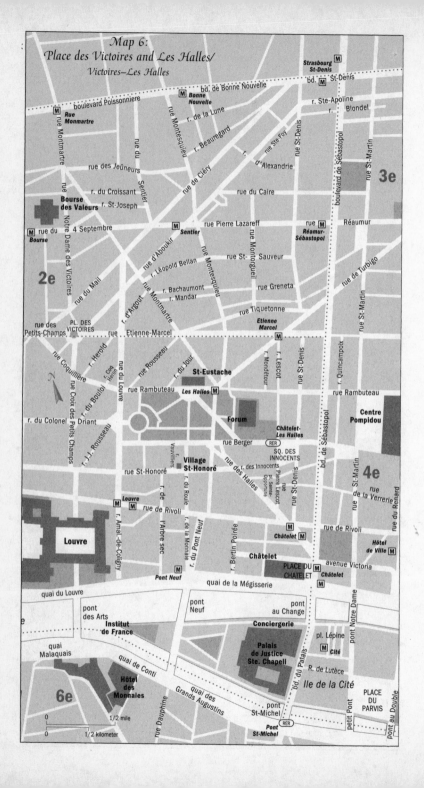

Map 6:
Place des Victoires and Les Halles/
Victoires–Les Halles

Strasbourg St-Denis
bd. St-Denis
bd. de Bonne Nouvelle
Bonne Nouvelle
r. Ste-Apoline
Blondel
boulevard Poissonnière
r. de la Lune
Rue Monmartre
rue Montmartre
rue du Sentier
rue Montesquieu
r. Beauregard
rue de Cléry
rue Ste-Foy
rue St-Denis
r. d'Alexandrie
rue St-Martin
3e
rue des Jeûneurs
rue du Caire
boulevard de Sébastopol
r. du Croissant
rue
Bourse des Valeurs
r. St-Joseph
rue du 4 Septembre
Bourse
Notre Dame des Victoires
rue Pierre Lazareff
Sentier
Réaumur-Sébastopol
Réaumur
2e
r. d'Aboukir
rue St-Sauveur
rue Montorgueil
rue de Turbigo
rue du Mail
r. Léopold Bellan
rue Montesquieu
r. Bachaumont
rue Greneta
rue St-Martin
r. Mandar
rue Montmartre
r. d'Argout
rue Tiquetonne
rue des Petits-Champs
PL. DES VICTOIRES
rue Etienne-Marcel
Etienne Marcel
r. Herold
r. Coq Heron
r. Rousseau
r. du Jour
St-Eustache
r. Lescot
r. Mondétour
rue St-Denis
r. Quincampoix
rue du Louvre
rue Rambuteau
Les Halles
rue Rambuteau
rue Coquillière
r. du Boulot
Centre Pompidou
r. du Colonel Driant
Forum
r. du Croix des Petits Champs
r. J.J. Rousseau
Châtelet-Les Halles
bd. de Sébastopol
rue St-Martin
rue Berger
RER
4e
Vauvilliers
Village St-Honoré
SQ. DES INNOCENTS
rue de la Verrerie
rue St-Honoré
r. des Innocents
pl. Sainte-Opportune
rue du Renard
Louvre
r. de Rivoli
rue des Halles
rue Pierre Lescot
r. du Roule
r. de l'Arbre sec
r. Amal.-de-Coligny
Louvre
Châtelet
Hôtel de Ville
r. du Pont Neuf
r. de la Monnaie
r. Bertin Poirée
Châtelet
rue de Rivoli
Pont Neuf
PLACE DU CHATELET
avenue Victoria
Châtelet
quai du Louvre
quai de la Mégisserie
pont des Arts
pont Neuf
pont au Change
pl. Lépine
pont Notre Dame
Institut de France
Conciergerie
Cité
quai Malaquais
quai de Conti
Palais de Justice Ste. Chapell
R. de Lutèce
Ile de la Cité
PLACE DU PARVIS
6e
Hôtel des Monnaies
quai des Grands Augustins
bd. du Palais
pont St-Michel
petit Pont
pont au Double
rue Dauphine
Pont St-Michel
RER

0   1/2 mile
0   1/2 kilometer

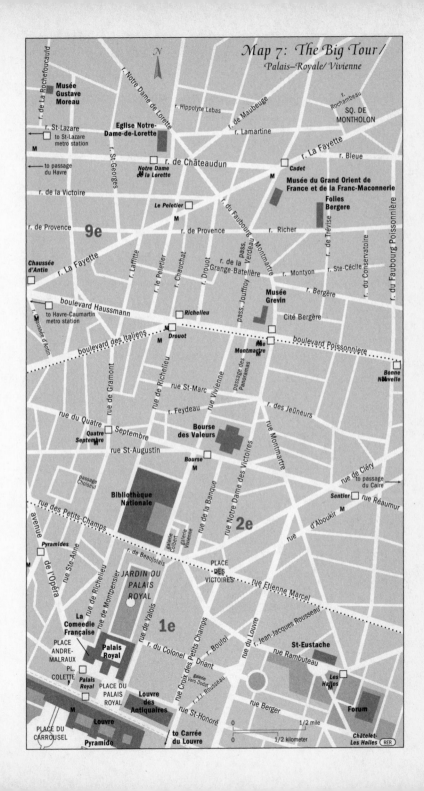

Map 7: The Big Tour / Palais–Royale/ Vivienne

N

Musée Gustave Moreau

r. de la Rochefoucauld

r. Notre Dame de Lorette

r. Hippolyte Lebas

r. de Maubeuge

r. Rochambeau

SQ. DE MONTHOLON

r. St-Lazare
to St-Lazare metro station

M

to passage du Havre

Eglise Notre-Dame-de-Lorette

r. de Châteaudun

r. Lamartine

r. La Fayette

r. Bleue

r. St-Georges

Notre Dame de la Lorette

Cadet
M

Musée du Grand Orient de France et de la Franc-Maconnerie

r. de la Victoire

Le Peletier
M

Folies Bergere

r. de Trévise

r. de Provence

9e

r. de Provence

r. du Faubourg Montmartre

r. Richer

r. Ste-Cécile

r. du Conservatoire

r. du Faubourg Poissonnière

Chaussée d'Antin

r. La Fayette

r. Laffitte

r. le Peletier

r. Chauchat

r. Drouot

r. de la Grange-Batelière

pass. Verdeau

pass. Jouffroy

r. Montyon

r. Bergère

boulevard Haussmann

to Havre-Caumartin metro station

Richelieu
M

Musée Grevin

Cité Bergère

Chaussée d'Antin

M

Drouot
M

boulevard des Italiens

r. Montmartre
M

boulevard Poissonnière

Bonne Nouvelle
M

rue de Gramont

rue de Richelieu

rue St-Marc

passage des Panoramas

rue Vivienne

r. des Jeûneurs

rue du Quatre

Septembre

r. Feydeau

rue Montmartre

Quatre Septembre
M

rue St-Augustin

Bourse des Valeurs

rue de Cléry

to passage du Caire

passage Choiseul

Bourse
M

rue de la Banque

rue Notre Dame des Victoires

Sentier
M

rue Réaumur

avenue de l'Opéra

rue des Petits-Champs

Bibliothèque Nationale

2e

rue d'Aboukir

Pyramides
M

rue Ste-Anne

galerie Colbert

galerie Vivienne

r. de Beaujolais

PLACE DES VICTOIRES

rue Etienne Marcel

rue de Richelieu

rue de Montpensier

JARDIN DU PALAIS ROYAL

rue du Louvre

r. Jean-Jacques Rousseau

St-Eustache

La Comeedie Française

rue de Valois

1e

r. du Colonel Driant

r. Boulor

rue Rambuteau

PLACE ANDRE-MALRAUX

Palais Royal

r. Croix des Petits Champs

galerie Vero-Dodat

Les Halles
M

PL. COLETTE

Palais Royal
M

PLACE DU PALAIS ROYAL

Louvre des Antiquaires

r. J.J. Rousseau

Forum

PLACE DU CARROUSEL

Louvre
M

rue St-Honoré

rue Berger

Châtelet-Les Halles   RER

Pyramide

to Carrée du Louvre

0   1/2 mile

0   1/2 kilometre

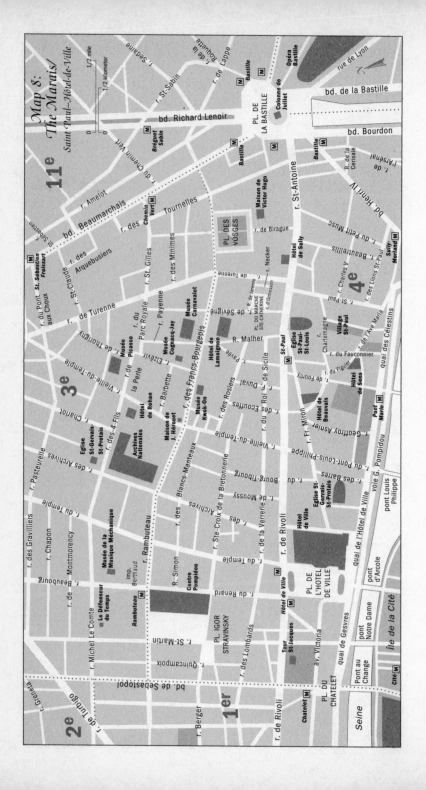

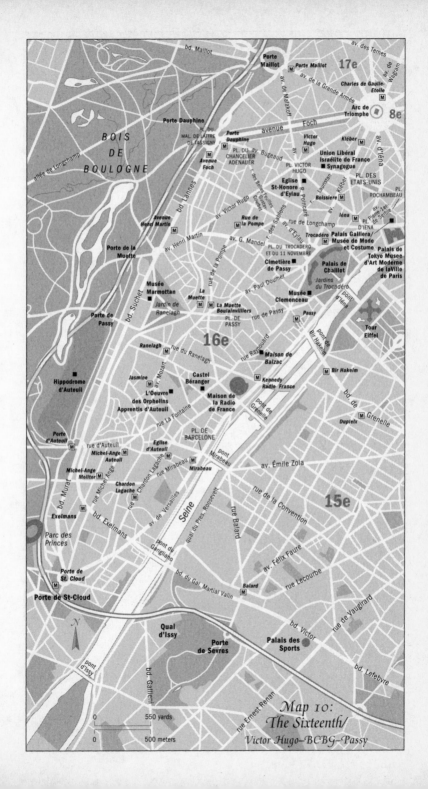

Map 10:
The Sixteenth/
Victor Hugo–BCBG–Passy

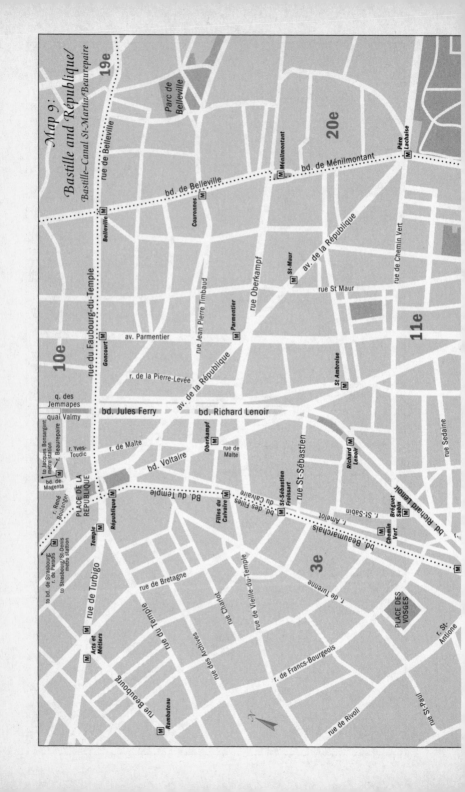

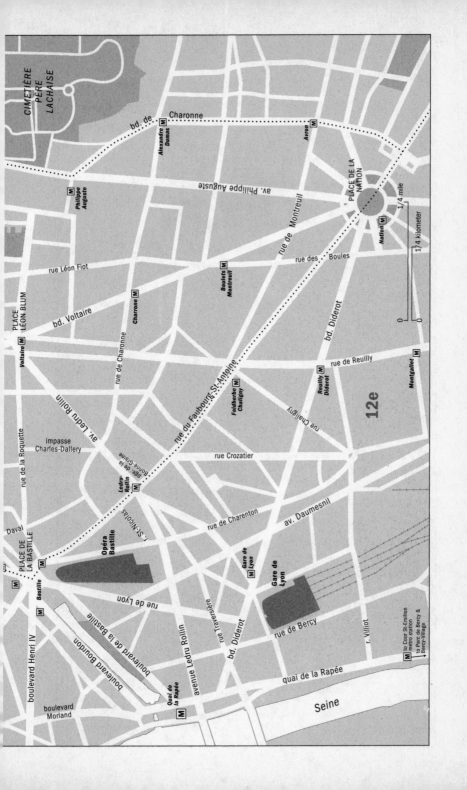

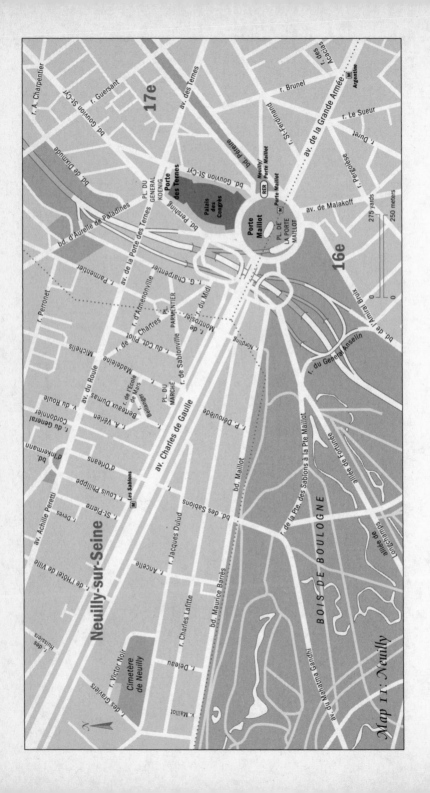

Map 11: Neuilly

I would like to hear from you.

As an author, a travel writer, and a travel enthusiast, I would enjoy hearing your impressions of various places of interest—both one that I have clued you in on and ones that you've discovered on your own.

I also conduct tours to France from time to time, so I'd love to be able to keep you abreast of my activities and offerings. Check out my Web site . . .

www.therichesof.com

. . . to learn more about my doings and to contact me. There you may also sign up to receive free travel and shopping bulletins.

MAUPINT☉UR ®

Luxury Escorted and Independent Vacations

EUROPE • ASIA • AFRICA • SOUTH AMERICA • AUSTRALIA/NEW ZEALAND • CANADA • USA

The Maupintour Advantage

Maupintour programs offer travelers distinct advantages

Limited group size, only 20 - 25 participants enables a more relaxed ambience, greater personal attention and increased comfort • Professional tour managers with an average 20 years of experience • Local, experienced English-speaking guides and historians • Scenic and centrally located 4 & 5 Star Hotels • More plated dinners and a-la-carte dining • Included meals feature regional wines and cuisine

Maupintour includes more tour elements

Special events • Tipping/porterage • Luggage handling
• Admission fees to exhibits, sites and entertainment
• Ample free time on all escorted tours to pursue individual interests

Maupintour offers comprehensive sightseeing, including both "must-see" and "off-the-beaten-path" treasures. Maupintour also includes entertainment and special events not customary with other tour operators. Our incredible escorted tours and independent packages to France as well as City Stays in Paris and throughout France are just a portion of what we offer throughout the world.

Independent personalized vacations

We can tailor any Maupintour product as a personalized package, creating your ideal getaway. This allows you to go when you want, where you want and include exactly what you want. With a distinctive range of escorted and independent programs, we also offer independent City Stays worldwide as well as river and canal cruises with MaupinWaterways. Maupintour is prepared to help you design the vacation of your dreams.

www.maupintour.com • 800-255-4266

GO FURTHER..

In France, travel as the locals do—by bicycle.

Rolling terrain and exhilarating views will keep you hard pressed to find rides more varied and dramatic. Savour the roads bathed in a special kind of light as you pedal through vineyards and orchards, alongside lavender fields and to famous hilltop villages. Does travel get any better than *boules* at sunset with a pastis in hand?

Since 1966, Butterfield & Robinson has been creating luxury biking and walking travel experiences for all ages. Call us at 1-800-678-1147 for more information or visit us at www.butterfield.com.

Butterfield & Robinson
BIKING AND WALKING SINCE 1966

www.butterfield.com 1.800.678.1147

SPEAK A FOREIGN LANGUAGE? SPEAK IT BETTER.

Join the thousands of top-tier professionals and frequent international travelers who depend on *Champs-Elysées, Schau ins Land, Puerta del Sol*, and *Acquerello italiano* to help them stay in touch with the languages and cultures they love. Designed to help you dramatically improve your listening comprehension, vocabulary, and cultural acuity, these unique European audiomagazines are guaranteed to reenergize your love of studying a language—or your money back!

Each audiomagazine consists of an hour-long program on CD or cassette. You'll hear interviews with prominent Europeans, segments covering current events and issues, as well as features on contemporary culture and beloved traditions. An accompanying booklet contains a complete printed transcript, a glossary averaging 600 words and expressions translated into English, plus extensive background notes. Subscribers can opt for Audio Flash Cards™ (on CD only) which give the correct pronunciation and translation of 100 words and phrases from each program.

If you want to make faster progress, order the study supplements (work sheets containing innovative listening exercises and grammar drills) that are available for each issue. Subscribers to the French have the option of adding *Champs-Elysées Plus* to your subscriptions. If your goal is to be able to understand native French easily, *Champs-Elysées Plus*, our new enhanced package, provides the extra help you need. *Champs-Elysées Plus* includes the basic *Champs-Elysées* audio program, the transcript and glossary, and a printed workbook with grammar exercises. In addition, you receive a cassette

or CD (your choice) with interactive audio exercises to help you with comprehension and vocabulary building. Audio flash cards™ of key words and expressions prepare you for listening. Several features from the program are read at a slower pace to make them easier to understand. After you listen to the segments, there are audio comprehension exercises to help you make sure you've understood everything you've heard. And just for fun, we've added a special feature—in English—in which we explore various aspects of the French language. Use this supplement on the go and see how fast your French progresses!

For product samples and information, or to request a brochure, go online to http://ads.champs-elysees.com/RP2.

Call Today
1.800.824.0829
Or Order Online
www.champs-elysees.com

Champs-Elysées, Inc.
Resources for intermediate-to-advanced language learners since 1983

Maribeth's Picks

for Top Online Shopping Experiences that are Distinctively French

Emilie Holland Paris
Exclusively Chic

Emilie Holland Paris, a sort of mini couture salon based in Paris, creates timelessly elegant fashions and accessories of the finest quality. And you'll find the prices to be *tout à fait raisonnable*. Embark upon your Right Bank shopping experience without even hopping on a plane!

www.EmilieHollandParis.com

Spirit of Provence offers an array of heartwarming and reasonably-priced gift items from this glorious sun-drenched region of Southern France. All are made by small family-owned and operated companies. Visiting their site is like shopping in a colorful Provençal open-air market filled with dried lavender bouquets, tablecloths and pottery, gourmet treats, and more.

www.spiritofprovence.com

Remember to go to www.therichesof.com to find more online shopping recommendations.